Curse of the Lost Memories

∝ Book 1 - Chronicles of the Celestial Chains ∝

GRIFFON LORE GAMES

CURSE OF THE LOST MEMORIES
BOOK 1 - CHRONICLES OF THE CELESTIAL CHAINS

Lead Designers & Writers
Christophe Herrbach (christophe@griffonloregames.com)
Anthony Pacheco (anthony@griffonloregames.com)

Production Manager: Anthony Pacheco

Cover Artist: Oliver Wetter www.fantasio.work
Cover Design: BZN Studio Designs covers.
bzndesignstudios.com
Original InDesign Template: Jonathan James
www.instagram.com/jonathanmjames
Page Layout Design: Justin Oefelein @ SPX Multimedia
Maps Artist (Campaign Maps): Anna Meyer
ghmaps.net
Maps Artist (Crossroads Village, Tactical Maps):
Tad Davis
Illustrations: deificat – Discord: deificat#1647
Play Testing, Feedback: Glenn Anderson, Brian Jones
& Maxine Chappuis
Editorial Assistance: Chrystelle de Valois, et. al.

Feedback, Questions and more:
info@griffonloregames.com
Discord Channel: discord.gg/KnSwfuG
Web & Online Store: griffonloregames.com
Facebook: facebook.com/griffonlore/

Curse of the Lost Memories is a 5E adventure for 4 Level 1 PCs. By the end of the adventure, characters should be 4th Level. This adventure is compliant with OGL rules.

5E Hardcover ISBN: 978-0-9883652-7-8

Griffon Lore Games LLC
704 228th Ave NE, Suite 741
Sammamish, WA 98074, USA

INTRODUCTION

A CHILLING WIND RISES ON THE MOOR, blowing at the jagged granite tors and slowly moving the banks of thick grey fog covering the treacherous bogs. Over the last few months, aberrations and crazed animals have been coming out of the moor and harassing the local populous, a much-beloved inn at an important rest stop along the Viscount's primary trade route. Long ago a battle was fought against demons in the moors, scattering its people to the neighboring lands, a battle no one remembers.

Curse of the Lost Memories for 5E takes players from Level 1 to Level 4 in hard fantasy romp where the stakes are high, mistakes can be deadly, and consequences for actions are everywhere. It is the first volume of a six-book campaign.

The player characters start the adventure with a curse of "their" own making.

Curse Origins

The PCs are reincarnated druids from ancient times where druids reigned supreme, arcane magic hadn't been introduced yet, and the Gods treated the Welt as just another realm that took precious resources away from their endless cosmic war against the demons.

These primordial Hierophants were able to peek into the future, but, as part of the first mortals to use magic to far-see, as they called it, they did not have the experience to recognize prophecies are dangerous and often self-fulfilling.

And that's the overarching cause of the PCs current predicament—they are trapped in a Self-Fulfilling Prophecy. And it isn't simply them, either, it's anyone throughout history with divination ability getting caught up with a problem of the Hierophants own making.

The Prophecy

Druids always viewed divination magics about the universe outside of nature with suspicion. The prophetic answer from their far-see only increased that suspicion.

Because of the Demon War, I see an endless sea of fire and torment everlasting, began from an angel's folly of corruption.

Only by storming the Gates of Elysia by those who are reborn can we save the damned, bring justice to the wronged and bring the false righteousness to heel.

To the Hierophants, the Prophecy was part-nonsense (what was an Angel?), part outside their purview (justice) part like the end of the world (the apocalypse), and part all too familiar (reincarnation).

The gods' last demon war was just recently concluded, in the gods' favor, so to the druids, this all seemed like The End Was Neigh. These druids, while primitive in the understanding of the workings of the gods, were not primitive in their understanding of cosmology. Mount Elysia was the first stepping-stone to each god's personal realm for a devoted priest. If there was something wrong with that and required them to storm its gates to do battle with this Angel to prevent the end of the world—well, that's what they needed to do.

Tempus Fugit

The druids assumed that the reincarnation aspects of the Prophecy were simply a map whereby their next lives would be in physically young bodies and that the interim time would be used to figure out who and what this Angel was, so they could do battle. They cast their titanic world-spell, shook off their mortal coil, and when born again, recaptured their memories and attempted to make sense of it all.

And then they died again. And then again, over and over until, at one point for each Hierophant, they simply forgot whom they once were.

The Prophecy was correct about a demon war.

It was simply a demon war, far, far off into the future.

Enter the Gods

While the Hierophants were on their thousands of years journey into the future, the gods were having a tough time with their endless demon wars. Thereupon they decided as a pantheon to become more powerful by encouraging worship amongst the mortal races and using the devotion and prayers of the faithful to give them power and further their own ends. As a reward, all mortals, not just their high priests, would enter heaven—the celestial kingdom known as Mount Elysia. Then after an undetermined time of heavenly paradise, they'd be sent to the realm of the god that held their devotion. Mortals failing to devote themselves properly were sent to Purgatory, like errant high priests of old, to purify themselves before entering Elysia.

Immortal and Eternal, the gods needed intermediaries to understand the workings of mortal people and appropriately grant spells and answer prayers. The gods created shepherds of the living and dead, and they were called celestials—angels. Lawful, given power and latitude to make decisions on their own, the celestials were both like mortals, and like gods. The most powerful amongst them were the archangels.

This plan worked. The gods became powerful enough to secure the realms against the endless, evil, entropy.

But mortals sometimes fail, and the PCs are caught up in a failure of epic proportions as one of the very celestials and guardians of the heavens becomes corrupted and starts to destroy it from within.

And it all starts with a love story.

Narakata and Chrystelle

Thousands of years after the Hierophants cast their ill-conceived reincarnation spells the Celestial Prince Narakata fell in love with the mortal Chrystelle de Valois, a half-elf of such beauty and grace that even the great Prince was enraptured by her.

The Prophecy was referring to Narakata—he is the angel that the PCs must defeat by storming the Gates of Elysia later in the campaign.

Secret Lovers

In secret, Chrystelle and Narakata both promised to cherish each other until the end of time. Narakata blessed his beloved with eternal life—Chrystelle would never age, for losing her would be unbearable. Both lovers retreated to the old elf tower on the moor and there spent hundreds of years in bliss.

Chrystelle's immortality eventually became known by the gods themselves when Prince Erebus, the celestial whose purview was preventing newly departed souls from being sucked into the Abyss or used for other nefarious purposes, became aware of Chrystelle's immortality through a taunt from his nemesis, the Demon Lord Orcus.

It was Erebus and his minions who made sure the souls of mortals departed to the proper god's realm, or if failing to be sorted thus—sent to Purgatory, an intermediate place where souls lingered. There they are purified until they identified with a deity and then stepped into Elysia to depart.

Erebus took exception that he was denied dominion over Chrystelle's soul and that Narakata's actions could unravel everything the gods put in place and plunge the Realms back into endless demon wars. Erebus, not knowing about the Prophecy, even used the druids of old as an example of how mortals interfering with the natural order of life and death could go so very wrong. The other celestials (some of whom pitied the old Hierophants), agreed with Erebus and asked (ordered) Narakata to limit Chrystelle's sphere of immortality to her little tower or let his wife die in peace.

Erebus was entirely correct—this was all folly. Narakata could not bear to see his wife die, so he chose the self-imposed exile.

Narakata chose poorly.

Trouble in Paradise

After 300 years, Chrystelle grew frustrated that she could not leave her tower and its grounds without taking the risk of seeing her great age catch up on her, for half-elves only lived approximately 180 years. Narakata spent as much time as he could

with her, but his duties called him away on multiple occasions. As time passed, her frustration turned into resentment, and the two lovers start to grow apart. Narakata visits to the tower became infrequent and spaced out. Chrystelle formed the (correct) impression that Narakata became bored with her. Even their lovemaking stopped holding passion.

It was after two more centuries when Chrystelle realized she had not seen Narakata in a hundred years—she had been set aside, without even the courtesy of her husband telling her it was over. She cursed him, and without being constantly in the presence of the Celestial, her mortal body started to grow old, even if she could not die of age.

Eventually, Chrystelle became a lich, neither dead nor alive, kept alive by the magic in her tower that was now a curse.

While she was not born out of evil, she gained the qualities of a lich, a powerful arcane wielder of spells. She taught herself arcane magic from her parents' old spell books.

Bored, lonely, and resentful, Chrystelle used powerful spells to summon creatures to her, looking for company. Using her summoning magic, she learned everything from warfare, current history, philosophy, and even engineering.

One fall and rainy day, Guillaume the shepherd found the entrance to her tower when he was leading his flock through the moor. Despite her understanding that Guillaume would one day die, and in her perspective all too soon, and that she would go on with her sorry existence, her loneliness overcame her bitterness, and she practically begged the young man to keep her company. She even revealed her true form to Guillaume, and the man took pity on her. Chrystelle may be the stuff of nightmares, but, the shepherd saw her heart was pure even if it was broken.

The Wailmoor Born

Chrystelle dedicated her time to educate and train the young shepherd she befriended. He grew into a noble and kind man, trained in the arts of magic, philosophy, and warfare. Over the years, Guillaume became a famous and beloved knight and was awarded by the King of Lothmar the lands he used to walk as a shepherd as his own barony. The Barony of Wailmoor was born.

The history of the Wailmoor picks back up in Chapter 2 – *Moortide Rising* but suffice it to say the Wailmoor was the epicenter of the Hierophants' prophecy. This is where the demon war happened, where Narakata started his path of corruption, and how the PCs realize they must storm the very Gates of Elysia to save it—if it can be saved.

Intro

Lost at the Beaux Seins

Moortide Rising

The Altar & the Anvil

Castle Wailmoor

Appendix

Adventure Summary

Curse of the Lost Memories is about the PCs learning just how cursed they are as they wander around the post-apocalyptic setting that is the Wailmoor, trying to do the right thing while not getting eaten by the corrupted monsters within. In the end, they are introduced to Chrystelle and must decide how to interact with the lich.

Chapters

Chapter 1 introduces the PCs to the Curse Mechanic and gives them clues about answers found in the Wailmoor. Chapter 2 glues all the various geographical locations together. Chapter 3 is the great Temple of Dvalin, while Chapter 4 concludes the adventure in the abandoned Wailmoor Castle, complete with Chrystelle stuck in her tower for all eternity.

Chapter 1: The Inn & the Viscount

The PCs curse manifests itself, and the PCs find themselves in a fight with Viscounty soldiers at the Crossroads Village. They learn their visions, while problematic and potentially life-threatening, are no mere visions of the past, but charged with power and purpose.

Prudent PCs will investigate recent events, such as why the Viscount was there at the remote inn in the first place and learn about the Wailmoor approximately five miles to the east.

Chapter 2: Moortide Rising

The PCs wander the landscape of the moor looking for answers and receiving clues in their previous lives' memories. There is a graveyard that holds their previous lives bodies, a mage tower, abandoned villages, impressive feats of engineering and finally an ancient battlefield where the Goddess of War attempts to help the PCs without making their predicament worse.

Clues from exploring the Wailmoor will lead to the Temple of Dvalin. Silas's Tower will hold secrets about the magic of the moor and give hints of a powerful immortal in ruins of old Castle Wailmoor.

The PCs learn that Castle Wailmoor itself is an elusive location, its walls translucent with auras of magic, the whole locked away in the Ethereal Plane.

Chapter 3: The Altar & the Anvil

The Temple of Dvalin is the key to understanding the depts of corruption in Wailmoor and the steps necessary to cause Castle Wailmoor to manifest itself.

The temple also holds weapons that are helpful in the concluding chapter and, if the PCs take it upon themselves to restore it, a place of sanctuary and divine power that can aid them throughout the rest of the Campaign.

Chapter 4: Castle Wailmoor

Clearing the corruption in the moor removes the Castle from the Ethereal Plane, and it manifests back into the waking world. The PCs can then complete their journey, thereby putting their previous lives' memories to rest and discovering the long-forgotten Chrystelle.

The PCs find a highly deceptive agent of Orcus in the castle and either do battle with the fell Dead-Knight, or expertly arrange his obliteration through their own subterfuge or superior tactics.

Here, at last, the PCs will meet with Chrystelle and must decide if she is friend or foe. The module concludes with this decision and their choices about what to do with the Wailmoor itself—it is either a place of continued abandonment and thus a place for the PCs to make their home without being bothered, or the beginning of the restoration of the Barony of Wailmoor and titles granted to them by the King of Lothmar himself.

Campaign

Chronicles of the Celestial Chains is a campaign in which the PCs fight their older memories to regain their agency and deal with Narakata's corruption. Demons, ever so resourceful (and in this case, smarter than Narakata), use his vanity and abandonment of his wife against him. As the PCs grow in power, so too does Narakata's corruption take hold and spread. Eventually, it becomes unbearable; the PCs must storm the Gates of Elysia itself and put an end to his terrible ways before he destroys it all from within.

The PCs become less reactionary and more of the arbiters of various fates—what to do with Chrystelle, solidifying their hold on the world by picking sides with Wailmoor's neighbors as war comes to Lothmar, dealing with Narakata and even putting events in motion that shake the world's cosmology to its very core.

Finally, the PCs have enough power to end their curse—if they choose to do so. In *Chronicles of the Celestial Chains*, everything has a price.

The Wailmoor

The Wailmoor is 7680 acres—a large barony. There's plenty of room for all sorts of shenanigans, and if the

PCs want to build out, they can extend their domain north or east.

While the PCs may wander away from the Wailmoor, this is the place they can always call home. If not Castle Wailmoor, Silas Tower, the Temple of Dvalin, a restored estate or even new construction on one of the many pristine places to build and expand.

They can spread the rumors that the moor is still haunted, and people will stay away, or, they can claim an end to the issues and welcome settlers. Here they can either rule the land, appoint rulers in their stead, or encourage someone else to take up the reigns of leadership.

Assuming Chrystelle is dealt with, one way or the other. She is an Enchantress Supreme, with centuries to hone her art.

THE CURSE MECHANIC

Right from the get-go, the players will realize their characters are screwed, and this Campaign is going to be difficult.

The *Curse of the Lost Memories* is both a description of what is happening to the PCs and a game mechanic.

Periodically, with one exception for a lone PC build, they will be asked to make a DC 20 Wisdom Saving Throw. If they fail, they are subject to a memory that consumes all their attention regardless of current circumstances.

Intro

Lost at the Beaux Seins

Moortide Rising

The Altar & the Anvil

Castle Wailmoor

Appendix

LOST MEMORY MECHANICS

Physically, a *Lost Memory* is a seizure with a vivid memory of the past attached to the temporary condition. Magically, it is the effect of constant reincarnation upon the mind. Spiritually, it is the very world, The Welt, trying to send the PCs a message.

- When triggered, a PC can choose to ignore the memory with a DC 20 Wisdom Save. If they save, they can choose to have the memory or ignore it. If they fail, the memory occurs.

- During the memory, the PC is *blinded* and *incapacitated*.

- Gerrdan or a custom PC with the +20 Wisdom Boon is not *incapacitated*, merely *blinded*.

- Because of their link as former Hierophants, *Lost Memories* are experienced by all the PCs that can see the PC who triggered the memory, even if the *Lost Memory* is only about a specific PC's former life.

- There are no memories of other prior lifetimes during *Curse of the Lost Memories*. Things are confusing enough as it is for the PCs. That comes later.

This curse will dog the PCs throughout the campaign until they either decide to end the cycle of reincarnation (and then die) or find ways to make a DC 20 Wisdom Saving Throw.

BOON OF THE LOST MEMORIES

With the curse comes boons that manifest itself as Epic Boons, feats (even at first level), extra skill proficiencies and other permanent conditions, each unique to the PC.

COMMON BOONS

All PCs are Proficient in Acrobatics, Stealth, and Athletics regardless of class or background. The rest of the boons use a combination of **feats** and **epic boons**, described in the 5E PHB and DMG.

PCs that wear medium armor have the feat Medium Armor Master, which allows them to use medium armor and use Advantage when moving with Stealth.

For all intents and purposes, the PCs past are commandos, able to move silently with precision and skill even if they have a class that normally doesn't lend itself to silent movement. As a group, they move with fell purpose, even if they're just out for a pint at the local.

PCs that are intrinsically stealthy are more so at lower levels than other PCs.

The PCs will need to take advantage of this added Stealth capability throughout the Campaign until they reach enough levels to warrant simply kicking in the front door. However, even then, the best results are attainable using stealth-based combined arms more so than not.

Most encounters assume the PCs are stealthy. PCs who bumble about without using their gifts are in for a tough time.

COMBINED BOON/CURSE

All PCs have the Epic Boon of Undetectability. While on the surface this seems like a long-term benefit, it is also a long-term detriment. Not only do they get a hefty bonus to any Stealth checks, greatly increasing their ability to be sneaky bastards even at lower levels, but they can't be scried or targeted by divination magics.

This Epic Boon is **absolute.** PCs cannot use divination magic on themselves. Simple auguries, divinations trivial and powerful, rituals and communing with the gods simply will not work on the PCs, even if a PC is the caster of the divination spell.

Divination magic cast by PCs about NPCs can work, but only if the answer has nothing to do with any of the PCs. If there is a possibility divination magic reveals any future or present detail about the PC, the spell or magical item simply ceases to function.

INDIVIDUAL BOON MATRIX

Players can use the pre-generated PCs, which come configured with their boons/curses, or if the DM allows, create their own PC using a boon from the following table. **PCs are not allowed to have the same individual boons.**

All encounters are designed with the expectation that the PCs will have access to Individual Boons—many are tough!

While all the pre-generated PCs will require more role-playing than most adventures, some PCs are designed for advanced role-players, as noted. As previously explained, all PCs have common skills of Athletics, Stealth, and Acrobatics.

HOW TO USE THE MATRIX

The matrix of the progenerated PCs can be used to create a custom PC by simply interchanging a Suggested PC Class with a different Suggested Individual Boons. For example:

- **Dagnerian** the female human Warlock with Increased Charisma and Strength/Able to change biological sex at will

- **Charles** the male human Monk with Boon of Immortality, Boon of Perfect Health, Medium Armor Master

- **Vesragoth** the male half-orc Paladin with Survival Background Skill Proficiency/Boon of Dimensional Travel

- Etc.

SUGGESTED PC CLASS	SUGGESTED INDIVIDUAL BOONS	ROLE-PLAY RATING
Gerrdan, the male human Fighter	Medium Armor Master +20 Wisdom Saving Throw	Moderate
Candara, the female elf Wizard	Increased Charisma and Strength Able to change biological sex at will	Advanced
Dagnerian, the female human Warlock	Survival Background Skill Proficiency Boon of Dimensional Travel	Normal to Moderate
Charles, the male human Monk	Rapier Weapon Proficiency +10 to Athletics Athlete Feat	Normal
Helena, the female human Cleric	Medium Armor Master Speaks 18 Languages Linguist Feat	Moderate
Hrog, the male human Barbarian	Boon of Recovery Medium Armor Master	Normal
Keshwan, the male elf Ranger	Boon of Immortality Boon of Perfect Health Medium Armor Master	Moderate
Mimi, the female gnome Druid	Heavily Armored Feat Medium Armor Master Many Weapon Proficiencies Giant Ferret Mount	Normal
Perrie, the female human Sorcerer	Increased Charisma War Caster Feat	Normal
Shervalee, the female half-elf Bard	Boon of Resilience Allergic to metal	Advanced
Tegan, the male human Rogue	Survival Background Skill Proficiency Dual Wielder Feat Skulker Feat	Normal
Vesragoth, the male half-orc Paladin	Dual Wielder Feat Medium Armor Master Well-Connected with Order Imperial University Educated	Advanced

For 5E class balance purposes, avoid giving a melee character the Boon of Resilience. Attached to the Bard in the pre-generated PCs, its powerful resistances are offset by a powerful aversion to metal.

Special Note on "Gerrdan"

The pre-generated Gerrdan has a +20 Wisdom Save, and he will never succumb to the *Lost Memory* reeve.

If using the custom options of building their own PCs using the boon matrix, the +20 Wisdom Save is in *addition* to any Ability or Proficiency bonus to the Wisdom Save.

Gerrdan will still see the vision of the memory, which will overlap what he is presently seeing. During this vision/memory overlap, Gerrdan only has the *Blinded* condition, and not Incapacitated.

Curse of the Lost Memories and the rest of the Campaign will work even without Gerrdan and his amazing willpower (or a PC with the same Individual Boon). But it sure makes things more interesting and sets the tone for the PCs wrestling their fates from their former lifetimes.

Custom Character Checklist

Here are the steps for creating a custom character rather than using the pre-generated PCs:

1. Pick Race
2. Pursue the Appendix for an applicable deity to worship (if appropriate given the PC's character history)
3. Pick Class
4. Add Bonus Proficiencies to Stealth, Athletics and Acrobatics
5. Adjust Abilities for Race
6. Apply 27 point-buy to Abilities
7. Apply Medium Armor Master Feat if the class is Proficient with Medium Amor
8. Apply a Suggested Individual Boon from the Individual Boon Matrix

Campaign Races

When using the *Chronical of the Celestial Chains* campaign setting, there are racial deviations from the 5E ruleset.

Campaign Breaking Race

Tieflings will break the campaign. There is no hell and thus no devils. *Infernal* is not even a word (although

diabolical is).

Avoid adding the concept or the place of Hell. Doing so will invalidate the last two modules in the campaign setting. The overall plot will break-down and require extensive modification by the DM.

Primary Campaign Races

Humans, **halflings**, **elves**, **dwarves**, **gnomes,** and **half-elves** are the standard races in the Empire and thus the Kingdom of Lothmar. They are listed in order of Kingdom population.

Optional Races with No Lore Backing

Goliath, Warforged, Simic Hybrids, and **Vedalken** receive no support in the *Chronical of the Celestial Chains* campaign setting.

Problematic Races

The purpose of a celestial is to guard the realms from outside influences (usually between themselves). Thus, **gith** does not fit within the lore, and the DM will need to modify such lore accordingly.

The lore around **changelings** and **shifters** is currently undetermined. DM implemented lore could conflict with lore presented in a later product.

Races That Deviate from Standard Lore

Dragonborn are not a distinct race, rather the rare product of sexual relations between a human and a dragon in human form. Dragonborn that try to mate produce attractive and unusually clever human offspring.

In the Empire, dragonborn are treated with a small amount of reverence.

Aasimar adheres to 5E lore but not previous edition lore. They are not the product of a liaison between a celestial and a mortal. Celestials cannot reproduce. The rare aasimar are souls pulled from Purgatory and given a chance to make the mortal realm a better place through chaos ass-kicking.

They are viewed as both blessed (the chosen of celestials) and with suspicion (souls that were not worthy enough to go to Mount Elysia).

Genasi are not an established race but rather, like dragonborn, the union of an elemental lord in human form and a human. They are born sterile—dragons are native to the Welt, but elementals are outsiders. How they are treated is dependent on where in the Empire they are. The more civilized and established Imperial Realms will view a genasi with suspicion. In wilder Imperial Providences or Holdings, such as the Viscounty of Kandra, they are a blessing from nature.

Orcs are not racial enemies of anybody except

Intro

Lost at the Beaux Seins

Moortide Rising

The Altar & the Anvil

Castle Wailmoor

Appendix

goblins. There is no orc pantheon—many magic-using orcs are simply druids or shamans. Orcs are more likely to worship dragons as not, although dragons don't answer prayers.

Most other races view orcs as primitive. Orcs view other races as people who don't help them with their endless wars with the goblins.

Half-orcs are often seen as the product of two war-like races (humans and orcs). Like dragonborn, they are treated with a small amount of reverence outside of their communities. Like half-elves making more half-elves, half-orcs, when they breed with each other, produce more half-orcs. When they do so, they tend to band together in remote places to have some semblance of their own culture without Imperial (human) influence.

Half-Elves are usually the union of an elf and an attractive human for the specific purpose of marrying a human noble in an arranged marriage. Some chafe at their lot, others revel in it. A half-elf mating with a human produces human offspring.

Half-elves who do not carry through with their arranged marriage are not exiled from elven lands, but they aren't made welcome, either. In human lands, these "escaped" half-elves are viewed with pity, and thus in campaign lore, they switch places with half-orcs to a small extent and are often sullen and broody.

There are cultural exceptions to this—half-elves that have banded together feel a very strong sense of community, and do not welcome elves in their midst. Nor do they let the "aw, poor half-elf" commentary bother them.

THE GEKK

Lizardfolk are called gekk, and like genasi, how they are viewed and treated is dependent on the local populous. They had a primitive, but a powerful empire that stretched across the Kingdom of Lothmar long ago. They were defeated in a holy crusade and now live in out-of-the-way places within the Kingdom. Outside of the Kingdom, they are viewed as primitive curiosities. Inside the Kingdom, feelings towards the gekk are as varied as feelings towards other races. The views of the gekk towards other races are a bigger factor—the gekk are people, according to the Empire, and thus crimes against them are as if a crime was committed against a human.

Most gekk enjoy their lives and place in the Empire. To them, the war was long ago. There are some diehard gekk longing for the days of old, but gekk are simply yet another race the Empire has brought to heel and swallowed in her borders.

Gekk historians are fully aware that "the good old days" of the gekk empires were very bad indeed. Many worshiped demons. There is evidence that there were things *worse* than demons directing the gekk empires.

NON-STANDARD RACES THAT FIT

The intent of this campaign is to support the 5E standard races in the PHB with a few exceptions, but there are races outside of the PHB supported in other products that work well.

Aarakocra, **bugbear**, **firbolg**, **kenku**, **tabaxi**, **triton**, **yuan-ti purebloods**, **tortle**, **kalashtar**, **centaur**, **loxodont** and **minotaur** all fit within the "rules" of the campaign. While rare, they could have local communities in various locations around the Kingdom and neighboring Imperial lands. In the more civilized parts of the Empire, not so much.

ANTAGONISTIC RACES

Goblins, **gnolls**, **kobolds**, **hobgoblins,** and **ogres** are at war with the other races. They are detained when found by soldiers and lawmen in the civilized portions of the Empire. On border holdings or provinces, they are attacked on sight.

PRIOR LIVES

The PCs eventually reincarnated as the Knights of Wailmoor, finally coming together after countless years apart. But they never remembered whom they were, and so, the Knights of Wailmoor were like ships passing in the fog. As they died one-by-one in the Demon War, the survivors felt deep sorrow and at times unbearable grief.

Some of the knights are mentioned by name in the *Lost Memories*. It isn't a necessity to tell attribute a past life to any PC, but if that's desired simply add to the following table:

KNIGHT	DETAILS
Jackon	Sir Jackon was a knighted Imperial War Wizard, holding a degree in War and Battle Studies, and served a tour with the Imperial Armed Forces as a special operations commissioned officer before taking up his duties in the Wailmoor
Heleshia	Dame Heleshia was an elf, a highly skilled swordsman augmented with both arcane and divine capabilities
Garret	Sir Garret was a weapon master and a lancer, in charge of security at Castle Wailmoor
Dannok	Sir Dannok was highly stealthy, at odds with this big frame and massive greatsword. He was the highest-ranking Knight in the service of the Baron when the Demon War broke out
Terri	Dame Terri was a Paladin of Platine and was proficient in channeling raw, almost uncontrollable radiant energy on her magical bastard sword
Carl (not discussed in the module)	Carl was both a Knight of Wailmoor and a Wailmoor Ranger. If there are six PCs, one of them could have the vision of Carl as he was investigating strange sightings along the eastern border of the Wailmoor. He was shot in the back of the head with an arrow, assailant unknown—the first causality of the Demon War.

DEATH MECHANIC

This is the life the Hierophants of old had been waiting for, and consequently, death is no escape from the *Curse of the Lost Memories.*

If a PC dies—fails three Death Saves—and not *raised* or *resurrected* within 5-minutes, the PC's body will wind up in the Great Tree's hallow at the stable in the Crossroads Village. This happens even if the PC is cremated or buried (both impressive feats for the time limit) or the body otherwise unavailable. Any gear on the PC is transporting to the Great Tree along with the body.

Once in the Great Tree, the PC is alive with 1d6 hit points and becomes conscious in 1d4 minutes.

DEATH MECHANIC VISUAL EFFECT

If anyone is viewing the body, it disappears after being struck by a lightning bolt, originating in the sky, even if underground or underwater. If the sky is clear, black rumbling clouds will roll in rapidly, complete with thunder and lightning flashes, swirl around the PC's body and with a mighty clap of thunder and flash of light, the PC will disappear.

DRUIDS AT THE STABLE

The Druids of the Stable will be surprised by this, but not hostile and *extremely* curious. The PC in question will have some explaining to do, or not, depending on their level of trust with the druids. What they can learn in this module about their true condition is scant.

STABLE CHANGES

The Great Tree is power, and the PC's resurrection in it reminds Jerimiah that the primal forces of the Welt can be chaotic and dangerous. After the Viscount and the Lancers leave, he closes the upper portion of the stable to everyone except the druids.

When Sir Walshan inquires about this change, he says "sometimes, the Great Tree is just dangerous." That explanation is good enough for the Knight.

DEATH PENALTY

The druidic tree resurrection at the stable carries with it a severe penalty. All six Ability Scores are lowered by one. This condition persists until the PC advances to the next level. If the PC dies repeatedly before leveling, each score can only be lowered to a minimum of 8. Once all scores are 8, the PC will continue to resurrect, but still must level to regain all ability scores lost in this manner.

Once the PC levels, all lost Ability scores lowered, either by the *Curse of the Lost Memory* Death Mechanic or through other means, are automatically restored.

This penalty is unavoidable; *restoration* magic or *curse removal* spells or items does not restore lost Ability points. PCs who die can avoid this mechanic by receiving a divine spell that *raises the dead,* such as within 5-minutes of expiring.

There is one *raise dead* scroll under the priest's bed in Castle Wailmoor, and another in the Reliquary in the Temple of Dvalin.

CUSTOM LOST MEMORIES

A DM familiar with this module can (and encouraged to do so) add *Lost Memories* for role-playing purposes. However, due to the intensity of the fall of Wailmoor as Knights of Wailmoor, memories of prior lives beyond their last one will not manifest themselves yet. It will be confusing enough as it is.

Clever players may suspect something deeper than unfinished business from the Demon War is going on, but assertive revelations of their place in the universe are for later modules in the *Chronicles of the Celestial Chains* Campaign.

Intro

Lost at the Beaux Seins

Moortide Rising

The Altar & the Anvil

Castle Wailmoor

Appendix

On Druids

Druids of today bear little resemblance of the druids of old before the gods invested themselves in the World. Druid PCs will not have any lore knowledge of either their past lives or the reincarnation ability of those ancient Hierophants.

Furthermore, the Viscounty of Kandra, druids are mighty horse trainers, animal shepherds, and agricultural advisors. Long has it been since druids in the Viscounty were akin to the primal nature runners of old.

In the vast stretches of untamed wilderness, "classic" druids do exist, but they are careful to not cause trouble within reach of the divine-centric Empire.

However, neither type of druid bears any similarity to the primal and elemental masters of old except only in the later levels of a current druid's career.

Which isn't to say druids can't regain their former glory—the power they tapped into, becoming extensions of The Welt itself—is still there.

And the PCs can recapture that primal magic but at a price. Everything has a price in *the Chronicles of the Celestial Chains*, and sometimes that price is a terrible, terrible thing to suffer.

Lost at the Beaux Seins Inn & Pub

"EVERY JOURNEY SHOULD START WITH A GOOD BEER. YOU SHOULD START A BAD JOURNEY WITH GOOD BEER, TOO!
(SIP)
"AND IF YOUR JOURNEY IS GONNA BE A BORING ONE, STARTING WITH A BEER SEEMS LIKE A PROMISING IDEA. IF THE JOURNEY IS ONLY A MIGHT POSSIBILITY, A FINE BEER WILL ALSO SET THE TONE. WHAT? DON'T GIVE ME THAT LOOK. THE VISCOUNTY HAS MORE THAN HORSES, YANNO. WE HAVE THE BEST DAMN BEER IN THE EMPIRE."
—EVAN THE BARKEEP, OVERHEARD JUST YESTERDAY

The Beaux Seins Inn & Pub in an important stop along the Viscounty's eastern border, simply to support travelers on the High Road, which travels from the barbarian elven-centric lands in the north, to the Duchy of Hardred to the south. The Kandra Road starts at the inn and runs all the way to the northwestern border of the Viscounty.

The inn, stables, a new manor home, and three farmhouses compose the small hamlet at the crossroads, with the farms only purpose to supply the inn and pub.

Travelers on the roads appreciate the inn mightily. The local populous enjoy the comforts of the pub. While the next village is twenty miles away, by horseback, it's an acceptable journey for outlying farms and herdsman for a change of pace (and a wench who isn't local).

The recent incursions of aberrations and rabid animals from the moors to the southeast were worrisome, but not a surprise, really. The place is haunted, after all.

That the Viscount himself showed up with two squads of Lancers after word was sent to the nearest guard post was odd, but not impossible. The benevolent, hands-on ruler often traveled the Viscounty.

No, things pretty much went bad when the player characters showed up.

Chapter One Summary

This chapter presents the crossroads village description, the people within, followed by The Curse Abides section, which starts the *Curse of the Lost Memories* adventure and *Chronicles of the Celestial Chains* campaign. The PCs all find themselves in a pub having a well-deserved beer, but the seemingly clichéd start isn't going to be what they expect.

The Crossroads village is more of a small hamlet than a bustling center of commerce. All the inhabitants are listed in the first section for the DM to use during the PCs investigation of what happened in the village. NPCs are listed with their motivations, and where warranted, how they act if they are Friendly, Indifferent or Hostile.

Areas

This section has all the areas in the Crossroads Village and all the NPCs therein. NPCs have listed motivations, attitudes, and anything they know about the mysterious events prior to the PCs arriving at the Beaux Semis.

First Encounter

The first encounter, The Curse Abides, starts on page
37. This encounter introduces the PCs to each other and people in the village beyond travelers seeking refuge and entertainment at the famous Pub.

Aftermath

Whatever happens in the Pub, the PCs are both impacting the world around them and being impacted by the same. This section covers the likely NPC reactions to The Curse Abides encounter.

Dungeon Mastering Note

The PCs can gain material and other support if they befriend the villagers. More so than that, how the PCs clean out the Wailmoor and how they interact with the Sir Walshan and the Dame has a profound impact on the village, which further increases the aid they can give to the PCs.

Skill Checks

There is a significant number of Skill check opportunities in this chapter, especially around soft skills (Persuasion, Insight, etc.) and in the later chapters around Skills Needed to Not Die.

Skill Checks, especially when they concern NPCs, are simply a means to an end with the almighty randomness factor built in on a die roll, not the end itself. Rolling a 1 and a 20, or a 2 and a 19, adds a significant amount of flavor to NPC interaction.

The investigation should reveal whom to talk to or what someone said, not a bulleted list of items revealed by the DM to the Players. Skill Checks are never supposed to be a metagame component—they are clues, directions and when they fail, obstacles—bound by the randomness of a roll with the benefits of Proficiency and progression.

In campaign play, the DM can slow down and provide the foundation for players to form their own narratives both as individual PCs and as an Adventuring Party™. For example, a player saying they are diplomatic and then rolling for Persuasion without revealing what they say is a story degradation. Trying to be persuasive and *then* rolling is advancing the story, rather than being advanced by the story. Skill rolls should have bonuses for good roleplaying and intra-party cooperation—but don't go easy on the players. **Failure on the way to success makes for dynamic 3-dimensional campaigns.**

Difficulty Challenge Checks and Saves in the *Chronicles of Celestial Chains* Campaign follow this pattern. Skills were always supposed to be part of a solution with a random element and the rules and framework around success or failure. They were never intended to be the actual success or failure.

THE CROSSROADS

Intro

Lost at the Beaux Seins

Moortide Rising

The Altar & the Anvil

Castle Wailmoor

Appendix

THE VILLAGE

The Beaux Seins Inn & Pub and its stable are the central features of the crossroads. Everything else at the crossroads, which includes the newly built manor for the newly installed knight, is there to support the inn and pub.

Most of the logistical support comes from the three farms that produce food for themselves and the inn, and now, to a small extent, the new manor.

THE VILLAGE AT A GLANCE

At the intersection between two paved roads lies a way stop for travelers comprised as an inn and connected pub. The crossroads are nestled against a plateau to the southeast, and an overgrown track winds its way to the top in lazy switchbacks.

The inn, pub and stable aren't the only features of the crossroads. Three farmhouses and their outbuildings lie on the northwestern side of the High Road, one to the southwest of Kandra Road and the other two to the northeast. The pie-shaped plotlines are lined with

hedges, trees, and stone fencing, denoting these farms have been here a long time.

The northeastern-most farm is clearly a halfling home, the home (but not the barn) burrowed into a small rise.

The farmhouses, their barns, and outbuildings are in good condition, and it is obvious the farmers enjoy some modicum of wealth. While not estate-like, each has been maintained with pride. The juxtaposition of the remote crossroads with the old-world feel throws many visitors off.

Southeast of the High Road and east-northeast of the inn, on a gentle hill rise, is a manor home, rising out of extensive gardens and various fruit trees.

It is obvious the Viscount treats his duties of the proper use and maintenance of Imperial Roads very seriously—the High Road and Kandra road are well maintained and in near-perfect condition, lined with pleasant, large-trunked ginkgo biloba trees whose roots do not intrude upon the road, but branches provide adequate shade from any summer sun.

The Farms

There are three farms, each with large, multi-level farmhouse, a barn—pastures for cows, sheep, horses, and pigs—that give way to fields of grain, hay, timothy, and vegetable plots. All the farms have beehives—essentially, each farm is a self-contained farm/ranch with specialties.

Each farmer owns the land underneath it. The farmers are the people who also, from the center of the crossroads extending five miles in any direction, are responsible for making any temporary repairs and notifying the road engineer of issues.

Prior to Sir Walshan's appointment last year as "The Knight of the Crossroads" and his subsequent building of the manor, the farms saw much autonomy. While they paid modest taxes to the Viscount, he was too far away to tithe a portion of the food they grew. Thus each farmstead was prosperous when good crop yields let them sell the reaming food to the lord west of the village, approximately twenty miles away.

This ended with Sir Walshan's appointment. There was some resentment on the impending income decrease, but it turned out the entirety of Sir Walshan's manor consisted of himself, his wife, his squire, Farmer Ted, and Devos, the gardener. Sir Walshan's estate is mostly self-sufficient.

Overriding Motivation

Any lingering disappointment over the dramatic change imposed by the Viscount was erased by Sir Walshan's defense of the village in a recent incursion of monstrous dogs from the haunted moors to the east. Without the knight's martial prowess and his ability to rally a small squad in defense of the village, there is little doubt they'd all be dead.

Thus, the farmers are motivated by *safety*. Their worldview went from wholesome substance provision to a poignant reminder of both their mortality and place in the Viscounty. Without support, the Inn cannot function. If the Inn cannot function, then the Viscount's obligation to the Empire cannot be fulfilled. While the Viscounty may be an Imperial Protectorate and not an Imperial Realm, the villagers have their pride. Failure is not an option.

This motivation bleeds into all their interactions with PCs. The PCs are seen both as a potential savior or another thorn in Sir Walshan's side. Either way, it all comes down to the PCs motivations. Do they care what happens in this thorp?

Becoming aware of ones or morality in a sudden way causes people to react. If a marriageable farm girl believes taking a jaded PC behind the barn so he'll be more empathic to their plight, she'll do it and fake it, and her parents will look the other way.

Are the PCs Heroes, or Hobos?

The Farms at a Glance

A closer look at the farms give the impression, because of the way the hedges and trees are planted, each is on pie-shaped lots with the wedge getting wider as the plot extends outward from the village.

As with most Viscounty food production, each has a mixture of farming and ranching, although none of them have the tale-tail signs of raising horses for exporting outside the Viscounty.

These are prosperous farms, the people seen no mere peasants, typical of land-owning farmers and ranchers in the Viscounty.

The Wilcox Farm

The Wilcox specialty is raising sheep, not just for mutton and lamb, but also selling the excess wool to the rest of the village and traders who stop by. They have extensive flower gardens to make dyes.

The Wilcox extended family currently is:

- **Ashner**, 60, the elder Wilcox that refuses to take it easy and his wife **Trudy** (55) who has mild dementia.
- **Gerry**, 30, first-born son and his wife **Anna** (28) and their children **Kate** (15), **Sherri** (14), **Hampton** (13), **Grego** (12) and **Nena** (5). Gerry's family has most of the farming duties.
- **Havlo**, 27 and his two wives, **Jani** (23) and **Yenifer** (20) and their 4 children **Amnar** (17), **Torrie** (15) by Jani and **Sam** (16) and **Lore** (14) by Yenifer. They live in a comfortable living area that makes up the upper half of the large barn.

Ashner's daughter **Hanna** died in a horseback riding accident many years ago before she could be married, while **Morena** (29) is married to Candors' senior son, and lives on the Candor Farm.

Ashner's other son, **Zander** (24) is an Imperial Courier, delivering messages along the High Road and Kandra Road. Zander is unmarried, but it is unknown if he has any children or not. The Wilcox clan wants to disapprove of his eternal bachelorhood, but an Imperial agent is a respectable and highly honorable position. He frequently stops at the family farm while executing his courier duties.

Friendly Attitude

The Wilcox matrons will make sure the PCs are always fed and invite them to dinner or breakfast. Dinner will consist of a leg of lamb and lamb stew. The PCs will always have a pie to take with them.

If the PCs perform any kind actions towards the Wilcox family, Anna will make sure available bachelors have a nice wool sweater in five days and drop hints that her daughter Kate is of marrying age.

Indifferent (Starting)

The Wilcox family refers all conversation to Gerry. Gerry will be polite and, if prompted, relate how their dogs all went missing right before the swamp dog attack.

Hostile

The family does their best to avoid PCs and alert the other villagers of trouble, running first to the Inn's two guards. While a Charisma (Persuade) check could improve their disposition, most likely the offending PC(s) will need to make amends for their transgressions with more than honeyed words.

The Candor Farm

The Candor Farm's specialty is beef (and so more of a ranch). They rotate cattle pastures with the wheat, timothy, and grain, essentially the cattle being a fertilizer factory for vital horse-centric crops.

The extended Candor family is:

- **Gillian** (62), widow of Jayson Candor
- **Fredrick**, 35, married to Morena (29) and their five children **Kemper** (16), **Peter** (14), **Josephine** (12), **Maxine** (10) and **Calvin** (8).
- **Lorrie Miller**, 21, and her husband, **William Miller** (25), and their 4 children **Bella** (8), **Joseph** (6), **Gwen** (5) and **Dax** (2). Lorrie is currently pregnant.

The Candors have extensive relatives farther west, relatives that have been siphoned off excess children for generations by arranging marriages and respectable work. William is the product of such an arranged marriage, wanting to ranch, and offered a wholesome and beautiful Lorrie in exchange for moving to the Candor Farm. William and his family live in the cozy living quarters in the upper part of the barn.

William has hired and imported a cattle hand, the Widower **Art** (26) and his son **Tom** (12), who live in a cabin northwest of the farmhouse.

It is the wives of the Crossroads repeatedly stated goal to have Art remarry, and there is a multitude of local options. Art, however, is still grieving over his lost wife and daughter, victims of a flash flood. Both Art and Tom seem content to roam with the cattle, but the wholesome girls-of-age may chip away at their self-imposed solitude.

Friendly Attitude

The Candor's matrons will make sure the PCs are always fed and invite them to dinner or breakfast. Dinner will consist of steak, roast beef, and beef stew. The PCs will always have a pie to take with them, along with beef jerky and pepperoni sticks.

If the PCs perform any kind actions towards the Candor family, Morena will drop hints that in a couple of years the beautiful Josephine will be of marrying age.

Intro

Lost at the Beaux Seins

Moortide Rising

The Altar & the Anvil

Castle Wailmoor

Appendix

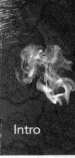

INDIFFERENT (STARTING)

The Candor family refers all conversation to Fredrick. Like Gerry Wilcox, he will be polite and, if prompted, relate how their dogs also went missing right before the swamp dog attack.

HOSTILE

The family does their best to avoid PCs and alert the other villagers of trouble, especially the Druids. While a Charisma check could improve their disposition, most likely the offending PC(s) will need to make amends for their transgressions with more than honeyed words.

THE HEARTHWARM FARM

The High Road runs between two gentle hills, and while the Manor sits on one, the halfling farmers have are invested in the other with a large and impressively comfortable halfling home.

The Hearthwarm Farm's specialty is pork. They make phenomenally tasty sausages, and pork products such as applewood smoked bacon.

The Hearthwarm extended family is:

- **Grampa Bill** (77) his wife **Grandma Shershi** (73), and the window **Grandma Nedia** (74)

- Unmarried offspring of Bill and Shershi: **Golo** (25), **Joanna** (23), **Hornlo** (21); unmarried offspring of Bill and Nedia: the twins **Serinma** (18) and **Sissy** (18)

- Married offspring of Bill and Shershi: **Groland** (45) and his wife **Pride** (42) have 4 children: **Sassi** (20), **Harold** (18), **Tribbi** (15), **Donal** (13) and **Kimie** (6)

The halflings also have 4 human farmhands who live in the living quarters in the upper part of the barn: **Cecile** (19), **Micha** (20) and **Odo** (18) and **Shap** (28). Cecile works at the Wilcox Farm, Odo works on the Condor Farm while Shap and Micha work directly for Groland. Groland is actively searching for more hands.

All three farms grow hops, but it is the Hearthwarm farm that turns it into beer.

FRIENDLY ATTITUDE

The Hearthwarm matrons will make sure the PCs are always fed and invite them to dinner or breakfast. Dinner will consist of ham and smoked sausages with endless amounts of tasty beer., roast beef, and beef stew. The PCs will always have a pie to take with them, and even a small keg.

Both Joanna and Sassi are of marrying age. Well-off and charming halflings are made to feel quite welcome at any time.

INDIFFERENT (STARTING)

All conversation is steered towards Groland. Groland has an alternate view on the recent unfortunate activities. He will relate that one of his ancestors came from the Wailmoor and he has explored it a bit. He said the place "thrums with power" and at night "the stars are misplaced." He talks about a creepy obelisk that seemingly overlooks the village, and that, when he tried to pay respects at the Old Graveyard gates, "the very air seemed to be thick with magic."

Groland is the reason no one visits the Wailmoor. He is not known as a person who exaggerates and is seen as brave—he told everyone to stay away lest they be cursed.

He doesn't know much else and is glad if the PCs ask about it as if he needed an excuse to get it off his chest. After talking about the moor, any kind word or friendly demeanor will change his attitude to friendly automatically.

HOSTILE

The family does their best to avoid PCs and alert the other villagers of trouble, especially the Dame. While a Charisma check could improve their disposition, most likely the offending PC(s) will need to make amends for their transgressions with more than honeyed words.

RELATIONS BETWEEN FARMS

These three farms are inter-dependent. They can't fulfill their duties to the Inn without cooperation and help from the other farms. For example, the Candor farm produces the mules required to work the land, while the Wilcox Farm supplies most of the cloth for clothing (they also trade the wool for cotton cloth bolts). The Hearthwarm Farm supplies most of the smoked meat. They are also dependent on the druids for animal health and long-term forestry management. The druids had farmers plant trees even outside settled lands for dozens of generations.

All three farms consequently are staunch allies and friends up to the point the whole could be considered a clan rather than a feudal relationship. They may have differences, but the three farms with their relative size work.

What doesn't work is a singular disaster would cause a catastrophic labor shortage, and it all comes crashing down. These farmers are not working 14-hour days and need be, can step it up. They are robust and advanced enough to weather the occasional bad crop.

Replacing people, on the other hand, is something altogether different.

Villagers' Stat Blocks

Human Commoner (male)

Medium Humanoid — Lawful Good
Armor Class 10 — **Hit Points** 7 — **Speed** 30 ft.

Statistics

STR	DEX	CON	INT	WIS	CHA
13 (+1)	11 (+0)	12 (+1)	10 (+0)	10 (+0)	10 (+0)

Skills Animal Handling +2, Athletics +3
Senses passive Perception 10
Languages Common, Halfling
Challenge 0 (10XP)

Actions

Dagger. Melee or Ranged Weapon Attack: +1 to hit, reach 5 ft. or range 20 ft./60 ft., one target.
Hit: 3 (1d4+1) piercing damage.

Spear. Melee or Ranged Weapon Attack: +3 to hit, reach 5 ft. or range 20 ft./60 ft., one target.
Hit: 4 (1d6+1) piercing damage or 5 (1d8+1) piercing damage if used with two hands to make a melee attack.

Human Commoner (female)

Medium Humanoid — Lawful Good
Armor Class 10 — **Hit Points** 7 — **Speed** 30 ft.

Statistics

STR	DEX	CON	INT	WIS	CHA
11 (+0)	10 (+0)	12 (+1)	10 (+0)	10 (+0)	12 (+1)

Skills Animal Handling +3, Athletics +2
Senses passive Perception 11
Languages Common, Halfling
Challenge 0 (1-XP)

Actions

Dagger. Melee or Ranged Weapon Attack: +0 to hit, reach 5 ft. or range 20 ft./60 ft., one target.
Hit: 2 (1d4) piercing damage.

Spear. Melee or Ranged Weapon Attack: +2 to hit, reach 5 ft. or range 20 ft./60 ft., one target.
Hit: 3 (1d6) piercing damage or 4 (1d8) piercing damage if used with two hands to make a melee attack.

These are the most common stats for a human farmer 13 or older. Assume that younger humans are non-combatants and will run at the first sign of battle (if able to) and if attacked, die on the first lethal blow.

These stats are general. For example, there are humans who are more and less wise, and more and less charismatic.

Humans in the Viscounty are a hearty, strong lot, known for their animal handling and advanced land stewardship. These are no exception.

Consider all farms to have access to all equipment needed for farming, such as mules, advanced plows, flails, and scythes.

Halfling Commoner (male)

Medium Humanoid — Neutral Good
Armor Class 10 — **Hit Points** 7 — **Speed** 30 ft.

Statistics

STR	DEX	CON	INT	WIS	CHA
11 (+0)	12 (+1)	12 (+1)	11 (+0)	11 (+0)	11 (+0)

Skills Animal Handling +2, Athletics +2
Senses passive Perception 10
Languages Common, Halfling
Challenge 0 (10XP)

Actions

Dagger. Melee or Ranged Weapon Attack: +1 to hit, reach 5 ft. or range 20 ft./60 ft., one target.
Hit: 3 (1d4+1) piercing damage.

Sling. Ranged Weapon Attack: +3 to hit, range 30 ft./120 ft., one target.
Hit: 3 (1d4+1) bludgeoning damage.

Spear. Melee or Ranged Weapon Attack: +0 to hit, reach 5 ft. or range 20 ft./60 ft., one target.
Hit: 3 (1d6) piercing damage or 4 (1d8) piercing damage if used with two hands to make a melee attack.

Halfling Commoner (female)

Medium Humanoid — Neutral Good
Armor Class 10 — **Hit Points** 7 — **Speed** 30 ft.

Statistics

STR	DEX	CON	INT	WIS	CHA
10 (+0)	12 (+1)	12 (+1)	11 (+0)	11 (+0)	12 (+0)

Skills Animal Handling +3, Athletics +2
Senses passive Perception 11
Languages Common, Halfling
Challenge 0 (10XP)

Actions

Dagger. Melee or Ranged Weapon Attack: +1 to hit, reach 5 ft. or range 20 ft./60 ft., one target.
Hit: 3 (1d4+1) piercing damage.

Sling. Ranged Weapon Attack: +3 to hit, range 30 ft./120 ft., one target.
Hit: 3 (1d4+1) bludgeoning damage.

Spear. Melee or Ranged Weapon Attack: +0 to hit, reach 5 ft. or range 20 ft./60 ft., one target.
Hit: 3 (1d6) piercing damage or 4 (1d8) piercing damage if used with two hands to make a melee attack.

These are the most common stats for a halfling farmer 16 or older. Assume that younger halflings are non-combatants and will run at the first sign of battle (if able to) and if attacked, die on the first lethal blow.

Halflings in the Viscounty have a reputation of being burly but attractive, friendly, enterprising, and nimble.

These have that reputation with a side of prolific child producers. The prior generation lost several siblings to wanderlust, and Groland and Pride have

Intro

Lost at the Beaux Seins

Moortide Rising

The Altar & the Anvil

Castle Wailmoor

Appendix

WALSHAN MANOR

been filling in the gap. She is pregnant with their fifth child. Joanna and Hornlo are ready to be married, and the mate search has commenced in earnest. The Hearthwarm family is prosperous, so any marriage will see generous support, especially if the couple stays on the farm.

SECRETS OF THE FARMS

Last year was a poor harvest but this year will be bountiful. These farms, though, are running hot—if it wasn't for the four farmhands living on the Hearthwarm farm, they would not be able to produce the amount of hay, timothy and grain the stable require and the amount of food the inn needs while feeding themselves—the genesis of the drama and handwringing when the Viscount appointed Sir Walshan as the Knight of the Crossroads and gifted him the inn, pub and stable. Coin taxes were the least of their worries—giving over a portion of their crops seemed like a disaster in the making.

Sir Walshan, however, hired a grander and a farmhand, with the farmhand tending their own 25 acres. Devos the gardener practices no-till techniques and tends to about 10 acres of vegetables. For now, the manor covers most of their food needs.

Imperial Agriculture techniques have vastly changed the Empire, and the Crossroads Village farms are no exception. A man-of-age with access to mules and advanced plows found in the Kingdom can tend

about 50 to 60 acres a year depending on the ages of the children or other laborers helping him. More acreage a year is dedicated to supplying the stables than the pub.

This is only of interest insomuch as the original land grant for each farm is 1800 acres. The farmers have considerably more land than they can farm.

Because of the amount of land, the three farms practice more advanced forms of crop rotation, and thus each acre is more productive than the typical Imperial farm. The extra land cannot effectively be farmed even if additional farmhouses are built—there is no local market for their food, the sale of excess crops only possible because the lord of the next manor comes and gets it. This is a remote location, miles, and miles from the next villages, and only exist to facilitate travel on the two Imperial Roads. The farms, inn, pub and stable exist in equilibrium. This equates to a low population.

And that is the start of the village downfall if not interrupted. They've lived for seven generations since the fall of the moors, relying on the travelers at the inn, and the druids of the stable, for relative security.

Unbeknownst to all, a ward stone at the western border of the moor kept wandering monsters and other nasty things from rising out of the bogs and prying upon the lowlands.

Recently, the last of these barriers fell to the relentless corruption festering in the moors, a mere four miles away from the village up the old road to the moor plateau. The result was the swamp dog attack, but there are other dire consequences in store sooner, rather than later.

And if the player characters are not successful in their quest to rid the moors of corruption, most everyone at the Crossroads Village, including the new knight and most of his household, will die.

THE MANOR

The Knight Sir Carl Walshan has a manor home befitting an honored knight, but the small household of a new appointment. Sir Walshan owns extensive land that starts with the inn, pub and stable and extends northeast and southwest, land that abuts the moor plateau and turns northwest and northeast to follow the property lines of the stable and Hearthwarm Farm, 3200 acres (5 square miles) in all—lands worthy of an influential lord.

5-square miles of fertile land, on the edge of the Viscounty, Kingdom, and Empire—Sir Walshan doesn't quite know what to make of it, but his friend and confidant the druid **Jerimiah** cautioned for a slow approach to any expansion.

It is obvious the Viscount now considers the remote crossroads of some import, but until the swamp dog attack, Sir Walshan had his doubts. It is the intersection of two Imperial Roads. Even from a remote standpoint, a safe place patrolled simply by the number of travelers and the occasional Kingdom and Viscounty patrols.

THE MANOR AT A GLANCE

At the top of a gentle rise northeast of the inn on the southern side of the High Road lies a manor home. The path is lined with shrubbery and flowers and ends in a large garden-like field that stretches around the hill before the manor home in what could only be described as a riot of color. A nearby barn is situated behind and to the northwest of the manor.

Both the gardens, the manor, and the barn look new. From the High Road, a pasture can't be seen, but it is likely there is one on the northeastern side of the hill.

PEOPLE OF THE MANOR

As the relationship between the farms, the pub, the inn, and the stables, the Walshan Manor is a tightly-knit group due to an atypical, small manor household. While Dame Walshan has forbidden her husband from doing any "woman's work," everyone else pitches in on cooking, cleaning, and maintaining the manor. Meals are hearty and delicious, cooked and served family style.

Everyone knows this can't last and someday there will be servants. But each is enjoying the intimacy of a small, cohesive group and friendship.

The Walshan household:

- **Sir Carl Walshan**, 22, Knight of the Crossroads, Protector of the Viscounty
- **Dame Melissai Walshan**, 22, his wife, a half-elf from the elven forests of Shaeniss.
- **Squire Dagmar**, 18, a skilled longbowman
- **Davos**, 40 a gardener and handyman
- **Ted**, 33, a farmer

SIR CARL WALSHAN

One day, Carl Walshan was training several new lads how to swing their swords, the next he was a knight, owner of a lucrative business, albeit a remote business and charged with defending people who had never been attacked in generations by anything fiercer than a frightened brown bear.

After his manor was built, he was then married to a stranger—a beautiful half-elf with magical powers and a pet cat that wasn't really a cat.

In between the time the manor was built and the swamp dog attack, Sir Walshan spent his time learning to farm from Ted, his hired farmhand, thinking that was going to be his focus in the remote, but seemingly safe, crossroads.

Sir Carl Walshan

Medium Humanoid — Fighter 5 — Neutral Good
Armor Class 19 (half plate, shield) — **Hit Points** 47 — **Speed** 30 ft.

Statistics

STR	DEX	CON	INT	WIS	CHA
16 (+3)	14 (+2)	12 (+1)	11 (+0)	11 (+0)	13 (+1)

Saving Throws STR +6, CON +4
Feats Blade Mastery
Skills Animal Handling +3, Athletics +6
Senses passive Perception 10
Languages Common, Halfling, Elvish
Challenge 2 (450 XP)

Actions

Longbow. *Ranged Weapon Attack:* +5 to hit, range 150 ft./600 ft., one target.
Hit: 6 (1d8+2) piercing damage.

Longsword. *Melee Weapon Attack:* +7 to hit, reach 5 ft., one target.
Hit: 9 (1d8+5) slashing damage or 8 (1d10+3) slashing damage if used with two hands to make a melee attack.

Carl's full stat block is on page 47. Sir Walshan's javelins and lance are a part of his horse gear. While Walshan is a good rider and a better swordsman, he is

Intro

Lost at the Beaux Seins

Moortide Rising

The Altar & the Anvil

Castle Wailmoor

Appendix

also a good archer and is never far from his massive longbow.

Currently, Sir Walshan is bedridden and will be so for a week longer unless he receives a magical disease cure. Once the disease has run its course, he will be permanently immune to it, so he has not gone out of his way to find an instant cure.

FRIENDLY ATTITUDE

Sir Walshan will offer his Manor home to the PCs as guests for the customary three days, and longer if they ask.

Sir Walshan's helpful disposition carries extensive political connections that can be used in the next module as the PCs assert themselves beyond a desperate group of adventurers. Carl is a Lord in all but name only—he has considerable connections to the two lords to the south and west of him, and of the elves to the north. Insightful PCs can accurately guess that he is going places.

INDIFFERENT

As noted later, Sir Walshan relates the tale of the swamp dog attack, but only after the PCs have the incident in the Inn with their unfortunate memories.

HOSTILE

The PCs has done goofed. Sir Walshan is no stranger to battle, and even sick has the same statistics and abilities. He will banish the PCs from the village with the backing of the two guards of the inn, his squire, and the druids, and then, while the PCs are gone, hire mercenaries to back up his authority should they return.

If the PCs attack anyone in the village, he replies with lethal force, assembling the same squad and focusing on killing obvious spellcasters first. Sir Walshan's experienced party will focus-fire and take out opponents one at a time. If the PCs have murdered anyone he will fight to the death and only accept surrender on the condition the guilty party's execution will be swift and painless.

INVESTIGATING THE SWAMP DOG ATTACK

Prudent PCs will want to talk to Sir Walshan. However, Dame Walshan will only allow access to him if the PCs did not draw steal during the incident in the Pub. Furthermore, still getting used to humans, she will not allow any men to talk to him, as she thinks that seeing him bedridden will weaken her husband in their eyes. If there are no females in the party, she could be persuaded with a good argument, with a +2 bonus to a Charisma (Persuasion) check if someone tries to persuade her in Elvish. To change her mind about a male visiting her ill husband requires

reassurance that the PCs won't think badly of her husband and a DC 13 Wisdom (Persuasion) check.

In any event, only *one* PC will be allowed to talk to him until he is no longer bedridden.

Sir Walshan's Motivations

Sir Walshan will appear pale and weak, but he is sitting up in bed and can converse through his mild fever. He will relate the details of the swamp dog attack and downplay his role, laying praise on his squire, his wife, Vergali the dwarf and even Evan.

Sir Walshan's goals are to get healthy, protect the village and get to know the PCs better. He'll ask about the incident in the Pub—but he won't judge.

Sir Walshan, is highly motivated for the PCs to investigate the moor and will tell them he's been there. He rode up the old road, saw a strange obelisk in the fog that he did not approach, and paid his respects at the Old Graveyard entrance. He did not venture further, as his duties were to protect the village, not expend resources exploring the moor.

He's a soldier. The best defense, to him, is an offense. The PCs will have whatever resources he can muster, but his primary duty is to protect the village. He will give a soldier's advice to the PCs if they are friendly: establish a base camp in the moor and clear the place out, mile by mile.

The Truth Behind Sir Walshan

If the PCs seem sincere, honest, and trustworthy, Sir Walshan can become an influential and helpful ally not just in *Curse of the Lost Memories*, but throughout the entire campaign. While this isn't a one-shot deal, events later will make Sir Walshan more cautious because of his elevated position not just in the Viscounty but also the Kingdom.

DAME MELISSAI WALSHAN

It is the somewhat-dirty-little-secret that elven clans near human kingdoms have a program in which they find exceptional humans to mate with and produce half-elves. They then train those offspring in all manner elf, diplomacy, and some type of martial, divine, or arcane arts—and then marry them to human nobles in arranged marriages.

The benefits, of course, lead to understanding and alliances, rather than ignorance and conflict. While the Empire has existed for over 5,000 years and the elves more than any other peoples have benefited from that control of human expansion, their memories are long.

Furthermore, under the right circumstances, the conflict between Kingdoms could be sanctioned by the Empire. That has never happened to the elves thus far, and they plan to keep it that way through any means necessary.

Melissai, or Melisa to her friends, was the product of a human bard and his elf mistress. Sometimes, products of such unions become bitter at their pre-determined lot and refuse to be bartered off—retreating to the wooden wildlands and finding peace with the wilder elves there.

Melisa thought she was one such half-elf until two things happened: one, the manifestation of her sorcerous blood at puberty which led to much welcome control training at a temple of Rhiannonie and two, her mentors allowed her to view Sir Walshan from afar before agreeing to the marriage.

And Sir Walshan, overseeing the construction of his manor, with his confident disposition and armed to the teeth, made her weak-in-the-knees at sight of the big, strong bundle of handsome man-candy.

She is thoroughly agog over Sir Walshan and has been careful to make sure she is the best wife that meets his expectations. Consequently, she is eight months pregnant.

Dame Melissai Walshan

Medium Humanoid — Sorcerer 1/Cleric 1 — Neutral Good
Armor Class 11 — **Hit Points** 11 — **Speed** 30 ft.

Statistics

STR	DEX	CON	INT	WIS	CHA
10 (+0)	12 (+1)	10 (+0)	11 (+0)	16 (+3)	16 (+3)

Skills Arcana +2, Medicine +5, Persuasion +5, Religion +2
Senses darkvision 60 ft., passive Perception 13
Languages Common, Halfling, Elvish
Saving Throws WIS +5, CHA +5
Challenge ¼ (50 XP)

Spells & Powers

Spell Slots cantrip: unlimited**,** 1st: 3

Cleric Spell Save DC 13 — Spell Attack +5
1st—*bless, bless, cure wounds, guiding bolt, protection from evil and good, shield of faith*
Cantrips—*light, sacred flame, spare the dying*

Sorcerer Spell Save DC 13 — Spell Attack +5
1st—*mage armor, magic missile*
Cantrips—*blade ward, fire bolt, friends, minor illusion*

Actions

+1 Staff. *Melee Weapon Attack:* +3 to hit, reach 5 ft., one target. *Hit:* 5 (1d8+1) bludgeoning damage or 5 (1d8+1) bludgeoning damage if used with two hands to make a melee attack.

Spell Attack. *Ranged Weapon Attack:* +5 to hit, range 0 ft., one target. *Hit:* As Spell damage.

Dame Walshan's full stat block is on page 47. With only two levels, one of cleric and one sorcerer, Dame Walshan is still no mere trophy wife. Using her sorcerer spells, she will engage opponents at the maximum distance possible and only close to heal allies.

Per her training, Dame Walshan avoids any lethal conflict unless necessary, and she will always cast *mage armor* beforehand. If it wasn't for her, everyone in the village would be dead, so she is somewhat confused about her place and wishes her husband would hire additional muscle.

Melissai is cognizant of the fact that her beauty has a profound effect on men (and elves) and makes women envious. She goes out of her way to foster good relations with the rest of the village.

FRIENDLY ATTITUDE

The Dame will make sure all the PCs are healed to the best of her ability. She will also give out one or two pies out of her ever-growing pie collection.

The Dame has extensive connections to the elves of the north (that's where she's from), but they are not political, rather religious, and social. These connections have enormous benefits to the PCs in the *Chronicles of the Celestial Chains* campaign if the PCs maintain her helpful attitude.

This is a two-way street. Out of everybody in the village, the Dame could use friendly advice and help as she transitions from her elven culture to the wife of a heroic knight going places.

INDIFFERENT

Melissai is cool to the PCs and will attempt to befriend them to have one less thing to worry about.

HOSTILE

The Dame, as pregnant, will withdraw to the best of her ability and seek help from her husband or the druids. She will only fight when cornered with no recourse and all able-bodied men the village will rally to her defense and fight to the death, giving no quarter.

INVESTIGATING THE SWAMP DOG ATTACK

Pregnant and somewhat bewildered, the extraordinary beautiful Dame Walshan will cautiously take the measure of the PCs and will be predisposed to half-elves, elves, PCs that can speak elvish and sorcerers and clerics. (in that order). In any event, she hosts well-cooked dinner with expertly roasted venison, so she can meet all the PCs and take their measure.

She will relate to the best of her ability the night of the swamp dog attack, but, more importantly, she will tell the PCs that there is something wrong with those swamp dogs beyond being unclean and infectious. She will claim they are corrupted and were vile, evil creatures. She is empathic in her use of the word *corruption*.

The PCs do not need a Wisdom (Insight) check to know she is frightened.

Dame Melissai Walshan is correct and underestimating the direness of the corruption

Intro

Lost at the Beaux Seins

Moortide Rising

The Altar & the Anvil

Castle Wailmoor

Appendix

because of her lack of experience.

Dame Walshan's Motivation

For the first time since her pregnancy, Melissai does not feel safe. *If* the Viscount left on Friendly or Helpful terms, none of the PCs used lethal force earlier, *and* a PC reassures her that they will try their best to rid the moors of corruption, she will take the PC cleric aside and gift her unattuned *staff of healing*—don't casually give this item away, it is a well-earned reward for role-playing heroes instead of *"Murder Hobos."*

Dame Walshan is a private person and is slowly coming to realize that she needs to understand more about humans, halflings and her duties as the Dame of the Crossroads. In some ways, she is a more powerful ally than her husband, and her friendship, alliance, and respect must be earned.

Squire Dagmar

A squire is a sought-after position in the Viscounty for both noble and non-noble young men. Dagmar is distantly related to the Viscount and is one of the rare Viscounty warriors that received formal training in the use of a longbow in support of a knight in battle, a fighting technique seemingly at odds with the lancer reputation of the Viscounty. But, for all the horses, close-combat longbowman is a coveted position.

Dagmar put his skills to use with devastating effect alongside Sir Walshan during the swap dog attack, and right now he is patrolling the village while Sir Walshan recovers from the disease he picked up by being bitten by swamp dogs.

Squire Dagmar

Medium Humanoid — Fighter 3| Lawful Good
Armor Class 16 (scale mail) — **Hit Points** 29 — **Speed** 30 ft.

Statistics

STR	DEX	CON	INT	WIS	CHA
14 (+2)	14 (+2)	13 (+1)	10 (+0)	10 (+0)	10 (+1)

Saving Throws STR +4, CON +3
Skills Animal Handling +2, Athletics +4
Senses passive Perception 10
Languages Common, Halfling
Challenge 2 (450 XP)

Actions

Battleaxe. *Melee Weapon Attack:* +4 to hit, reach 5 ft., one target.
Hit: 6 (1d8+2) slashing damage or 7 (1d10+2) slashing damage if used with two hands to make a melee attack.

Longbow. *Ranged Weapon Attack:* +6 to hit, range 150 ft./600 ft., one target.
Hit: 6 (1d8+2) piercing damage.

Squire Dagmar's full stat block is on page 48. Dagmar is a plausible swordsman and lancer, but his

training is close-combat support via sinking longbow-driven arrow shafts into foes already engaged. This was an effective technique against the swamp dogs, but he was only one archer and the foes many. So, Dagmar had embarked on training new ranged combatants. In the brief time since the swamp dog attack, he's trained two.

Devos

Devos is the former bartender of the Beaux Seins Pub, advocating the position to the more talented Evan, his son-in-law. He always wanted to garden and farm *his* way, and Sir Walshan said he had more land than he knew what to do with—so go for it. And so, he did.

He's been an adept addition to the household, and while Farmer Ted brings in the staples, Ted also must grow timothy and hay for the horses and mule who need supplemental feed in the winter and after any major activity, especially the warhorses. Devo's ten acres of vegetables and herbs serve the manor well, and Dame Walshan loves all the flowers.

Devos is also a good cook and did indeed cook meals for the Pub on occasion.

Devos

Medium Humanoid — Neutral Good
Armor Class 10 — **Hit Points** 16 — **Speed** 30 ft.

Statistics

STR	DEX	CON	INT	WIS	CHA
13 (+1)	11 (+0)	12 (+1)	10 (+0)	10 (+0)	10 (+0)

Skills Animal Handling +2, Athletics +3
Senses passive Perception 10
Languages Common, Halfling
Challenge ¼ (10XP)

Actions

Light Crossbow. *Ranged Weapon Attack:* +2 to hit, range 80 ft./320 ft., one target.
Hit: 4 (1d8) piercing damage.

Dagger. *Melee or Ranged Weapon Attack:* +3 to hit, reach 5 ft. or range 20 ft./60 ft., one target.
Hit: 2 (1d4) piercing damage.

Sickle. *Melee Weapon Attack:* +3 to hit, reach 5 ft., one target.
Hit: 2 (1d4) slashing damage.

Like Ted, Dagmar is training Devos in simple weapon usage. He is also no warrior, although he does have experience breaking up bar fights and his crossbow is from his old barkeeping days. He never fired it in the bar, but he did take it down on a rare occasion, the act stopping the current drunken damage to the Pub.

Over the years, Devos has saved a considerable amount of coin for a commoner.

Farmer Ted

Ted is an import from the northwest. Fathering children at an early age, rather than have his sons wait around for him to die to inherit, he titled his farm and left, the memories of his late wife too much to bear in the family home.

He met Sir Walshan on the road to the village after hearing there was work to be had at the Hearthwarm farm. Sir Walshan gave him a position in his household instead.

Ted is quiet and keeps to himself. He lives in the typical Viscounty barn/stable living quarters.

During harvest and planting seasons, all the manor defers to Ted for work-schedules for the crops, including the knight and dame, a down-to-earth work ethic Ted appreciates mightily. The extra help dramatically increases his production and gives him time to help maintain the manor and grounds.

Ted

Medium Humanoid — Lawful Good
Armor Class 10 — **Hit Points** 16 — **Speed** 30 ft.

Statistics

STR	DEX	CON	INT	WIS	CHA
12 (+1)	12 (+1)	12 (+1)	10 (+0)	10 (+0)	10 (+0)

Skills Animal Handling +2, Athletics +3
Senses passive Perception 10
Languages Common, Halfling
Challenge ¼ (10XP)

Actions

Dagger. *Melee or Ranged Weapon Attack:* +3 to hit, reach 5 ft. or range 20 ft./60 ft., one target.
Hit: 2 (1d4) piercing damage.

Longbow. *Ranged Weapon Attack:* +3 to hit, range 150 ft./600 ft., one target.
Hit: 4 (1d8) piercing damage.

Spear. *Melee or Ranged Weapon Attack:* +3 to hit, reach 5 ft. or range 20 ft./60 ft., one target.
Hit: 3 (1d6) piercing damage or 4 (1d8) piercing damage if used with two hands to make a melee attack.

Since the swap dog attack, Dagmar has been training Ted with the basic usage of weapons and has even given him his spare longbow. Ted is no warrior, but he understands the basics and a proficient longbowman, even as a commoner, can make a difference.

Ted has been using his bow to hunt wild game that he comes across while farming, decreasing the meals the household must eat at the Pub. His latest catch was a much-appreciated large deer.

Secrets of the Manor

In the basement of the manor is a hidden floor vault, where Sir Walshan stores his considerable savings. As the owner of the inn, pub and stable, and the large dowry from his marriage, he has over 5,000 gold pieces worth of platinum, gold, and silver. Sir Walshan knows he needs to spend more money to have a proper manor (in the village sense of the word) but is taking Jerimiah's advice to heart—don't overextend and don't change the character of the village too dramatically.

But that isn't the dirty-little-secret of the manor, and the secret in question is *dirty*.

The elves that share a border with the Viscounty, free spirits, and life-loving people, are also long-lived and experienced enough to make hard choices.

Leaving their forest by the High Road and traveling south, the Crossroads is the first "village," and when the elves learned of a knight appoint therein, they pulled some strings inside the Viscounty and put forth their most beautiful and talented half-elf as an arranged marriage.

And they gave her a tailored, magical love potion to make sure that marriage happened and that the wedding night was filled with wanton lust and abandon.

The *charm* has since worn off, but Melissai is still just as enamored with her husband as she was when she was flush with magically-enhanced hormones. Sir Walshan is a man's man, a leader and, more important than ever, a bundle of violence as a death-dealing sword master—the Viscount knew what he was doing when he knighted him.

The elves were positive the effects of the charm would wear off, and if Sir Walshan was reputed to be the good and strong man that he was, nobody would be the wiser and the marriage would continue, reliant on the couple's true love and attraction to each other. After all, the elves have done this before.

They weren't counting on the druid Jeremiah, a perceptive druid with a cautious streak enough to back up a small suspicion with a discretely cast *detect magic* cantrip.

He'll never tell.

The Stable

The village might not be much of a village, but the Inn certainly has a proper stable by the tough Viscounty standards. It is staffed by the druidic stablemaster and two acolyte ostlers, all three holding traditional and respected positions. It is typical of the Viscounty's stables for a Lord and the large towns to have stables

Intro

Lost at the Beaux Seins

Moortide Rising

The Altar & the Anvil

Castle Wailmoor

Appendix

THE STABLE

such as these. The Crossroads, as an important trade route and the conjunction of two Imperial roads, certainly warrants the large effort and resources dedicated to the stable.

One could argue in the Viscounty, the Inn and Pub, and the farms that support the same and now the manor, are there to support the stable.

In the middle of the stable is the Great Tree. It is large enough that the druids sleep in a hollow-room in its trunk on the ground floor.

THE STABLE AT A GLANCE

Like all central stables in the Viscounty, this large square (75' each side) stable on the other side the road from the inn is built around a giant sequoia tree that rises beyond its roof, its branches stretching out as if sheltering the well-built complex. There are generous fields to the northwest and north of the stable. The fences are all whitewashed and lined with hedges. A training ring is off to one side.

Two barn doors are to the southwest and northeast, respectively. Facing the road is another sliding barn door, open to the path that leads to the High Road thirty feet away. Through the doors, a cobblestone floor encircles the great sequoia tree.

The stable is the standard two story-affair, the second story lodging for riders not wishing to be separated from their mounts. Twenty feet from the stable to the north is a hay shed. There are hearths in all four corners of the stable, away from the trunk of the tree.

THE DRUIDS

It is one thing to hear that in the Viscounty, horses are a religion, and quite another for newcomers to realize all the stable masters and ostlers are druids, and thus *literally* a religion.

"A man without a horse is no man at all"—a wives' saying.

The druids are there to protect and take care of the horses and are the spiritual backbone of the village. They also train horses, so they can be ridden, which includes battle training.

- **Jeremiah**, aged 32, the stablemaster
- **Kenidad**, aged 17, an ostler, twin brother to **Yurgana**
- Yurgana, aged 17, an ostler, twin sister to Kenidad

The druids actually sleep inside the tree, the tree grown around a 20' diameter circular room with a short, domed ceiling.

STABLEMASTER JEREMIAH

One day, Jeremiah was an initiate of the great Druidic Tradition of Sable Mastering, beholden to no one except the owner of the Inn, certainly a junior position but one with the benefits of not answering to a Lord.

The next the Viscount himself bought the inn which carried the pub and stable with it, gifted it to a knight, and here he was, beholden, maybe not to a lord, but certainly to the nobility hierarchy.

With taxes. *Taxes.* Jeremiah should have known that the Crossroads, under the protection of the Viscount rather than Lord Fermont twenty miles west on Kandra Road, would eventually receive an appointed knight. He just never expected to see it in his lifetime.

Whatever negativity towards Sir Walshan was built in his mind fled when he took one look at the young knight and concluded that he was more uncomfortable with the current events than Jeremiah was. Walshan told him to keep the same financial arrangements he had with the prior inn owner and call it good for now.

Indeed, the man endeared himself when he insisted on being called "Carl" and to leave out the *Sirs* even around strangers. Over the course of the year, Jeremiah became the knight's confidant, Carl even going so far as to admit his sorcerous-priestess of a wife was difficult to know because she came from the elven lands.

Jeremiah laughed and clapped the man on his shoulder. "She's very pretty, and all women want one thing when they get naked for you, no matter what land they come from."

It was with no small amount of terror when Jeremiah could only watch from the *hallowed* stable grounds as the horde of swamp dogs attacked the knight and his undersized, hastily assembled squad. His duty is to protect the horses, and it was all he could do to not lead them all into battle, lance in hand, his acolytes at his back.

And that is what he was contemplating when Dame Walshan galloped forth on a conjured mount with her extended, pregnant belly, and proceeded to lay waste to the remaining swamp dogs by shooting bolts of fire from her hands.

Well okay then.

Jeremiah — Medium Humanoid

Druid 3/Fighter 1 — Neutral
Armor Class 13 (leather armor, shield) — **Hit Points** 21 — **Speed** 30 ft.

Statistics

STR	DEX	CON	INT	WIS	CHA
13 (+1)	10 (+0)	11 (+0)	11 (+0)	16 (+3)	12 (+1)

Saving Throws WIS +5, INT +2
Skills Animal Handling +5, Insight +5, Medicine +5, Nature +2, Perception +5
Senses passive Perception 15
Languages Common, Draconic, Druidic, Elvish, Halfling
Challenge 1 (200 XP)

Actions

Scimitar. Melee Weapon Attack: +3 to hit, reach 5 ft., one target.
Hit: 4 (1d6+1) slashing damage.

Spell Attack. Ranged Weapon Attack: +5 to hit, range 0 ft., one target.
Hit: As Spell damage.

Spells

Druid spells memorized (CL 3rd)
Spell Save DC 13 — Spell Attack +5
2nd— (2 slots) *invisibility, pass without trace*
1st— (4 slots) *animal friendship, cure wounds, healing word, longstrider, speak with animals, thunderwave*
Cantrips—*druidcraft, mending, produce flame*

His full stat block is on page 48. Jeremiah's lance, spear, and other horse gear are stored in the stable.

Jeremiah is a reoccurring power-player in the *Chronicles of the Celestial Chains* Campaign (assuming he lives).

Friendly Attitude

Jeremiah will be a powerful ally. While he will not leave the Stable to adventure, he has considerable influence in the village and part of the druidic and ranger organizations. He can even lend the PCs money if they require it. If the PCs keep him appraised of the goings on in the Wailmoor, he will do his utmost to support them.

Jeremiah knows there is something very wrong with the moor on the plateau.

Finally, if the PCs throw caution to the wind and describe their visions, he is the very first NPC to suggest that the PCs sound like they have been reincarnated from the Knights of the Wailmoor. All he knows is reincarnation is an ancient druidic rite no longer practiced since the founding of the Empire.

Out of all the people in the Crossroads Village, Jeremiah has the best near-term benefits to the PCs: he alone can offer not only advice about their visions, but he will also do his best to cover their asses, especially if the *Curse of the Lost Memories* death mechanic.

In 30 days, Jeremiah can train a group of warhorses to *Pride of the Viscounty* warhorse standards.

Indifferent (Starting)

Jeremiah will heal wounded PCs without prompting. He doesn't have any horses for sale now but can have 1d4 (normal) warhorses in 5 days if a PC expresses interest.

Hostile

Jeremiah is a trained warrior. He will defend the Stable to the best of his ability but will retreat with his acolytes if necessary and then attack the PCs in an ambush using overwhelming numbers after summoning druidic network allies (Challenge Rating of 12).

Ostlers Kenidad & Yurgana

Kenidad and Yurgana are twins, feral humans barely civilized by Jeremiah. An elven ranger dropped them off at the stable a little under three years ago, saying they spoke a smattering of druidic, which was odd to him, since he found them living by themselves in the mountain portions of the elven lands, alone in a wizard tower with no wizard.

Jeremiah has since learned that the pair was indeed raised by a wizard—a wizard with druidic powers and ties to the hierarchy—and they spoke *nature's tongue*, albeit crudely.

When taught more of the language, the pair revealed that the wizard was a kind, if puzzling, old-man who claimed to have rescued them from an abandoned village. Oddly, they know sylvan and draconic as well, saying the wizard used all three languages with them. They speak and write draconic fluently.

Kenidad & Yurgana

Medium Humanoid — Druid 1 — Neutral
Armor Class 13 (leather armor, shield) — **Hit Points** 8 — **Speed** 30 ft.

Statistics

STR	DEX	CON	INT	WIS	CHA
13 (+1)	10 (+0)	11 (+0)	11 (+0)	16 (+3)	12 (+1)

Skills Animal Handling +2, Medicine +2, Nature +2, Religion +2
Senses passive Perception 10
Languages Draconic, Druidic, Sylvan
Saving Throws WIS +2, INT +2
Challenge 1/8 (200 XP)

Actions

Sickle. Melee Weapon Attack: +2 to hit, reach 5 ft., one target.
Hit: 1d4 slashing damage.

Spell Attack. Ranged Weapon Attack: +2 to hit, range 0 ft., one target.
Hit: As Spell damage.

Spells

Spell Save DC 10 — Spell Attack +2
1st— (2 slots) *cure wounds*
Cantrips— *druidcraft, mending*

Intro

Lost at the Beaux Seins

Moortide Rising

The Altar & the Anvil

Castle Wailmoor

Appendix

The acolytes' full stat blocks are on page 50. Their spears are normally stored in the stable when they are on horseback.

The twins will actively hide from anybody who attempts to talk to them beyond their stable duties. For one, they don't know the Common tongue although they understand most speech when it concerns taking care of horses.

The other reason is they are indeed feral, barely tamed by Jerimiah and only then, trusting the man because he spoke Druidic better than they did.

Jerimiah taught them druidic craft more out of channeling their idle hands into non-selfish pursuits. Each teen is now well-versed in the facts of life (having witnessed and helped when Jerimiah helped deliver Dax Candor), and now, at least, their glances of the opposite sex are now on the sly. While their mentor is convinced they won't be taken advantage of, he is unsure their shyness is a product of spending so much time alone after the wizard died.

While they haven't talked about their earliest childhood memories, Jerimiah thinks they have suffered some trauma neither remembers, perhaps with a genesis in the abandoned village the wizard mentioned. He worries about them.

Friendly Attitude

The only way to reach this attitude with the ostler-druids is if a PC speaks a language they know. Both will come out of their shy shell and answer any questions to the best of their ability.

Yurgana will accompany the PCs if asked (and prompt if not asked) into the Wailmoor as a camp and horse guard. She is a dangerous combatant when employing trained warhorses, able to command them on a round-by-round basis if they are in the line-of-sight and if they are in a hearing distance of her signal whistle, she can summon them or have them return to the stable.

Indifferent (Starting)

If questioned, Yurgana will relate that she saw the ranger that was courting Sarah the Wench ride up the old road and has never seen since. They will heal any wounds without prompting.

Hostile

Their training calls for them to summon the remaining horses and await instructions from Jeremiah. If the Druid falls, they will, per instructions, flee with the horses and any villagers they can immediately rescue.

Secrets of the Stable

While no secret, the villagers only have general knowledge that the stable is built on *hallowed* grounds,

THE BEAUX SEINS

with a permanent, extended *hallow* spell radiating from the central tree.

The *hallow* spell extends 5' past the stable and has all the standard features of the spell, including *fire resistance* via *energy protection*.

The Pub

The Pub attached to the inn and simply known as "The Pub" or "The Crossroads Pub" or "The Beaux Seins" is a well-visited place that soundly rejects pretentiousness yet does not delve into the dive-bar territory. It opens early in the morning and closes when there are no more customers spending money. If there are people spending the coin, the pub will stay open. As the last customers leave (or stumbles away), the Pub closes, and the doors lock. If people are lingering and not spending the coin, they are informed the pub is closing, and they must leave.

This operational philosophy sometimes makes for difficult days when the nights were long (or never-ending during the few festivals), but the extra coin makes up for it. Travelers frequent a pub with the reputation of tasty beer with a wide selection, busty, nubile wenches, and clean rooms next door—even though the pub has a lock on business, they are experts at offering services that cause travelers to gladly spend the coin.

Pub at a Glance

The Pub is two stories, and basement access can be seen from the northernmost side. The lower half of the first floor is stone and mortar, while the rest of the pub is in wood siding with a wood shingled roof.

In the middle of the pub is the expertly constructed,

halfling-crafted hearth composed of attractive river-rock rather than the stone and mortar theme found in the surrounding domiciles. Long rectangular tables or large round tables surround the hearth—there are no private, small tables or intimate booths here—seating is in "family style" and strangers are encouraged to mingle with other strangers or the locals.

The Pub enjoys glass windows that can be shuttered on every wall except where it opens into the inn. Festooned at intervals are copper, hooded lanterns with *continual flame* cast on the wicks.

The bar seats six customers in front, and two on each side. There are eight taps, each unique handle carved as a naked nymph loitering against a tree.

On a wall near the bar is a chalkboard with the three meals on it corresponding to poor, common, and good. Customers who order a meal and eschew jug wine or pitcher beer for more expensive purists receive a discount on their first drink order.

In one corner there is a small stage with a stool, an obvious place for a singular bard or musician.

FOOD AND DRINK

The pub serves cold beer, wine (several vintages, the ones their elf customers usually request) and ale.

The pub also brews its own house beer which is not for sale except to drink in the pub. Or, unless you are the Viscount.

As with most of the Viscounty, the beer is produced by the halfling populous while most of the wine is produced in vineyards run by humans to the south past.

The food is simple and hearty fare, expertly cooked with the goal of filling hungry men's bellies. Sausages, pork chops, marinated goose, beef, lamb and mutton, pheasant, duck, occasionally venison and small amounts of fish. All vegetables are seasonal, with winter fair consisting of dried fruits, onions, turnips, and basic winter greens.

The three nearby farms supply the pub with almost all its food needs. The Pub also purchase fish and game from fishermen and hunters and baked goods from the farms when the inn is full. If the kitchen staff have too much work for three people, the pub hires supplemental help from a farm girl, or, if available, asks Devos in the manor to help.

PUB STAFF

The kitchen staff is a well-oiled, integrated and coin producing machine. Most of the combined Inn, Pub and stable income come from the Pub.

COOKS

The Pub's three cooks that split up the day and help the other cooks as needed depending on the number of customers (morning, day, and evening shifts). Each takes pride that the Pub is renowned for fare a traveler can really appreciate. The cooks are:

- **Mari** is the oldest at 39 and has the evening shift
- **Kera**, 25 years old, has the morning shift
- **Jenna**, the youngest at 15, has afternoons.

The cooks have the same stats as the Human Female Farmers, p17.

Jenna is the new addition and the trainee on the job, given the relatively easy day shift. She is a buxom and lithe—but athletic—girl, but her father in the village north could not find her a suitable husband, so by Lord Fermont's advice, she put her cooking skills to use at the Pub until better opportunities avail themselves. She has no interest in being a serving wench despite the dramatically better pay (and tips) and would rather hold on to her virginity until marriage, as encouraged by the other staff, including the wenches.

Mari has two grown children and is a recent window. She has the coin from her previous marriage but dislikes both her empty nest and the lack of company her husband provided, so she enjoys the sociability of the Pub's kitchen.

Kera is **Evan's** pretty and shapely wife and has two girls **Deni** and **Jacki**, 10 and 8, respectively. The girls help both their mother and father in the Pub but disappear if the evening gets rowdy. Kera is pregnant with another child and hopes it is a boy.

Mari and Jenna share a pleasant room off the pub's wine cellar, next to the hearth that extends down into the basement.

EVAN THE BARKEEP

Evan is a tall, charismatic, able-bodied 28-year-old man with a warm smile, a jovial attitude, and righteous handlebar mustache. He is the singular reason for the pub's current success—not only is he the resident barkeep, but he is also a highly proficient restaurateur: he can out cook the cooks, his brewery talent is extensive and if he put his mind to it, he could probably out wench the wenches. He is so popular and successful that Hayro the Innkeeper lets Evan takes 50% of the Pub's profits, and the other 50% goes to Sir Walshan, who is now making more with that split than the prior owner was by taking all the profits. This suits Sir Walshan well, as the Pub and Inn profits go straight to his war chest, his manor home being mostly self-sufficient.

Intro

Lost at the Beaux Seins

Moortide Rising

The Altar & the Anvil

Castle Wailmoor

Appendix

Evan lives with his wife, Kera, and his two daughters, Deni and Jacki, in the small apartment above the pub.

Evan

Medium Humanoid — Neutral Good
Armor Class 11 — **Hit Points** 29 — **Speed** 30 ft.

Statistics

STR	DEX	CON	INT	WIS	CHA
12 (+1)	12 (+0)	12 (+1)	11 (+1)	10 (+0)	14 (+2)

Feats Lightly Armored, Weapon Master
Skills Animal Handling +2, History +3, Insight +2, Persuasion +4
Senses passive Perception 10
Languages Common, Halfling
Challenge ½ (100 XP)

Actions

Heavy Crossbow. *Ranged Weapon Attack:* +3 to hit, range 100 ft./400 ft., one target.
Hit: 6 (1d10+1) piercing damage.

Light Crossbow. *Ranged Weapon Attack:* +3 to hit, range 80 ft./320 ft., one target.
Hit: 5 (1d8+1) piercing damage.

Javelin. *Melee or Ranged Weapon Attack:* +3 to hit, reach 5 ft. or range 30 ft./120 ft., one target.
Hit: 4 (1d6+1) piercing damage.

Warhammer. *Melee Weapon Attack:* +3 to hit, reach 5 ft., one target.
Hit: 5 (1d8+1) bludgeoning damage or 6 (1d10+1) bludgeoning damage if used with two hands to make a melee attack.

Evan is always armed with his dagger. He keeps the heavy warhammer behind the bar, and the heavy crossbow is hanging, visible, next to the whiskey shelf. He is proficient with throwing javelins from horseback but is not a lancer.

When he gets out his warhammer, impending bar fights either dissipate or are stopped short.

Evan was a young man of no-small intellectual skills on his way to an Imperial University when, while traveling the High Road, he met, seduced, and impregnated Kera, whom he later married after her brother and father tracked him down. Kera's father, Devos, was the barkeep back then.

Thinking that Evan was a worthless, prissy mam, Devos still tried to teach the lad some craft, least his almost-dishonored daughter be destitute with her new husband. With his natural talents, it wasn't long until Evan was running the Pub.

In his spare time, Evan loves to ride his warhorse **Scotette**, although he is not a warrior. Secretly his wife thinks he likes to ride the wenches and simply hasn't been caught. Evan, however, while appreciating young women with beautiful breasts, is a proper husband. The drama would be bad for business, and he thinks

the world of this daughters.

That Evan has always paid homage to The Maiden, is sometimes an awkwardness around the Pub.

Evan is also versed in Innkeeping. He and Hayro the Innkeeper (also trained in tending bar), occasionally spot each other.

The recent swamp dog incursion from the moors and the subsequent wounding of Sir Walshan has rocked Evan's previously naive world. On the battlefield, Sir Walshan was like a god while Evan felt like a child. Intellectually, Evan knew there were monsters in the world, but it was quite another to have the moors haunts extend to the small village. Evan put on his chain shirt, grabbed the warhammer behind the bar and the heavy crossbow when he heard the fighting.

He even killed one of the terrible, vicious, sick things with a bolt right through its skull, but by the time he could get his shaking hands to reload the crossbow, Dame Walshan had ended the fight with her sorcerous magic.

Evan's singular motivation now is, when Sir Walshan recovers from his wounds, to receive warrior training and have the knight sanction a small militia.

He is confident Sir Walshan will have no problems with that idea.

FRIENDLY ATTITUDE

The beer is free.

INDIFFERENT (STARTING)

Evan will tell the PCs anything he knows within reason. He will come across as an educated man's man.

HOSTILE

Evan summons the druids from across the street and backs up his words with the warhammer behind the bar. He'll do his best to make the PCs be reasonable.

WENCHES

The Beaux Seins Pub seems overstaffed in serving wenches until one realizes that the wenches are all prostitutes, and professional ones at that.

Unlike most establishments, each wench has her own, albeit small, room down a stairway dedicated to their privacy. They will certainly go back to the Inn with a customer instead of their room, but all five have agreed that only 2 can be away from a full pub at any given time, regulating customers who want a lingering, all night encounter to wait until the Pub is closed for the evening.

The wenches are all friendly, busty, athletic and range from doe-eyed pretty to dangerously stimulating. They are:

- **Sarah,** a leggy, honey-blonde 16-year-old with

a touch of elf blood and the pretty girl-next-door look. She used to be a chambermaid in the inn, but slept with one of the customers and was fired by Hayro, and then recruited by Kerri as a Bastet Acolyte.

- **Kerri**, a short raven-haired 20-year-old with a glib tongue and is either "flirty" or "sleeping."

- **Mimi**, 18, is a red-head with sharp cheekbones and odd accent, with the look of the traveling people.

- **Priss**, a 17-year-old blonde with large blue eyes, who plays up the innocent angle until she sees the weight of her patron's coin purse.

- **Carole**, an 18-year old athletic brunette with seductive brown eyes and a love of fine whiskey.

Wenches

Female Medium Humanoid — Chaotic Neutral
Armor Class 10 — **Hit Points** 7 — **Speed** 30 ft.

Statistics

STR	DEX	CON	INT	WIS	CHA
10 (+0)	12 (+1)	11 (+0)	9 (-1)	9 (-1)	15 (+2)

Skills Acrobatics +3, Athletics +2, Insight +1, Persuasion +4
Senses passive Perception 9
Languages Common, Halfling
Challenge 0 (1-XP)

Actions

Bastet Stiletto. *Melee or Ranged Weapon Attack:* +3 to hit, reach 5 ft. or range 20 ft./60 ft., one target. *Hit:* 3 (1d4+1) piercing damage.

Additional Details

Bastet Acolyte While wearing the silver holy symbol of Bastet, a female acolyte is infertile and unable to conceive children. If removed, if the female was fertile prior to wearing the symbol, the fertility chance for the acolyte to conceive a child is 100% for approximately 21 days, after which the fertility chance decreases to the normal rate for her race.

The symbol has no effect on males.

All five wenches are Imperial sanctioned acolytes of Bastet—the goddess of sex, seduction, and pleasure—and as such carry, a dagger called the *bastet stiletto* along with their required silver holy symbol.

As an Imperial regulated profession, they are obligated to wear their silver holy symbols (not necessarily around their necks) and pay 20% of their income in Imperial taxes rather than to a local tax authority.

FRIENDLY ATTITUDE

She'll never lower her rates, but she will listen and be attentive to any personal issues the PC might have.

INDIFFERENT (STARTING)

She will try her best to be friendly with the PC. Only Sarah will talk about the swamp dog attack, however, or has anything meaningful to say.

HOSTILE

Before a PC arrives at this state, mention that Bastet Acolytes are under an Imperial charter and the Empire's reach is everywhere an Imperial Road reaches, be it Realm or Protectorate.

While the Wenches will simply surrender or run, they have the legal right to appeal to any Imperial authority, not just to the local lord. PCs that result in physical violence, robbery, theft, or other ill-fated deeds towards the women will eventually result in arrest and transport to trial.

However, the offended Acolyte will make sure the PC never arrives for trial by seducing the guards, and the PC will be listed as "fatally wounded while trying to escape" and will appear in the Great Tree after several days of abuse from their captors.

DANO

The only other pub staff is **Dano** the 20-year-old bartender and handyman who relieves some bartending and heavy lifting pressure from Evan.

Dano

Medium Humanoid — Lawful Good
Armor Class 10 — **Hit Points** 12 — **Speed** 30 ft.

Statistics

STR	DEX	CON	INT	WIS	CHA
13 (+1)	10 (+0)	12 (+1)	10 (+0)	10 (+0)	10 (+0)

Senses passive Perception 10
Languages Common, Halfling
Challenge 1/8 (25 XP)

Actions

Heavy Crossbow. *Ranged Weapon Attack:* +2 to hit, range 100 ft./400 ft., one target.
Hit: 5 (1d10) piercing damage.

Dagger. *Melee or Ranged Weapon Attack:* +3 to hit, reach 5 ft. or range 20 ft./60 ft., one target.
Hit: 3 (1d4+1) piercing damage.

Warhammer. *Melee Weapon Attack:* +3 to hit, reach 5 ft., one target.
Hit: 5 (1d8+1) bludgeoning damage or 6 (1d10+1) bludgeoning damage if used with two hands to make a melee attack.

Intro

Lost at the Beaux Seins

Moortide Rising

The Altar & the Anvil

Castle Wailmoor

Appendix

Dao's full stat block is on page 50. His listed javelins and spear are with his horse. The warhammer and heavy crossbow are the weapons Evan stores at the bar.

One would think the quiet (but still friendly) Dano would be an ill match for Evan's people-person personality. However, Evan views Dano as the brother he never had, and they both have a love of horseback riding. Like many a Viscounty young man, Dano spent all his coin first on his holy symbol and then on a warhorse (named Scrappy). Like Evan, while being stronger than the older man, he is no warrior and simply enjoys riding a clever horse. Evan will sometimes have the innkeeper tend bar so he and Dano can go out riding.

Dano knows Evan will insist he receives warrior training and serves in the soon-to-be commissioned militia. Dano doesn't know how he feels about this, but, shy as he is, even he knows that a warrior is popular with young women.

Dano's singular vice, and the probable cause of his unmarried status: he finds it enjoyable and easier to simply pay one of the wenches for a dalliance. He feels a modicum of guilt for this habit, as he was in a liaison with Mimi in her room during the incursion of swamp dogs from the moor.

His room is next to the cook's room. Sometimes he wishes it was upstairs away from the wenches, but at least they don't use the same stairway and do not pass each other in the basement.

Friendly Attitude

Dano will offer to go horseback riding. He will show the PCs all the nice fishing spots and give the occasional free beer while bartending. He will also gossip.

Indifferent (Starting)

Dano doesn't have much to say about anything. He is receptive to talking about other people in general details.

Hostile

Dano is pragmatic. He'll withdrawal from any hostile situation, and people he believes are prone to violence.

Secrets of the Pub

As a well-kept, but over one hundred-years-old attached building to the inn, the Beaux Seins Pub his its share of secrets.

SECRET	WHO KNOWS
The central hearth has preservation magic, even though it is made of river rock and mortar. Why the Halflings who built it wanted to add preservative magic to stone, nobody alive today knows. It has a faint aura of alteration magic if detected.	A passing elf sorcerer told Evan this to be seductive. She failed in her seduction, but Evan found preservation magic on *stonework* highly amusing.
There is a secret door between the wench's rooms and the pub's cellar.	All the staff. Like the hearth, nobody remembers why. The current pub building was a replacement for an older, rundown building that was also a pub. Evan has theories it was made by some dwarf gotten drunk by the same halflings that made the hearth.
The beer storage is magically cold, and the keg housing in the bar is insulated.	All the staff and the innkeeper. The Pub's first owner paid a considerable amount of coin for this enchantment. The cold radiates from a central column in a room situated away from the hearth.
The brass hooded lantern directly above the bar in the middle radiates a permanent *magic circle against evil*.	Nobody. Obviously, if magic is detected the lantern will have a moderate abjuration enhancement as compared to just the weak evocation magic of the *continual flame* spell. But if anyone has noticed, nobody has mentioned it. If taken, the lantern requires attunement.

The Beaux Seins Inn

The Inn, built at the same time and attached to the pub, enjoys a hospitable reputation as a quiet, always cozy place to rest while traveling the High Road. As the eastern terminus of Kandra Road, the Inn also sees travelers and trade caravans with an east or west destination and a desire to travel along a paved, well maintained Imperial road rather than the wagon-rutted tract that, while more of a direct route, winds its way around farms and connects villages rather than offer a straight line to the neighboring Barony of Hardred (south) or the elven woods (north).

Traveling by horseback, it is faster to take one of the more direct routes. With a wagon or carriage, the High Road to Kandra Road is always faster. However, even horsemen will go out of the way to use the paved roads simply because the stops along the way are more pleasant, the inns better quality and usually a wench or two to spend the coin on rather than flirting with a shy farm girl with her father glaring from afar.

Travel between the Barony of Hardred and the elf lands is almost exclusively via the High Road.

The Beaux Seins Inn is a popular stop.

Inn at a Glance

The inn is a well-built two-story affair built in the same style of the pub—lower half of the first floor is stone and mortar, while the rest of the inn is in wood siding with a wood shingled roof.

From the southern side of the inn, there are visible basement stairs leading down to a thick oak door. Behind the inn is a large herb and flower garden with apple trees. A gazebo stands amongst the flowers and wild hedges, a place for guests to meet outdoors and relax.

There is a large sign next to the inn door: *The Beaux Seins Inn & Pub*, with the Imperial stamp of the courtesan on one corner. On the opposite corner is a coat of arms: a shield with two swords with the shield face a cross with four dots next to each intersection's corner. The sign looks new.

Three chimneys can be seen protruding from the middle of the roof, spaced evenly along the length of the inn.

Staff

The inn has a smalls staff consisting of the innkeeper, three chambermaids, a handyman who also serves as a guard in the daytime, and a night watchman.

- **Hayro**, aged 30, a polite, charismatic halfling with a professional demeanor and an eye for detail
- **Donatella**, 16, a chambermaid and a niece of Farmer Wilcox
- **Joline**, 16, a maid and daughter of the farmhand Shap, who works for the Hearthwarm halfling farmers. Her mother died in childbirth
- **Penelope**, also 16, a chambermaid from the

Barony of Hardred, whose father died in the inn several years ago.

- **Timothy**, 20, a handyman and daytime guard
- **Vergali**, a dwarf night watchman

Hayro

The young (for a halfling) Hayro is a pro. Not much gets by him, and he takes his hospitality duties very seriously. While he is relentlessly professional, his philosophy is guidance rather than stern correctness (although he does have limits as the Courtesan Sarah found out) and is much appreciated by the staff. The happy staff treats their guests with a smile, adding to the reputation that halflings make infectiously good hosts.

Intro

Lost at the Beaux Seins

Moortide Rising

The Altar & the Anvil

Castle Wailmoor

Appendix

Hayro

Medium Humanoid — Neutral Good
Armor Class 10 — **Hit Points** 10 — **Speed** 30 ft.

Statistics

STR	DEX	CON	INT	WIS	CHA
9 (-1)	13 (+1)	9 (-1)	13 (+1)	13 (+1)	13 (+1)

Skills Insight +3, Persuasion +3
Senses passive Perception 13
Languages Common, Common, Dwarvish, Halfling
Challenge ¼ (50 XP)

Actions

Dagger. *Melee or Ranged Weapon Attack:* +3 to hit, reach 5 ft. or range 20 ft./60 ft., one target.
Hit: 3 (1d4+1) piercing damage.

Sling. *Ranged Weapon Attack:* +3 to hit, range 30 ft./120 ft., one target.
Hit: 3 (1d4+1) bludgeoning damage.

Unarmed Strike. *Melee Weapon Attack:* +1 to hit, reach 5 ft., one creature.
Hit: 1 bludgeoning damage.

Hayro always carries his sling and bullets with him in his belt pouch.

The inn's reputation, to Hayro, is his honor. He has a good working relationship with Sir Walshan. As the village's resident halfling bachelor of some means, he has the eye of all the halfling farmers' daughters.

Hayro has modest room in the basement with a ground-side window facing the inn's back, overlooking the herb and flower garden, which suits him just fine. He takes his meals in the pub, usually at the bar.

Friendly Attitude

Hayro, perhaps, has the best benefit of establishing friendly relations: he will convert a room on the first floor of the inn (used now as a large storage room) into a small shop. He will stock most of the equipment found in the *Player's Handbook* in 3d4 days.

Indifferent

Hayro didn't know much about anything outside of the inn and was sleeping during the swamp dog attack. He will state he is very happy to have hired the guards that he did, and suggest PCs talk to them.

Hostile

Hayro will be confused at one anyone would be hostile towards him and retreat to the presence of his guards.

Chambermaids

The Viscounty has a reputation of athletic women, and the chambermaids are no exception. Where the wenches are wanton slatterns, the chambermaids are attractive, youthful prime wife material.

The chambermaids have the same stats as the Human Female Farmers, p17.

Chambermaids without exception find a husband in one to two years of working, an eventuality of attractive feminine staff in cute uniforms that Hayro has grudgingly accepted. At least the inn always has a reputation for pretty and young chambermaids.

The chambermaids refer horny guests to the Pub, and the wenches, in turn, will tip the chambermaid making the referral. The chambermaids will bring female or mix-sex guests' food from the Inn, but now leave deliveries to single men to one of the guards.

They share a windowless, but comfortable room with a hearth downstairs in the basement.

Chambermaid

Female Commoner — Medium humanoid — lawful good
Armor Class 10 — **Hit Points** 10 — **Speed** 30 ft.

Statistics

STR	DEX	CON	INT	WIS	CHA
12 (+1)	11 (+0)	10 (+0)	10 (+0)	10 (+0)	11 (+0)

Senses passive Perception 10
Languages Common
Challenge 1/8 (25 XP)

Actions

Dagger. Melee or Ranged Weapon Attack: +1 to hit, reach 5 ft. or range 20 ft./60 ft., one target.
Hit: 3 (1d4+1) piercing damage.

The inn could get by with only two chambermaids. Hayro's service focus compels him to put some money where his mouth is, however. Once he made the decision to hire another maid, the benefits of the increased hospitable reputation soon followed.

Friendly Attitude

All three chambermaids will drop not-so-subtle hints they would like to find a nice husband and settle down. They will not sleep with any of the PCs but can be courted for marriage over the course of the adventure. The most they will do is hold hands and kiss. The Acolytes in the pub are a vivid example of what happens to unmarried Viscounty girls who do more than that.

If a PC has gone a'cour'n and proposed to any of the chambermaids at the end of *Curse of the Lost Memories*, they will say yes.

Adventurers aren't exactly the best spouses (they tend to die), but they are heroes and certainly not boring.

Indifferent

The chambermaids are respectful and courteous.

Hostile

They run, summon one of the guards, and hide.

Timothy

Timothy is one rather large, imposing, intimidating young man, and used to be a hunter for the inn and village until an unfortunate security incident with Sarah (then a chambermaid) and a guest. Hayro then offered him a well-paying job of simply helping with lifting heavy things, delivering the occasional meal to unaccompanied male guests, and looking like he could kick the crap out of drunk people.

Timothy thought about that, and to him, that sounded like a respectable job, and he has been the inn's resident handyman/day guard ever since. During the pub's more rowdier times, he sometimes moonlights as a bouncer.

Timothy is quite a nice guy to his friends and fellow staff members, at odds with his "resting- kick-your-ass-face."

Timothy

Medium Humanoid — Fighter 2 — Lawful Good
Armor Class 18 (chain mail, shield) — **Hit Points** 20 — **Speed** 30 ft.

Statistics

STR	DEX	CON	INT	WIS	CHA
16 (+3)	12 (+1)	12 (+1)	10 (+0)	10 (+0)	11 (+0)

Saving Throws STR +5, CON +3
Skills Animal Handling +2, Perception +2
Senses passive Perception 12
Languages Common, Halfling
Challenge ¼ (50 XP)

Actions

Longsword. Melee Weapon Attack: +5 to hit, reach 5 ft., one target.
Hit: 7 (1d8+3) slashing damage or 8 (1d10+3) slashing damage if used with two hands to make a melee attack.

Unarmed Strike. Melee Weapon Attack: +5 to hit, reach 5 ft., one creature.
Hit: 4 bludgeoning damage.

Timothy's full stat block is on page 50. His spear, lance, and javelins are on his horse (or in the stable with the horse). Due to recent festivities, if he's not sleeping, Timothy's wearing his armor.

Timothy is an honorable fellow and has grown fond of being part of the protectorate of the inn. So, it was with much disappointment and no small amount of anger that Vergali didn't wake him when he detected something wrong in the village and went straight to Sir Walshan instead. Timothy's room, being in the basement, masked the sounds of the battle and he slept through it.

The next day Timothy had words with Vergali. The dwarf paused for a moment, admitted his error, and apologized. Then he asserted they would never get past his grievous transgression on the young man's honor unless they settled it like real warriors, and punched Timothy in the face.

Timothy and Vergali then proceeded to kick the crap out of each other. They then went to the Pub and drank expensive whiskey all night, and then stumbled around the Hearthwarm Farm's sheep pens yelling "Baaaaah! Baaaah!" at the top of their lungs. They've been best friends ever since.

Timothy is motivated to find a nice girl and marry, and the chambermaids all suit his eye. If only they didn't swoon pathetically every time Sir Walshan came to the Pub. Beyond that, as a competent lancer, he aspires to own a heavy warhorse.

Friendly Attitude
Timothy, while he won't abandon his job as the inn's day guard, will go out of his way to help PCs in any way possible.

Indifferent (Starting)
Timothy will embarrassingly admit he slept right through the prior swamp dog troubles.

Hostile
Timothy will summon Vergali, and together they will form a plan with Hayro on how to deal with difficult PCs. If cornered and threatened (or witnessing violent crimes), Timothy will blow on his guard whittle continually while attacking the offending PC(s).

Vergali
Whereas Timothy appears and is intimidating, Vergali looks like he will split you lengthwise with his oversized dwarven war axe and beat whatever is still warm with his shield until it is room temperature—while smoking a pipe.

Vergali

Hill Dwarf — Male — Medium Humanoid — Fighter 2 — Lawful Good
Armor Class 19 (splint, shield) — **Hit Points** 24 — **Speed** 25 ft.

Statistics

STR	DEX	CON	INT	WIS	CHA
16 (+3)	10 (+0)	14 (+2)	10 (+0)	11 (+0)	10 (+0)

Saving Throws STR +5, CON +4
Skills Acrobatics +2, Athletics +5, Intimidation +2, Perception +2
Damage Resistances poison
Senses darkvision 60 ft., passive Perception 12
Languages Common, Dwarvish, Halfling
Challenge ¼ (50 XP)

Actions

Battleaxe. *Melee Weapon Attack:* +5 to hit, reach 5 ft., one target. *Hit:* 7 (1d8+3) slashing damage or 8 (1d10+3) slashing damage if used with two hands to make a melee attack.

Light Crossbow. *Ranged Weapon Attack:* +2 to hit, range 80 ft./320 ft., one target. *Hit:* 4 (1d8) piercing damage.

Unarmed Strike. *Melee Weapon Attack:* +5 to hit, reach 5 ft., one creature. *Hit:* 4 bludgeoning damage.

Vergali's full stat block is on page 50. Unlike everyone else in the village, including Sir Walshan, the young Vergali is a veteran of several battles during the Brief War of Detestation between the Cliffside Mountains' East Brigade and the Ogre Incursion in the Imperial Year 5009.

When the brief war was over, Vergali woke up one morning and walked south down the Imperial North Road. He kept walking until the road turned into Kandra Road and proceeded across the Viscounty. When the road finally ended at the inn, he asked the halfling, the first non-farming non-human he found at the crossroads if he had any work to be done. Hayro, a bit took back at first, rapidly concluded that the quiet, but lethal arsenal on short legs would be well suited for a night-time guard duty.

It was Vergali that noticed that Go-Go, the inn's guard dog, was missing. A quick examination found that the guard dog that slept outside the stable was also gone, but the horses inside the stable were calm and asleep.

That's when Vergali went to Sir Walshan's manor and politely knocked on the door. Walshan eventually opened it, holding his longsword scabbard and quickly realized his guard dog too, was missing. The knight had his squire and wife help him don his armor while Vergali guarded the front door. The three of them—Vergali, Sir Walshan, and Squire Dagmar—then proceeded to the crossroad's well.

Then, as they say, it was on.

Vergali is a veteran haunted by too many battle

Intro

Lost at the Beaux Seins

Moortide Rising

The Altar & the Anvil

Castle Wailmoor

Appendix

memories and simply wants to be somewhere where he belongs. Since the swamp dog attack, where he fought side-by-side with Sir Walsham, he has been feeling uneasy and nervous. He catches himself fingering his holy symbol of Dvalin.

Vergali is convinced the hamlet's troubles are only the beginning.

Friendly Attitude

Vergali is the only NPC that will not readily tell his story on the swamp dog night without moving his Attitude from Indifferent to Friendly. If any of the PCs have the solider background, a simple salute will move his attitude to Friendly.

A simple beer or an easily made Charisma (Persuasion) check (DC 12, DC 10 with beer and +1 bonus per beer) will also move his attitude to Friendly.

Once loosened up, he will talk about anything the PCs want to know and will lend tactical advice bordering on strategic:

- PCs should establish a supply line to a base of operations in the Wailmoor

- PCs should immediately destroy anything that remotely resembles a corruptive element

- PCs next step should be discovering the swamp dog lair in the Wailmoor and kill the villager's missing dogs before the corruption sets in

- PCs, if they have horses, should enlist the aid of a druidic acolyte to watch their horses and camps, and will tell them, if they are not familiar with Viscounty warhorses, that a singular druid with her warhorses is more than enough guard for a simple camp

- Vergali has a thing for female halflings and female gnomes—and being in the village with a bunch of cute halflings has made things a mite—difficult—because in the Viscounty, interspecies get-togethers are not the norm, unlike the barbarian lands he is from. If the party has either of his preferences, he offers to buy dinner and then at dinner offers to get a room. He shrugs off rejection. He's seen it all, and there are plenty more cute gnomes or halflings in the world.

The dwarf Vergali is well-traveled, cosmopolitan, experienced, and a trained killer. Beyond his friendly attitude advice, Vergali will warn the PCs that amongst his clan, there were warnings about "Viscounty Demon Humping Witches" that "skulk in the background and strike from the shadows." He specifically warns any witch or warlock PCs to watch their back—the covens of the Viscounty undermine non-Viscounty witches whenever possible.

Indifferent (Starting)

Vergali will politely answer questions about the village, inn, and pub, and will seem animated when talking about the beer Evan has been making. He really likes beer. He mentions this several times. Sometimes randomly. Even in his sleep.

Hostile

Vergali has a challenging time understanding Viscounty citizens, and his stoic, experienced nature prevents him from becoming Hostile unless the PCs resort to violence.

So, he is either Indifferent with non-violent confrontations, summoning allies to help him kill the PCs, or is in the process of killing PCs. He's a soldier. He doesn't mess around.

Investigating the Swamp Dog Attack

When questioned, Vergali will flat out say that the dogs disappearing seems like they up and left on their own and that, even now, they are being *corrupted and twisted into vile, disease-infested fonts of evil.* "They'll be back, those demon swamp dogs, mark my words!"

He will tell the PCs anything they want to know, but, like everyone else, realizes the actual protection of the village is thin. Too thin. He won't leave his post to go adventuring.

Vergali, if asked if he knows anything about the Wailmoor besides his suspicion of corruption, will go back to his room and fetch a silver amulet that he bought off one of the villagers that asked him what it was (the symbols look dwarven) and shows it to them. It is a Silver Holy Symbol of Dvalin, with the hammer and anvil art on one side and a multitude of dwarven-like symbols on the other.

If the PCs go back to the Crossroads Village *after* discovering the Temple, he will mention that he has a "fancy and pretentious Dvalin symbol" and give the party the amulet.

Secrets of the Inn

The Beaux Seins Inn has no secrets per se, but its recent place in the Viscounty is certainly unusual.

A year ago, the Viscount's wife, a priestess of The Maiden, informed her husband that the crossroad's inn was of great importance to the Viscounty and of importance to The Maiden from a religious perspective.

The Viscount found this odd, but he had given up several years ago trying to understand his politically arranged marriage, barbarian-raised wife and just went with the flow, as his wife was fond of saying. Whatever the flow meant. He was never quite sure what his wife was talking about when she discussed religious matters, often in a dialect he had trouble understanding.

Viscount Merris Argona pondered what he considered the un-ponderable, took out a map and looked at the Crossroads Village. He noticed a faint road marking going east, remembering there was indeed some overgrown trail the last time he visited. Consulting an older map, Argona learned that the Kingdom extended up into a moor-filled land of beauty. Curious on why a king would abandon an entire barony, and essentially any expansion beyond said barony, Argona eventually read the King at the time disowned the area because everyone in it had *died*. He had always assumed the Emperor, with his methodical, constant expansion, simply didn't have the time, resources, or inclination to have the King push beyond the Viscounty's southeast border.

Intellectually, the Viscount knew that the lands to his east were haunted. Reading about a demon war drove home that perhaps The Maiden, though his wife, was telling him to get his shit together and secure his rear.

Merris's actions where immediate. He purchased the inn, pub and stable and knighted one of his personal guards, Carl Walshan. Carl was so good with a sword that he oversaw training of Argona's personal guard in swordcraft. Argona gifted the young lad with the land, titled the stable, inn and pub to him, knighted him and arranged a lucrative political marriage to a beautiful half-elf from a rich elven clan to the northeast.

And that was that. Nobody, including Sir Walshan, understood the Viscount's motivations, although Merris did tell Sir Walshan that it was time to secure the intersection of two Imperial roads, even if it was, throughout known history, to never be in danger.

Why didn't the Viscount tell his loyal subject of the prior barony to the east?

His wife told him it was not Sir Walshan's place. Such is the mysterious ways of barbarian princesses who receives the occasional omen from her goddess.

The Curse Abides

When word reached the Viscount that his new knight saved the Crossroads from something rather vile belching forth from the moor plateau in the middle of a night, he turned to his (pregnant) wife—was this the trouble she had divined earlier, he asked the Viscountess?

"Of course. And it's not yours to solve, or Sir Walshan's to solve. There is no *solution*. Troubled people at the crossroads awaits your leadership. They need your help—they are lost in a fog, and they don't even know how terrible their lives are. No sword or lance or spell will protect the crossroads, but their righteousness will cleanse all corruption."

And with that Viscount Merris Argona threw up his hands, put his personal guard in charge of his wife's safety, commandeered two random squads of Lancers and set forth post haste to the crossroads, muttering under his breath over the folly of marring barbarian princesses.

The Viscountess was completely correct. Her goddess, The Maiden, has a vested interest in the player character's well-being. More so than that, this is the PCs story.

Everyone else is along for the ride, and it's up to the PC to not leave swaths of destruction in their wake. Starting here on the edges of the Viscounty.

The Curse Abides Encounter is in five parts:

- **Setup:** Setting the Stage for the encounter.
- **Trigger:** Trigger the *Lost Memory*.
- **PC Choices:** What the PCs, who saved, can choose to do.
- **Choice Consequence:** All actions have consequences in *Curse of the Lost Memories*.
- **NPC Reactions:** NPCs reactions to the *Lost Memory*

Setup

This encounter introduces the PCs to the Viscount and in the aftermath, the village beyond the Pub, which includes Sir Walshan, the knight.

It also introduces just how messed up their lives really are. How they deal with their curse will define them. Action is character.

Just what types of characters do the players have?

Over the course of a month, the "visions" you have been experiencing now seem more like memories. Talking to people you've never talked to. Fighting battles, you've never fought. Kissing a lover that you've never met. The memories are confusing and ethereal, and when trying to make sense of it all, they skitter away as if hiding from something dark.

Most of the memories seem to be about a beautiful land, a moor with lonely tors situated on a plateau. Sometimes in the vision, the moor is haunted. It's probably no coincidence that on the eastern edge of the Viscounty, there is a haunted moor.

Kandra Road leads right to the place, its terminus a crossroads with the High Road, an inn, stable and lively pub for travelers such as yourself.

That's why the PCs are in the pub. They have not met each other, but they are about to do so—in a big way.

The Pub

Curse of the Lost Memories starts in the Pub, and the pub

Intro

Lost at the Beaux Seins

Moortide Rising

The Altar & the Anvil

Castle Wailmoor

Appendix

is full. There are soldiers, locals, and travelers in the Beaux Seins Pub, although the Inn still has available room for the PCs. The soldiers are sleeping in the living quarters above their horses. The Knight and the Dame are not currently in the Pub.

The Staff

Evan and the wenches are holding down the front of the house while Mari, with help from Jenna, holds down the back of the house. At the beginning of the encounter, Mimi and Carole are entertaining guests in their quarters.

The Soldiers

Lancers ride hard, fight hard and drink hard. They're not going to get drunk this evening, but, why waste an opportunity to have some mighty fine beer in the company of might fine wenches? They are thoroughly enjoying this assignment, and the friendly and pragmatic Viscount has made this assignment thus far interesting without bloodshed.

Disposition

The soldiers in the inn, the Viscount and the soldiers in the stable have the Indifferent Attitude for the PCs and will stay that way unless the PCs use lethal force in their presence. Then they will turn Hostile but will still try to get the PCs to surrender before someone (probably the PCs) get killed.

If the PCs do not resort to lethal force, they can be moved to Friendly by making nice with the Viscount.

While what is going to next transpire is certainly an odd occurrence, this won't be the first time these Lancers have been in a bar fight. If nobody drew steel, they're good.

There are two squads of soldiers in the village, elite rapid-response Lancers. The prior squad had an early dinner and are in the stable with the Viscount, relaxing with a keg of beer after a hard ride through the Viscounty. They aren't drunk—but they are feeling good, enjoying the company of the Viscount who seems genuinely interested in whom they are.

The Lancers in the inn sitting at a large round table closest to the small stage are:

- **Sergeant Lorral**, 26-years-old
- **Phelip**, 18
- **Jereme**, 19
- **Kando**, 18
- **Relf**, 22
- **Svern**, 20
- **Arney**, 23

Sergeant Lorral

Lorral is a man used to operating within the chain of command and making sure his men stay alive. Reporting directly to the Viscount on this "mission" makes him nervous, and he is drinking a much-needed beer (or two) when the PCs make his life interesting.

Sergeant Lorral

Medium Humanoid — Fighter 3 — Lawful Neutral
Armor Class or 17 (scale mail and/or shield) — **Hit Points** 29
Speed 30 ft.

Statistics

STR	DEX	CON	INT	WIS	CHA
14 (+2)	12 (+1)	13 (+1)	10 (+0)	10 (+0)	10 (+1)

Saving Throws STR +4, CON +3
Skills Animal Handling +2, Athletics +4
Senses passive Perception 10
Languages Common, Halfling
Challenge ½ (100 XP)

Actions

Unarmed Strike. *Melee Weapon Attack:* +4 to hit, reach 5 ft., one creature.
Hit: 3 bludgeoning damage.

Warhammer. *Melee Weapon Attack:* +4 to hit, reach 5 ft., one target.
Hit: 6 (1d8+2) bludgeoning damage or 7 (1d10+2) bludgeoning damage if used with two hands to make a melee attack.

Sergeant Lorral's full stat block is on page 51. His shield, lance, spear, javelins, and light crossbow are with his horse, along with the other horse gear. He is armed with his warhammer and dagger.

Lancers

These are technically light lancers, and part of the Viscounty rapid-response soldiers, given fast horses and equipment to quickly move to different areas in the Viscounty in a recon-in-force configuration.

Lancers

Medium Humanoid — Fighter 1| Lawful Neutral
Armor Class 15 or 16 (chain mail and/or shield) — **Hit Points** 10 —
Speed 30 ft.

Statistics

STR	DEX	CON	INT	WIS	CHA
13 (+3)	11 (+01)	12 (+1)	11 (+0)	11 (+0)	11 (+0)

Saving Throws STR +3, CON +3
Skills Animal Handling +2, Athletics +3
Senses passive Perception 10
Languages Common, Halfling
Challenge 1/8 (25 XP)

Actions

Unarmed Strike. *Melee Weapon Attack:* +3 to hit, reach 5 ft., one creature.
Hit: 2 bludgeoning damage.

Warhammer. *Melee Weapon Attack:* +3 to hit, reach 5 ft., one target.
Hit: 5 (1d8+1) bludgeoning damage or 6 (1d10+1) bludgeoning damage if used with two hands to make a melee attack.

The Lancers' full stat block is on page 51. Their shields, lances, spears, javelins, and light crossbows are with their horses, along with the other horse gear. They are armed with warhammer and dagger.

The Soldiers at the at the Stable

Having finished their dinner and respite, there are soldiers at the stable, relaxing in the living quarters on the second floor. They are:

- Viscount Merris Argona, 30
- **Sergeant Harris**, 25
- **Johnny**, 20
- **Herbal**, 24

- **Jerro**, 18
- **Devan**, 18
- **Carlo**, 19
- **Sigred**, 21

- **Kris** the Pack Master, 22
  - o Guard Dog **Wogro**
  - o Guard Dog **Bowser**
  - o Guard Dog **Tregger**
  - o Guard Dog **Boo-Boo**

The Sergeant and Soldiers at the stable have the same stat blocks as their counterparts in the club.

The Viscount Merris Argona

Unlike the rest of the Kingdom where his barons hold hereditary positions, the Viscount is an appointed position by the King, chosen when the current Viscount retires from old age or dies. Picked from a pool of three candidates as put forth by the Horse Lords of Kandra, with the implied stipulation the house that supplies the best horses to the Kingdom and the Empire is the one that is chosen by the King.

Merris Argona is the current pick, chosen by the King in a contentious and political appointment. The King is young, and the horse lords did not consider he would pick someone he knew, trusted, and was the youngest of the candidates to boot.

Viscount Merris Argon

Medium Humanoid — Nobel (5 HD) / Fighter 3| Lawful Good
Armor Class 22 (+1 scale mail, shield) — **Hit Points** 84 — **Speed** 30 ft.

Statistics

STR	DEX	CON	INT	WIS	CHA
19 (+4)	12 (+1)	14 (+2)	12 (+0)	12 (+0)	16 (+3)

Saving Throws STR +7, CON +5
Skills Animal Handling +4, Deception +6, Insight +4, Perception +4, Persuasion +6
Senses passive Perception 14
Languages Common, Elvish, Halfling
Challenge 6 (2,300 XP)

Actions

+1 Longsword. *Melee Weapon Attack:* +8 to hit, reach 5 ft., one target.
Hit: 9 (1d8+5) slashing damage or 10 (1d10+5) slashing damage if used with two hands to make a melee attack.

Magical Items

Splint +1, Longsword +1, Gauntlets of Ogre Power, Potion of Greater Healing (x2)

The Viscount's full stat block is on page 52. Merris's javelins and lance stay with his trusty warhorse.

Sergeant Harris

Sergeant Harris has the same stats as Sergeant Lorral. He is a pragmatic man and not prone to excitement unless someone is trying to kill him on the battlefield. That to him is excitement.

Packmaster Kris

Kris had a talent for dog handling, and is the Lancer who trains, takes care of, and uses the guard dogs. The highly trained dogs are loyal to Kris.

Packmaster Kris

Medium Humanoid — Fighter 1/Ranger 2| Lawful Neutral
Armor Class 16 or (scale mail) — **Hit Points** 29 — **Speed** 30 ft.

Statistics

STR	DEX	CON	INT	WIS	CHA
13 (+1)	13 (+1)	13 (+1)	10 (+0)	13 (+1)	10 (+1)

Saving Throws STR +3, CON +3
Skills Animal Handling +3, Athletics +3, Survival +3
Senses passive Perception 11
Languages Common, Dwarvish, Elvish, Halfling
Challenge ½ (100 XP)

Actions

Heavy Crossbow. *Ranged Weapon Attack:* +5 to hit, range 100 ft./400 ft., one target.
Hit: 6 (1d10+1) piercing damage.

Unarmed Strike. *Melee Weapon Attack:* +3 to hit, reach 5 ft., one creature.
Hit: 2 bludgeoning damage.

Warhammer. *Melee Weapon Attack:* +3 to hit, reach 5 ft., one target.
Hit: 5 (1d8+1) bludgeoning damage or 6 (1d10+1) bludgeoning damage if used with two hands to make a melee attack.

Kris's full stat block is on page 52. His lance, spear, and javelins are with his warhorse.

Guard Dogs

These large dogs are intimidating and loyal, although their function is tracking and cornering prey and guarding camp, not direct battle engagement.

Intro

Lost at the Beaux Seins

Moortide Rising

The Altar & the Anvil

Castle Wailmoor

Appendix

Guard Dogs

Medium Beast — Mastiff | Unaligned
Armor Class 12 — **Hit Points** 5 — **Speed** 40 ft.

Statistics

STR	DEX	CON	INT	WIS	CHA
13 (+1)	14 (+2)	12 (+1)	3 (-4)	12 (+1)	7 (-2)

Skills Perception +3
Senses passive Perception 13
Challenge ½ (100 XP)

Abilities

Keen Hearing and Smell. The mastiff has Advantage on Wisdom (Perception) checks that rely on hearing or smell.

Actions

Bite. *Melee Weapon Attack:* +3 to hit, reach 5 ft., one target. *Hit:* 1d6+1 piercing damage. If the target is a creature, it must succeed on a DC 11 Strength Saving Throw or be knocked prone.

GUESTS & MALCONTENTS

The Pub currently has three other notable people (to the DM):

- Zander Wilcox (24), Imperial Courier
- **Gillian Flanders** (22), a bard and spy
- **The Shadow** (35), a counter-intelligence agent and assassin

ZANDER WILCOX

Zander keeps his lance and javelins with his horse. Zander is recognizable as an Imperial Courier by his distinctive black and red uniform—only Imperial martial-based functionaries or soldiers may wear black and red. Zander is an unassuming man, even in his uniform, but is highly trained and a skilled combatant, able to fire arrows with accuracy even from horseback.

Zander Wilcox

Medium Humanoid — Fighter 1/Ranger 3 | Neutral Good
Armor Class 20 (Mithral Half Plate) — **Hit Points** 38 — Speed 30 ft.

Statistics

STR	DEX	CON	INT	WIS	CHA
13 (+1)	14 (+2)	12 (+1)	12 (+0)	13 (+1)	10 (+1)

Saving Throws STR +5, CON +3
Skills Animal Handling +3, Athletics +3, Survival +3
Senses passive Perception 11
Languages Common, Dwarvish, Elvish, Halfling
Challenge 1 (200 XP)

Actions

Shortsword. *Melee Weapon Attack:* +4 to hit, reach 5 ft., one target. *Hit:* 5 (1d6+2) piercing damage.

Zander's full stat block is on page 53. He is relaxing with relatives in the Pub and is on his way north on Kandra Road.

GILLIAN FLANDERS

Gillian Flanders is a spy for the Duchy of Hardred, who is halfway through long-term Viscounty subversive campaign of blackmail, bribery, and intimidation to pick up agents. She's a thoroughly wicked woman—using her bardic skills, powerfully passive-aggressive magic, and raw sex appeal to accomplish her goals. She is a patient—despite her youthful appearance and outward demeanor—and takes great delight in getting people to do things they would normally never do. Her superiors call her The Corruptor.

Gillian's stat block is on page 53. Gillian is performing in the pub, belly-dancing with her symbols and coin scarf in a seductive style that put the wenches to shame. She currently has her ring, headband, and amulet on, and little else. Her rapier and cloak are behind the bar. All her other gear is in her room.

Gillian has yet to determine which person at the Crossroads she is going to seduce and charm (or charm and seduce).

The soldiers, however, have given her some pause, along with the Viscount himself relaxing in the stable quarters. She knew only rumors about the swamp dog attack but was more interested in learning that she needs to avoid the stablemaster and Dame Walshan.

THE SHADOW

The Shadow is a reoccurring character in the *Chronicles of the Celestial Chains* campaign. Here, he is neither friend nor foe, but the PCs could run-afoul of his duties to the Viscounty.

When the Emperor was having a nice dinner at an exquisite, but demure restaurant with his favorite assassin, The Shadow, he told the man of an honored imperial tradition. Since he has lived to achieve the highest assassin rank in the Empire, the Shadow was welcome to leave the Emperor's employ and serve his homeland instead. Or, alternatively, become a member of the Imperial Court.

The Shadow asked only one question: when was the last time someone had achieved such a rank?

"1,000 years," was the Emperor's reply.

The Shadow paused and considered his options. He knew better than to ask the Emperor his preference.

"The Viscount of Kandra, Merris, is my cousin. Growing up, he was my only friend and the only person to ask me to stay home."

The Emperor nodded, pleased at the choice.

This is how the Viscount acquired a Shadow, acting as a quasi-bodyguard and one-man counterintelligence organization. The Viscount doesn't even know The Shadow exists. To him, his cousin is a bitter-sweet childhood memory, his best friend who left to seek fortune elsewhere in the Empire.

The Shadow's stat block is found on page 54.

CURSE OF LOST MEMORIES

Each pre-generated PC on their character sheets has a boon. This boon, however, comes with a curse (and is labeled as such)—they experience visions, and sometimes those visions manifest themselves in ways that are confusing, but then fade away before it has any adverse effects.

Until now. They aren't visions, but memories. Their memories of a different time. And these memories will not abide.

ALL FOR ONE, AND ONE FOR ALL!

If the PCs are within sight of each other, all it takes is one PC to trigger a *Lost Memory* for the rest of the party to experience it. The PCs all cast the reincarnation spell on themselves together, as a group—but this is also a game-play mechanic. It prevents the DM from keeping track who has those memories.

While it's interesting to keep track of which PC is the reincarnation of a Knight of Wailmoor, it isn't necessary to advance the adventure.

Once a PC triggers a *Lost Memory*, everyone must save—DC 20 Wisdom. Those who fail, experience the memory. Those who save can choose to ignore it or accept the vision.

One of the pre-generated PCs operates different with the *Lost Memories*—they have a +20 to a Wisdom Save. They automatically save unless they have some extensive penalty to their Wisdom at the time of the trigger.

That pre-generated PC is Gerrdan. The below setup assumes he (if not by name, then by boon) is a part of the party, but it isn't necessary—if the party doesn't have a PC with the +20 Wisdom Save bonus, well, then that's that—skip those sections.

THE TRIGGER

After the intimal intro, choose *one* variation to run, depending on who saves and who doesn't, and if there is a Wisdom Save Boon in play.

The Inn at the crossroads at the bottom of the moor plateau seems the obvious place to rest before embarking on a journey to make sense of the visions, memories, or whatever they are that have been running around in your mind.

The pub attached to the inn only has large tables, so you are sitting next to locals and other travelers. The beer is good and the food expertly cooked, and an extraordinary attractive bard just finished belly-dancing

provocatively around the pub, much to the delight of the soldiers sitting at their own table—elite Viscounty Lancers by the look of them.

"Gah!" one of the soldiers yells out, and by the cup on the floor, the wet uniform, and the wide-eyed serving wench, you can guess she spilled beer on him. He reaches out and smacks her on the bottom, and she yelps and jumps in place.

"Damn it, girl, get your game on. Don't just stand there, bring me another beer!"

The young woman, however, indeed just stands there, tears streaming down her face, and she starts to sob.

That's when you realize she looks familiar. Your vision goes red. Make a Wisdom Save—DC 20—and then roll for initiative.

The wench that was smacked on the butt by the annoyed Lancer, Sarah, is a direct descendant of a noblewoman whom the PCs, in their last and fateful incarnations, saved—at great cost—from an onslaught of demons. Sarah looks just like her ancestor.

This situation has forced all the PCs memories as Knights of the Wailmoor into the forefront of their brains but in a scattered way. The *Lost Memories* have caused the PCs to think Sarah is this noble woman, and that she was just abused by a soldier under their command!

The exception is those that made their Saving Throws and Gerrdan. Gerrdan and his unearthly Wisdom Save is completely immune to the *Lost Memories* subverting his conscious will.

THE RESULT

PCs failing the DC 20 Wisdom Save start kicking the crap out of the soldiers in hand-to-hand combat, neither drawing steel or trying to deal lethal damage.

PCs who did save have to make a choice.

Drop into initiative; it's on.

PC CHOICES

The PCs need to decide what they do base on what they see. However, this section is only for PCs who saved. PCs who didn't save are simply smacking around the Lancers like high-level monks. Which, in previous lives, they all were at some point or the other.

PC CHOICE: "GERRDAN" VARIATION

Gerrdan (or another PC who has his Epic Boon) is immune to taking any action against his will, manifested as a permanent +20 Wisdom bonus. This boon, however, does not prevent memories of his past lives from being remembered. His memories come as visual overlays. The real world doesn't disappear from

Intro

Lost
at the
Beaux
Seins

Moortide
Rising

The Altar
& the
Anvil

Castle
Wailmoor

Appendix

him, one memory asserts itself as a vision and overlaps what he is seeing.

Such as right now. After initiative is rolled, and one of the PCs has Gerrdan's Boon (or is Gerrdan himself), proceed below:

Several other patrons leap to their feet at the sight of the crying barmaid, but what *you* see is confusing. It is as if you are sitting in two pubs, with one intersecting the other, people sitting and standing, drinking, and singing, but some in one pub and some in a different pub. Some of the guests are even sitting on other guests when the tables and chairs in this vision of two pubs overlap.

The visual oddity is nauseating as if you can't find your balance sitting in your own seat.

What is apparent, however, that several patrons are engaged in a rather robust bar fight with Viscounty soldiers—except the vision is overlaid on top of a bar fight that doesn't contain *any* soldiers. In one vision, one set of patrons is smacking the virtual and sometimes literal snot out of each of the soldiers. In the other, it simply looks like a bunch of cheerful young men having a drunken row.

It is at that moment of observation that you see a man who looks familiar smack the table in front of him with his hand and shouts, "Stop this nonsense right now!"

The impressive table smack gets the attention of all the young men fighting. That group stops and glances about sheepishly and then starts laughing and shaking hands, helping each other up. But the other group, which you realize are people you've seen entering the pub before your vision—indeed, the other vision is now gone entirely—they didn't hear the man shout for an end to this foolishness because that was a vision, and *this* is the real world.

Amidst the fisticuffs, the barmaid is standing in the middle, crying her eyes out. What do you do?

PC CHOICE: SAVED, WITH GERRDAN

This variation is used when one or more other PCs Saved, *and* there is a Gerrdan or someone who has his Save Boon, in the group. Proceed first with Gerrdan, *then* below for the PCs who saved—but only if he doesn't smack the table. No need for additional setup; those PCs made their Wisdom Save and none the wiser.

One moment you're having a great beer, the next some barmaid gets a smack on the butt— as countless barmaids have and countless barmaids, unfortunately, will—and then some travelers jumped from their seats and started kicking the crap out of Viscounty Lancers. They aren't trying to kill the Lancers, but they are, without a doubt, engaged in the most awesome display of expert fisticuffs you've ever seen. And the Lancers, who are elite soldiers, might as well be pikers.

That's when you have a sudden and odd-thought.

All of this seems like it happened before. You call up a memory where there is a vigorous bar fight, and you smack the table to get everyone's attention and shout, "Stop this nonsense right now!" and everyone stops fighting.

But it doesn't seem like *your* memory.

Amidst the fisticuffs, the barmaid is standing in the middle, crying her eyes out. And there is this other person watching the barfight looking mightily confused and that he's about to hurl chicken pot-pie chunks all over the table. What do you do?

PC CHOICE: SAVED, NO GERRDAN

This variation is for when one or more other PCs saved, and they *don't* have Gerrdan's unique "visual overlay" curse.

Even if it is only *one* PC that failed, that PC is, single-handedly, smacking the soldiers around like a Kung-Fu master. The soldiers are all bewildered, hesitant (see NPC Reactions) and embarrassed—the soldier who smacked Sarah's butt did not mean for Sarah to cry.

One moment you're having a great beer, the next some barmaid gets a smack on the butt— as countless barmaids have, and countless barmaids will—and then some travelers jumped from their seats and started kicking the crap out of Viscounty Lancers. They aren't trying to kill the Lancers, but they are, without a doubt, engaged in the most awesome display of expert fisticuffs you've ever seen. And the Lancers, who are elite soldiers, might as well be pikers.

That's when you have a sudden and odd-thought. All of this seems like it happened before. You call up a memory where there is a vigorous bar fight, and you smack the table to get everyone's attention and shout, "Stop this nonsense right now!" and everyone stops fighting.

But it doesn't seem like *your* memory.

Amidst the fisticuffs, the barmaid is standing in the middle, crying her eyes out. What do you do?

CHOICE CONSEQUENCES

Either the table gets smacked, or it doesn't. It's a choice. As soon as one person smacks the table, then that's it— no need to blow up the Pub multiple times.

SOMEONE SMACKED THE TABLE

Each PC has lived countless lives, some of them ascribing to dizzying heights of magical power—only to die and forget it all, reborn back unto the Welt without going to Elysia no matter how well-deserved.

But that's over now. The Hierophants' World-Spell is asserting itself. Everyone gets off easy.

Well, everyone except the PC that smacked the table.

Your actions immediately stop the bar fight—although not in the way the fight ended in the vision.

From your location, a visible, circular shockwave rolls through the pub in all directions. People are pushed to the floor, across tables, off their feet. All the glass bottles at the bar shatter, and the soldiers are scattered this way and that. The patrons fighting the soldiers are pushed over. One goes flying into the air, crashes into the ceiling, and falls to the floor with a thud. The pub's windows explode outward in a loud shattering of glass.

You cough, spitting out blood. You're on the ground, feeling as if your insides are coming undone. You embrace the oblivion that comes to take the pain away.

At this point, the other PCs regain their faculties and pick themselves up. But that's not all that happens. Substitute "His/He" or "Her/She" for "They/Theirs" below.

Everyone picks themselves up. The Pub is trashed, but nobody is seriously injured.

Or maybe not—there is a moan from the middle of the pub. The person who smacked the table has a hand over their eyes. They take their hand away hands away, and they drip with blood—blood is flowing out of the eyes like tears. They cough blood and collapse to the floor.

What do you do?

Describe the PC on the floor as someone clearly dying: his breath is shallow and gurgling, there is blood coming out of his eyes, and his skin is turning blue.

The PC is thoroughly unconscious, bleeding, and at 0 HP. Stay in initiative and keep track of time. The PC bleeding out with internal injuries is on the death track and needs to make Death Saves.

If nobody helps the poor sot, the Viscount comes in and heals the PC with his *potion of greater healing* before he or she expires.

Hopefully, a PC with healing ability will step in and do the right thing. Assuming that's not the PC on the ground.

NOBODY SMACKED THE TABLE

Never fault a player for not taking the obvious route, it could be a trick. This is a trick all right—smacking the table blows up the pub. Sure, nobody died. But still. Smack! Ruined beer! Broken whiskey bottles! Havoc!

PCS WHO DIDN'T SAVE

Blowing up a tavern is one way to get player's attention, but the "blink-and-you're-in-a-bar-fight" can be just as disconcerting, if a bit less messy.

You find yourselves in the middle of a bar fight, mid

punch, with Viscounty soldiers without quite knowing how you got there. Something about a barmaid crying. Or was it a spilled beer?

In any event, the Lancers you all were in the process of throttling are looking at you with surprised expressions and grimaces, but they also seem to be holding back, hands well away from their weapons.

"Hey, are you guys OK?"

You turn to the man who talked from the doorway, clearly a noble and a warrior from his fancy armor and highly functional, but also expensive, clothes. Oh, now you remember—you saw him earlier. The Viscount. Of Kandra. The liege of the man who owns the inn and pub. He's looking right at you.

Whoops.

EVERYBODY SAVED

While it is highly unlikely everyone can make a DC 20 Wisdom Save at 1st level, it is possible to do so especially if there are only 3 or so players at the table, everybody has a Wisdom based class, etc. Reward players with a reveal by having them all experience a *Lost Memory*. Without blowing the pub up or punching Viscounty Lancers.

This *Lost Memory* happens to all the PCs.

The barmaid crying and standing alone seems familiar, and one moment you're studying her face and the next you're in armor, swords drawn, running down steps to waiting horses, the young woman now in an expensive and fancy-dress noble lady would wear, slung over someone's shoulder.

Only, you're not. You're clearly in the pub, but it's as if you're somewhere else too, at the same time. Images from the pub and this vision jumble together, making you dizzy.

But you forget about being dizzy when a low, reverberating growl comes from behind you. Everyone turns to look up the stairs, and a large demon with four arms, two of them ending in crab claws, immerges from the manor ruins.

"I'll take that virgin," the demon says in a perverse and vile voice.

A woman in armor that was running with you steps back up the stairs, her bastard sword suddenly glowing with arcane runes, wisps of smoke rising from the blade.

"No," is all she says and light bursts from the sword, blinding you.

You blink your eyes, and you're back in the pub, laying on the floor along with several other people. A human man in fancy banded mail is standing over you.

"Hey, are you guys OK?" he asks, holding out his riding-gloved hand.

The man is Viscount Marris Argona, and he tells the characters that as one of the soldiers was going to apologize to the barmaid, the PCs collapsed on the floor. All at the same time.

Intro

Lost at the Beaux Seins

Moortide Rising

The Altar & the Anvil

Castle Wailmoor

Appendix

NPC Reactions

Reactions are divided into two sections: during the period, some PCs are not themselves, and after.

During the Lost Memory

During the fight, there is little time for the people to react, but some can.

Soldiers: The soldiers received orders from the Viscount himself to not engage in any lethal combat and that there could be people in the village who "need our help but don't know it" and to keep an eye out for something strange. PCs kicking their asses like high-level monks fit that bill.

Zander Wilcox: Zander acts exactly to training. At the odd occurrence of fast-fists-of-ass-kicking, he bolts for the door grabs his horse from the stable and immediately rides to his next destination. Zander is not a coward; this is the training Imperial Couriers receive: disengage and continue the mission.

Gillian Flanders: Gillian is caught off guard, enjoying a glass of expensive elven wine one of the wenches poured her for her outstanding and provocative dance performance—they expect business will be good tonight. Gillian slithers away from the soldiers.

The Shadow: Gillian's expert reaction is what causes him to notice her beyond a man's appreciation for a professional and provocative dance performance. He starts to study her in earnest in a way a Grandmaster Imperial Assassin can. He could care less about the PCs.

The Wenches: Carole and Mimi are entertaining customers in their rooms. Priss and Kerri grab Sarah and drag her away from the soldiers. They don't know what is going on; the Sarah they knew would laugh at the smack and buy the soldier a round, and then seduce him later and pry most, if not all, his coin out of his purse.

Evan: Evan is unsure what to do. Clearly, there is something odd going on; he is contemplating fetching the other soldiers in the stable when he sees Zander leave, and assumes Zander went for help.

The Viscount: Merris Argona catches word something is amiss in the bar and immediately thinks of his wife's strange omen. His men, however, insist he stays in the stable while one of them checks it out.

Patrons: The other patrons are too stunned to do anything right now.

Dispelled or Dissipated Lost Memory

Once the *Lost Memory* ends, either by someone smacking the table—or having it run its course—the various NPCs will react to the player's reactions.

Soldiers: If the characters keep fighting hand-to-hand without trying to stab or crush them dead, the soldiers try to contain the situation. Whatever monk mojo the PCs had is gone.

If there are only two soldiers left conscious, one swallows his pride and blows on his signal whistle, which summons the soldiers in the Stable in earnest.

If the PCs chose to start stabbing, crushing, or using damaging spells, they discard their orders and respond in kind. Things will now get ugly.

Gillian Flanders: Gillian continues her non-observation observation of events from behind the bar, Evan, also behind the bar, thinks she is trying to get somewhere safe and doesn't think anything of it.

The Shadow: Unfortunately for Gillian, The Shadow recognizes her *ring of mind shielding*. He's seen it before, and now he's interested in why a bard would have a spy's ring. He then quickly observes she is wearing an *amulet of proof against detection and location*, sealing her fate. Gillian is good, but she is not Grandmaster Imperial Assassin good.

The Wenches: The wenches stay out of the fight but, like everyone else, they are riveted at the spectacle.

Evan: Evan thinks that interfering with Viscounty soldiers falls into the category of "things you just don't do," so he grabs the warhammer but stays put. If anybody responds with trying to draw blood, he grabs his crossbow and tells the offender(s) to stand down. He'll use it if they don't.

The Viscount: If things go badly for the first set of soldiers, the second set comes in, this group with their shields and warhammers out, but still determined to use non-lethal force.

If by chance the second group runs into trouble, the Viscount engages the PCs himself and choosing not to kill the PCs when they drop to 0 or less HP. Have all the PCs make a Wisdom (Insight) skill check, DC 12. Those that make the skill check knows the man is a noble of the Viscounty. With a DC 15, they think he's the Viscount himself.

If the PCs use lethal force against the second group of soldiers, they try to keep them away from the Viscount while trying to wear the offenders down.

If the PCs engage the Viscount in lethal force, The Shadow turns invisible using his cloak and assassinates the PC. Don't bother with exactly how he does it, he's 20th Level, and they are 1st.

Any PCs who didn't use lethal damage are spared and simply see people dropping to the floor with a missing eye, spleen removal, etc.

Patrons: The other patrons back away from any confrontation.

AFTERMATH

From a narrative sense, the entire village description and the inhabitants described within is the backbone to the PCs investigation of the moors and the related problems after the "incident" in the Pub. There is a wealth of knowledge available and depending on how the PCs acted when their curse manifested itself, material support.

THE VISCOUNT

The Viscount is a goodly, but pragmatic, man. He is also religious, worshiping Platine. He does put great faith in his wife, and therefore, also her faith, the barbarian goddess The Maiden. He tries to do the right thing and is a shrewd diplomat.

He arrived at the village to lend support to his new knight, to assess the situation and try to make sense of his wife's omens.

Argona is a competent lancer, but his soft skills are better: Deception +6, Insight +4, Persuasion +6. He is also perceptive at Perception +4.

The Viscount will absolutely talk to the PCs, even if they resorted to lethal force (against the Lancers—against him they are killed by The Shadow), to assess what they know and whom they are. In his mind, they are blameless for their actions, but if the PCs react with hostility his desire to protect his subjects will override his wife's advice.

PCs AND THE TRUTH

Play the Viscount as a clever man. He will absolutely use Insight on the PCs and if the PCs are hedging their words or outright lying, and he can sense it, he will encourage the PCs to come clean, so he can help them. Insight on the Viscount reveals he has no hidden agenda, although a Wisdom (Insight) of DC 20 or more will reveal he seems hesitant about something.

That hesitation is about his wife's omens. He says it is obvious that the PCs are connected somehow to the abandoned, haunted moors, and the swamp dog attack is part of a larger picture. Depending on how the PCs talk to him, he may or may not reveal The Maiden has been sending omens about the crossroads and the PCs. He is hesitant because in his experience omens can be misinterpreted and cause harm.

PCs ACTIONS IN THE PUB

How the PCs reacted will influence the Viscount. Even if smacking the table made a mess of things, if the PCs did not respond with trying to murder-stab people when given a chance to disengage, his Attitude towards the PCs is "Parental" (Indifferent), and the PCs can easily move him to Friendly.

PCs DIDN'T TRY TO KILL PEOPLE

Argona will back the PCs expedition to Wailmoor and gift them his finest warhorses **and** a supply wagon full of goods, pulled by a mighty draft horse. The PCs handled themselves in an honorable manner and didn't turn a tough situation worse.

The Viscount will also pay for the bar damage and tell the PCs they have enough to worry about.

Reward the PCs 50 XP each.

PCs TRIED TO KILL PEOPLE, NOBODY DIED

Argona's disposition will be Indifferent. If the PCs try to make amends, he will become Friendly, and he rewards them with the wagon and the draft horse **but not the warhorses.** Only if someone makes their case for more aid move his Attitude to Friendly via Charisma (Persuasion) DC 15, will he release the prized warhorses in this scenario. The druids or the Dame can heal wounds, after all.

Reward the PCs 25 XP each.

PCs RESORTED TO MURDER, SOMEONE DIED

Argona is Hostile to the PC(s) who killed someone and will hang that person from the nearest tree, and his now organized soldiers will draw steel on anyone who attempts to interfere. He will be Hostile to the other PCs, but if the PCs make their case that they didn't know that person, or if they tried to stop that person, he can be moved to Indifferent, with further Charisma (Persuasion) and easing of tensions be moved to Friendly. He then rewards them with warhorses and the wagon of supplies, or just the draft horse and wagon if he stays at Indifferent.

The PCs get 25 XP if they make their case to the Viscount and move his disposition to a more favorable position.

If the Viscount hangs a PC, his or her body disappears with the *Curse of the Lost Memory* <u>Death</u>

Intro

Lost at the Beaux Seins

Moortide Rising

The Altar & the Anvil

Castle Wailmoor

Appendix

Mechanic. This is seen only by the druids on the ground floor. One of them knocks out the PC and revives them after the Viscount has left. Awkward conversations with Jerimiah ensue, in which he advises the murderous PC to mend his or her ways—and keep their body out of his tree!

PERCEPTIVE PCS

Perceptive PCs don't need an Insight check to note that the Viscount came with a wagon of supplies and extra warhorses (and prized Viscounty warhorses at that). He knows more than he is letting on, and that is his wife's omens. If politely asked about the coincidence, just as if they successfully Wisdom (Insight) DC 20 on him, he will talk about the omens and how similar to a prophecy, they are difficult to decipher and sometimes do more harm than good.

THE WAGON OF SUPPLIES

The wagon of supplies is literally a wagon *full* of supplies. PCs cannot ride in the wagon unless they hitch another (expensive) draft horse or offload heavier supplies somewhere else.

Arrows (x100)
Ball bearings (bag of 1,000)
Barrel (empty)
Basket (empty) (x2)
Bedroll (x6)
Bit and bridle
Blanket (x6)
Block and tackle
Bucket (x2)
Case, crossbow bolt (empty) (x2)
Case, map or scroll (empty)
Chain (10 feet) (x2)
Chalk (x2)
Climber's kit (x2)
Crossbow bolts (x100)
Crowbar (x2)
Fishing tackle (x2)
Grappling hook (x2)
Hammer (x2)
Hammer, sledge
Healer's kit (10 uses) (x2)

Hunting trap
Ladder (10-foot)
Lances (x6)
Lantern, bullseye (x2)
Mess kit (x6)
Oil (flask) (x10)
Paper (x7)
Pitcher
Piton (x10)
Pot, iron
Rations (x20)
Rope, hemp (50 feet) (x3)
Rope, silk (50 feet) (x2)
Sack (empty) (x6)
Sealing wax (x2)
Shovel (x3)
Signal whistle (x2)
Soap (x6)
Spikes, iron (x3)
Tankard (x6)
Tent, two-person (x3)
Tinderbox (x3)
Torch (x15)
Waterskin (x6)
Whetstone (x3)

TOBY THE DRAFT HORSE

To a small statured person, Toby the draft horse is a scary-big horse. He's really a sweetheart, though.

While large and very muscular, Toby is not a warhorse. He is trained as a workhorse. Toby is amazing to look at, a figure of pure equine, almost larger than life.

Toby isn't skittish, but he is very perceptive. Like all non-warhorses, he doesn't like blood, sounds of battle, loud noises, creepy animals, predators, odd things blowing in the breeze and mean people.

Toby the Draft Horse

Draft horse — Large beast, unaligned
Armor Class 10 — **Hit Points** 20 — **Speed** 40 ft.

Statistics

STR	DEX	CON	INT	WIS	CHA
20 (+5)	10 (+0)	12 (+1)	2 (-4)	11 (+0)	7 (-2)

Skills Athletics +7, Perception +4
Senses passive Perception 14
Languages —
Challenge 1/4 (50 XP)

Actions

Hooves. Melee Weapon Attack: +7 to hit, reach 5 ft., one target. *Hit:* 10 (2d4+5) bludgeoning damage.

PRIDE OF VISCOUNTY WARHORSES

The warhorses' stat blocks are in the appendix starting on page 209. Merris brought six horses with him (in addition to the wagon of supplies), some of the best warhorses the Viscounty has to offer, steeds usually reserved for Lancer officers, the horse lords, and their families or honored knights.

Merris is a competent lancer. Like any Viscounty mounted knight, he's predisposed to throwing horseflesh at a problem until it goes away—hence his extraordinarily generous gift.

PCs obviously not mounted warriors will receive a quick lesson on how to handle their horses. This won't add any skills or increase a skill check, but it will prevent the horses from completely dominating the lower-level PCs.

BRINGING THE PCS TOGETHER

Up until now, it's been uncoordinated action and the Viscount's show. He will ask if the PCs know each other (they do not) and suggest that they work together to get to the bottom of these "visions" they have been having. He also, to the group, points out that divine omens and visions don't act this way. He will, sadly, reveal that the PCs may be cursed.

If the PCs are slow on the uptake, point out that meeting other people like themselves is the first time something meaningful has happened in their difficult lives. And if the occurrence in the pub is an indication, they better start working together to figure it out.

The Viscount's Next Actions

Merris will try to help the PCs with logistical support, confer with Sir Walshan and leave to try to get home before his wife gives birth. He'll leave with several pies for the Viscountess, but they won't make it that far.

Inn and Pub Staff

The Pub staff will be bewildered at the PCs actions, no matter what they were.

Evan

Any apologies to Evan for any mess will be met with a dismissive smile and a handshake. The Viscount paid for the damages, and Sir Walshan owns the Pub. He's the guy that makes beer and pours drinks—no permanent harm, no foul.

The apology will go a long way with him, however, and he will be on Friendly terms thereafter.

Sarah the Wench

There is more to Sarah's story—it was never her intention to be a prostitute. She made a youthful indiscretion and turned to the sanctioned Imperial Courtesan profession, partly out of the desire to feed herself, partly for the escape. She has no family.

Any PC kind enough to inquire about her has her appreciation. Shallow PCs can take advantage of her hospitality, but that's not the real benefits Sarah has to offer—information is.

Sarah was upset that day because earlier she met a man named Kenneth, who paid for her services on several occasions. Kenneth, however, convinced her that this life wasn't for her and she should come with him. He had a hunting cabin, and they could make a good life of it.

Sarah was dubious but hopeful, and against her cynical nature, agreed. Kenneth told her he would be back in a fortnight with an extra horse. He never showed.

She describes him as a "tall, blonde man with a massive longbow that had glowing elven runes on the wood."

What Really Happened to Kenneth

Kenneth was a ranger, part of the roaming network of rangers that are the eyes and ears of the formal druid hierarchy and was in the village to introduce himself to the stablemaster. Sensing something odd about the plateau, he proceeded up the trail to investigate.

A few miles into the moor, he was set upon by moor demon gators, dragged into a bog, drowned, and eaten.

PCs with divination magic, or who questions one of the druid twins, can find out Kenneth went to the moor and never came back. His bow is a *+1 longbow* and sits at the bottom of a bog.

Sarah's Motivation

Sarah feels motivated by survival. If a PC talks to Hayro on her behalf, he will say he just can't take her back—he would have to fire another chambermaid.

Thinking PCs could petition Dame Walshan to have Sarah as a servant, and if they miss this Hayro will mention it. Dame Melissai at first is hesitant, but the truth is, she could use the help and agrees.

Award the PC who helped Sarah 10 XP, and if it was a party effort award them all 25 XP each. She is very thankful.

Sarah won't waste this chance. She won't even try to seduce Sir Walshan. She will be thoroughly loyal to the Dame.

The Village

The villager's disposition to the PCs depends on the Dame Walshan's disposition, more so than anyone else including the Viscount. Since the swamp dog attack, they have gotten over their caution about her and considered her the Dame of the Crossroads both in title and spirit. They are constantly bringing her food, and indeed, if the PCs visit The Dame, she will offer them a villager-baked pie or two. Or three. She already feels fat.

The Druids

Jerimiah would like to provide the PCs with whatever help they need but must say in the village. He can offer to heal. If questioned by the PCs about Dame Walshan's corruption comments, he will agree and state that he's noticed odd things since the swamp dog attack, mainly bats flying erratically. He claims he doesn't want to be dramatic but thinks Dame Walshan might be correct and perhaps underestimating the malevolence of the moor. He'll flat-out says looking up at the old road at night makes his skin crawl.

Yurgana the druid, if cautiously approached using a language she speaks (not Common), will shyly tell the PCs she was admiring the ranger Kenneth when she saw him stare up the plateau, and then ride up the old road.

It is up to the PCs if they tell Sarah this or not. If they do, award the PCs 10 XP each, or 15 XP for a singular PC.

Yurgana is the only PC in the village that can be convinced to accompany the PCs—but only to guard their camp and horses. If the PCs have no warhorses,

Intro

Lost at the Beaux Seins

Moortide Rising

The Altar & the Anvil

Castle Wailmoor

Appendix

then she won't offer her services.

Jerimiah will be thrilled with this as a sign of breaking out of her shell. Her twin—not so much, but Kenidad knows she is not a child.

THE MALCONTENTS

The people in the bar were an interesting lot. Zander rode off and if anybody noticed, give the PCs a chance to learn about Imperial Couriers (they wouldn't necessarily know) and that such was normal.

Gillian Flanders leaves right after the Viscount and can't wait to tell her superiors what she witnessed, but The Shadow catches up to her soon afterward, and that is the end of Gillian. Over the course of a month, Hardred agents in the entire Kingdom meet similar ends, and the ones recalled out of panic never make it home. Hardred itself then purged of anything resembling an intelligence officer. And then a week later, the Duke of Hardred's beloved daughter will go missing on her way to the castle's chapel to get married, in her wedding dress, never to be seen again. Any divinations or investigations will not reveal any information at all.

The Shadow isn't exactly an ally of the PCs. He is a nation unto himself—he dominates whatever the situation is in his immediate vicinity with the experience and talents of the highest rank of Imperial Assassin. However, he is one man.

If the PCs become invested in the Viscounty, they will cross paths again.

THE PCS

In the aftermath of the *Lost Memories* trigger in the Pub, PCs should absolutely talk to various NPCs to see if anything unusual happened before they blew up the local tavern.

INVESTIGATION

All the people who live in the village will talk about the swamp dog attack that injured their knight-protector—he is still bedridden, recovering from some diseased bite.

Prudent PCs will want to investigate the odd circumstances before their odd arrival. All the NPC entries earlier detail what they know about the attack on the village or any other prudent, post-pub-explosion details.

NPC KNOWLEDGE SUMMARY

- The farmers don't know much, other than their dogs went missing and the dogs that attacked the village didn't look like any of the village dogs.

- One of the halfling farmers has visited the moor.

- Vergali can relate numerous things and give great advice to the PCs (as he was a soldier). He is the one that recognized there was an attack about to happen on the village. He believes the dogs to be corrupted by demon taint and that more will be back.

- Evan was present during the attack.

- Sarah the Wench has intel about Kenneth the Ranger, who disappeared before the attack.

- Jeremiah has supportive intel, and one of the druid's acolytes has specific information about Kenneth the Ranger.

- Sir Walsham, his squire and Dame Walshan all participated in defense of the village during the swamp dog attack, with Sir Walshan receiving wounds. Dame Walshan has specific intelligence about the swamp dogs and may give one of the PCs a healing staff if they meet certain criteria.

THE PIECES

The pieces are in place—the swamp dog attacks, the ominously missing village dogs, the PCs visions that don't seem like visions, one of which almost got them killed and the Viscount's direct support, assuming the PCs did the right thing when offered the chance. There's a missing ranger, and the village's cleric claims something is wrong with the moor.

It is time to gear up and take their fate into their own hands and find the answers.

MILESTONE XP

If using milestone experience, while the PCs only had one meaningful encounter, there was considerable opportunity for role-playing with NPCs and investigating the prior events before their arrival. Therefore, PCs are near Level 2, and after the encounter with the Corrupted Obelisk, they are ready to level. Suggested milestones needed to progress:

- Chapter 1 and the Plateau Obelisk Encounter get to Level 2.

- Exploring the Wailmoor and destroying the Bog Obelisk gets to Level 3.

- Defeating the Witch Haeggra and destroying the Crypt Obelisk gets to Level 4.

- Surviving Castle Wailmoor and defeating the Dead-Knight Harakan get to Level 5, at the end of the module.

COMPLETE STAT BLOCKS

Sir Carl Walshan

Medium Humanoid — Neutral Good — Fighter 5
Armor Class 19 (half plate, shield) — **Hit Points** 47 — **Speed** 30 ft.

Statistics

STR	DEX	CON	INT	WIS	CHA
16 (+3)	14 (+2)	12 (+1)	11 (+0)	11 (+0)	13 (+1)

Saving Throws STR +6, CON +4
Feats Blade Mastery
Skills Animal Handling +3, Athletics +6
Senses passive Perception 10
Languages Common, Halfling, Elvish
Challenge 2 (450 XP)

Abilities

Blade Mastery. Master the shortsword, longsword, scimitar, rapier, and greatsword.

Action Surge (1/short rest). Can attack twice, instead of once, whenever he takes the Attack action on his turn.

Critical Hits. Blade attacks score a critical hit on a roll of 19 or 20.

Second Wind (1/short rest). On his turn, can use a bonus action to regain hit points equal to 1d10 + 5

Military Rank. Has military rank.

Actions

Dagger. Melee or Ranged Weapon Attack: +6 to hit, reach 5 ft. or range 20 ft./60 ft., one target.
Hit: 7 (1d4+5) piercing damage in melee or 5 (1d4+3) piercing damage at range.

Javelin. Melee or Ranged Weapon Attack: +6 to hit, reach 5 ft. or range 30 ft./120 ft., one target.
Hit: 8 (1d6+5) piercing damage in melee or 6 (1d6+3) piercing damage at range.

Lance. Melee Weapon Attack: +6 to hit, reach 10 ft., one target.
Hit: 9 (1d12+3) piercing damage.

Longbow. Ranged Weapon Attack: +5 to hit, range 150 ft./600 ft., one target.
Hit: 6 (1d8+2) piercing damage.

Longsword. Melee Weapon Attack: +7 to hit, reach 5 ft., one target.
Hit: 9 (1d8+5) slashing damage or 8 (1d10+3) slashing damage if used with two hands to make a melee attack.

Unarmed Strike. Melee Weapon Attack: +6 to hit, reach 5 ft., one creature.
Hit: 4 bludgeoning damage.

Dame Melissai Walshan

Medium Humanoid — Sorcerer 1/Cleric 1 — Neutral Good
Armor Class 11 — **Hit Points** 11 — **Speed** 30 ft.

Statistics

STR	DEX	CON	INT	WIS	CHA
10 (+0)	12 (+1)	10 (+1)	11 (+0)	16 (+3)	16 (+3)

Skills Arcana +2, Medicine +5, Persuasion +5, Religion +2
Senses darkvision 60 ft., passive Perception 13
Languages Common, Halfling, Elvish
Saving Throws WIS +5, CHA +5
Challenge ¼ (50 XP)

Spells & Powers

Spell Slots: 3

Cleric spells memorized (CL 1st) — Spell Save DC 13 Spell Attack +5
1st—bless, bless, cure wounds, guiding bolt, protection from evil and good, shield of faith
Cantrips—light, sacred flame, spare the dying

Sorcerer spells known (CL 1st)
Spell Save DC 13 — Spell Attack +5
1st—mage armor, magic missile
Cantrips—blade ward, fire bolt, friends, minor illusion

Familiar Sharrisi the Cat (tiny beast)

Abilities

Disciple of Life. Adds 3 HP to 1st Level or above healing spells

Fey Ancestry. Advantage on Saving Throws against being charmed, and magic can't put to sleep.

Tides of Chaos (1/day). Gain advantage on an attack, ability check or save. Recharges on long rest, or a roll on the Wild Magic Surge Table (see Wild Magic Surge).

Wild Magic. Experts in the use of wild magic, chaos sorcerers, derive their power from the terrible and wondrous forces of the planes of power and Elemental Chaos.

Wild Magic Surge. When casting cast a Level 1 or higher spell, can trigger a wild magic surge.

Actions

+1 Staff. Melee Weapon Attack: +3 to hit, reach 5 ft., one target.
Hit: 5 (1d8+1) bludgeoning damage or 5 (1d8+1) bludgeoning damage if used with two hands to make a melee attack.

Spear. Melee or Ranged Weapon Attack: +2 to hit, reach 5 ft. or range 20 ft./60 ft., one target.
Hit: 3 (1d6) piercing damage or 4 (1d8) piercing damage if used with two hands to make a melee attack.

Spell Attack. Ranged Weapon Attack: +5 to hit, range 0 ft., one target.
Hit: As Spell damage.

Intro

Lost at the Beaux Seins

Moortide Rising

The Altar & the Anvil

Castle Wailmoor

Appendix

Squire Dagmar

Medium Humanoid — Fighter 3| Lawful Good
Armor Class 16 (scale mail) — **Hit Points** 29 — **Speed** 30 ft.

Statistics

STR	DEX	CON	INT	WIS	CHA
14 (+2)	14 (+2)	13 (+1)	10 (+0)	10 (+0)	10 (+1)

Saving Throws STR +4, CON +3
Skills Animal Handling +2, Athletics +4
Senses passive Perception 10
Languages Common, Halfling
Challenge 2 (450 XP)

Abilities

Action Surge (1/short rest). Can attack twice, instead of once, whenever he takes the Attack action on his turn.

Second Wind (1/short rest). On his turn, can use a bonus action to regain hit points equal to 1d10 + 3

Sharpshooter. The Sharpshooter is a master of ranged combat. An excellent sniper and eagle-eyed scout, this fighter is a perilous foe who can defeat an entire war band so long as they are kept at the range.

Steady Aim (3/short rest). As a bonus action on his turn can take careful aim at a creature seen within the range of a wielded ranged weapon. Until his end of turn, ranged attacks ignore half and three-quarters cover. On each hit, the weapon deals 3 HP additional damage to the target

Actions

Battleaxe. *Melee Weapon Attack:* +4 to hit, reach 5 ft., one target.
Hit: 6 (1d8+2) slashing damage or 7 (1d10+2) slashing damage if used with two hands to make a melee attack.

Longbow. *Ranged Weapon Attack:* +6 to hit, range 150 ft./600 ft., one target.
Hit: 6 (1d8+2) piercing damage.

Javelin. *Melee or Ranged Weapon Attack:* +4 to hit, reach 5 ft. or range 30 ft./120 ft., one target.
Hit: 5 (1d6+2) piercing damage.

Lance. *Melee Weapon Attack:* +4 to hit, reach 10 ft., one target.
Hit: 8 (1d12+2) piercing damage.

Unarmed Strike. *Melee Weapon Attack:* +4 to hit, reach 5 ft., one creature.
Hit: 3 bludgeoning damage

Jeremiah

Medium Humanoid — Druid 3/Fighter 1 — Neutral
Armor Class 13 (leather armor, shield) — **Hit Points** 21 — **Speed** 30 ft.

Statistics

STR	DEX	CON	INT	WIS	CHA
13 (+1)	10 (+0)	11 (+0)	11 (+0)	16 (+3)	12 (+1)

Saving Throws WIS +5, INT +2
Skills Animal Handling +5, Insight +5, Medicine +5, Nature +2, Perception +5
Senses passive Perception 15
Languages Common, Draconic, Druidic, Elvish, Halfling
Challenge 1 (200 XP)

Spells

Druid spells memorized (CL 3rd) — Spell Save DC 13 — Spell Attack +5
2nd— (2 slots) *invisibility, pass without trace*
1st— (4 slots) *animal friendship, cure wounds, healing word, longstrider, speak with animals, thunderwave*
Cantrips— *druidcraft, mending, produce flame*

Abilities

Natural Recovery (1/long rest). Can regain some magical energy by sitting in meditation and communing with nature

Protection. When a creature he sees attacks a target other than Jeremiah that is within 5 feet of him, he can use his reaction to impose disadvantage on the attack roll. He must be wielding a shield.

Second Wind (1/short rest). On his turn, can use a bonus action to regain hit points equal to 1d10 + 1

Wild Shape (2/short rest). Can use action to magically assume the shape of a beast that Jeremiah has seen before.

Actions

Dagger. *Melee or Ranged Weapon Attack:* +3 to hit, reach 5 ft. or range 20 ft./60 ft., one target.
Hit: 3 (1d4+1) piercing damage.

Lance. *Melee Weapon Attack:* +3 to hit, reach 10 ft., one target.
Hit: 7 (1d12+1) piercing damage.

Scimitar. *Melee Weapon Attack:* +3 to hit, reach 5 ft., one target.
Hit: 4 (1d6+1) slashing damage.

Sickle. *Melee Weapon Attack:* +3 to hit, reach 5 ft., one target.
Hit: 3 (1d4+1) slashing damage.

Sling. *Ranged Weapon Attack:* +2 to hit, range 30 ft./120 ft., one target.
Hit: 2 (1d4) bludgeoning damage.

Spear. *Melee or Ranged Weapon Attack:* +3 to hit, reach 5 ft. or range 20 ft./60 ft., one target.
Hit: 4 (1d6+1) piercing damage or 5 (1d8+1) piercing damage if used with two hands to make a melee attack.

Spell Attack. *Ranged Weapon Attack:* +5 to hit, range 0 ft., one target.
Hit: As Spell damage.

Unarmed Strike. *Melee Weapon Attack:* +3 to hit, reach 5 ft., one creature.
Hit: 2 bludgeoning damage.

Kenidad & Yurgana

Medium Humanoid — Druid 1 — Neutral
Armor Class 13 (leather armor, shield) — **Hit Points** 8 — **Speed** 30 ft.

Statistics

STR	DEX	CON	INT	WIS	CHA
13 (+1)	10 (+0)	11 (+0)	11 (+0)	16 (+3)	12 (+1)

Saving Throws WIS +2, INT +2
Skills Animal Handling +2, Medicine +2, Nature +2, Religion +2
Senses passive Perception 10
Languages Draconic, Druidic, Sylvan
Challenge 1/8 (25 XP)

Spells

Druid spells memorized (CL 1st)
Spell Save DC 10 — Spell Attack +2
1st— (2 slots) *cure wounds*
Cantrips—*druidcraft, mending*

Actions

Dagger. *Melee or Ranged Weapon Attack:* +2 to hit, reach 5 ft. or range 20 ft./60 ft., one target.
Hit: 1d4 piercing damage.

Sickle. *Melee Weapon Attack:* +2 to hit, reach 5 ft., one target.
Hit: 1d4 slashing damage.

Sling. *Ranged Weapon Attack:* +2 to hit, range 30 ft./120 ft., one target.
Hit: 1d4 bludgeoning damage.

Spear. *Melee or Ranged Weapon Attack:* +2 to hit, reach 5 ft. or range 20 ft./60 ft., one target.
Hit: 1d6 piercing damage or 1d8 piercing damage if used with two hands to make a melee attack.

Spell Attack. *Ranged Weapon Attack:* +2 to hit, range 0 ft., one target.
Hit: As Spell damage.

Dano

Medium Humanoid — Lawful Good
Armor Class 10 — **Hit Points** 12 — **Speed** 30 ft.

Statistics

STR	DEX	CON	INT	WIS	CHA
13 (+1)	10 (+0)	12 (+1)	10 (+0)	10 (+0)	10 (+0)

Senses passive Perception 10
Languages Common, Halfling
Challenge 1/8 (25 XP)

Actions

Heavy Crossbow. *Ranged Weapon Attack:* +2 to hit, range 100 ft./400 ft., one target.
Hit: 5 (1d10) piercing damage.

Light Crossbow. *Ranged Weapon Attack:* +2 to hit, range 80 ft./320 ft., one target.
Hit: 4 (1d8) piercing damage.

Dagger. *Melee or Ranged Weapon Attack:* +3 to hit, reach 5 ft. or range 20 ft./60 ft., one target.
Hit: 3 (1d4+1) piercing damage.

Javelin. *Melee or Ranged Weapon Attack:* +3 to hit, reach 5 ft. or range 30 ft./120 ft., one target.
Hit: 4 (1d6+1) piercing damage.

Quarterstaff. *Melee Weapon Attack:* +3 to hit, reach 5 ft., one target.
Hit: 4 (1d6+1) bludgeoning damage or 5 (1d8+1) bludgeoning damage if used with two hands to make a melee attack.

Warhammer. *Melee Weapon Attack:* +3 to hit, reach 5 ft., one target.
Hit: 5 (1d8+1) bludgeoning damage or 6 (1d10+1) bludgeoning damage if used with two hands to make a melee attack.

Intro

Lost at the Beaux Seins

Moortide Rising

The Altar & the Anvil

Castle Wailmoor

Appendix

Timothy

Medium Humanoid — Lawful Good — Fighter 2
Armor Class 18 (chain mail, shield) — **Hit Points** 20 — **Speed** 30 ft.

Statistics

STR	DEX	CON	INT	WIS	CHA
16 (+3)	12 (+1)	12 (+1)	10 (+0)	10 (+0)	11 (+0)

Saving Throws STR +5, CON +3
Skills Animal Handling +2, Perception +2
Senses passive Perception 12
Languages Common, Halfling
Challenge ¼ (50 XP)

Abilities

Action Surge (1/short rest). Can attack twice, instead of once, whenever he takes the Attack action on his turn.

Protection. When a creature he sees attacks a target other than Timothy that is within 5 feet of him, he can use his reaction to impose disadvantage on the attack roll. He must be wielding a shield.

Second Wind (1/short rest). On his turn, can use a bonus action to regain hit points equal to 1d10 + 2

Actions

Dagger. Melee or Ranged Weapon Attack: +5 to hit, reach 5 ft. or range 20 ft./60 ft., one target.
Hit: 5 (1d4+3) piercing damage.

Javelin. Melee or Ranged Weapon Attack: +5 to hit, reach 5 ft. or range 30 ft./120 ft., one target.
Hit: 6 (1d6+3) piercing damage.

Lance. Melee Weapon Attack: +5 to hit, reach 10 ft., one target.
Hit: 9 (1d12+3) piercing damage.

Longbow. Ranged Weapon Attack: +3 to hit, range 150 ft./600 ft., one target.
Hit: 5 (1d8+1) piercing damage.

Longsword. Melee Weapon Attack: +5 to hit, reach 5 ft., one target.
Hit: 7 (1d8+3) slashing damage or 8 (1d10+3) slashing damage if used with two hands to make a melee attack.

Spear. Melee or Ranged Weapon Attack: +5 to hit, reach 5 ft. or range 20 ft./60 ft., one target.
Hit: 6 (1d6+3) piercing damage or 7 (1d8+3) piercing damage if used with two hands to make a melee attack.

Unarmed Strike. Melee Weapon Attack: +5 to hit, reach 5 ft., one creature.
Hit: 4 bludgeoning damage.

Vergali

Hill Dwarf – Male – Fighter 2 – Lawful Good
Armor Class 19 (splint, shield) — **Hit Points** 24 — **Speed** 25 ft.

Statistics

STR	DEX	CON	INT	WIS	CHA
16 (+3)	10 (+0)	14 (+2)	10 (+0)	11 (+0)	10 (+0)

Saving Throws STR +5, CON +4
Skills Acrobatics +2, Athletics +5, Intimidation +2, Perception +2
Damage Resistances poison
Senses darkvision 60 ft., passive Perception 12
Languages Common, Dwarvish, Halfling
Challenge ¼ (50 XP)

Abilities

Action Surge (1/short rest). Can attack twice, instead of once, whenever he takes the Attack action on his turn.

Protection. When a creature he sees attacks a target other than Vergali that is within 5 feet of him, he can use his reaction to impose disadvantage on the attack roll. He must be wielding a shield.

Second Wind (1/short rest). On his turn, can use a bonus action to regain hit points equal to 1d10 + 2

Dwarven Resistance. Advantage on Saving Throws against poison, and resistance against poison damage.

Military Rank. Has military rank.

Stonecunning. Whenever Vergali makes an Intelligence (History) Check related to the origin of stonework, he is considered proficient in the History skill and adds double his proficiency bonus to the check

Actions

Battleaxe. Melee Weapon Attack: +5 to hit, reach 5 ft., one target.
Hit: 7 (1d8+3) slashing damage or 8 (1d10+3) slashing damage if used with two hands to make a melee attack.

Light Crossbow. Ranged Weapon Attack: +2 to hit, range 80 ft./320 ft., one target.
Hit: 4 (1d8) piercing damage.

Dagger. Melee or Ranged Weapon Attack: +5 to hit, reach 5 ft. or range 20 ft./60 ft., one target.
Hit: 5 (1d4+3) piercing damage.

Handaxe. Melee or Ranged Weapon Attack: +5 to hit, reach 5 ft. or range 20 ft./60 ft., one target.
Hit: 6 (1d6+3) slashing damage.

Unarmed Strike. Melee Weapon Attack: +5 to hit, reach 5 ft., one creature.
Hit: 4 bludgeoning damage.

Sergeant Lorral & Sergeant Harris

Medium Humanoid — Fighter 3 — Lawful Neutral
Armor Class 16 or 17 (scale mail and/or shield) — **Hit Points** 29
Speed 30 ft.

Statistics

STR	DEX	CON	INT	WIS	CHA
14 (+2)	12 (+1)	13 (+1)	10 (+0)	10 (+0)	10 (+1)

Saving Throws STR +4, CON +3
Skills Animal Handling +2, Athletics +4
Senses passive Perception 10
Languages Common, Halfling
Challenge ½ (100 XP)

Abilities

Action Surge (1/short rest). Can attack twice, instead of once, on an Attack action on his turn.

Protection. When a seen creature attacks a target other than Vergali that is within 5 feet of him, he can use his reaction to impose disadvantage on the attack roll. He must be wielding a shield.

Second Wind (1/short rest). On his turn, can use a bonus action to regain hit points equal to 1d10 + 3

Military Rank. Has military rank.

Born to Saddle. Mounting or dismounting a creature costs only 5 feet of movement, rather than half speed. In addition, has Advantage on Saving Throws made to avoid falling off his mount. If falling off his mount can automatically land on feet if not incapacitated

Implacable Mark (3/short rest). When hitting a creature with a melee weapon attack, the target is marked by until the end of the fighter's next turn. A creature ignores this effect if the creature can't be frightened. The marked target has Disadvantage on any attack roll against a creature other than the fighter or someone else who marked it.
   If a target marked is within 5 feet of the fighter on its turn and it moves at least 1 foot or makes an attack that suffers Disadvantage from this feature, the fighter can make one melee weapon attack against it using a reaction. This attack roll has Advantage, and if it hits, the attack's weapon deals +3 HP extra damage.

Knight. When a creature the knight can see attacks a target other than the knight that is within 5 feet of the knight, the knight can use a reaction to impose disadvantage on the attack roll. Requires wielding a shield.

Actions

Warhammer. *Melee Weapon Attack:* +4 to hit, reach 5 ft., one target. *Hit:* 6 (1d8+2) bludgeoning damage or 7 (1d10+2) bludgeoning damage if used with two hands to make a melee attack

Light Crossbow. *Ranged Weapon Attack:* +3 to hit, range 80 ft./320 ft., one target.
Hit: 5 (1d8+1) piercing damage.

Dagger. *Melee or Ranged Weapon Attack:* +4 to hit, reach 5 ft. or range 20 ft./60 ft., one target.
Hit: 4 (1d4+2) piercing damage.

Javelin. *Melee or Ranged Weapon Attack:* +4 to hit, reach 5 ft. or range 30 ft./120 ft., one target.
Hit: 5 (1d6+2) piercing damage.

Lance. *Melee Weapon Attack:* +4 to hit, reach 10 ft., one target.
Hit: 8 (1d12+2) piercing damage.

Spear. *Melee or Ranged Weapon Attack:* +4 to hit, reach 5 ft. or range 20 ft./60 ft., one target.
Hit: 5 (1d6+2) piercing damage or 6 (1d8+2) piercing damage if used with two hands to make a melee attack.

Unarmed Strike. *Melee Weapon Attack:* +4 to hit, reach 5 ft., one creature.
Hit: 3 bludgeoning damage.

Lancers

Medium Humanoid — Commoner/Fighter 1| Lawful Neutral
Armor Class 15 or 16 (chain mail and/or shield) — **Hit Points** 10
Speed 30 ft.

Statistics

STR	DEX	CON	INT	WIS	CHA
13 (+3)	11 (+1)	12 (+1)	11 (+0)	11 (+0)	11 (+0)

Saving Throws STR +3, CON +3
Skills Animal Handling +2, Athletics +3
Senses passive Perception 10
Languages Common, Halfling
Challenge 1/8 (25 XP)

Abilities

Action Surge (1/short rest). Can attack twice, instead of once, whenever he takes the Attack action on his turn.

Second Wind (1/short rest). On their turns, can use a bonus action to regain hit points equal to 1d10 + 1

Military Rank. Has military rank.

Actions

Warhammer. *Melee Weapon Attack:* +3 to hit, reach 5 ft., one target.
Hit: 5 (1d8+1) bludgeoning damage or 6 (1d10+1) bludgeoning damage if used with two hands to make a melee attack.

Light Crossbow. *Ranged Weapon Attack:* +2 to hit, range 80 ft./320 ft., one target.
Hit: 4 (1d8) piercing damage.

Dagger. *Melee or Ranged Weapon Attack:* +3 to hit, reach 5 ft. or range 20 ft./60 ft., one target.
Hit: 3 (1d4+1) piercing damage.

Javelin. *Melee or Ranged Weapon Attack:* +3 to hit, reach 5 ft. or range 30 ft./120 ft., one target.
Hit: 4 (1d6+1) piercing damage.

Lance. *Melee Weapon Attack:* +3 to hit, reach 10 ft., one target.
Hit: 7 (1d12+1) piercing damage.

Spear. *Melee or Ranged Weapon Attack:* +3 to hit, reach 5 ft. or range 20 ft./60 ft., one target.
Hit: 4 (1d6+1) piercing damage or 5 (1d8+1) piercing damage if used with two hands to make a melee attack.

Unarmed Strike. *Melee Weapon Attack:* +3 to hit, reach 5 ft., one creature.
Hit: 2 bludgeoning damage.

Intro

Lost at the Beaux Seins

Moortide Rising

The Altar & the Anvil

Castle Wailmoor

Appendix

Viscount Merris Argona

Medium Humanoid — Nobel (5 HD) / Fighter 3| Lawful Good
Armor Class 22 (+1 scale mail, shield) — **Hit Points** 84 — **Speed** 30 ft.

Statistics

STR	DEX	CON	INT	WIS	CHA
19 (+4)	12 (+1)	14 (+2)	12 (+0)	12 (+0)	16 (+3)

Saving Throws STR +7, CON +5
Skills Animal Handling +4, Deception +6, Insight +4, Perception +4, Persuasion +6
Senses passive Perception 14
Languages Common, Elvish, Halfling
Challenge 6 (2,300 XP)

Abilities

Action Surge (1/short rest). Can attack twice, instead of once, on an Attack action on his turn.

Second Wind (1/short rest). On his turn, can use a bonus action to regain hit points equal to 1d10 +3

Born to Saddle. Mounting or dismounting a creature costs only 5 feet of movement, rather than half speed. In addition, has Advantage on Saving Throws made to avoid falling off his mount. If falling off his mount can automatically land on feet if not incapacitated

Implacable Mark (3/short rest). When hitting a creature with a melee weapon attack, the target is marked by until the end of the fighter's next turn. A creature ignores this effect if the creature can't be frightened. The marked target has Disadvantage on any attack roll against a creature other than the fighter or someone else who marked it.

   If a target marked is within 5 feet of the fighter on its turn and it moves at least 1 foot or makes an attack that suffers Disadvantage from this feature, the fighter can make one melee weapon attack against it using a reaction. This attack roll has Advantage, and if it hits, the attack's weapon deals +3 HP extra damage.

Knight. When a creature the knight can see attacks a target other than the knight that is within 5 feet of the knight, the knight can use a reaction to impose disadvantage on the attack roll. Requires wielding a shield.

Protection. When a seen creature attacks a target other than Merris that is within 5 feet of him, he can use his reaction to impose disadvantage on the attack roll. He must be wielding a shield.

Actions

+1 Longsword. *Melee Weapon Attack:* +8 to hit, reach 5 ft., one target.
Hit: 9 (1d8+5) slashing damage or 10 (1d10+5) slashing damage if used with two hands to make a melee attack.

Reactions

Parry. The noble adds 2 to its AC against one melee attack that would hit it. To do so, the noble must see the attacker and be wielding a melee weapon.

Magical Items

Splint +1, Longsword +1, Gauntlets of Ogre Power, Potion of Greater Healing (x2)

Packmaster Kris

Medium Humanoid — Fighter 1/Ranger 2| Lawful Neutral
Armor Class 16 or (scale mail) — **Hit Points** 29 — **Speed** 30 ft.

Statistics

STR	DEX	CON	INT	WIS	CHA
13 (+1)	13 (+1)	13 (+1)	10 (+0)	13 (+1)	10 (+1)

Saving Throws STR +3, CON +3
Skills Animal Handling +3, Athletics +3, Survival +3
Senses passive Perception 11
Languages Common, Dwarvish, Elvish, Halfling
Challenge ½ (100 XP)

Abilities

Second Wind (1/short rest). On his turn can use a bonus action to regain hit points equal to 1d10 +

Favored Terrain. (Grasslands)

Favored Enemy. (Humans, Halflings). Has extensive experience studying, tracking, hunting, and even talking to a certain type of enemy.

Actions

Heavy Crossbow. *Ranged Weapon Attack:* +5 to hit, range 100 ft./400 ft., one target.
Hit: 6 (1d10+1) piercing damage.

Dagger. *Melee or Ranged Weapon Attack:* +3 to hit, reach 5 ft. or range 20 ft./60 ft., one target.
Hit: 3 (1d4+1) piercing damage.

Javelin. *Melee or Ranged Weapon Attack:* +3 to hit, reach 5 ft. or range 30 ft./120 ft., one target.
Hit: 4 (1d6+1) piercing damage.

Lance. *Melee Weapon Attack:* +3 to hit, reach 10 ft., one target.
Hit: 7 (1d12+1) piercing damage.

Spear. *Melee or Ranged Weapon Attack:* +3 to hit, reach 5 ft. or range 20 ft./60 ft., one target.
Hit: 4 (1d6+1) piercing damage or 5 (1d8+1) piercing damage if used with two hands to make a melee attack.

Warhammer. *Melee Weapon Attack:* +3 to hit, reach 5 ft., one target.
Hit: 5 (1d8+1) bludgeoning damage or 6 (1d10+1) bludgeoning damage if used with two hands to make a melee attack.

Unarmed Strike. *Melee Weapon Attack:* +3 to hit, reach 5 ft., one creature.
Hit: 2 bludgeoning damage.

Zander Wilcox — Medium Humanoid

Fighter 1/Ranger 3| Neutral Good
Armor Class 20 (Mithral Half Plate) — **Hit Points** 38 — **Speed** 30 ft.

Statistics

STR	DEX	CON	INT	WIS	CHA
13 (+1)	14 (+2)	12 (+1)	12 (+0)	13 (+1)	10 (+1)

Saving Throws STR +5, CON +3
Skills Animal Handling +3, Athletics +3, Survival +3
Senses passive Perception 11
Languages Common, Dwarvish, Elvish, Halfling
Challenge 1 (200 XP)

Abilities

Second Wind. (recover 1d10+1 HP, 1/short rest)

Colossus Slayer. (1/round). Zander's tenacity can wear down the most potent foes. When he hits a creature with a weapon attack, the creature takes an extra 1d8 damage if it's below its hit point maximum. He can deal this extra damage only once per turn.

Primal Awareness. Can use action and expend one ranger spell slot to focus awareness on the region around Zander.

Favored Terrain. (Grasslands)

Favored Enemy (Humans, Halflings). Has extensive experience studying, tracking, hunting, and even talking to a certain type of enemy.

Actions

Hand Crossbow. *Ranged Weapon Attack:* +6 to hit, range 30 ft./120 ft., one target.
Hit: 5 (1d6+2) piercing damage.

Dagger. *Melee or Ranged Weapon Attack:* +4 to hit, reach 5 ft. or range 20 ft./60 ft., one target.
Hit: 4 (1d4+2) piercing damage.

Javelin. *Melee or Ranged Weapon Attack:* +3 to hit, reach 5 ft. or range 30 ft./120 ft., one target.
Hit: 4 (1d6+1) piercing damage.

Lance. *Melee Weapon Attack:* +3 to hit, reach 10 ft., one target.
Hit: 7 (1d12+1) piercing damage.

Longbow. *Ranged Weapon Attack:* +6 to hit, range 150 ft./600 ft., one target.
Hit: 6 (1d8+2) piercing damage.

Shortsword. *Melee Weapon Attack:* +4 to hit, reach 5 ft., one target.
Hit: 5 (1d6+2) piercing damage.

Unarmed Strike. *Melee Weapon Attack:* +3 to hit, reach 5 ft., one creature.
Hit: 2 bludgeoning damage.

Gillam Flanders

Medium Humanoid — Bard 10 — Lawful Evil
Armor Class 12 — **Hit Points** 62 — **Speed** 30 ft.

Statistics

STR	DEX	CON	INT	WIS	CHA
13 (+1)	14 (+2)	12 (+1)	12 (+0)	13 (+1)	10 (+1)

Saving Throws Dex +6, Cha +9
Feats Actor, Master of Disguise
Skills Acrobatics +3, Animal Handling +2, Arcana +3, Athletics +2, Deception +12, History +3, Insight +2, Intimidation +8, Investigation +9, Medicine +2, Nature +3, Perception +4, Performance +12, Persuasion +12, Religion +3, Sleight of Hand +3, Stealth +3, Survival +2
Senses passive Perception 14
Languages Common, Halfling
Challenge 7 (2,900 XP

Spells

Bard spells known (CL 10th) — Spell Save DC — 16 Spell Attack +8
5th— (2 slots) *dominate person, modify memory*
4th— (3 slots) *compulsion, confusion, instant audience*
3rd— (3 slots) *fear, speak with dead, tongues*
2nd— (3 slots) *invisibility, knock, zone of truth*
1st— (4 slots) *animal friendship, charm person, cure wounds*
Cantrips— *friends, minor illusion, prestidigitation, vicious mockery*

Abilities

Bardic Inspiration (d10, 4/short rest). The bard can inspire others through stirring words or music. To do so, Gillian uses a bonus action on her turn to choose one creature within 60 feet of Gillian who can hear her. That creature gains one Bardic Inspiration die, a d6.

Once within the next 10 minutes, the creature can roll the die and add the number rolled to one ability check, attack roll, or Saving Throw it makes. The creature can wait until after it rolls the d20 before deciding to use the Bardic Inspiration die but must decide before the GM says whether the roll succeeds or fails. Once the Bardic Inspiration die is rolled, it is lost. A creature can have only one Bardic Inspiration die at a time.

Countercharm. Can use musical notes or words of power to disrupt mind-influencing effects. As an action can start a performance that lasts until the end of the bard's next turn. During that time, she, and any friendly creatures within 30 feet of have Advantage on Saving Throws against being frightened or charmed. A creature must be able to hear the bard to gain this benefit. The performance ends early if the bard is incapacitated or silenced or if the bard voluntarily ends it (no action required).

Jack of All Trades. Bard bonus to Skill Checks.

Song of Rest (d8). Sing for allies during short rest to heal them an extra 1d8 hit points.

Bard College Expertise. Extra Proficiency bonuses for 4 skills.

Font of Inspiration. Regain all expended uses of Bardic Inspiration when finishing a short or long rest.

Magical Secrets. By 10th level, the bard has plundered magical knowledge from a wide spectrum of disciplines. Choose two spells from any class, including this one. A spell she chooses must be of a level she can cast, as shown on the Bard table, or a cantrip.

The chosen spells count as bard spells for Gillian and are included in the number in the Spells Known column of the Bard table.

Actions

+1 Silver Rapier. *Melee Weapon Attack:* +6 to hit, reach 5 ft., one target.
Hit: 6 (1d8+2) piercing damage.

+1 Silver Dagger. *Melee or Ranged Weapon Attack:* +6 to hit, reach 5 ft. or range 20 ft./60 ft., one target.
Hit: 4 (1d4+2) piercing damage.

Magic Items

+1 silver rapier, +1 silver dagger, Elixir of Health, Philter of Love x3, Potion of Invisibility, Potion of Mind Reading, Potion of Speed, Ring of Mind Shielding, Ring of Protection

Intro

Lost
at the
Beaux
Seins

Moortide
Rising

The Altar
& the
Anvil

Castle
Wailmoor

Appendix

The Shadow

Medium Humanoid — Rogue 20/Fighter 1 — Lawful Evil
Armor Class 16 — **Hit Points** 151 — **Speed** 30 ft.

Statistics

STR	DEX	CON	INT	WIS	CHA
23 (+6)	20 (+5)	12 (+1)	14 (+2)	11 (+0)	14 (+2)

Feats Dual Wielder, Keen Mind, Master of Disguise, Skulker
Saving Throws STR +13, CON +8, WIS +7
Skills Acrobatics +19, Animal Handling +7, Arcana +9, Athletics +13, Deception +16, History +9, Insight +7, Intimidation +9, Investigation +16, Medicine +7, Nature +9, Perception +7, Performance +9, Persuasion +9, Religion +9, Sleight of Hand +12, Stealth +19 (Advantage on checks to move silently), Survival +7
Senses truesight 60 ft., passive Perception 17
Languages Common, Draconic, Dwarvish, Elvish, Halfling, Orc, Thieves' Cant
Challenge 20 (33,000 XP)

Abilities

Sneak Attack. Once per turn, you can deal an extra 10d6 damage to one creature he hits with an Attack if he has Advantage on the Attack roll. The Attack must use a Finesse or a ranged weapon.

The Shadow doesn't need advantage on the Attack roll if another enemy of the target is within 5 feet of it, that enemy isn't Incapacitated, and you don't have disadvantage on the Attack roll.

Assassinate. Has advantage on attack rolls against any creature that hasn't taken a turn in the combat yet. In addition, any hit scored against a creature that is surprised is a critical hit.

Death Strike (DC 20 CON). When The Shadow attacks and hits a creature that is surprised, it must make a Constitution Saving Throw. On a failed save, double the damage against the creature.

Cunning Action. Can use a Bonus Action to take the Dash, Disengage, or Hide action.

Uncanny Dodge. Can use a reaction to halve an attack's damage if The Shadow can see the attacker.

Evasion. When subjected to the effect that allows The Shadow to make a Dexterity Saving Throw to take only half damage, he instead takes no damage if he succeeds on the Saving Throw, and only half damage if he fails.

Impostor. Ability to unerringly mimic another person's speech, writing, and behavior after studying victim, gain Advantage on any Charisma (Deception) check made to avoid detection.

Blindsense. if The Shadow can hear, he is aware of the location of any hidden or invisible creature within 10 feet.

Slippery Mind. Gains proficiency in Wisdom Saving Throws.

Elusive. No attack roll has Advantage against The Shadow while he isn't incapacitated.

Stroke of Luck (1/short rest). At 20th level, if The Shadow's attack misses a target within range, he can turn the miss into a hit. Alternatively, if he fails an ability check, he can treat the d20 roll as a 20.

Reliable Talent (all Skill Checks). Whenever The Shadow makes an ability check that lets him adds his proficiency bonus, he can treat a d20 roll of 9 or lower as a 10.

Infiltration Expertise. Unfailingly creates false identities after proper legwork

Second Wind. (recover 1d10+1 HP, 1/short rest)

Boon of Skill Proficiency. Imperial Assassins are proficient in all skills.

Boon of Truesight. At 10th level, the Emperor grants Imperial Assassins the Epic Boon of Truesight.

Advanced Attunement. Imperial Assassins at 10th level or above can attune two additional magical items.

Legendary Actions

The Shadow can take 3 legendary actions, choosing from the options below. Only one legendary action option can be used at a time and only at the end of another creature's turn. He regains spent legendary actions at the start of its turn.

Legendary Cunning (1 action). The Shadow can Dash, Disengage, or Hide.

Speed of Death (1 action). The Shadow doubles his movement rate until his next turn.

Retribution of the Emperor (2 actions). The Shadow can make a melee or ranged attack with a held weapon, or an unarmed attack.

Actions

+3 Rapier. *Melee Weapon Attack:* +16 to hit, reach 5 ft., one target. *Hit:* 13 (1d8+9) piercing damage. Sneak attack for 10d6 if applicable.

Dagger of Venom. *Melee or Ranged Weapon Attack:* +14 to hit, reach 5 ft. or range 20 ft./60 ft., one target. Sneak attack for 10d6 if applicable.
Hit: 9 (1d4+7) piercing damage.

+2 Crossbow, Hand. *Ranged Weapon Attack:* +14 to hit, range 30 ft./120 ft., one target. Sneak attack for 10d6 if applicable.
Hit: 10 (1d6+7) piercing damage.

Unarmed Strike. *Melee Weapon Attack:* +13 to hit, reach 5 ft., one creature.
Hit: 7 bludgeoning damage.

Magic Items

Amulet of Proof Against Detection and Location
Belt of Stone Giant Strength
Boots of Elvenkind
Cloak of Greater Invisibility
Dimensional Shackles
Figurine of Wonderous Power (Ebon Fly)
Goggles of the Night
Philter of Love., Potion of Climbing, Potion of Flying, Potion of Gaseous Form, Potion of Vitality
Ring of Free Action
Ring of Mind Shielding

Intro

Lost
at the
Beaux
Seins

Moortide
Rising

The Altar
& the
Anvil

Castle
Wailmoor

Appendix

MOORTIDE RISING

"HOPELESS!

"THIS IS HOPELESS. THEY ARE ALL LEAVING—SOON, IT WILL BE JUST YOU AND ME, TWO OF THE OPPOSITE—UNITED IN OUR MUTUAL LOATHING FOR EACH OTHER."

"INTERESTING THAT YOU SAID LOATHING AND NOT HATE. LET ME LEAVE, MAGE. WHEN YOUR SOUL COMES BACK TO ME, I MIGHT FORGIVE SOME OF YOUR ACTIONS." EVEN IMPRISONED, THE DEMON DISPLAYED AN ARROGANT SMILE TO GO ALONG WITH HIS CONDESCENDING TONE.

"YOU ARE JUST A TOOL HERE, DEMON. I NEED TO FIND WHO STOOD BEHIND ALL THIS, EVEN IF IT IS TOO LATE FOR THE BARONY."

"I HAVE TO ADMIT I ENJOY THIS BITTERSWEET TONE OF YOURS, MAGE. IT'S EXTREMELY DELICIOUS."

—THE MAGE SILAS AND HIS PRISONER, THE DEMON MERGA

The overarching goal for the PCs in this chapter is to find the two corrupted Obelisks, destroy them, and then mount an expedition to the Temple of Dvalin to destroy the third (Chapter 3), thereby giving the PCs access to Castle Wailmoor (Chapter 4).

Whereupon Chapter 1 was all about bringing the PCs together and getting them acquainted with how they've gotten the short end of the stick—and establishing NPCs for the adventure and campaign—Chapter 2 is all about the Barony, the Wailmoor. This is an open-world, designed for PCs to roam about, getting into, and staying out of trouble.

The Wailmoor is a primal, beautiful place. At the height of its power, there were still many untamed areas where people did not tread. The engineering, magical usage, and agricultural advancements did not require large farming communities. As the PCs piece together what happened, the knowledge they gain does bring understanding, and they are burdened not only with the corruption and critters within trying to kill them but the realization that the Wailmoor is a place worth dying for and 150-years ago—it was soaked in blood.

Chapter 2 is divided up into four sections.

THE CELESTIAL CHAINS

This section sets the context for the adventure in the overall campaign.

At the end of *Curse of the Lost Memories,* the Wailmoor should be the seat of the PCs power and base of operations. Also included is information helpful to maintain continuity between modules and lore.

THE LOST MEMORIES

This section outlines all the *Lost Memories* the PCs can encounter and their possible actions. As a part mechanic, part lore device and open-world guidance system, the *Lost Memories* require the DM to take a step back and evaluate their impact at the time they are given—you may need to modify a memory, so it makes sense as someone viewing a conversation, or action, rather than participating it.

Role-playing centric players may respond to the memories negatively because when they trigger it can temporarily remove some of their agency. Encourage those players to view the memories as what they are—a curse. If the player doesn't want the past to keep haunting them, then they need to find out as much information about them as possible, which will require them to become allies with Chrystelle, the Enchantress trapped in her tower connected to Castle Wailmoor.

Some players may respond to the memories as a unique role-playing opportunity. If your players fall into this category, the DM could outline all the prior Knights of the Wailmoor (Jackon, Heleshia, Garret,

Dannok and the rest) with their backstories to provide additional memories.

MOOR ENCOUNTER LOCATIONS

All encounters and their sites throughout the Wailmoor are detailed in this section based on location. To guide the PCs through the story by leaving clues, *Lost Memories* point the way:

- The Old Bridge will provide a vision about Silas and his tower
- Silas's Tower will guide PCs to the Temple of Dvalin
- The Temple of Dvalin contains further references to Chrystelle, the Enchantress trapped in the elf tower, and the final corruption that must be cleansed before Castle Wailmoor is pulled back into reality

Some PCs will be explorers and not in need of such guidance. Some parties may be motivated to find the swamp dog Lair as their primary goal. There's no memory that points the way, so they will need to explore and track.

Other parties will view tramping about the 12-square-mile hex that is the Lost Barony of Wailmoor as the explorational adventure itself. Use the many online references and videos on the Dartmoor National Park in the UK for additional reference and inspiration.

AFTERMATH

This summarizes any NPC reactions based on the PCs activities and provides context for Chapter 3, *The Altar & the Anvil.*

THE CELESTIAL CHAINS

The Wailmoor should be the PCs base of operations for the entire campaign. When tromping through the former barony, there are places and circumstances that hold weight and meaning beyond *Curse of the Lost Memories.*

MAGICAL PROPERTIES

The *Lost Memory M6 – The Spell* alludes to a series of rituals Silas used to attempt to ward the barony from further demonic intrusion—after all, the Knights of Wailmoor were down to two, Heleshia and Jackon and Silas was an old man. And the wards worked— demons could no longer *gate* or be summoned into the Wailmoor.

Now, however, the objects of the rituals, the Obelisks, are corrupted, and for the PCs to manifest Castle

Wailmoor and the old Elven Tower within, they must remove the corruption by destroying the Obelisks and the remaining demons in the Wailmoor.

As Sir Jackon, Knight of Wailmoor alludes to, linking the magic of the wards to the spell-engine in the dam, while expedient, was detrimental in the long term. The dam is both an engineering marvel and highly magical. In *CC2 – Beneath a Dreary Wave*, PCs must tame this magic, or the fabric of reality will spin away, dragging much of the barony to the Ethereal Plane.

It is advisable for the DM to not dangle the dam in front of the players even though it comprises the later chapters of *Beneath a Dreary Wave*, as they need the blueprints to get inside the thing. It's supposed to be mysterious, so whatever the PCs conjure up in their own minds for *Curse of the Lost Memories* is an optimal outcome. For now, references to the dam that the PCs can find are kept at a minimum.

CURRENT WAILMOOR MAGICAL ISSUES

Until the PCs destroy all three Obelisks, these magical problems occur anywhere in Barony.

TELEPORTATION

Until the three Obelisks are destroyed, *dimension door* and *teleportation* are by line-of-sight-only. If you can't see the destination, you can't teleport there. Creatures with an innate teleport can only *teleport* once and then *are never able to teleport in the Wailmoor again*. Only magic users that can memorize the spell (having the capability of "reloading" their *teleport*) can repeatedly *teleport*—by line-of-sight.

Teleportation circles (such as in the old Elven Tower in Castle Wailmoor, function insofar as their destination is measured in feet—500ft. maximum, to be exact. If someone were to try to build a new circle beyond that, it wouldn't work.

Teleporting *into* the Wailmoor, unless the caster can *see* the destination, fails.

GATE

Gates are also problematic. Opening a *gate* results in a rip in the fabric of reality much like an Ethereal Cyclone. The *gate* simply sucks the caster into it and deposits them on the other end and then the *gate* closes.

The remaining demons have seen this effect and aren't sure what happens, so they don't attempt to open a *gate* unless they are losing a battle, and then only as a matter of retreat (all but one, trapped in Silas Tower, lack *gate* capability).

It is possible that a PC sharing the same space of a demon is sucked into a *gate* that successfully opens and sucks the demon through. Instead of winding in the

Abyss with the demon (!), the PC is *gated* to the hollow of the Great Tree in the Crossroad Village's stable.

Opening a *gate* to the Wailmoor from somewhere else simply fails.

BLINK

Blinking will cause 1d4 force damage (no Saving Throw) every time the blinking entity moves in *and* out of the Ethereal Plane.

MAGIC MISSILE

This spell uses the Ethereal to create bolts that don't miss (in elvish the spell translates to "ethereal bolt") and the dam powers these missiles, giving them an additional 1d4 damage, at the expense of the caster taking 1d4 damage (no Saving Throw).

PLANE SHIFT AND ASTRAL PROJECTION

Neither of these spells works in the Wailmoor and result in catastrophic damage to the caster and anyone else in a 30ft. radius, for 8d8 of non-typed damage (no Saving Throw).

Using these spells to attempt to enter the Wailmoor fail spectacularly. Travelers find themselves in an Ethereal Cyclone and take 10d8+10 force damage, (DC 20 Constitution Save for half-damage). They then spit out in another Realm (randomly determined by the DM).

OBELISK DESTRUCTION

Once the PCs destroy all three Obelisks, none of these magical issues occur, although some places are *hallowed* ground or *forbiddance*, or, like the Old Graveyard, wards powered by a spell-engine and still in effect.

NATURE DEITIES

A giant fresh-water octopus known only as The Guardian dwells in the Wailmoor, and he is a reclusive demigod, one of the many "children" of nature gods Cernunos and Rhiannonie.

Nature deities such as The Guardian can grant cleric access to the domain focuses of Animal, Plant, Air, Earth, Fire or Water as appropriate. Physically, they are the natural area in question (a lake, a forest, a mountain, etc.) but can manifest simple avatars. Thus, the Guardian of the Lake is the lake and manifests its avatar as a giant fresh-water octopus.

A nature deity can only grant spells to 20 Levels of clerics. For example, the deity could have twenty 1st Level clerics, one 20th Level cleric, two 3rd Level clerics or any other combination that does not total more than 20.

The Guardian of the Lake does not have any clerics at this time, but he had one during the Demon War.

Intro

Lost at the Beaux Seins

Moortide Rising

The Altar & the Anvil

Castle Wailmoor

Appendix

The Guardian of the Lake

Secretive and inquisitive, the deity that is the lake next to the Temple of Dvalin and the ruined town of Graspen can manifest itself as a fresh-water octopus. He can turn *invisible* at will and can secrete an ink cloud that is a *charm person* and causes the ability to *breathe underwater*.

The Guardian serves a minor function—at the very bottom of the lake (which is himself), there is a portal to the Plane of Water. The Guardian does not let anyone, or anything through the gate from either side.

This gate is quite dangerous. Should its magic fail, water from the Plane of Water could leak into the Lake and cause flooding or the manifestation of water elementals.

The Guardian is telepathic and may talk to a PC if he or she is highly intelligent (Intelligence 16 or more), or an attractive, young woman. If his avatar is confronted beyond conversing, it simply retreats to the bottom of the lake and hides with its great stealth ability, or, if pressed, dissipate his avatar entirely to reform sometime later.

When warranted, The Guardian will recruit a cleric if events around its immediate vicinity give him concern. The Demon War was one such incursion. The cleric he recruited was murdered by possessed villagers, but not before performing the tasks The Guardian set for her. His cleric domains are Plant and Water.

The Guardian has trouble thinking in short timespans. To him, the Demon War was a minor annoyance. The only practical advice he can give is a chastisement to the PCs for not destroying the corrupted Obelisks if they have not already. To him, it's an obvious course of action, and he will tell the PCs to use radiant energy to do so. If there is a paladin in the party, the Guardian will call the paladin stupid for not using Divine Smite on the things. He will give detailed, sarcastic directions to their locations.

Witch Digression

There are references to "witches" throughout *Curse of the Lost Memories*. Witches are female warlocks that usually organize themselves into covens, but not always.

If one of the PCs is a witch (warlock), then there is a nuance to consider. Like today, during the time of the Demon War, there were several factions of witches/warlocks. This below information is for the DM to consider if one of the PCs is a warlock class or a sorcerer that considers herself a witch.

Witches 150-Years Ago

There were three factions of Witches during the time of the Demon War, only one of which exists today in the Imperial Year 5011.

Wailmoor Covens

There were several covens in the Wailmoor throughout history. They were esoteric and not popular because the Guardian of the Lake, a mysterious entity, did not entreat witches, so he worked behind the scenes to maneuver them to a wizard, druid, or clerical pursuits.

During the Demon War, the singular witch coven in the Barony of Wailmoor was assassinated by the Kandra Witches. They were some of the first causalities of the war.

Viscounty of Kandra Witches

When the King of Lothmar set out to conquer the Horse Lords—the continual political thorn-in-the-side of the grasslands of Kandra—he also had a holy crusade in mind. Kandra was not a place of clerics and priests of the Three Dragons of Law nor any of their "untidy offspring" (in his view). It was a place of barbaric horse clans, wild druids, and chaotic witches.

Those three factions joined together through packs of blood, sex, and magic, and stomped the Lothmarian forces into oblivion in a series of brilliant strategic maneuvers, superior tactics, and surprisingly better magical abilities. Indeed, any Imperial War Wizard or Imperial University graduate will have studied this bit of Lothmarian dirty laundry at length, along with Emperor's wise peace offering, which eventually achieved the King's original goals over the course of several hundreds of years without warfare.

The witch faction of Kandra, however, never lost their grudge against Lothmar and by extension, the Empire. Over time, they turned to patrons that corrupted them, and thus, while they hold political power—the lack of a formal clerical structure in the Viscounty and that druids became primarily horse breeders—removed the checks and balances keeping the witches from straying to the dark. Almost all the covens now use demons to further their goals, and they are thoroughly evil.

Duchy of Hardred

In the Duchy, witches were licensed and regulated and were, for all intents-and-purposes, a formal guild specializing in mysticism and scholarly ruminations of the universe. Hardred warlocks were seekers of the knowledge that lies hidden in the intersection of space and time. Like the Kandra witches, the witches, and warlocks of Hardred held political power, but for the warlock in Hardred, this was a matter of noble sponsorship and breeding. Like music patrons, it was a symbol of wealth to afford to sponsor a mysterious witch that spent her time delving esoteric, arcane secrets. Subsequently, after birthing an heir, the spare heir, a priest—fourth and fifth noble children were given reign to explore scholarly purists. Some turned to mysticism.

Before the Demon War, the current Duke of Hardred gave secret monetary support to the Kandra Witches, as both his father and grandfather had long had their eyes on the Wailmoor, and the current Viscount was even out of favor to the King. He thought it money well spent.

What he didn't know is the Kandra Witches were in bed (sometimes literally) with demons. And when the Demon War broke out and possessed refugees was playing havoc with his border villages—the Duke did not panic, but there was a certain urgency in figuring out just what his secret allies were doing. For all, he knew it was the Wailmoor allying with demons. He dispatched the Aether Witch, a highly respected (and beautiful) Hardred warlock with noble blood, to investigate.

He sent Lady Leighandra Rothcannon, Scion of Hardred, Wizard of the Higher Order, Mistress to Baron Amschel Mayer Carl, Ninth Weaver of Broken Dreams, the Aether Witch, to see if the demon rumors were true. He surmised nobody would dare mess with her due to her political connections and arcane competency and that she was a witch herself would lend weight to her investigations.

Upon arriving at the Wailmoor, she was, through trickery, possessed by a major demon and wreaked terrible havoc with her latent magical ability and powerful magical items.

The Aether Witch was able to penetrate Castle Wailmoor, in which she was blown into the Deep Ethereal by Chrystelle the Enchantress. There she still is, a place where time flows differently. Although she is no longer possessed, she is not fully conscious and is more of a "power thought" that persists in the Deep Ethereal rather than a living person.

As his border with the Wailmoor became worse and worse, and reports trickled in that the Aether Witch had gone rogue, The Duke played the only card he had left. He outlawed sponsorship of warlocks, and to this day, while witches aren't burnt at the stake, they are usually told to ply their trade elsewhere by the threat of Sanction by the Church of Tiamat, usually by a Tiamat Paladin.

The PCs will have a chance to rescue the Aether Witch later in the Campaign, should they choose to do so.

NATION-BUILDING SUPPLEMENTS

The next installment, *Beneath a Dreary Wave*, is the first module where PCs are of the level (or approaching thereof) where they can embark not only making the Wailmoor theirs but also expanding its borders and utilizing its vast resources to their benefit.

If your PCs are into nation-building, then the next module in the series has an option for them to do just that. There are several third-party products for 5E that can add structure in rebuilding the Barony of Wailmoor besides the loose guidelines presented by the module itself.

These products and the concept of nation-building (or in this case, barony building) is optimal, of course, and mentioned here for DMs that want to invest the time to weave additional campaign locations and encounters using the *Lost Barony of Wailmoor* map.

There are several important documents PC can find to help make a legal claim for the Wailmoor.

REVISITING THE CROSSROADS

The Crossroads provides a respite from adventuring, and the inn contains warm beds, the pub's friendly wenches, and good food and even better drink.

This is all assuming the PCs destroy the first Obelisk just east of the Crossroads on the plateau that is the start of the moor.

If they do not destroy it in 24-hours, coming back will immediately show the small hamlet in complete disarray with Sir Walshan slain, and potentially other villagers, too.

It is possible for the PCs, having failed to destroy the Obelisk for over 3 days, to come back to a village empty of anything alive, scattered bodies here and there, and the manor shuttered and locked tight.

IF PCs DESTROYED THE OBELISK IMMEDIATELY

What happens depends on whom the PCs talk to and what they say.

THE WALSHANS

If the PCs tell Carl and the Dame about the Plateau Obelisk and other trouble they've taken care of, they are both immensely grateful, and if their Attitude is not already friendly, it becomes that now.

If the PCs talk about their *Lost Memories*, for now, both the Dame and Sir Walshan believe that is simply part of the curse that seems to inhabit the Wailmoor, and for the PCs to continue. After all, they know through the Viscount that the PCs are connected to the Wailmoor in some way.

Intro

Lost at the Beaux Seins

Moortide Rising

The Altar & the Anvil

Castle Wailmoor

Appendix

The Druids

Jeremiah's disposition depends on not only the tale the PCs relate, but also if one of the PCs had died and had their body resurrected in the Great Tree of the stable.

If the none of the PCs died, and if the PCs prattle on about their *Lost Memories*, Jeremiah is the first person they are to encounter that thinks there is something going on greater than the Demon War so long ago. He just has no idea what. He emphatically tells the PCs to keep the *Lost Memories* to themselves, and he'll try to help them after they finish cleaning out the Wailmoor.

If told about the Obelisks, he will assert that if the PCs need to find any more of them and destroy them as soon as they are encountered.

Other NPCs

The other NPCs see the PCs are dangerous (due to the encounter in the Inn in the previous chapter) heroes, anti-heroes, or murder hobos. Either way, the PCs are exciting, and if the PCs show or talk about loot found and (probably drunkenly) brag about their shenanigans, this simply increases their reputations, whatever their reputations are. The PCs start to attract attention from members of the opposite sex (or, in the case of the Bastet Acolytes, either sex). They are the most exciting thing to happen to the village since the swamp dog attack.

The Second Visit

If the PCs visit the Crossroads village a second time after successfully destroying the first Obelisk (in 24-hours), and at least a day has passed, there will be a weapons merchant, and armor merchant and a general merchant in town, setting up a small trade fair. The PCs can buy (at 100%) and sell (at 50%) most goods. They do not have any magical items. They do have common spell components, and esoteric items such as scroll tubes, ink, paper, etc.

Visiting After Leaving the Obelisk Intact

Night after night, the Crossroads is attacked if the Obelisk above the village is discovered but not destroyed.   Unless the PCs are there to help, on the first night the corrupted monsters kill Sir Walshan. On the second, they probe around the village defenses (such as they are), and some villagers flee. On the third night, the corrupted swamp dogs manage to kill the druids in the village.

Once that occurs, the Crossroads Village is abandoned, and it will be 1d10 days before a platoon of Viscounty Lancers arrives escorting a grim, but determined, Dame Walshan to guard the Crossroads and fulfill the Imperial obligation of keeping travelers on the road free from molestation. The attacks stop (the elite warriors destroy anything thrown at them), but small consolation to the Dame of an abandoned village. She sets out to get the inn and the farms working again, vowing her husband's brave sacrifice will not go in vain.

The PCs have the capability of impacting everything that occurs including Sir Walshan's death—but they need to be in the village at night. Run the encounter E4.9 Swamp Dog Hunter Pack in the village each night the Plateau Obelisk remains undestroyed, and the PCs are present. If they are not present, proceed with the results as outlined.

Visiting within the time before the Lancers arrive reveals an abandoned village. After the Lancers arrives, the Commanding Officer (**Lieutenant Willis**) talks the PCs and his attitude towards them is determined by the attitude of the Dame before the PCs sent out and the Viscount after he met the PCs.

- If his attitude is **Friendly**, he'll ask for intelligence about the moor, and then steer PCs towards destroying the Obelisk on the plateau as soon as possible. He will ask the PCs if they need anything. He can supply them with any non-magical equipment and weapons (but not armor).

- If his attitude is **Indifferent**, he'll ask for intel and ask the PCs to destroy any evil edifices they encounter.

- If his attitude is **Hostile**, he is still professional, appearing stoic and inquisitive. If the can get the PCs talking about the Obelisk, he will take them on a tour of the abandoned village, stop at Sir Walshan's grave—and then blame them for it. He'll tell them they owe a debt to the Dame, and that, in the future, should the PCs encounter an Evil Obelisk Close to a Village, might they want to destroy it immediately?

- If the PCs don't shift the platoon's attitude away from **Hostile** in 2d4 days, at the end of the allotted time they and the Dame will attack when the PCs visit the village next—concluding rightly or wrongly the PCs are to blame for the village's destruction. There are a 100 Lancers, 10 of them sergeants, and a Lieutenant. Unless the PCs disengage, they don't make it and must figure out how to sneak their way out of the Stable.

THE LOST MEMORIES

As PCs explore the moor and come up with hints and revelations helping them to put together the story of the events that unfolded 150-years ago, they will experience confusing memories about the moor and its inhabitants.

Not only are these memories instrumental in revealing the plot of the module and creating a personal connection between PCs and the story, but they also are used as the core mechanism to guide players through their exploration of the moor—it's a big place. The DM should describe the memories to the players as they trigger but should let players decide how they want to react to them. Some players will decide to follow each memory as they happen, some will choose to ignore them, or dynamically prioritize and deprioritize them depending on what their current goal is.

There is **no order** that players must follow when it comes to acting on these memories.

LOST MEMORY MECHANICS

To recap:

- A PC can choose to ignore the memory with a DC 20 Wisdom Save. If they save, they can choose to have the memory or ignore it. If they fail, the memory occurs.

- During the memory, the PC is *blinded* and *incapacitated*

- Gerrdan or a custom PC with the +20 Wisdom Boon is not *incapacitated*, merely *blinded*

- Because of their link as former Hierophants, *Lost Memories* are experienced by all the PCs that can see the PC who triggered the memory, even if the *Lost Memory* is only about a specific PC's former life.

- There are no memories of other prior lifetimes during *Curse of the Lost Memories*. Things are confusing enough as it is for the PCs. That comes later.

MEMORY	TRIGGER	POSSIBLE ACTIONS
M1 The Obelisk	80ft of the obelisk as PCs enter the moor plateau	Destroy the obelisk and slowly remove the curse
M2 Silas and his Wilderness Tower	Crossing the old bridge on the west side of the main road	Visit the tower of the mage Silas
M3 The View of Belver Tor	Seeing Belver Tor from anywhere on the moor.	Identifies other locations and POIs on the moor
M4 The Battlefield	Second evening on the moor	Visit the battlefield south of Castle Wailmoor
M5 The Lady in the Woods	Injured character	Find the statue of the mysterious woman in the woods
M6 The Spell	Trying to force trigger a memory	Hints to bring castle Wailmoor back from the ethereal plane
M7 Blessings of Dvalin	See Dvalin's rune at the center of the village of Graspen	Get subtle hints on how to bypass the Iron Golem and the first clue in retrieving the cleric's mighty warhammer
M8 The Witch	See Kavita's tattoo on any Kandra bandit	Information about the witch Coven of Kandra and their role in the fall of the barony
M9 The Commandos	More than one PC purposely using Stealth	Lore vision of all the PCs moving through the landscape unmolested
M10 The Graveyard	Visit the Graveyard	Retrieve the Staff of Ishtari and have a vision of the Maiden
M11 The Warhorses	2 or more PCs are galloping on warhorses	The exact location of the battlefield
M12 After the Graveyard	Sleeping outdoors after visiting the graveyard once	None
M13 Rescuing Sarah	Seeing the ruined estate foundations of Harenvale	Realize the barmaid at the Pub is a descendant of a Wailmoor noble.

M1 -THE OBELISK

TRIGGER

This *Lost Memory* triggers as the PCs climb up the trail climbing from the crossroads to the moor plateau. The obelisk is there, on the side of the road and impossible to miss. Pick one character at random (or the character which makes the highest Wisdom (Perception) check for the target of this memory.

Intro

Lost at the Beaux Seins

Moortide Rising

The Altar & the Anvil

Castle Wailmoor

Appendix

A man in a mithril chainmail slumps against the tall, black ward stone that is glowing with wispy, blue runes.

"It is done," he says, voice shaky. "The last of the wards, and the most important. The Kingdom will not meet the same fate. It won't."

"Good work, Jackon. Let's get you to the Crossroad's pub and get some food in you," you say, your normally melodic elven voice sounding almost as tired as the wizard looks. You reach out your hand, and Jackon grasps it, but before you can pull him to his feet, you notice the hand is cool and pale.

"I am sorry, Heleshia," he says in perfect elvish, "the strength of the barrier is only as good as the sacrifice."

"No! You're all that's left! I cannot be alone! I will heal you…"

"For leaving you alone, I am truly sorry. Bury me in the Knight's Graveyard, will you? I can't bear the thought of resting anywhere… else…"

Jackon closes his eyes.

His hand lets go of yours.

Jackon is dead.

Heleshia was a Knight of the Wailmoor, as was Jackon. But, as the player saw in this vision, she's now the last—or was back then.

HELESHIA'S LOST MEMORY OPTION

Note which PC seems to be the reincarnate of Heleshia. As an elf as her last reincarnation, her memories are especially vivid. During other *Lost Memory* visions, allow this PC a few moments of lucidity:

- The person in the vision is obviously a knight, dressed in decorative armor or clothing

- Even common folk do not look like peasants

- A companion, also a knight, seems to talk to someone who is not visible

- A Cleric of Dvalin is standing nearby, a grim but knowing look about his face

- She catches one of the other knights staring at her butt, which is silly because it's in armor, but the knight winks at her

- During a memory about a battle, a knight next to her whispers "Goddess of War, hear my prayer, so that I may honor your name when I die in righteous battle."

- Etc.

M2 – THE MAGE SILAS & HIS WILDERNESS TOWER

TRIGGER

This *Lost Memory* occurs as the PCs cross the old bridge of the road connecting the old graveyard with Castle Wailmoor. It is an old stone bridge, covered in moss and mud. The *Lost Memory* triggers as players either approach the bridge from its west side or as they gaze down south from the middle of the bridge. This memory affects all PCs and gives them the location of Silas Tower, just south of The Old Bridge.

As you stand by an old bridge, a vision takes hold, and now the sun is high in the sky—it must be a summer day with flowers, birds and the sound of a rapid stream flowing under the
bridge. The road is in much better condition, well-maintained with quite some traffic on it. Wagons and carts cross the bridge from both directions, and you hear the excited chatter of merchants and simple folk enjoying their day of work in the Barony.

Coming from the east, you spot a covered carriage rapidly approaching, a carriage pulled by summoned horses, their hooves glowing green and not even touching the ground. The carriage is driven by the mage Silas. He nods with a kind smile in your direction as the carriage passes in front of you, then turns south, following the river after it crossed the bridge. You see the carriage disappear behind a nearby hill, on its way to Silas's tower southwest of Belver Tor, taking a track that parallels the great bog.

POSSIBLE PC QUESTIONS AND ACTIONS

Describe the vision above and feel free to make it as confusing as possible—the contrast of then and now is stark. Currently, the bridge has not seen traffic in a long time, and while made of stone, it is worn and has the aura of abandonment. The river below is filled with overgrown reeds and does not flow as nicely anymore. Even the road to the south, DC 13 Wisdom (Perception) Check to spot, is now looking like a faded game trail.

PCs may be surprised that they were able to put a name on their vision of the mage character driving the carriage. Similarly, they seem to remember vividly that this mage was the court wizard to the Barony and lived in his own lone tower, a few miles south from the bridge on the west side of the river.

What the players know after experiencing this memory:

- The name of the mage is Silas; he is a trusted advisor to the Baron (the name of the Baron, however, seems still buried in their memories and they cannot remember it—for now)
- Silas spends his days in the Castle serving the Baron but lives on the west side of the moor, in his own private tower
- Silas is a friendly and joyful character, but he takes the security of the Barony very seriously, and he oversees its magical protection
- The Silas Tower is in the wilderness, about 3 miles south from the bridge
- Let the reincarnate of Heleshia and Jackon remember Silas as a malevolent and deadly impromptu War Wizard, far different than his impression from the M2 vision.

M3 - BELVER TOR

TRIGGER

This memory triggers at the sight of Belver Tor, a tall hill that rises south of the river and west of the lake and Castle Wailmoor. DMs may choose to trigger it if players visually inspect the outstanding landmark or simply inquire about it.

The Baron Mark Wailmoor addresses you and the other Knights kneeling in front of him: "... and to conclude this ceremony, I will bless you with the benediction of our beloved King, Benedict of Lothmar. You now shall stand and rise as Knights of the Wailmoor!"

As you stand up on your feet, your heavy sword clings on your side and your gaze capture the vista of the moor that the top of Belver Tor offers. With warmth in your heart and a gushing pride, you embrace with your sight the lands you are now bound to protect and become the Keeper of Secrets as all Wailmoor Knights must be.

POSSIBLE PC QUESTIONS AND ACTIONS

This memory sends the PCs to when they were Knights of the Wailmoor, the sworn defenders of the Barony. As an optional visit, they might decide to climb up the Tor to see the platform where they were sworn in and observe once again the breathtaking vista over the moor.

On a clear day the PCs can see the entire Wailmoor from the top of the tor, and on a clear night, quite the glow fest.

M4 - BATTLEFIELD MEMORY

TRIGGER

This memory happens as the PCs spend their second night on the moor (or at the Inn if the PCs choose to move back to Crossroads at night).

The memory could also trigger at the sight of the Seat of Barbu.

The battle rages around you. It was a good run, but death is certain. You're almost to the grotesque throne looming above the battlefield, its very sight supposed to fill you with anguish, but rage is all you're feeling—well that and a mighty blow on your back.

"Will you just die already, you warded human!" You manage to turn around, and there's Barbu. He can't touch you, but he's holding a longbow bigger than yourself. Another arrow shaft flies and enters your armor, your flesh, your heart, and out the back.

"Garret!" You hear Mark scream your name as if far away. "Men! Ignore Barbu! Kill as many of his bodyguards as possible! For the Wailmoor!"

"For the Wailmoor!" come quiet voices, almost like whispers. You hear a distant explosion, but the heat is on your face. You wish you could chastise Mark for his excellent change in strategy—because it's going to kill him.

Death seems like a drawn-out fade to shadows, but your final thoughts are of holding Madeline in your arms.

POSSIBLE PC QUESTIONS AND ACTIONS

The target PCs might decide to explore the battlefield, especially if they recognize the seat of Barbu in the distance. It is still an evil thing that good PCs should destroy—but they will need to deal with the possessed warriors guarding it first.

M5 - THE LADY IN THE WOODS

TRIGGER

This memory happens to the first time they take a rest with one of the PCs significantly injured (injury threshold at the discretion of the DM).

Intro

Lost at the Beaux Seins

Moortide Rising

The Altar & the Anvil

Castle Wailmoor

Appendix

You are walking through the woods; your hearts are light and joyful. The sun bathes your shoulders like a warm cloak and while your sharp sword clings on your side; you surprise yourself by whistling a song from your childhood. Then abruptly, she appears—the Lady in the Woods! A tall statue in the middle of the forest built a long time ago. The precision of the sculpture is uncanny, and she feels almost alive. You lift your shirt and look again at the nasty bruise you gained as a price at the tournament. It is painful, all purple and swollen. But you know that a night's rest in the Lady's arms will have you cured.

POSSIBLE PC QUESTIONS AND ACTIONS

This memory is a hint for injured PCs to potential find some help in healing their wounds from the Lady's statue in the woods and explore the moor in that direction.

M6 - THE SPELL

TRIGGER

The only way to trigger this *Lost Memory* is for PCs to ask for it.

This memory triggers when PCs are confused enough with the influx of *Lost Memories* that they will likely try to focus and make one happen on demand. The trigger occurs at DM discretion (when dreaming in their sleep, focusing through meditation, contemplation of scenery or an item, usage of mushrooms, etc.).

This memory only happens on the moor.

You are in a cave, with the elven Knight Heleshia and the Dvalin Elf-Priestess Merisee, standing in front of a black stone obelisk beset with magical runes. Only yesterday did you and Silas place it here and enchant it.

"Silas. Jackon. Putting the Obelisk in the bog drained you both. This one seemed to almost kill you," says Heleshia.

Her warning has merit. Before you can say anything, Silas speaks up.

"This time I felt—something. Ethereal. I think I know why the Old Elven Tower in the castle disappeared when we put up the first stone. Poking at the Ethereal is triggering some defensive mechanism—well, that is a minor problem. To be fixed later."

Silas turns to you, meeting your eyes "I know you have doubts, Jackon." He isn't talking about Heleshia's comments.

You do have doubts. When the ritual concluded you too felt—something. "We're too hasty." You don't need to say anything else. Silas is a wizard.

Silas stares at you. You know he is far from stupid, and over the years has guessed the Knights know the Tower holds a secret that not even he is privy to.

After a moment, however, he just shrugs. "It is what it is. How many dead haunt us booth because at the beginning we were too cautious, old friend?"

A very good question. You turn away.

"Too many, Silas. Too many."

"This is so fascinating! Don't see magic like this every day," Merisee the Priestess interrupts your melancholy, cheerfully writing in her ever-present book.

POSSIBLE PC QUESTIONS AND ACTIONS

This memory is quite important or at least unveils the events that precipitated the fall of Wailmoor and gives broad hints to why it eventually went so very wrong. Silas and Jackon had all the best intentions. Both would be shamed beyond measure to learn their handiwork—like everything else when demons remain unpurged—succumbed to corruption and chaos.

M7 - BLESSINGS OF DVALIN

TRIGGER

This memory happens when PCs come across one of Dvalin runes marked on the fountain in <u>Graspen</u> or on various stones throughout the barony (DMs can choose to add runes where they see fit).

Beram Oakheart, the revered High Priest of Dvalin in Wailmoor, turns towards you with a broad smile. "The last spell out of so many it makes me tired—and hungry—to think of them all!" he says, as he finishes casting a powerful spell, imbuing an over-sized statue of iron with powerful Dwarven magic.

"This beautiful piece of engineering and magic shall protect the Temple from the demonic intruders, and well, whoever is foolish enough to enter this sanctum without paying respect to its holiness. I want these entrance rooms to be clean and polished, in the name of Dvalin!"

Beram then pulls a massive hammer from a large velvet bag tied to his belt. "The Golem and this Hammer are my last creations. One guards the temple, and the other protected by it."

The High Priest slaps his large belly. "Well, out of the ashes, something good, eh?" he says, his smile fading at the memory of so, so many dead.

POSSIBLE PC QUESTIONS AND ACTIONS

This memory is a hint on how to bypass the golem guarding the Temple of Dvalin (See Chapter 3) the easy way: cleaning up the room the golem is in, along with the rooms to the left and right of the entrance will cause the Golem to let the PCs past.

But, when Beram means clean, he means *cleaning* it. The golem does not attack anyone thusly, only if they try to move past it without restoring that portion of the temple. The High Priest was a neat freak, but he sure could carve a great rune.

M8 - The Witch

Trigger

This memory happens when one of the PCs sees the tattoo of the ancient Witch Kavita on the arm of any Kandra bandit they come across as they explore the barony.

There is tension in the hall as an old, small, and crooked woman, Kavita the Witch, holding a staff of gnarled wood, discusses with the Baron of Wailmoor.

"Do not stand in my way, Baron Mark. I know what is happening here; I have studied the unlikely rise of your family and barony. There is a power behind your throne that we cannot tolerate. I will bring her down, whether you help me or not. You cannot expect to stay her puppet forever..."

"I deny this power, Kavita the Witch. I find your ways quite rude and aggressive. You shall turn your back on me, and not return to Wailmoor with such attitude again."

"Ah!" says the witch, stunned with the lack of fear the Baron manifested from her open threat. "We shall then see what becomes of you and the place she cherished."

The witch leaves the hall with the cackling voice of a deranged augur.

There is silence in the hall after she leaves.

"A powerful witch, but not powerful enough," says Jackon. The sapphire glow from the top of his staff seems to glow brighter, as if in agreement.

"It's the other two that could pose the real threat," says Knight Dannok.

"At least she kept her Evil Monolog to a minimum," says Knight Heleshia, moving her hand off the hilt of her elven longsword.

Possible PC Questions and Actions

This memory is more about lore. It will help PCs position factions and understand the role of the Witches of Kandra in the terrible events that unfolded on the Wailmoor.

M9 - The Commandos

Trigger

This memory happens to the PCs when two or more of them are operating in Stealth.

Heavily armed and armored, you and your fellow Knights are still moving about the copse of trees as if you were silent cats stalking prey. Off to one side, the clomping of boots and baying of demon hounds is a stark contrast to your movement as you and your fellow knights slip from shadow to shadow.

Soon the baying is ahead of you, and Knight Dannok raises his hand. As one, you stop. He motions again. Three and six and four. Three priests of Orcus. Six possessed humans. Four demon dogs. He motions again. You and

the fellow knights fan out as you put a magical bolt onto the crossbow, the wicked sharp bolt seeming to vibrate with eagerness. You immerge from the trees.

"Tracking us?" Dannok asks, eldritch magic already forming on his great blade.

The demonic party doesn't even have a chance to turn around before the first is cut down.

Possible PC Questions and Actions

Unknown to the Knights of the Wailmoor, the *Curse of the Lost Memories* was manifesting itself during the Demon War. Their memories came in hazy dreams, each thinking nothing of it—the stress of war.

Moving silently was something they were good at, augmented by their nascent *Lost Memory* boons.

If the PCs poke about this memory, tell them they remember all the hand signals for silent, squad-based coordination. It's up to the players if they wish to pursue this type of tactical combat.

Either way, they're *very* good at it. When they move as a group, it's with deadly purpose, and hushed fell intentions, whether they are strolling to the Pub or flanking an enemy. Periodically, have NPCs startle because they did not hear the PC(s) approach, or forgot they were there, etc.

M10 - The Graveyard

Trigger

PCs may visit the graveyard for a variety of reasons, one of which is it was mentioned in the vision with Jackon (and PCs quick on the uptake may be after his staff), or, equally as likely; they worry that's where the monsters come from.

This memory triggers when the PCs views the graveyard. It is dramatically different than all other memories.

As soon as you see the graveyard, a vision slams into you like the mental fist of the gods. This vision is different, where before, you were seeing out of someone's eyes, here, it feels as if you see from a—gravestone. Or something perched on a gravestone. That's when you realize—this is the Knight's Graveyard. You're watching from your resting place.

The elven Knight Heleshia is piling rocks on a fresh grave, burying Jackon and his staff, silently crying all the while until the last rock is placed.

She lays down on the grave, the stones a rocky mattress. She draws her long, slender blade and holds it to her as if she was the one buried.

"Goddess of War hear my prayer, so that I may honor your name when I die..."

And then Heleshia dies—an elf's burden when faced with too much sorrow.

Intro

Lost at the Beaux Seins

Moortide Rising

The Altar & the Anvil

Castle Wailmoor

Appendix

Heleshia is dead, and from the perch on your own grave, you fade away into the darkness once more.

SPECIAL TRIGGER FOR MAIDEN WORSHIPERS

This *Lost Memory* is optional for the DM. Continue below only if one of the PCs is a cleric, paladin, or worshiper of the Maiden. This *Lost Memory* is campaign and world-building specific and that PC is open to receiving a lore-dump that poses more questions than answers.

If no PCs meet the criteria for the trigger, the *Lost Memory* does not occur.

Instead of the vision ending, the vision grows sharper; you see more detail, not less, hear all the sounds are around you, not a few, the smell the fresh earth and the floral scent that always followed Heleshia fading in the lonely wind.

Behind Jackon's grave, the air shimmers, the very scene behind the grave morphing into a wavy field full of stars, and a rip in the very air appears. A blonde-haired warrior woman steps out, clad in ancient armor, wielding a round shield and battleaxe.

Both of which she drops when she sees Heleshia.

"No!" The woman's voice carries power, but also heartache. She sits on the ground with a heavy thud. She pulls Heleshia to her, cradling her, peering into her dead eyes. She rocks the elf, her own tears falling. It seems as if she cries forever, but she finally reaches up, closes Heleshia's eyes and kisses her softly on the lips.

Suddenly, the woman's head snaps up, and she is gazing at you.

The cosmic rend the shield maiden steps through flashes and starts to suck all the things around it into the star field. First the discarded shield and battleaxe, then Heleshia's body. The abrupt gale pulls at the woman, and she leans forward, grasping your translucent, outstretched hand.

The woman's eyes are wide, not in terror, but in surprise and calculation. She is off her feet, the rift pulling mightily at her body. One of her boots comes off.

Her eyes seem to blaze as they gaze at yours, pieces of armor and then clothing are ripped from her and then she is naked, her beautiful, sword-scared body almost painfully, athletically perfect. Then her very skin starts to rip away.

The silent woman is determined to not let go of you. But as another strip of skin is pulled off her body, the mighty rift will have her, one way or another.

What do you do?

PCs may not be expecting a question about doing something during a *Lost Memory*. Turn to a Cleric of the Maiden, a War-Paladin of the Maiden, or a worshiper of The Maiden (in that order) for an answer. The question is for one PC that meets the criteria and that PC alone.

POSSIBLE PC QUESTIONS AND ACTIONS

Knight Heleshia dying on Jackon's grave isn't a literary license. Elves can die of overwhelming sadness, a burden of their primal, empathetic nature. Jackon's death after the Knights' hollow victory was more than she could bear by far. She loved Jackon with her mind and body. He was the only thing she had left.

The first part of the vision is confirmation that Jackon was buried with his staff, the *Staff of Ishtari*. There is no sacrilege in digging up the grave and retrieving the staff, it, is, after all, Jackon's staff and one of the PCs is the reincarnate of Jackon the War Wizard.

The Shield Maiden from the Additional Trigger is none other than the Maiden, the only god in the Pantheon besides Dvalin who did not write off the Hierophants as crack-pot mortals playing with immortality spells they didn't understand. Heleshia's prayer called to her, and, despite the difficulties (and danger) of a god traveling to the Welt, she came.

The gods' existence is not exactly linear. The Maiden saw into future—aided by a full manifestation of Hierophant that worships her (the PC the DM turned to for an answer on what they do in the vision)—tried to cross the boundary of space and time to save the PC's soul from its endless cycle of death and rebirth.

The Hierophant's spell is backed by the power of the Welt itself, and here in the Wailmoor, it reigns supreme. Not even a goddess can change it, and power of the Graveyard pushed the Maiden away.

There is no win or lose condition with this memory/vision/encounter. The PCs are involved in a war, not of their own making (at least in this life), and sometimes dreadful things happen to good people.

- If the PC tries to talk to the Maiden, communication is not possible, the audible energy of the tear both physical and mental, drowning all sound.

- If the PC let's go, the Maiden nods as she is pulled into the rift. It closes, and the *Lost Memory* ends.

- If the PC doesn't let go, the Maiden is (literally) ripped to shreds, and in a mighty bang, the rift implodes. The PC is torn out of the vision and holding a skeletal arm, which soon turns to dust. The rift has even ripped strips of flesh from the PC. He or she is at 0 hit points, a severely wounded arm, and blood coming out the eyes and ears. Without healing, death will come soon if the PC fails their Death Saves.

The dust is not magical and had no divine properties. The Maiden takes no offense at the last grim outcome (although it was extremely painful). She's not a mind reader, here on the Welt. She guessed the PC understood she is the Maiden and cannot die.

M11 - The Warhorses

Trigger

If more than one PC is galloping on a warhorse, this *Lost Memory* will trigger (and only trigger once) for all the PCs on or near their warhorse. This memory only triggers when riding warhorses, and not riding horses, draft horses, or a giant ferret.

Riding on your mighty steeds, lances in hand, you gallop at a furious pace through the Wailmoor, and soon you are at the mighty battlefield, charging into the flank of undead that was just about to eat a phalanx of archers.

Possible PC Questions and Actions

The only information this *Lost Memory* departs is the location of the battlefield. As the memory is so tactile, those lost ride their warhorses all the way to the Old Battlefield and only regain their composure when they get there.

PCs who make their Saving Throws or are not riding warhorses can only follow—short of physical violence, the PCs in the vision will not stop. Gerrdan, or the PC with the +20 Wisdom Save, can follow, but the interposing vision on top of a galloping steed makes him nauseous, applied as the *poison* condition (no Saving Throw) until the horse stops.

M12 - After the Graveyard

Trigger

This *Lost Memory* only triggers *after* the PCs have visited The Old Graveyard once *and* are sleeping outdoors. It is unique as it carries with a magical effect caused by Jackon's and Silas's old wards mutating from lack of maintenance.

PCs who fail their *Lost Memory* Saving Throws wake up in the morning on top of a grave in the graveyard, having been physically moved there through the Ethereal.

Anybody on watch or observing the PC sleeping sees them fade from view as soon as they fall into a deep sleep.

You startle awake, realizing you are not where you went to sleep. You are back in the graveyard, sleeping on a grave.

Possible PC Questions and Actions

The PCs wake up on their graves when they were Knights of the Wailmoor. If the DM mapped the prior lives of the PCs as the Knights of the Wailmoor to a PC, then the PC that was Heleshia wakes up on Jackon's

grave, as does the PC that was Jackon. If more than one PC succumbs to this memory by failing their Saving Throw, then they all wake at the same time. Since the *Lost Memory* occurs while they are sleeping, PCs don't receive a choice to accept the vision or not, only the Saving Throw (DC 20 Wisdom) matters.

After the first trigger, every night the PCs sleep *outside* in the Wailmoor, there is a 1 to 3 chance on a 1d10 this will repeat.

The only way to prevent this from occurring is to make the DC 20 Wisdom Save, stop sleeping outdoors in the Wailmoor or destroy all three Obelisks.

PCs affected by M12 wake up refreshed from a long rest, regardless.

M13 - Rescuing "Sarah"

Trigger

This *Lost Memory* triggers when the PCs are exploring Harenvale and poking at the ruins.

You know Heleshia is somewhere in the collapsing manor, as you skip down the manor home's steps two at a time, the young lady slung over your shoulder in her nightgown. She's now the last of her family, and you've decided that she's not going to die this night. She weeps softly. You're amazed she's still conscious.

A low, reverberating growl comes from behind you. Everyone turns to look up the stairs, and a large demon with four arms, two of them ending in crab claws, immerges from the manor ruins.

"I'll take that virgin," the demon says in a perverse and vile voice.

This is not good. You're not too sure your staff has any remaining energy. In the excitement, you lost count how many times you used it today. Was it five? Six?

"No," says the paladin Terr turning back up the steps as her sword glows painfully bright.

The air shimmers behind the demon. "Yeah, nope," says Heleshia as she bashes the demon in the back of its head with a mighty blow from her magical shield with one hand, stabbing it with her glowing sword with the other.

The demon doesn't reply. It just looks surprised as it turns to goop that starts running down the stairs.

As the vision fades you realize as the girl you put down looks like Sarah, the bar wench from the pub at the Crossroads.

Possible PC Questions and Actions

PCs might be wondering on the legalities of a direct-heir to family property—titled landowner nobility.

In Lothmar, noble lineage is often verified by divination magic when it is in question.

Sarah is indeed the descendant of the young woman in the vision.

Intro

Lost at the Beaux Seins

Moortide Rising

The Altar & the Anvil

Castle Wailmoor

Appendix

MOOR ENCOUNTER LOCATIONS

The Wailmoor is the size of a large medieval barony. This section describes the more obvious places a PC can discover. When moving about the Wailmoor, or by doing certain things, the PCs will trigger *Lost Memories*. Please reference the *Lost Memory* section and the summary table for when and why they happen.

The Ascent from the Crossroads

Getting the moor plateau is easy—just walk or ride up the "trail" which is a 150-year-old neglected paved road. The last Baron Wailmoor installed the road with the thought of petitioning the Imperial Road Authority (IRA) of extending Kandra Road up to the plateau and all the way through it to the southeast border of his barony. The IRA was considering doing that very thing—until the moor fell, that is.

This faint road, while not difficult to walk or ride, isn't in any shape to have a wagon pulled to the top. There are numerous washouts, fallen trees, and a granite rockpile.

A PC with an engineering background, a dwarf, or a DC 15 Wisdom (Perception) Check will return an estimate of two days to clear the road to get the wagon to the top of the plateau—one day to clear the random obstructions and to fill in a couple of washouts, another to move a large, heavy rock slide.

Nothing untold happens if the PCs embark on this impromptu road repair. In any event, riding or walking back to the inn is easy enough, and rooms are available in the inn or the stable. If Dame Walshan is Friendly to the PCs, they can stay at the manor. These options will always be available to the PCs throughout the adventure.

If the PCs scout ahead and trigger a run-in with the Obelisk, however, the 24-hour clock to destroy it triggers.

Another Chance for Druidic Help

If the PCs work on the road to get the wagon to the top, and they have not taken the young Druidess Yurgana's help yet, the acolyte will come out of her shell and deliver a picnic basket of sandwiches, cheese, bread, milk and cookies and jugs of beer while they are toiling away. If the PCs are on good terms with the village (Friendly to either Evan, Jerimiah, either Walshan or Hayro), she will offer to watch their horses and camp for them—assuming there is a PC that speaks one of the languages she does (Druidic, Sylvan or Draconic).

Pick a charismatic PC with a Strength 12 or over—attraction is Yurgana's real motive, but she's still shy. She will smile and be predisposed to that PC if the PC isn't abusive or cruel. Odd behavior does not bother Yurgana. Even occasional meanness is akin to how some animals act. However, if the PC doesn't reciprocate or isn't occasionally nice and kind, her infatuation will cease.

This offer to help is only if the PCs have warhorses. If they don't, there isn't any way for Yurgana to secure their base of operations or camp, and she will simply be a kind person delivering a much-welcomed (and free) meal.

Exploring the Wailmoor

The Wailmoor is a dangerous place. 150-years-ago, it was a wealthy and safe barony, one of the rising jewels on the crown of the King of Lothmar. But a terrible demonic invasion brought the Barony to its knees, caused its people to flee to other lands and saw its behind-the-scenes benefactor, the Enchantress Chrystelle de Valois, cast into the Ethereal Plane. While most demons of the army of Barbu have returned to the Abyss since losing the war, some of them are still roaming the Wailmoor with the slim hope in finding a way inside the Castle and redeeming their shame in losing. The greatest strength and weakness of demons is pride, after all.

On top of these formidable enemies, the moor is populated with wild animals, some of them tainted by the demonic corruption lingering over the Barony and magnified by the three Obelisks. As players explore the moor and try to figure out the story behind these *Lost Memories* that dragged them to this barren place, they will encounter creatures that need dispatching.

Whether they are making their way through the moor or decide to 'clean up' the moor from monsters, they will run into creatures for every 5 miles they wander in the Wailmoor (some locations have their own encounter tables).

If the PCs are moving in Stealth, either make the normal Dexterity (Stealth) vs. Wisdom (Perception) Check or simply reward the players on the spot by having them spot the encounter subjects first.

Wailmoor Random Encounters

Once the PCs destroy both outdoor Obelisks, for every random encounter where they immerge victorious, replace the entry with "No Encounter."

D10	ENCOUNTER	AVG. CR
1	1d4 Swamp Dogs	2
2	No Encounter	N/A
3	1d10 Giant Bats	1/2
4	1d8 Boars	1
5	1 Dire Boar	2
6	No Encounter	N/A
7	1d4 Dire Wolves	2
8	1d4 Giant Spiders	2
9	Swarm of Bats	1/4
10	2 Demonic-Tainted Wolves	2

Intro

Lost at the Beaux Seins

Moortide Rising

The Altar & the Anvil

Castle Wailmoor

Appendix

The Inn at the Crossroads

Obelisk

Tombs

THE CAIRNS

E0 – The Obelisk Encounter

Approaching the Obelisk triggers the _M1 Lost Memory_.

The first thing the PCs encounter on the moor plateau is the Obelisk. They can't miss it; it's a literal hole in the Welt sucking up corruption in the moor and gathering it as vile fuel for terrible purposes.

Tic-Tock, Start a Clock

Once the PCs are at the top of the plateau and see the Obelisk, the peruviol clock is ticking. They have 24-hours, once sighted, to deal with the corrupted ward stone or the Crossroads Village faces attack after attack from the corrupted canines, mutated into swamp dogs—or worse.

This is 150-years of corruption coming to fruition. It could be that the PCs as a group just doesn't care about the village below. All arcane and divine actions have arcane and divine consequences, including neglect.

The Obelisk at a Glance

As the crest of the trail four miles from the Crossroads Village, you come across an Obelisk, 3 feet thick, 4 feet high somewhat circular granite-looking slab with profane runes pulsating with a sickly, snot-colored glow, 85 feet from the edge of the plateau.

60-feet in all directions from the stone, the ground churns with slimy, churning maggots in a thick, carpet-like mass that also contains bones of small animals—birds, rabbits, other small game, maybe fox and badger bones.

The grotesque carpet gives off a low, gurgling noise as if a sea of maggots were writhing in a gravel pile.

Corrupted Plateau Obelisk

Demonic Ward Stone
Armor Class 17 (natural armor) — **Hit Points** 220 — **Speed** 0 ft.

Statistics

STR	DEX	CON	INT	WIS	CHA
-	-	20 (+5)	-	-	-

Damage Immunities poison, disease, necrotic
Damage Resistance All except bludgeoning, radiant, force
Damage Vulnerabilities bludgeoning, radiant, force
Condition Immunities blinded, charmed, deafened, exhaustion, frightened, paralyzed, petrified, poisoned
Senses -
Languages —
Challenge Rating 4 (3,900 XP)

Abilities

Enticing Trail. If approached, the churning mass parts, revealing wet, but unbroken ground to walk on without difficulty. However, as soon as someone gets within 5ft. of the corrupted plateau obelisk, the enticing trail disappears as the goop moves into the previously vacated space. The obelisk then animates the bones within the mass.

Animate Crawling Hand Swarm. The corrupted plateau obelisk spends it first (and only) Action animating its cadre of clawing hands, turning the churning mass into a swarm.

Anchored in Place. The corrupted plateau obelisk cannot move, and automatically fails all Dexterity Saving Throws.

Churning Mass of Slippery Horror. Regardless of the obelisk animated its crawling hands, stepping on the churning mass must make an Acrobatics DC 12 roll or the terrain is difficult. Every attempt at moving within the churning mass requires a new DC roll.

Obelisk Fate. When destroyed, any undead created by the corrupted plateau obelisk also is destroyed. Any created undead immediately turn to dust.

Inner Obelisk Workings

The corrupted plateau obelisk is a hole in material reality that extends to the Ethereal Plane. The Ethereal is the barrier between the world and chaotic forces such as the base elemental planes, but also the swirling forces of entropy. As the Astral Sea is the space between planes, and specifically the Welt and the outer, the Ethereal is often referred to as "the barrier" between raw, elemental entropy and the world.

And this is how the ward stones used to work. They extended their magic circle and *hallowed*-like effects at the border facing the moor, essentially creating a rather formidable barrier to the Ethereal which is, unto itself, a barrier. Nobody could *teleport* or *gate* into the Barony or use any other dimensional means of locomotion for entry, such as *plane shift, arcane gate,* or *astral projection.*

Unfortunately, the corruption in the Wailmoor, some of which was caused by demons *still* roaming the Barony (and now trapped), had nowhere to go. So, over time, the wards stones were perverted. Now they are parodies of their original construction, perverse and an affront to life. Instead of warding against corruption—they soak it up like a sponge.

The Obelisks Strengths

Before animating its "defender," the mix of bones and maggots has immunity to all damage except radiant, which it is vulnerable, and then all radiant damage is then transferred to the Obelisk itself. This effect ends when the Obelisk animates the crawling hand swarm.

If PCs don't take its offered "trail," stepping on the churning maggot carpet has consequences. Regardless if the bones inside the evil goop are animated or not, the maggots are difficult terrain unless a PC makes a Dexterity (Acrobatics) DC 12 check for each round of attempted movement.

As soon as one PC approaches within 5ft. of the Obelisk, it animates the swarm and the swarm attacks immediately. It will attack anyone in its area and within 5ft. of its 60ft-radius.

Attackers of the swarm have Disadvantage to the parts of the swarm when 10ft. or closer to the Obelisk. This Disadvantage only impacts the swarm closest to the Obelisk, not the Obelisk itself.

Animated Crawling Hand Swarm

60ft. radius of undead, neutral evil
Armor Class 12 — **Hit Points** 111 — **Speed** 0 ft

Statistics

STR	DEX	CON	INT	WIS	CHA
13 (+1)	14 (+2)	11 (+0),	5 (-3)	10 (+0)	4 (-3)

Damage Immunities poison, necrotic
Damage Resistance fire (within 10ft. of Obelisk)
Damage Vulnerabilities bludgeoning, force, radiant
Condition Immunities charmed, exhaustion, poisoned
Senses blindsight 60 ft. (blind beyond this radius), passive Perception 10
Languages —
Challenge 4 (1,100 XP)

Abilities

Pre-Animation Defense. Before animated by the Obelisk, the animated crawling hand swarm is immune to all damage except radiant, which it is vulnerable, and then all radiant damage is then transferred to the Obelisk itself.

Turn Immunity. The animated crawling hand swarm is immune to effects that turn undead.

Swarm. The animated crawling hand swarm can occupy another creature's space and vice versa, and the swarm can move through an opening at least 2 inches square. The swarm can't regain hit points or gain temporary hit points.

Obelisk Protection. Within 10ft.-radius of the Corrupted Plateau Obelisk, attackers have Disadvantage on the swarm (the Obelisk itself does not have this Disadvantage protection).

Actions

Carpet of Bones Multiattack. The animated crawling hands swarm attacks all PCs in the space it occupies, but only once per PC.

Claw. Melee Weapon Attack: +3 to hit, reach 5ft of all space occupied by the swarm
Hit: 3 (1d4+1) bludgeoning or slashing damage (creature's choice) damage.

The Obelisk's Weaknesses

Once destroyed, The Obelisk crumbles to dust, and there is no longer an aura of evil around it.

It is susceptible to blunt, force or radiant damage. If its animated swarm is defeated before it is, the Obelisk cannot animate another.

Consequences of Not Destroying the Obelisk

Not destroying the (blatantly-corrupted-super-evil-most- scariest-thing-the-PCs-have-encountered-in-their-lives-thus-far) Obelisk results in an attack on the village below the next evening. See <u>Visiting After Leaving the Obelisk Intact</u> for a timeline of events.

Intro

Lost at the Beaux Seins

Moortide Rising

The Altar & the Anvil

Castle Wailmoor

Appendix

SILAS'S TOWER

1ST FLOOR

2ND FLOOR

3RD FLOOR

BASEMENT

E1 - SILAS TOWER

PCs find out about the tower through the _M2 Lost Memory_ by crossing or examining The Old Bridge north of Silas Tower.

APPROACHING THE TOWER

The tower is visible from at least a mile out coming from the north and stands on top of a medium-sized hill, overlooking the bog to the east. From the tower to the east, the players can see the tall Belver Tor (and might experience the _M3 Lost Memory_ if it was not triggered before) about 2 miles in the distance.

From the outside, the tower looks like a ruin. PCs can spot windows in its walls and figure that the first two floors of the tower are intact. The upper floors, however, were destroyed in some unknown event and now, ruined walls crown the top of the tower, which strangely looks like it got chopped in half by either the assault of time, a nasty military siege or a dangerous spell gone bad.

On the south side of the tower, a flight of steps rises to a set of double doors which are the main and only entrance into the tower. The doors are made of solid wood and are closed. The doors are not trapped mechanically or magically and are not locked. When pushed on, they open inside the tower in a sinister creak.

E1.1 - ENTRANCE VESTIBULE

There are two doors that lead from this entrance vestibule deeper into the tower. One, opposite the entrance door, leads to the main room and the other open on top of a stairway that descends into the darkness of the basement. Both doors are locked and require a DC 15 Dexterity (Thieves' Tools) check to open.

You entered a large and dusty room that occupies a good half of the tower first level. The stone floor is dirty with neglect and shows no marks or tracks of visitors in a long time. On the left side of the entrance double doors, you see a simple wooden desk and a chair. Dust covers the surface of the desk as well.

The desk does not have anything on it. This desk was used by Humbert, the tower guard as a station for when Silas was in the tower. He sat there, preventing visitors from entering the tower unannounced and providing security should someone try to break into the tower. After the last battle in the Barony, Humbert took everything that was his in the tower and left. He traveled to the Viscounty of Kandra where he died there, like many Wailmoor survivors.

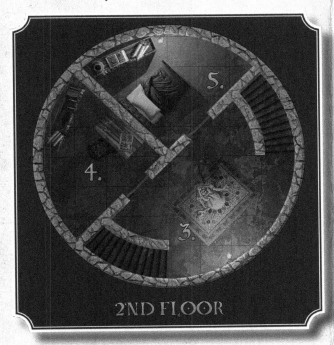

2ND FLOOR

E1.2 – MAIN ROOM

There are many things in this room for the PCs to find.
Here, the PCs will start to learn more about the fate of Silas and his tower. They can search through the room and looking for clues or information about Silas. At this point, they do not remember anything about the mage but for the *Lost Memory* of him traveling on the bridge.

This is a large room at the base of the tower. A big table occupies its center. It is made in rich mahogany, a surprising note of luxury in the simple décor of the place. The table is empty but shows marks of common usage from meals taken there. On the right corner of the room, a simple kitchen is organized around a deep sink and cupboards containing plates and cups. On the opposite wall, you see shelves covered with books and scrolls.

If the PCs search through the room and the kitchen area, this is what they can learn based on the DC of their Intelligence (Investigation) Checks:

- **DC 10** – Not more than two people used to live here. No one has lived in this tower for a least a hundred years based on the amount of dust on the furniture and the deterioration of the wood.

- **DC 13** – Dishes, plates, and utensils are well ordered in the kitchen, whoever lived here had access to magical means (Silas used to rely on an Unseen Servant) to clean up the kitchen.

- **DC 18** – PCs find a hidden compartment on the bookshelf that reveals a small cache containing a *potion of healing*.

Searching through the bookshelves, PCs will find another set of interesting facts, even if they quickly realize these shelves only contains mundane books and that the mage's arcane library is to be found elsewhere:

- **DC 13** – There are many books covering the local history of the Wailmoor and the Kingdom of Lothmar. Silas seemed passionate about the history of the Wailmoor barons.

- **DC 15** – Some of the local history tomes are annotated by Silas. These notes highlight mentions of the powers at play between the Witches of Kandra, the cults of Dvalin, the religion of Tiamat in the Duchy and the rising tensions with Wailmoor.

- **DC 20** – The personal notes of Silas indicate surprise at the story of the Wailmoor being founded by a simple shepherd about 800 years ago. This seems to make Silas doubtful about this story, a specific note says:

There must be more about this history—what is the origin behind the early scholarly power behind the Barony? There's no record of Imperial University graduates founding the Barony, which was my (wrong) assumption. Is there a reason why the Knights of the Wailmoor seem so secretive sometimes?

E1.3 – STATUE OF ISHTARI

Walking past the magical statue towards the doors without touching it and saying "Ishtari" triggers the trap. The statue is a large magic item.
The two doors behind the statue led to the private apartments of Silas. The magical (one-time-use) trap on the statue that can be disabled with a DC 20 Intelligence (Arcana Check). The statue radiates magical energy of Alternation and Summoning.

Intro

Lost at the Beaux Seins

Moortide Rising

The Altar & the Anvil

Castle Wailmoor

Appendix

A tall statue of the goddess of magic users and knowledge—Ishtari—stands in the middle of the large stair landing. Magical torches light the room, adding to the majesty of the statue, casting flickering shadows in the hall. Two closed doors behind the statue are made of rich wood and still perfectly stained, giving them the feel of luxury. The statue itself is about 8ft. tall and depicts Ishtari waving her arms as if casting a powerful spell.

The first part of the trap has the statue casting an *alarm* spell that was mentally connected to Silas's mind. Since Silas is now long dead, the spell does not do much. The next effect summons two giant spiders.

Two Giant Spiders

Large beast, unaligned
Armor Class 14 (natural armor) — **Hit Points** 26
Speed 30 ft./climb 30 ft.

Statistics

STR	DEX	CON	INT	WIS	CHA
14 (+2)	16 (+3)	12 (+1),	2 (-4)	11 (+0)	4 (-3)

Skills Stealth +7
Senses blindsight 10 ft., darkvision 60 ft., passive Perception 10
Languages —
Challenge 2 (450 XP) each

Abilities

Spider Climb. The spider can climb difficult surfaces, including upside down on ceilings, without needing to make an ability check.

Web Sense. While in contact with a web, the spider knows the exact location of any other creature in contact with the same web.

Web Walker. The spider ignores movement restrictions caused by webbing.

Actions

Bite. *Melee Weapon Attack:* +5 to hit, reach 5 ft., one creature. *Hit:* 7 (1d8+3) piercing damage. The target must make a DC 11 Constitution Saving Throw, taking 9 (2d8) poison damage on a failed save, or half as much damage on a successful one. If the poison damage reduces the target to 0 hit points, the target is stable but poisoned for 1 hour, even after regaining hit points, and is paralyzed while poisoned in this way.

Web (Recharge 5-6). *Ranged Weapon Attack:* +5 to hit, range 30 ft./60 ft., one creature.
Hit: The target is restrained by webbing. As an action, the restrained target can make a DC 12 Strength check, bursting the webbing on a success. The webbing can also be attacked and destroyed (AC 10; hp 5; vulnerability to fire damage; immunity to bludgeoning, poison, and psychic damage).

E1.4 - SILAS' LABORATORY

The real treat from this room is the arcane library of Silas that still has magical books in it. All the books have a magical trap on them.

A study room occupies a quarter of this floor of the tower. A beautiful desk crafted out of rich mahogany rests against the center wall with crumpled notes and empty vials laying on it. On the outside wall, a few shelves are filled with thick leather-bound books, in a different state of preservation.

The notes on the desk are all consumed by time and will fall to dust as they are picked up by the PCs. If they find a smart way to handle them, they should be able to read part of them, discovering a correspondence between Silas and Lord Masmen, a high-ranked politician at the court of the King of Lothmar. Lord Masmen seem to request news from the Barony and whether it is now safe from the demonic army. In other letters, Silas was drafting an answer that there is still demonic taint and given the terrible ordeal of the war, and it is doubtful the good folks will ever return to the Wailmoor.

The bookshelves are not trapped, but Silas has placed a magical trap on *each* book in the form of a custom spell, *silas's explosive book trap*. Since traps are placed on individual books, PCs who will want to check them will have to detect magic for each book, and then make a DC 15 Intelligence (Arcana) Check to disable the magical trap. The password to turn the traps off and on is "Abby," Silas's first girlfriend.

Triggering the trap has a 40% chance of destroying the book.

Silas's Explosive Book Trap

Type magic; DC 15 Intelligence or Arcana to disable
Trigger: Touch (on a book) without a password. The caster does not have to utter the password; the trap does not trigger for him or her
Reset none
Effect spell effect (minor explosion, 1d6 fire damage, 1d6 thunder damage, combine damage then DC 12 Dexterity save for half)

PCs will be able to find the following books:

- An unmarked, crimson leather-bound tome: This book contains the following spells: *charm person, enthrall, dispel magic, invisibility*

- A mysterious purple tome marked "CdV": This is one of Chrystelle de Valois' early spellbooks containing the following spells: *enlarge/reduce, longstrider, jump, protection from energy, fog cloud, enlarge person, expeditious retreat, jump, arcane lock, protection from arrows, fog cloud, arcane lock, web*

- *The War Between Angels and Demons*: This is not a spellbook but a religious book describing how Angels and Demons are in an eternal struggle for the souls of mortals, especially between the Celestial Prince Erebus and the Demon Lord Orcus. Oddly,

the book makes this struggle seem like a minor war in the "grander scheme of things." The book also describes a complicated ritual that sorcerers and wizards can use to entrap a demon for a very long time, based on tricking the demon into stepping on a blue arcane glyph. The book is not a ritual book, but rather a book someone used to describe the ritual's effects.

- This book detects magical but is not trapped. The cover seems to be made of clockwork, and the whole required a DC 20 Dexterity (Thieves' Tools) Check to pick the complicated lock. Once open, the title is *Treaty on Dvalin Weaponry*. The book mentions the art and craft of dwarven and elven weaponsmiths and covers an extensive list of magical items and their locations. It mentions the *Hammer of Dvalin*, located on the Wailmoor and the *Elven Mace of Disruption*, located in the capital city of Ereska. There is also an extensive chapter on the smithing techniques for cold iron and silver weapons, including a description of a cold iron forge and the technique for silvering a weapon without it losing its strength.

- *A hard tome bound with ivory*: When opened, this item reveals to be a small chest the size of a thick book. It contains a few scrolls rolled-up individually: *magic missile, shield, mage armor*

- A *wooden cube used as a book holder*: This item is also trapped per above. When opened, this item reveals to be a small chest the size of a thick book. It contains a few scrolls rolled-up individually: *invisibility, darkvision, knock*

PCs may notice they are not finding Silas's spell books. He kept his books, and his treasure, in a *leomund's secret chest*. When he died, there was no way to refresh the spell, so it ended. His spell books, his ritual books, and monies are lost in the Ethereal Plane.

E1.5 - SILAS' CHAMBERS

This set of notes found here contain important clues as to where to go next.

You stepped in a small but richly decorated bedroom. A large bed with a thick wooden frame sits in the middle of the room, with a large side table next to it, covered with letters and notes. The bed is covered with a layer of dust. Under the bed, a well-crafted rug casts red and yellow light into the room.

There is not much to be found in Silas' chambers. The mage did not spend a lot of time here and occupied his time studying in his laboratory next door or socializing with Humbert in the kitchen downstairs. There are two sets of notes on the side table:

- Some notes are piled together and list farms and locations on the Wailmoor that has seen demonic taint problems or local wildlife perverted by it. These notes seem to have been authored by local peasants and farmers requesting help from their local mage. Silas put personal annotations on some describing his lack of faith and ability in solving the problem.

- Another set of notes are written by Silas. All these notes, almost like a journal if it was not for the absence of dates, mention Silas growing intrigued thinking about an old, hidden, magical power under Castle Wailmoor. Silas is noting that he believes a lot of his questions should find answers in the library of the *Temple of Dvalin*, on the northern side of the Lake, where the history and events of the Wailmoor are recorded. There is mention that he suspects one of the unspoken duties of the Knights of the Wailmoor is to protect this supposed magic or protect the Barony from it, he isn't sure.

- Another note talks about the swamp to the east and southeast, and the rumination of if the location would be a good place for a wading stone since that's where a lot of "malcontent animals and surly monsters come from."

Intro

Lost at the Beaux Seins

Moortide Rising

The Altar & the Anvil

Castle Wailmoor

Appendix

E1.6 - The Blue Sphere

This room contains a trapped demon.

As the Court Wizard of the Barony of Wailmoor, Silas's duty was mainly an overseer function of the civilian wizards in the Barony, approving, sponsoring, and helping the various wizards of each Lord's manor with arcane projects and beneficial magic research.

At the end of the war, Silas was a battle-hardened ruthless survivor, replacing his cheerfulness with stoicism. He was no Imperial War Wizard, but he was a quick learner, and there was a reason him and Jackon were two of the few survivors of the Demon War—Silas took to war like a thirsty man walking in from the desert drank water. He was good at it.

So, when the demon Merga came to kill him, Silas used deception and trapped him. It was almost too easy.

The debris-covered stairs lead up to this platform, once a floor to the tower. Now the sky serves as its ceiling, and the ruined remnants of the tower walls surround the platform like the broken spikes of a sinister crown. On the middle of the platform, a blue sphere, about 7 feet in diameter, floats above the ground. It is pulsating arcane energy and slowly hums. Inside the sphere, a horned demon looks at you with a gaze of longing and malevolence. Its voice echoes through the sphere and is directed at you: "Well, greetings strangers..."

3RD FLOOR

Merga is a powerful demon imprisoned there by Silas about 150-years ago. Merga survived the last assault of the Wailmoor Knights and decided to visit a less-than-formable opponent—their supporting ally, the mage Silas—and kill him. Silas was old, after all.

Silas, however, trapped him with a demon-trapping ritual. Since then, Silas has left the tower and Merga is waiting for someone to free him.

This encounter gives players some hints about the events that precipitated the fall of the Wailmoor, who were the players in the plot at that time, and some hints about the existence of Chrystelle, the immortal enchantress who lives in the Elven Tower of Castle Wailmoor. Should the PCs decide to free Merga and fight him, things won't go so well for them—at least for a few rounds.

Merga is not up for a fight. He will use his malice, his velvet voice, and cunning mind to convince players to free him. He will sometimes tell the truth, or lie, for players to agree to wipe the pentagram drawn under the blue sphere. While patient and able to slip into a catatonic-like reeve state, he can feel the tug of Silas's errant warding spell from the Obelisk in the swamp and wonders if it is going to suck him into the Deep Ethereal for all of eternity, or simply consume him. He has spent the last 150-years imprisoned in this sphere and just wants to gate back to his realm in the Abyss.

ON DEMONS

Demons do not hate mortals, rather, view them as food and playthings to corrupt morally, philosophically, sexually, and mentally. Demons in the *Chronicles of the Celestial Chains* campaign can consume corrupted souls—the longer it took to corrupt the soul, the more delicious the consummation, especially if it was done without consent. Demon corruption is the personification of the absence of choice.

A demon's *teleport* is a formattable ability but no longer functions in the Wailmoor once used, and a *gate* never works to summon other demons. The *gate* will, however, suck a demon out of the Wailmoor who cast it. Merga has seen this effect and is banking on using it as his escape route.

ROLE-PLAYING MERGA

It should be a fun moment for the DM to roleplay Merga and try convincing players to free him. He is sleazy and sarcastic. Merga will exchange information to get PCs to agree to set Merga free or at least try. Merga has no interest in hiding information from them, that battle is long lost, but he is afraid that showing all his cards without guarantees will just make the players turn around and leave him there.

If the players free Merga, he'll open his gate and be sucked away. He could kill these mortals for the fun of it, but something feels wrong about them and the state of their souls. Merga is not able to see the Hierophants reincarnated through the PCs but he smells something awfully fishy, and it scares him. Rather than figure out what bothers him and risk ending up trapped here *again*, he leaves.

Some roleplay tips for Merga might include using both seduction and threat to influence the players. Merga is an intelligent demon with patience. He knows the arts of deception, bluff, and intimidation.

If the players obtain information from Merga that will allow them to further explore the moor and the adventure plot, award them XP as if they defeated a CR 4 monster.

Whether Merga is free or remains captive does not change the course of the next events.

Merga

Large demon, chaotic evil
Armor Class 16 (natural armor) — **Hit Points** 136
Speed 30ft./fly 60. ft

Statistics

STR	DEX	CON	INT,	WIS,	CHA
19 (+4)	17 (+3)	20 (+5	5 (-3)	12 (+1)	13 (+1)

Saving Throws Str +7, Con +8, Wis +4
Damage Immunities poison, disease
Damage Resistances cold, fire, lightning; bludgeoning, piercing, and slashing from nonmagical attacks
Damage Vulnerabilities radiant, force
Condition Immunities poisoned
Senses darkvision 120 ft., passive Perception 11
Languages Abyssal, telepathy 120 ft.
Challenge 8 (3,900 XP)

Abilities

Magic Resistance. Merga has an advantage on Saving Throws against spells and other magical effects.

Gate Demonic Ally. (1/day) Merga can *gate* a demonic ally from the Abyss, either a vrock, a succubus, or a glabrezu (summoner)

Actions

Multiattack. Merga makes three attacks: one with its bite and two with its claws.

Bite. Melee Weapon Attack: +7 to hit, reach 5 ft., one target. Hit: 15 (2d10+4) piercing damage.

Claw. Melee Weapon Attack: +7 to hit, reach 5 ft., one target. Hit: 11 (2d6+4) slashing damage.

Tactics: Before Combat

While trapped in the blue sphere, Merga cannot move or use any ability.

Tactics: During Combat

Merga can practically feel the PCs latent power, and he wants nothing to do with it. He will open a gate and be sucked back into the abyss at the nearest opportunity.

PCs who are observing the platform might be able to notice the pentagram is drawn right under the blue floating sphere, DC15 Perception (Wisdom) or Intelligence (Investigation). If not, Merga will mention it at some point in the conversation. The pentagram

was created with magical chalk and while immune from the elements, can be erased by a simple swipe from a 'PCs foot. When the pentagram is altered or erased, the blue sphere vanishes and Merga is set free.

MERGA'S REVEALS

The information below can/will be revealed by Merga in his attempt to convince the PCs to free him:

- The owner of this tower, Silas, is long gone. He left the tower more than a hundred years ago and never returned.

- Merga was trapped by Silas after he came here to kill the mage. Silas was a force that needed to be dealt with if the demons were going to try again to retake the Wailmoor. Although at the end of the war, the Barony seemed empty to him.

- About 150-years ago, the Demon Lord Barbu lead an army here on the moor to siege the castle. Merga does not know why. The demons lost the battle as Barbu was defeated, but the taint and the devastation from that siege caused most people to flee and leave the barony, never to return.

- The Knights of Wailmoor won the battle against the demons. They were highly trained warriors and tacticians, led by an Imperial War Wizard and were helped with impressive

Intro

Lost at the Beaux Seins

Moortide Rising

The Altar & the Anvil

Castle Wailmoor

Appendix

enchanted gear and weapons as well as powerful boons. The demons killed most of them but when Barbu was brought down, most of the demons *gated* back to the Abyss.

- Merga suspects a powerful undead thing of the like the Welt has never seen resides under Castle Wailmoor and is involved in defeating the demonic army.

- There are other demons in the Wailmoor who have not left through personal decisions our inability. He doesn't know whom they are or what they are, even, only that Silas talked to him about it before he disappeared.

E1.7 - HUMBERT'S QUARTERS

This room has a note from Silas's guard to Silas, along with a magical item.

This small room contains simple furniture: a wooden cupboard with an empty ceramic bowl and a rudimentary, but comfortable bed. Everything is covered in dust and has not been used for a long time.

This room that was used by the tower guard, Humbert, as his personal quarters. The room has not been used in a century and a half and dusty. The sheets and pillows of the bed are degraded by time, beyond use and will turn to shreds in the hands of the PCs trying to manipulate them.

Under the bowl on the cupboard, PCs can easily find a handwritten note, left here by Humbert for Silas to read (he never did). The note says:

Master Silas,

After many years at your service protecting the tower and the Barony, I am sorry to announce through this letter than I am leaving the tower and returning to my brother's farm in Kandra.

You left the tower three weeks ago, looking for answers to questions I do not understand, in the ruins of Castle Wailmoor. Since you have not returned, I can only assume you are dead and that my services are not needed anymore.

I also find it very difficult to live with this demon under our roof. I hope Lady Ishtari protects you,

Your humble servant, Humbert

PS: I am leaving the sword you gave me under the bed, as I shall not keep what was your property and was just trusted with me, so I can perform this job for you.

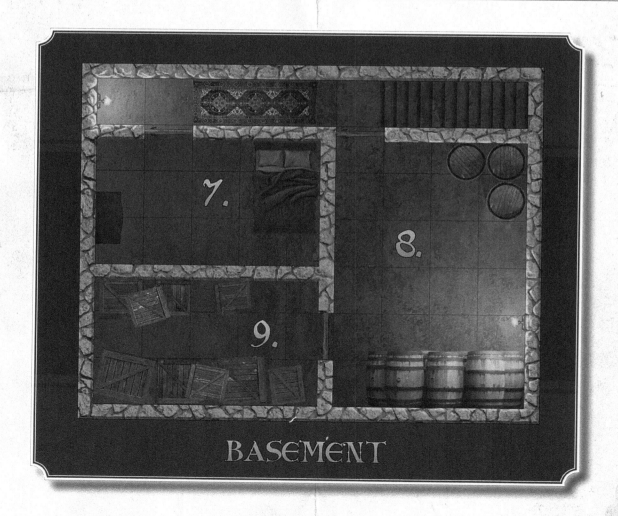

BASEMENT

Under the bed, PCs will be able to find a *+1 short sword* in its scabbard.

E1.8 - THE CELLAR

There are giant rats here and some wine and wine-turned-vinegar.

Wine barrels and food crates are lined up against the wall of this small cellar under the tower. The dust-covered floor is marked with the footprints of many little, some not-so-little, rodents.

A group of eight giant rats live here in the cellar, arriving via a crack in the basement wall, and will attack players trying to move through the room or check the content of the crates and barrels. They were attracted originally to the dry basement, but now seem to bask in the corruption that seeps from demon taint from the trapped demon upstairs. The statue doesn't blast them to bits, but if they get any bigger, it might.

Eight Giant Rats

Small beast, unaligned
Armor Class 12 — **Hit Points** 7 — **Speed** 30 ft.

Statistics

STR	DEX	CON	INT	WIS	CHA
7 (-2)	15 (+2)	11 (+0)	2 (-4)	10 (+0)	4 (-3)

Senses darkvision 60 ft., passive Perception 10
Languages —
Challenge 1/8 (25 XP) each

Abilities

Keen Smell. The rat has Advantage on Wisdom (Perception) checks that rely on smell.

Pack Tactics. The rat has Advantage on an attack roll against a creature if at least one of the rat's allies is within 5 feet of the creature and the ally isn't incapacitated.

Actions

Bite. Melee Weapon Attack: +4 to hit, reach 5 ft., one target. Hit: 4 (1d4+2) piercing damage.

Going through the cellar, PCs can find 5 gallons of wine (of spectacular quality, 300 GP per gallon), and about 10 gallons of wine-turned-vinegar (but would make great salad dressing).

E1.9 - STORAGE ROOM

There are magical potions to find in this room.

Crates and boxes are stacked up in this storage room. The ground is dusty. No one has entered this room in a long time.

The storage room is not trapped or protected by spells but contains crates. Crates are locked with simple locks, DC 15 Dexterity (Thieves" Tools), which are not meant to prevent thieves from opening them but rather protect them from rats and other rodents. Many of the crates were empty; others filled only with a straw. Some crates have rotted supplies even when filled with straw and items wrapped in burlap bags.

Three crates contain usable content:

- **Crate 1** contains 3 blankets, 2 fur coats (100 GP each) and 20 candles.

- **Crate 2** contains a rope (100feet), a set of blank parchment scrolls (5 pages) in a scroll tube as well as a vial of ink and a quill. The ink will need a drop or two of water and remixing before use.

- **Crate 3** contains 2 vials of oil, a bullseye lantern, 1 vial of *alchemist fire* and *potion of healing*.

WHAT HAPPENED TO SILAS

PCs might put the following facts and story together: after the fall of the demon Barbu, most of the demonic army departed from the Wailmoor, leaving a desolate place behind them. He and Jackon set up the ward stones, but, alas, Jackon died from performing the last ritual, perhaps intentionally.

Silas stayed in his tower for a few years, working to remove the demonic taint from the moor and return it to a habitable place.

During that time, the demon Merga, among the demons who stayed behind, moved to murder Silas and found himself his prisoner instead. Through study and conversations with Merga, Silas figured out there was power hiding within Castle Wailmoor. Without knowing her identity, he discovered the existence of Chrystelle de Valois and her influence on the Barony. He even wondered if she was the reason behind the demonic siege.

Silas was greatly impacted by Jackon the War Wizard's death and, not being able to enter the Knight's Graveyard, could not find closure. One morning in gloom and depression—determined to find the secret Jackon hid from him so well—he left his tower and managed to enter Castle Wailmoor. But when he used his *leomund's secret chest* to fetch a ritual book, drawing his magical chest from the Ethereal Plane, his spell malfunctioned, just as the Old Elven Tower's original wards malfunctioned when the Obelisks went up. His poking at the Ethereal triggered the entire Castle to follow the Tower, trapping him inside.

Silas shortly encountered two demons, and while he took them out, he quickly succumbed to his wounds. PCs will be able to find the fate of Silas and his skeleton in Chapter 4 when they visit Castle Wailmoor.

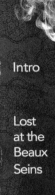

Intro

Lost at the Beaux Seins

Moortide Rising

The Altar & the Anvil

Castle Wailmoor

Appendix

The Old Bridge

BELVER TOR

E2 - BELVER TOR

ASCENDING THE TOR

Before arriving, the PCs will most likely have experienced the *Lost Memory M3 - Belver Tor.* If not, trigger it before they ascend to the top. On a clear night, there is also a multitude of glowing objects to be seen. There're also 2 demon hounds here, a formidable encounter for low-level PCs.

The tor is steep and the climb strenuous. On foot, it takes about an hour to reach the top, following a narrow path, cluttered with big granite rocks that rolled onto the trail. The trail is unmaintained and has returned to a wild state, the path disappearing on many instances over a few dozen feet. Unless the PCs attempts to climb up the Tor at night (in that case, make them roll a DC 15 Wisdom (Survival) Check to avoid another hour to the total climb), the ascension does not require extraordinary efforts.

THE TOP OF THE TOR

At the top, PCs will find a large flat area that offers a 360-view of all directions.

There is a 60 ft.-diameter circular stone-paved platform at the middle of tor top where the Baron of Wailmoor used to swear in the new recruits of the Knights of the Wailmoor. Before the PCs can reach the platform of white stones, they are ambushed by 2 demon hounds who are hiding in the nearby bushes (demon hounds' Stealth vs. PCs' Perception to spot the ambush).

Two Wailmoor Demon Hounds

Medium demon, chaotic evil
Armor Class 15 (natural armor) — **Hit Points** 45 — **Speed** 50 ft.

Statistics

STR	DEX	CON	INT	WIS	CHA
17 (+3)	12 (+1)	14 (+2)	6 (-2)	13 (+1)	6 (-2)

Skills Perception +5
Damage Immunities fire
Damage Vulnerability cold, radiant
Senses darkvision 60 ft., passive Perception 15
Languages understand abyssal but doesn't speak it
Challenge 3 (700 XP) each

Abilities

Keen Hearing and Smell. The hound has Advantage on Wisdom (Perception) checks that rely on hearing or smell.

Actions

Bite. *Melee Weapon Attack:* +5 to hit, reach 5 ft., one target. *Hit:* 7 (1d8+3) piercing plus 7 (2d6) fire damage.

Fire Breath (Recharge 5-6). The demon hound exhales fire in a 15-foot cone. Each creature in that area must make a DC 12 Dexterity Saving Throw, taking 21 (6d6) fire damage on a failed save, or half as much damage on a successful one.

Tactics: During Combat

The demon hounds will move to position themselves between the PCs and the stone platform at the top of the tor. The platform is *hallowed* ground, and the demon dogs cannot enter its limits. Once onto the platform, PCs can use range weapons to defeat the demon hounds. If out of their reach, the demon dogs will retreat and decide to ambush the PCs again as they climb down the tor.

Once the PCs reach the platform (and the demon hounds defeated), they will feel at ease and in great comfort, protected by the consecration of the place (the platform is permanently consecrated, via a *hallow* spell to Platine, a Dragon of Law). Spending the night there or a full rest will heal the PCs of their wounds but could trigger the <u>Lost Memory that drags them to the Old Graveyard</u> if they've visited it previously.

The Panorama at the Tor

On a lovely day, the view allows visitors to see the entire Barony and well beyond, their view only being blocked by mountainous terrain. On a clear night, the PCs can see quite the glow-fest. They won't be able to see features details other than the glow:

- The most obvious illumination, a large shaft of light shining far into the sky as if some lost beacon of hope from the fountain in Harenvale

- The faint glow from the Lady's Statue

- If the demon is still trapped, the blue glow from Silas's Tower

- The green glow from both outside Obelisks (if still undefeated)

- While the plateau obscures the village, faint glow from the inn, pub, farms, and manor

- A slight green glow from the well at the Temple of Dvalin

- A slight red glow from the Shrine of the Maiden

- A green-purple glow from the Seat of Barbu on the Old Battlefield

- The ever-present slight glow from the wards around Castle Wailmoor

In the day, looking to the north, PCs see a vast forest (the Lady's Woods) that extends far beyond the limits of the moor plateau. With a DC 12 Wisdom (Perception) check, they will be able to spot the ruined buildings of the village of Harenvale about 6 miles north on the east side of the forest.

To the west, they see the road that connects the Kings Road with the old bridge on the moor. This is likely to be the way they came.

Looking south and southwest, a vast bog opens before the eyes of the PCs. They clearly see the lone tower of the mage Silas on a hilly promontory above the moor. Further south, maybe ten miles out, the horizon is blocked by taller hills, not quite mountains but still a steep rocky ridge known as the Harden Hills. With a DC 18 Wisdom (Perception) check, PCs will be able to discern the entrance holes of the copper mine and the quarry pits at the foot of these hills.

To the east (and northeast), they will be able to observe several interesting locations that, combined with upcoming *Lost Memories*, they will receive, might encourage them to pay these locations a visit:

- **The Lake and the Temple of Dvalin**—they see a deep lake of dark waters with a large building poking out of a carved half-hill on its northern shore. The building can easily be identified as a temple of some kind.

- **Castle Wailmoor** towers above the lake, perched on a hill on its southern shore. The castle bears the marks of a rough siege even if all its walls still stand. One mysterious note about the castle— it seems to glimmer and flicker as if fading in and out of existence. This is even more noticeable at night or dawn when the castle is bathed in an eerie green light.

- **The Village of Graspen** is built at the foot of the castle. It appears to be deserted and extensively ruined. The PCs can spot some intact building, and on a creek, an intact waterwheel house.

- **The Battlefield**—a vast gray plateau extends between the Tor and the Lake, barren and sinister. Marks and remnants of heavy siege weaponry indicate a long and strenuous battle happened there, a long time ago. On east easternmost side of the battlefield, PCs can notice a small ruin, maybe a shrine or a small temple.

E3 - The Lady's Woods

This location contains random encounters and a magical statue that can heal the PCs and possibly see and hear them remotely.

Into the Woods

The Lady's Woods used to be a well-groomed forest, maintained by the skilled rangers of the Barony, and used for the Barons' hunts and entertainment. Now they are a dense, un-welcoming place with bramble-wrapped trees and thick undergrowth. Movement through the woods is considered difficult terrain and most roads are faded from sight under a mattress of fallen leaves and twigs. A DC 15 Wisdom (Survival) Check will allow PCs to move through the woods at their movement rate by following game trails. Animal presence in the woods is limited to pack of hungry wolves, rabbits, and rodents. Majestic stags and deer have long left the Lady's Woods.

Intro

Lost at the Beaux Seins

Moortide Rising

The Altar & the Anvil

Castle Wailmoor

Appendix

For every three hours spent in the woods, roll an encounter for the PCs on the suggested table below:

2D6	ENCOUNTER	AVG. CR
2	1 Swarm of Bats	1/4
3	1d4 Giant Spiders	2
4	1d4 Giant Bats	4
5	1d8 Boars	1
6	1 Dire Boar	2
7	The Lady's Statue	N/A
8	1d4 Dire Wolves	2
9	1 Ettercap and 2 Giant Spiders	4
10	1 Swarm of Wasps	1/2
11	2 Demonic-tainted Wolves	4
12	No encounter	-

THE LADY'S STATUE

Deep within the woods, there is a tall (10ft. high) alabaster statue of a regal and noble woman with some type of preservation magic on it that gives it a minor glow at night. The statue is covered with leaves and brambles but still easy to spot as PCs will travel through the forest. The statue has its eyes looking down at whoever would stand before it, and its arms opened wide in a welcoming and protective embrace. It radiates with magical energy.

This statue was erected here by Terrance, the 7th Baron of Wailmoor as an homage to Chrystelle de Valois, his beloved tutor, and mentor. If Chrystelle has been directly involved in supporting and educating all Wailmoor barons, Terrance was the first of them to fall in love with her. Terrance was a kind soul who saw Chrystelle's heart underneath her undead appearance.

Today, the statue acts as a sensory extension to Chrystelle herself. Normally the PCs are not scryable, but the magic used in linking Chrystelle to the statue is more telepathic-and-necromantic-based. This is the one place that Chrystelle can see and hear everything the PCs do remotely—if the Elven Tower was not shut away into the Ethereal Plane. Unless the PCs have destroyed all three Obelisks, Chrystelle's psychic link to the statue does not function.

The aura around the statue, a large magical item, will also heal living creatures for a maximum a 20 HPs per character for every night rest spent within 30ft. of the statue (in addition to other healing they may receive).

HARENVALE

This area contains bandits. This location can trigger the M8 – The Witch Lost Memory by viewing the witch's tattoo on a bandit's arm, and the Lost Memory, M13 – Rescuing "Sarah." The fountain in the middle of the town ruins shines a bright light, straight up, and can be seen anywhere from an elevated position within the Barony on a clear night.

Before the Barony fell a hundred and fifty years ago, the village of Harenvale was a wealthy community on the northern border of Wailmoor. It operated as a commercial gateway between the Barony of Wailmoor and the middle portions of the Viscounty of Kandra to the west and the elves and their barbarian allies of the untamed lands directly north. Grain, pelts, food items and all manner of things such as metal tools, weapon, and armor were publicly traded at the marketplace as often as 3 times a week.

Harenvale was also a place of where the nobles and the upper class had estates, much like they did in Graspen to the south. The function of these estates, however, was primarily for recreation, hunting in the woods and having a good time with other nobles and rich folks, and the serenity and well-crafted construction of each estate were more of a status symbol than a necessity.

But there was a lot of money to be had in trade in Harenvale. In the time leading up to the war, the hum barbarians to the north were interested in being social with their neighbors, wanting to learn the arts of agriculture and civilized, Imperial ways.

THE DEMON WAR

While Harenvale was spared by the demonic army (through the leadership efforts of Jackon, the Imperial War Wizard and Knight of Wailmoor) and did not receive much of the nefarious taint covering the rest of the moor, the town did not survive the fall and was deserted by its inhabitants. At several points, it suffered several catastrophic fires.

This is the location that Sarah, the pub wench's ancestor comes from. Sarah looks just like her, the noble bloodline, while now mixed with common blood, is strong enough to randomly assert itself on a generation.

If Sarah's lineage is somehow traced, she is the legal heir (and of noble blood) of two 5-acre estates, one in Harenvale and one in Graspen (both destroyed, but the land is still intact), and four extensive farms southeast of the Old Graveyard and southeast of the road. Her father was a Lord, who had three knights overseeing two to five farms each. He was well-respected (in addition to being handsome and rich) and ran several businesses in Harenvale, but the land for those businesses was rented. Her full name is Lady Sarah Wailcourt.

HARENVALE NOW

In current days, Harenvale is a ghost town with crumbled wooden buildings and ever-growing roots covering its once paved streets.

This small town at one point must have been picturesque, and by the stone foundations and the odd standing brick walls, wealthy, but now it is a ruin having suffered at least one catastrophic fire. In the middle of town are two stone buildings that were spared the confabulation. One looks like a town hall, the other, a granary. Between them is a granite fountain, devoid of flowing water.

The center of the town has a few stone buildings still standing.

- The old town hall—although the windows are long gone, the slate roof has withstood the march of time. 3 bandits are here.

- The village granary—this building was made entirely of the same cement formula as the dam was far to the south. Nothing has degraded its structure or damaged it.

- The granite fountain—both buildings stand opposite from each other, across a largely paved marketplace with a granite fountain at its center. The fountain stopped working long. At night, a shaft of light radiates from the fountain far into the night sky. 2 bandits guard here.

THE GIRL

There is a northern barbarian teen girl in the Town Hall that "willingly" attends to the bandit's needs. However, unbeknownst to them, she is simply *charmed* by Haeggra and is thoroughly ensorcelled. She gives herself to the bandits and considers them her friends. Once a month, Haeggra gives her a contraceptive in the form of an herbal concoction. Her name is Catherin.

The young woman is dressed provocatively but has traveling clothes in addition to her lingerie. She is well-fed and clean. Any PC talking to her with a Wisdom (Insights) DC 12 Check will recognize that she isn't quite right in the head and might be a simpleton. An Intelligence (Arcana) Check DC of 15 will reveal she has been thoroughly *charmed*.

Charming young women to be playthings is thoroughly illegal in all Imperial lands with sanction from Paladins of Bastet. Charming and coercion is a sin against the church (and an Imperial crime) and perpetrators are dealt violently and with extreme prejudice. Returning the girl to a Bastet Priestess or Paladin of Bastet (both of which can be found with the help of a Bastet Acolyte) garners favor with the church,

along with a private party for *one* PC and his or her two preferred Bastet Acolytes.

Apothecary contraceptives are also illegal both in the Viscounty and the Duchy of Hardred.

The girl is a non-combatant. If attacked with lethal intent, she dies in one blow.

THE BANDITS

These are men from the remote sections of the Viscounty of Kandra (and there are many such places) who've been hired by the Witch Haeggra to support her investigations of the Wailmoor (see Haeggra description and motives in E10 - The Temple of Dvalin). They are currently waiting for her to come back from one of her expeditions and are growing restless that their hard coin payday keeps getting delayed. They are aggressive and have no interest in conversation with the PCs.

There are 5 bandits, 2 outside by the fountain and 3 inside the old town hall. Among the bandits inside the town hall, PCs should be able to also single out Berar, their leader, a stout man with a cunning gaze.

The bandits outside are gathered around a campfire on which they are grilling sausages. They do not expect anyone to come from within Wailmoor and should be easy for PCs to surprise and spot (listen/smell) from some distance. To them, the Wailmoor has been one big empty space punctuated by intense visits from their employer, whom they refer to as The Bitch Witch.

Between all the bandits, there is 67 GP and 391 SP.

Five Kandra Bandits

Medium humanoid, chaotic neutral
Armor Class 12 (leather armor) — **Hit Points** 20 — **Speed** 30 ft.

Statistics

STR	DEX	CON	INT	WIS	CHA
13 (+1)	12 (+1)	12 (+1)	10 (+0)	9 (-1)	10 (+0)

Senses passive Perception 10
Challenge 1/2 (100 XP) each

Actions

Light Crossbow. *Ranged Weapon Attack:* +4 to hit, range 80 ft./320 ft., one target.
Hit: 5 (1d8+1) piercing damage.

Scimitar. *Melee Weapon Attack:* +4 to hit, reach 5 ft., one target.
Hit: (1d6+2) slashing damage.

The bandits here favor ranged attacks. Normally opportunists, their witch employer both rewards (both occasional coin payment as promised, and what they think is a paid prostitute, the teen girl in the town hall). They do not retreat but could be captured by a variety of different methods.

Intro

Lost at the Beaux Seins

Moortide Rising

The Altar & the Anvil

Castle Wailmoor

Appendix

Berar, Bandit Captain

Medium humanoid, chaotic neutral
Armor Class 15 (studded leather) — **Hit Points** 65 — **Speed** 30 ft.

Statistics

STR	DEX	CON	INT	WIS	CHA
15 (+2	16 (+3)	14 (+2)	14 (+2)	11 (+0)	14 (+2)

Saving Throws Str +4, Dex +5, Wis +2
Skills Athletics +4, Deception +4
Senses passive Perception 10
Challenge 2 (450 XP)

Actions

Multiattack. The captain makes three melee attacks: two with its scimitar and one with its dagger. Or the captain makes two ranged attacks with its daggers.

Dagger. Melee or Ranged Weapon Attack: +5 to hit, reach 5 ft. or range 20 ft./60 ft., one target.
Hit: 5 (1d4+3) piercing damage.

Scimitar. Melee Weapon Attack: +5 to hit, reach 5 ft., one target.
Hit: 6 (1d6+3) slashing damage.

Reactions

Parry. Berar adds 2 to its AC against one melee attack that would hit it. To do so, the captain must see the attacker and be wielding a melee weapon.

Tactics: During Battle

Berar and his 5 bandits are a tough encounter if the PCs fight them together. As soon as attacked, the 2 bandits outside call for help and Berar and the 3 other bandits join him within the next round. With some planning and the Advantage of surprise, it would be easy for smart PCs to split the bandits apart and reduce their numbers piecemeal.

If PCs manage to capture and interrogate one of the bandits, a DC 15 Charisma (Intimidation) or Charisma (Deception) Check will have him share some information.

- They were hired by a witch or a sorceress from Kandra. Her name is Haeggra. She is mean and short of temper.

- They do not know her objectives. She asked to be guarded traveling the moor and has left them here for about a week. She said she was going to a temple to Dvalin, somewhere south.

If PCs manage to capture and interrogate Berar, he knows a little more:

- Haeggra is a member of a powerful coven that has numerous political ties in the Viscounty of Kandra and the Duchy of Hardred. The ancient witch Kavita runs this coven.

- The coven has a long feud with Wailmoor and acts still to this day to make sure the Barony never recovers from its fall.

If these bandits are taken alive back to the closest local authority, Sir Walshan in the Crossroad Villages, Sir Walshan thanks them profusely and has them hanged on the spot. He gives the PCs 400 Imperial Gold Crowns to split amongst themselves—he hates bandits, but he mightily appreciates the PCs bringing the bandits to him. To him, that makes the PCs less roaming killers and more Good Men and Women That Do Violence and is keen on rewarding lawful behavior.

If Dame Walshan is presented with the bandit's plaything, she takes care of the girl's recovery and sees the PCs as the heroes they are. Catherin becomes a member of her household as a chambermaid.

Ruins

If the PCs are exploring, it's obvious from the foundations and ruins, despite the fires that destroyed the town, that it was a place of wealth and prosperity (spacing between houses, foundations with basements giving an indication of large manor houses, surviving stonework, etc.). In one of the manorial ruins is a *bullseye lantern*, with a *continual flame* cast inside. Picking up the lantern triggers M13 – Rescuing "Sarah" if the PCs have not triggered it before.

Also, of note is a well-constructed sewer system and a copper pipe network for indoor plumbing—both Imperial designs out of place in a far-flung Imperial Protectorate and odd given the spacing in-between estates.

Graveyards

The two temples in Harenvale were burned and looted and then burned again. Little remains. PCs looking for temples, or graveyards, will discover graveyards where the graves were dug up.

Defenders of the Wailmoor dug up all the buried bodies, save those in the tombs in the Hardred Hills, and cremated them to prevent them from being defiled, animated or worse by demonic forces.

E4 The Bog

PCs must brave the bog to destroy the Corrupted Bog Obelisk. It's a rough place for bumbling PCs.

The bog is a nasty environment where many people have died, either chased down by the demons as they were trying to flee from the battlefield to the north, or to the corrupted creatures ambushing refugees on their way out of the Barony. People not familiar with The Bog (as locals called it), found themselves in treacherous landscape without realizing how dangerous it is.

DMs who would want to encourage their players to 'clean up the barony' can point the bog as a good place to start.

CRITTERS

If the Bog Obelisk hasn't outright corrupted a critter in the swamp, it made it either irritated or sick. This swampy area is dangerous, filled to the brim with all sorts of nasty things—and some nice treasure.

Not displayed on the map is the ever-present low-lying mist, and while it can hide PCs, it also can hide critters.

CRITTERS AND STEALTH

If the PCs are moving stealthily, make sure the encountered creatures make a proper Wisdom (Perception) check to notice they are there. This area, more so than other places, pays to move as Stealthy as possible.

The inverse applies. Creatures with Stealth use it constantly unless otherwise noted.

THE CORRUPTION

The two most corrupted critters are the swamp dogs and demon crocs. Once the Bog Obelisk and those two groups are destroyed, even if there are still other occasional nasty things (such as the psychic leech swarm), The Bog is considered "cleaned." Within 1d20 days, the other tainted creatures die of disease or starvation, unable to receive nourishment from food once the PCs destroy the Obelisk.

TERRAIN

Any time an encounter occurs, assume the PCs are on mostly dry land on an east/west 10-foot wide trail or a north/south trail, depending on their travel direction. Off the trail is difficult terrain (bog/swamp/marsh/muck) unless otherwise noted.

BOG RANDOM ENCOUNTERS

The location of these encounters occurs when the encounter comes up. Everything except the corrupted vapor, sounds and Boo are leaving tracks or evidence of their movement. If the PCs want to clean out the bog and they have a tracker, then skip the random check and proceed to the table to see what critter the ranger found.

Random encounter checks are made every two hours until the Obelisk is destroyed and the demon crocs, along with the swamp dogs, are defeated. Then the encounters are no longer random, leaving the DM to place any remaining exploration-based encounters as he or she sees fit. Encounters 2-12 are not infinite if the PCs destroy the Bog Obelisk within a week of first entering the Bog. If the PCs find and deal with one of these groups of creatures, then they no longer are available as random encounters and the resultant roll results in "No Encounter." Boo the Owl can be

encountered multiple times.

If the PCs ignore the Obelisk, refer to the Bog Obelisk's modified encounter table.

BOG ENCOUNTER TABLE

2D8	ENCOUNTER	AVG. CR
2	Wailmoor Demon Crocs	4
3	Lost, Sad Dog	-
4	3 Sickly Dogs	-
5	2 Slightly Corrupted Crocs	2
6	4 Wailmoor Giant Leeches	1
7	4 Wailmoor Giant Leeches in Trees	1
8	Corrupted Psychic Leech Swarm	5
9	Swamp Dog Hunter Pack (5)	5
10	Corrupted Vapor	5
11	2 Demonic-Wolves	4
12	Boo the Owl	5
13-16	Creepy Sounds	-

E4.2 TWO SLIGHTLY TAINTED CROCODILES

These crocs only have avoided most of the Obelisk taint but have enough that they hunt in a pair and fight to the death, enjoying snapping their jaws around flesh a little too much.

They will attack horses first, and then people, but will switch to targets that do them damage. If the PCs are dragging a wagon with them with a draft horse, the draft horse panics and immediately overturns the wagon, which slips into the muck and becomes stuck.

Two Slight Tainted Crocodiles

Large beast, unaligned
AC 12 (natural armor) — **HP** 25 — **Speed** 20 ft., swim 30 ft.

Statistics

STR	DEX	CON	INT	WIS	CHA
15 (+2)	10 (+0)	13 (+1)	2 (-4)	10 (+0)	5 (-3)

Skills Stealth +2
Senses passive Perception 10
Languages —
Challenge 1 (200 XP) each

Abilities

Hold Breath. The crocodile can hold its breath for 15 minutes.

Actions

Bite. Melee Weapon Attack: +4 to hit, reach 5 ft., one creature. *Hit:* 7 (1d10+2) piercing damage. The target is grappled (escape DC 12). Until this grapple ends, the target is restrained, and the crocodile can't bite another target.

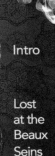

Intro

Lost at the Beaux Seins

Moortide Rising

The Altar & the Anvil

Castle Wailmoor

Appendix

Within the bog near this encounter, players will be able to find a different wagon covered in reeds and mud (if the encounter repeats, there isn't a new wagon). The petrified skeleton of two oxen, as well as the bodies of a human family, can be found scattered around it. These poor peasants got trapped in the bog as they were trying to leave the Barony and were attacked by crocodiles. Since getting to the wagon will probably require players to encounter a few monsters from the table above, you can reward them with some loot found among the properties of the late family. A *ring of protection +1* can be found around the finger of a teenage boy skeleton in the wagon, and *bracers of protection +1* can be found around the wrist of the father, deep under the bog's mud (*detect magic* will allow players to locate it through the mud).

E4.3 Lost, Sad Dog

This young mix-breed dog is wet, tired, hungry, and confused. It's a matter of time before he succumbs to the call of the Bog Obelisk, but for now, he is in full control of his faculties. He's a sprinter and a good swimmer and all around a Good Boy.

He is attracted to the party as *people*. If the PCs are not moving with Stealth, he slinks towards them on his belly, whimpering. If fed and shown kindness he is fiercely loyal, but he must be removed from the Wailmoor if the Bog Obelisk isn't destroyed or he will succumb to its call.

If he doesn't perceive the PCs, then he simply is found in the middle of the trail, sad and forlorn.

There is no XP award for killing Lost, Sad Dog. He will die on a single blow.

E4.4 Three Sickly Dogs

These dogs are sick and are simply lying on a patch of dry ground. They growl at anyone that approaches but can't even muster the energy to bite. If petted they will whine pitifully. In 24-hours the corruption will consume them, and they will be swamp dogs forever more. At that point, the process is irreversible without a *remove curse*.

If the dogs are healed, DC 15 Wisdom (Medicine) with a or a *cure disease*), the only way to prevent them from being corrupted again is by destroying the Bog Obelisk.

There is no XP award for killing the Three Sickly Dogs; they will die on a single blow.

E4.5 Two Demon Crocs

The ranger from chapter one, Kenneth, knew that something was (very) wrong with the Obelisk above the Crossroads Village, but didn't have the expertise to do something with it. As a scout, he decided to go scouting before heading back to the village and talking to the Druid Jeremiah. He found dog tracks leading to The Bog and was waylaid by the two demon crocs.

His magical *+1 longbow* lies in a 20ft deep, 40ft wide putrid pound that the demon crocs inhabit. The pound is murky with visibility only at 5-feet, although the glow of *detect magic* from the edge of the pound will show something in the murk.

> The trail you're attempting to use and stay dry in this forsaken bog sidelines a murky pound ringed with trees and trailing vines.
> And no sooner do you think that this place might be dangerous, two red, glowing crocodiles burst out of the water and come right out you with a disgusting, loud roar halfway between a gurgle and a hiss.

Two Wailmoor Demon Crocodiles

Large demonic beast, chaotic evil
Armor Class 13 (natural armor) — **Hit Points** 30
Speed 20 ft., swim 30 ft.

Statistics

STR	DEX	CON	INT	WIS	CHA
15 (+2)	10 (+0)	13 (+1)	4 (-3)	10 (+0)	5 (-3)

Damage Immunity necrotic
Damage Vulnerability radiant, force
Saving Throws Dex +2, Int -1
Skills Acrobatics +2, Athletics +4, Deception -1, Perception +2, Stealth +4
Senses passive Perception 12
Languages Abyssal
Challenge 2 (450 XP) each

Abilities

Hold Breath. The crocodile can hold its breath for 15 minutes.

Actions

Bite. Melee Weapon Attack: +4 to hit, reach 5 ft., one creature. *Hit:* 7 (1d10+2) piercing damage. The target is grappled (escape DC 14). Until this grapple ends, the target is restrained, and the crocodile can't bite another target.

The demon crocs go right for anybody with a holy symbol to a good deity regardless of tactical significance.

PCs can attempt a DC 12 Dexterity (Acrobatics) Check to grab one of the vines hanging over the pound to prevent from sinking under. At that point, the vine operates as a rope, giving Advantage to break the grapple.

E4.6 Six Giant Leeches

These disgusting giant leeches are merely hungry. They will attack anybody within 5-feet reach of the difficult terrain they inhabit.

Giant leeches are horrific in appearance. They are bloated, slimy creatures with a large circular mouth with rows and rows of teeth.

Six Wailmoor Giant Leeches

Medium beast, unaligned
Armor Class 13 (Natural Armor) — **Hit Points** 27
Speed 20 ft., swim 40 ft.

Statistics

STR	DEX	CON	INT	WIS	CHA
15 (+2)	15 (+2)	15 (+2)	1 (-5)	8 (-1)	1 (-5)

Damage Vulnerabilities fire, radiant
Senses Blindsight 40 ft. (blind beyond this radius), Passive Perception 9
Languages —
Challenge 1/4 (50 XP) each

Abilities

Amphibious. The leech can breathe air and water.

Salt Hater. The giant leech reacts badly to salt. A vial's worth causes 2d6 hit points of damage and causes the leech to detach if attached to a victim.

Blood Gorge. If the leech absorbs 24 or over hit points of blood from victims within a day, it explodes, killing it instantly.

Actions

Blood Drain. Melee Weapon Attack: +4 to hit, reach 5 ft., one creature. *Hit:* 4 (1d6 + 1) piercing damage and the leech attaches to the target. While attached, the leech doesn't attack. Instead, at the start of each of the leech's turns, the target loses 4 (1d6 +1) hit point due to blood loss.
If fire, radiant damage, or salt is applied to the giant leech, it detaches from its current victim but will attempt to reattach itself during its next action.

Intro

Lost at the Beaux Seins

Moortide Rising

The Altar & the Anvil

Castle Wailmoor

Appendix

E4.7 Another 4 Giant Leeches

The PCs can avoid this encounter by avoiding the body. This may be a deadly encounter for one swimming PC if the party is not familiar with the dangerous giant leeches.

Off to the side of a trail, an emaciated body floats in the bog face down about 80-feet away. The man is wearing leather armor and is gripping a spear.

10-feet off the trail the difficult terrain turns into water, 15ft. deep.

This is one of the bandits (from either group) that had a vivid nightmare and fled down a trail in the darkness and got lost. PCs that attempt to swim to the body are attacked by the leeches when they are 10-feet away from it.

The body has 5 GP and 10 SP and an old silver holy symbol of three eyes and very odd (and somewhat disturbing) runes on the back. A DC 20 Intelligence (Religion) check reveals this is a witch coven's symbol from Kandra, and any High Priest of any of the gods will pay up to 200 GP for it, as these symbols are secretive and subversive. Each one is different, and there is an active hunt to acquire more by several different factions opposed to the Kandra witch covens.

Stirring the muck with a long stick, pole-arm or any long-bladed weapon will reveal the leeches with a DC 15 Wisdom (Perception) check. The giant leeches only attack when someone is swimming to the body.

E4.8 Corrupted Psychic Leech Swarm

Another monstrosity birthed from the Bog Obelisk, this horrific encounter in some ways is deadlier than the Obelisk that spawned it and may have PCs questions their choice of moving around without Stealth (or adventuring career).

With a sickening slurping sound, out of the bog arises a form that could only be described as a floating cloud of tiny leeches. The leeches swirl about and then forms into a 10-foot tall humanoid shaped monstrosity that walks with foul purpose, each step a sickening slurp in the muck from the churning mass of leeches.

There is some type of demonic laughter in your head along with words that seem almost too terrible to recognize. Roll for initiative.

The corrupt psychic leech swarm occupies a large space (10ft. x 10ft.) and is 10ft. tall. It attempts to move into a position where it can occupy the same square of as many creatures as its large size will accommodate for its *swarm aura* to do the most damage to the party as possible.

If losing the battle, the corrupted psychic leech swarm attempts to flee back into the bog, never to be encountered again.

The language it is screeching in the PCs mind is abyssal, and it is saying "Yum, yum, more blood for me!"

Corrupted Psychic Leech Swarm

Large aberration, chaotic evil
Armor Class 14 (Natural Armor) — **Hit Points** 49
Speed 30 ft./fly 30 ft.

Statistics

STR	DEX	CON	INT	WIS	CHA
15 (+2)	15 (+2)	15 (+2)	10	10	1 (-5)

Damage Resistance bludgeoning, psychic
Damage Vulnerabilities fire, radiant, thunder
Senses Blindsight 60 ft. passive Perception 10
Languages Abyssal, telepathy (line of sight)
Challenge 4 (1,100 XP)

Abilities

Amphibious. The corrupted psychic leech swarm can breathe air and water.

Swarm Aura. The amorphous corrupted psychic leech swarm can (and will) move through and occupy spaces already occupied. Any creature in the swarm's location takes 4 (1d6 +1) hit points of damage due to blood loss at the beginning of their turn.

Action

Fist of Psionic Leeches Slam Attack: +5 to hit, reach 10ft, one creature
Hit: 10 (2d6+3) psychic damage

E4.9 Swamp Dog Hunter Pack

If the PCs randomly encounter this pack and defeat them, then Bog Obelisk is not able to call upon the pack to its defense. They are a major component of the bog's corruption.

These five swamp dogs are eager to eat the PCs and fight to the death. They attack the weakest party member first, which to them is someone in cloth or no armor, then light armor, then medium and finally heavy. Despite their small size, they are vicious and thoroughly evil. They fight to the death.

Mangy, diseased, glowing with a disgusting green and red aura, these dogs seem to move with fell purpose and coordination out of proportion to their disheveled appearance.

Their low growls and salivating stares leave no doubt they want you as their next intended meal.

Five Swamp Dogs

Small monstrosity, chaotic evil
AC 12 — **HP** 39 — **Speed** 40 ft.

Statistics

STR	DEX	CON	INT	WIS	CHA
15 (+2),	14 (+2)	14 (+2)	3 (-4)	13 (+1)	6 (-2)

Damage Immunity necrotic, disease
Damage Resistance poison
Damage Vulnerability radiant
Conditional Immunities poisoned
Skills Perception +5, Stealth +4
Senses darkvision 120 ft., passive Perception 15
Languages —
Challenge 1 (200 XP) each

Actions

Multiattack. The dog makes two bite attacks.

Bite. *Melee Weapon Attack:* +4 to hit, reach 5 ft., two targets or one target.
Hit: 5 (1d6+2) piercing damage. If the target is a creature, it must succeed on a DC 12 Constitution Saving Throw against disease or become poisoned until the disease is cured.

Every 24 hours that elapse, the creature must repeat the Saving Throw, reducing its hit point maximum by 5 (1d10) on a failure. This reduction lasts until the disease is cured. The creature dies if the disease reduces its hit point maximum to 0.

Once a person is bitten by a swamp dog and has been diseased and successfully cured, then 24 hours later that person is immune to the disease from a swamp dog's bite.

E4.10 CORRUPT VAPOR

The Bog Obelisk is out of control, sucking energy from the dam, combining it with the ever-pervasive demon taint and spewing out monstrosities almost daily. And if the Plateau Obelisk is still intact, then that edifice calls upon the monsters the Bog Obelisk manufactures to attack the Crossroads Village below.

This mist is one such monstrosity. The corrupted vapor is technically a demonic presence and cannot penetrate *protection from evil* unless it is attacked first.

If the PCs have not acquired magical weapons, or cannot resort to fire, thunder, or radiant energy attacks, this can be an encounter that punches above its rating. The corrupt vapor peruses victims relentlessly and fights to the death.

> Out of the fog, greenish-red pulsating vapor streaks
> through the air. It morphs into the form of a cloaked
> figure made of swirly vapor, shadowy claws extended to
> suck the life force from you. While it doesn't have a face,
> you somehow intuit it seems happy and content that it
> has found a victim.

Corrupted Vapor

Medium monstrosity, chaotic evil
Armor Class 13 — **Hit Points** 45 — **Speed** 0 ft., fly 30 ft. (hover)

Statistics

STR	DEX	CON	INT	WIS	CHA
6 (-2),	16 (+3)	16 (+3	6 (-2)	12 (+1)	7 (-2)

Saving Throws Wis +3
Damage Immunities poison, necrotic
Damage Resistances acid, cold, lightning; bludgeoning, piercing, and slashing from nonmagical attacks
Damage Vulnerabilities fire, radiant, thunder
Condition Immunities charmed, exhaustion, grappled, paralyzed, petrified, poisoned, prone, restrained
Senses darkvision 60 ft., passive Perception 11
Languages —
Challenge 3 (700 XP)

Abilities

Life Attraction. The corrupted vapor can sense living creatures within a radius of 60 feet.

Misty Form. The corrupted vapor can occupy another creature's space and vice versa. In addition, if air can pass through a space, the corrupted vapor can pass through it without squeezing. Water is difficult terrain for the corrupted vapor. The corrupted vapor can't manipulate objects in any way that requires hands; it can apply simple force only.

Actions

Blood Drain. One creature in the corrupted vapor 's space must make a DC 13 Constitution Saving Throw (demons, undead and constructs automatically succeed). On a failed save, the target takes 10 (2d6 + 3) necrotic damage, its hit point maximum is reduced by an amount equal to the necrotic damage taken, and the corrupted vapor regains hit points equal to that amount. This reduction to the target's hit point maximum lasts until the target finishes a long rest. It dies if this effect reduces its hit point maximum to 0.

E4.11 THREE DEMONIC WOLVES

These are wolves from outside of the barony, having heard the call of the Bog Obelisk. Made of heartier stuff than a mere dog, they were possessed by demonic spirits called from the Old Battlefield and attached to the wolves (by the Bog Obelisk) while they were sleeping.

Now, they roam the bog, specifically looking for people, tasty good people, specifically. They attack paladins first, followed by clerics and then anyone else with a good aura. They are cunning and thoroughly evil. Once they have Advantage due to pack tactics, they *smite good* at the earliest opportunity.

> These wolves move silently with a glowing red gleam in
> their eyes. They seem to blend into their surroundings,
> moving fast with fell purpose.

Intro

Lost at the Beaux Seins

Moortide Rising

The Altar & the Anvil

Castle Wailmoor

Appendix

Three Demonic Wolves

Medium demon, Chaotic Evil
Armor Class 14 (natural armor) | **Hit Points** 12 — **Speed** 50 ft.

Statistics

STR	DEX	CON	INT	WIS	CHA
12 (+1)	15 (+2)	12 (+1)	6 (-2)	12 (+1)	6 (-2)

Skills Perception +3, Stealth +4
Damage Resistances necrotic, cold
Damage Vulnerabilities radiant, fire
Senses passive Perception 13
Languages abyssal (can speak)
Challenge 1 (200 XP) each

Abilities

Keen Hearing and Smell. The demonic wolf has Advantage on Wisdom (Perception) checks that rely on hearing or smell.

Pack Tactics. The demonic wolf has Advantage on attack rolls against a creature if at least one of the wolf's allies is within 5 feet of the creature and the ally isn't incapacitated.

Champion of Evil: Once a day, the demonic wolf can *smite good.*

Actions

Bite. *Melee Weapon Attack:* +4 to hit, reach 5 ft., one target. *Hit:* 7 (2d4+2) piercing damage. If the target is a creature, it must succeed on a DC 11 Strength Saving Throw or be knocked prone.

Smite Good. (1/day) *Melee Weapon Attack:* +4 to hit, reach 5 ft., one target. Hit: 2d8 points of necrotic damage and 2d4+2 piercing damage.

E4.12 Boo the Owl

Boo the Owl is a recent arrival to the Barony of Wailmoor, arriving from the far north. He is an owl that is a druid, not a druid in owl form.

History

Boo is a magically enhanced owl given intelligence and the ability to reason by a powerful archmage who was attempting to ally herself with a reclusive druid grove to harvest some rare and elusive flowers.

Such are the goals of esoteric hermit wizards.

Her plan worked, and over the years the druids and the archmage became friends (and lovers).

Sadly, both the wizard and druids are dead, and Boo finds himself as a magical owl that doesn't age. He's been flying aimlessly for the last few decades but has arrived at the Barony, specifically The Bog. He is studying the Bog Obelisk and its corruption, in an academic way.

Current Boo

Boo doesn't necessarily seek out or speak to the PCs on his own accord unless the DM wishes—he's cautious. However, if encountered, he will be sitting on a tree branch studying the PCs. If they say hello, he'll say hello back. He's a very large owl, medium sized.

Boo is friendly but a recluse and not a combatant; at the first hint of danger, he will fly away. His attitude is Indifferent. If moved to Friendly, he will answer questions about what he's seen; but not about himself:

- He recently arrived in the Barony and was attracted to the glow of the Bog Obelisk while flying at night.

- He knows the Obelisk is somehow linked to the Ethereal Plane and thinks it is a ward stone but is somehow corrupted, possibly from all the lingering demons in the barony.

- He can give directions to the Bog Obelisk and reveal it is guarded by a roaming group of "swamp dogs."

- He will describe all the monsters that are in the Bog but only in a general sense (what the look like, if they roam or where they are). He has no experience in combat or monster hunting. He describes the corrupted psychic leech storm as "an affront against nature and the gods."

- Boo will trade healing for bacon or sausage.

- Boo relates that many things glow at night and for PCs to find a high vantage point on a clear night to see these glow themselves.

- He will emphatically suggest that whatever the Obelisks were, they are now "fonts of evil" and should be destroyed as soon as possible.

- All Boo will say about himself (for now) is that he is a druid of modest power, likes cooked pork products, and has recently arrived in the Barony.

Once the PCs destroy the Bog Obelisk, Boo the Owl leaves and hangs out near Olaf's Dam.

Chatty PCs

If the PCs simply tell everything they have encountered thus far including their *Lost Memories*, Boo the Owl will be very empathic in his council—the PCs are not to tell *anyone* about their *Lost Memories* without careful thought and attention. "Sounds like a good way to get burned at the stake in far-flung Imperial Providences. Yanno, like *this* area."

Boo promises to help. And he will, in *CC2-Beneath a Dreary Wave,* if still around.

Boo as a DM Device

If the DM desires, floundering PCs who need a little more hand-holding can get it from Boo. Simply have Boo contact the PCs, cautiously, and state that he sees the PCs as "the only good things in this gods-forsaken abandoned land" and give out hints as a druid needing help cleansing a primal land. He'll immediately tell the PCs to destroy the three Obelisks and give directions to them if necessary. He's seen the green glow from the well and guessed about the Crypt Obelisk but will readily admit to the PCs the Temple of Dvalin is going to be a tough nut to crack.

Boo the Owl

Male Giant Owl Druid 5 — Medium beast, neutral
Armor Class 12 — **Hit Points** 44 — **Speed** 5 ft., fly 60 ft.

Statistics

STR	DEX	CON	INT	WIS	CHA
13 (+1)	15 (+2)	12 (+1)	10 (+0)	16 (+3)	10 (+0)

Saving Throws Int +2, Wis +5
Skills Arcana +2, Nature +2, Perception +7, Stealth +4
Senses darkvision 120 ft., passive Perception 17
Languages Druidic, Giant Owl, Common, Elvish, Sylvan
Challenge 4 (1,100 XP)

Spells

Spell Save DC 15 — Spell Attack +5
3rd— (2 slots) *call lightning, meld into stone, plant growth, speak with plants*
2nd— (3 slots) *barkskin, gust of wind, hold person, spider climb*
1st— (4 slots) *animal friendship, cure wounds, healing word, speak with animals*
Cantrips— *druidcraft, guidance, mending, shillelagh*

Abilities

Boon of Immortality. Boo stopped aging and became immune to any effect that would cause him to age. He cannot die from old age.

Flyby. Boo doesn't provoke opportunity attacks when it flies out of an enemy's reach.

Keen Hearing and Sight. Boo has Advantage on Wisdom (Perception) checks that rely on hearing or sight.

Wild Shape (2/short rest). Magically assume beast shape seen previously

Natural Recovery (1/long rest). Recover up to 2 spell slots (either one 2nd Level spell slot or two 1st level spell slots)

Actions

Talons. *Melee Weapon Attack:* +3 to hit, reach 5 ft., one target. *Hit:* 8 (2d6+1) slashing damage.

E4,13-16 CREEPY SOUNDS

Until the PCs destroy the Bog Obelisk, they will hear odd sounds outside of what is natural for a bog—moaning, warbling, reverberating hissing, slurping plunks in water, abnormally loud snapping branches, creepy faint howling, etc.

E4,13-16 THE BOG OBELISK

This encounter is like the Obelisk near the Crossroads Village. Other than the location, the Obelisks are physically identical. They operate differently, however.
The primary defense of this Obelisk is its locations—

PCs had to slog through a swampy bog to get here. Its immediate defense is calling the Swamp Dog Hunter Pack to its aid. If the PCs have encountered and defeated the swamp dog pack, the Bog Obelisk is defenseless. It can, however, create new swamp dogs once a week.

THE BOG OBELISK AT A GLANCE

The Bog Obelisk sits in the middle of 80ft of bubbling, putrid muck arranged in a perfect circle. The air smells of sulfur. A contrast to the creepy sounds of The Bog thus far, it is silent here. Like the Obelisk near the Crossroads Village, it is 3 feet thick, 4 feet high somewhat circular granite-looking slab with profane runes pulsating with a sickly, snot-colored glow.

Corrupted Bog Obelisk

Demonic Ward Stone
Armor Class 17 (natural armor) — **Hit Points** 220 — **Speed** 0 ft.

Statistics

STR	DEX	CON	INT	WIS	CHA
-	-	20 (+5)	-	-	-

Damage Immunities poison, disease, necrotic
Damage Resistance all except bludgeoning, radiant, force
Damage Vulnerabilities bludgeoning, radiant, force
Condition Immunities blinded, charmed, deafened, exhaustion, frightened, paralyzed, petrified, poisoned
Senses -
Languages —
Challenge Rating 4 (3,900)

Abilities

Difficult Terrain. In an 80ft radius around the bog obelisk, the terrain is muck and mud and is difficult to traverse.

Call Swamp Dog Hunter Pack. If approached within 80ft. the bog obelisk summons the swamp dog hunter pack, which attacks the next round. The swamp dog hunter pack is not affected by the difficult terrain around the bog obelisk

Create Swamp Dog Hunter Pack. (1/week). Until the bog obelisk is destroyed, it re-creates the swamp dog hunter pack by replacing falling pack members with new additions (up to 5 swamp dogs).

Intro

Lost at the Beaux Seins

Moortide Rising

The Altar & the Anvil

Castle Wailmoor

Appendix

Not Destroying the Bog Obelisk

If the PCs don't destroy the Bog Obelisk, it simply continues to keep the Bog supplied with corrupted wolves, swamp dogs, and giant leeches and such. Use this modified encounter table every two hours:

1D20	ENCOUNTER	AVG. CR
1	2 Wailmoor Demon Crocs	4
2	Swarm of Centipedes	1/2
3	4 Giant Leeches	1
4	4 Giant Leeches in Trees	1
5	Corrupted Psychic Leech Swarm	5
6	Swamp Dog Hunter Pack (5)	5
7	Corrupted Vapor	5
8	Boo the Owl	5
9-12	Creepy Sounds	-
13-20	No Encounter	-

If the PCs defeat one of these encounters, they are "No Encounters" until a week passes, and then the Bog Obelisk refreshes its evil list of corrupted creatures.

E5 - Hardred Hills

The Hardred Hills is an optional area for PCs to explore on the moor. They are not tied to plot elements that PCs will need to resolve to progress on the campaign—in the first module.

However, they offer some flavorful encounters as well as important resources for players fond of world-building and PCs who would want to settle on the moor and participate in its rebirth.

While adventuring through the Hills, use the suggested encounter table below for every 6 hours the PCs will spend there.

D10	ENCOUNTER	AVG. CR
1	Swarm of Bats	1/4
2	1d2 Phase Spiders	3
3	1d4 Assassin Vines	5
4	2d12 Wailmoor Stirges	5
5	1d2 Otyugh	5
6	1 Shambling Mound	5
7	1d2 Trolls	5
8	1d4 Giant Spiders	2
9	1d4 Dire Wolves	2
10	1 Black Pudding	4

Tombs

E CAIRNS

⊗ Copper Mine

HARDRED HILLS

Brief History of the Hardred Hills

These hills used to belong to the Duchy of Hardred, owned by the Hardred family. During a period of Hardred expansion, the then Duke over-extended his family and sold these lands to an early Baron of Wailmoor who had (back then) a surprising amount of coin. The Baron and the Duke became friends, so the Baron renamed the hills "Hardred Hills" as a tribute to the Duke.

The hills were always supposed to be developed, but for reasons lost in history, early Barony nobility started to bury their dead in Cairns along the hill. Development of the lands stopped saved from an abortive copper mine.

After the Demon War, the hills remain a buffer between the Barony and the Duchy. There is also 5-miles no-mans-land south of the hills, which is off-limits by Duchy law.

Hardred Hills Resources

The Hardred Hills are rich in mineral resources. There are copper, silver, and lead in and around the hills, some of it concentrated around the tombs.

There are also considerable granite and gravel deposits, some of which were quarried at various times in the Barony's history.

Unknown but suspected every now and then, are the gemstone deposits usually associated with some granite-rich areas. The hills are rich with the associated minerals to granite, which includes beryl, chrysoberyl, corundum, diamond, garnet, feldspar, peridot, quartz, spinel, topaz, tourmaline, and zircon.

To give up these gem secrets requires extensive mining, engineering and exploration techniques that were not available to the early Barony and Duchy peoples. An Imperial University graduate holding various degrees, with considerable resources and personnel, can mine the extensive deposit in and beneath the granite.

E5.1 The Cairns

The early Wailmoor barons had their graves set on these rocky hills, their cairns facing north and observing the lands they once ruled and loved.

There is no plot hook here or undead ghosts within the Cairns. It is mostly a place of political importance: with the presence of old Wailmoor nobility in the southern parts of the moor, it sets a clear border with the Duchy of Hardred to the south. If players take on rebuilding the Barony as a possible follow-up to the conclusion of this module, they will likely have to establish the former borders of the barony and provide historical proof of its location. The Cairns of the old Wailmoor Barons provide that.

Dungeon Mastering Note

If you want to add more content to the module and the moor open-world, you could easily locate a small dungeon or a tomb to explore at this location. Rewards should include equipment bearing the arms of the Wailmoor, such as a shield or an engraved breastplate, and wondrous magical items created under the tutelage of Chrystelle the Enchanter. These items will come a long way to establish legitimacy and credibility for players driving a Wailmoor revival.

The Copper Mine

This Copper Mine contains an oversized black pudding at Challenge Level 8.

The old copper mine is abandoned, and its equipment rusted beyond use. The veins are still rich, and plenty of ore is yet to be mined. The entrance of the mine opens on the side of a tall hill and is 'guarded' by a dangerous black pudding lurking by the entrance and feeding from hares and deer who look for shelter in the mines.

If players defeat the black pudding, they will gain access to the whole mine complex. A PC with training in mining or geology will understand there is a lot of money to be made from this mine. Should workers and miners be brought back to the Wailmoor, this mine would yield profits in the hundreds of gold Imperials per week.

Intro

Lost at the Beaux Seins

Moortide Rising

The Altar & the Anvil

Castle Wailmoor

Appendix

Giant Black Pudding

Huge ooze, unaligned

Armor Class 9 — **Hit Points** 117 — **Speed** 20 ft., climb 20 ft.

Statistics

STR	DEX	CON	INT	WIS	CHA
16 (+3)	5 (-3)	16 (+3)	1 (-5)	6 (-2)	1 (-5)

Damage Immunities acid, cold, lightning, slashing
Damage Vulnerabilities fire
Condition Immunities blinded, charmed, deafened, exhaustion, frightened, prone
Senses blindsight 60 ft. (blind beyond this radius), passive Perception 8
Languages —
Challenge 8 (3,900 XP)

Abilities

Amorphous. The pudding can move through a space as narrow as 1 inch wide without squeezing.

Corrosive Form. A creature that touches the pudding or hits it with a melee attack while within 5 feet of it takes 4 (1d8) acid damage. Any nonmagical weapon made of metal or wood that hits the pudding corrodes. After dealing damage, the weapon takes a permanent and cumulative −1 penalty to damage rolls. If its penalty drops to −5, the weapon is destroyed. Nonmagical ammunition made of metal or wood that hits the pudding is destroyed after dealing damage. The pudding can eat through 2-inch-thick, nonmagical wood or metal in 1 round.

Spider Climb. The pudding can climb difficult surfaces, including upside down on ceilings, without needing to make an ability check.

Actions

Pseudopod. Melee Weapon Attack: +6 to hit, reach 10 ft., one target.
Hit: 6 (1d6+3) bludgeoning plus 18 (4d8) acid damage. In addition, nonmagical armor worn by the target is partly dissolved and takes a permanent and cumulative −1 penalty to the AC it offers. The armor is destroyed if the penalty reduces its AC to 10.

Reactions

Split. When a pudding that is Medium or larger is subjected to lightning or slashing damage, it splits into two new puddings if it has at least 10 hit points. Each new pudding has hit points equal to half the original pudding's, rounded down. New puddings are one size smaller than the original pudding.

E6 - The Old Battlefield

A *Lost Memory* can reveal The Battlefield before the PCs visit it.

A Desolated Land

The area on the moor south of the castle is where most of the "traditional" combat happened between the defenders of the Wailmoor and the demonic army led by Barbu, about 150-years ago. For days, blood was spilled on the battlefield; fiery spells were cast, scorching the land and hundreds of demons *gated* in and out of the Abyss to support the siege of the Wailmoor. Where other places in the barony are tainted by that nefarious demonic presence, the battlefield remains a place where evil reeks and spouts from the pores of the earth.

When approaching the Old Battlefield for the first time, PCs can practically feel the despair and terror from imagining the strength of how demons clashed their malice against the defenders of the moor.

The battlefield is approximately 3 miles long and 1 mile wide and very flat. It is covered with a thick, almost mud-like layer of ashes that mixed with blood and filth, and a strong odor of musk still exhales from the ground, 150-years later.

All movement on the battlefield is considered difficult terrain. It is easy, due to the flat terrain, to spot places of interest and creatures on the battlefield from a respectable distance. No one should be taken by surprise, whether it is the PCs or their enemies unless otherwise noted.

For encounters on the battlefield, use the suggested table below. Roll 2d10 every hour spent on the battlefield.

2D10	ENCOUNTER	AVG. CR
2	Aggressive Vermin	1
3-6	Sick Fauna (deer, rabbit, turkey, etc.)	0
7	1 Troll	5
8	1 Ettin	4
9	1d6 Dretches	1
10	2d6 Skeletons	2
11	1d2 Trolls	4
12	1d4 Giant Spiders	2
13	1d4 Dire Wolves	2
14	1d4 Satyrs	1
15	Random PC sinks into the muck to the waist. Roll again. Previous stuck PCs do not become more stuck (but another roll is made).	-
16-20	No encounter	N/A

A flat, desolate field of turned up soil appears before you, scorched earth, burnt bones, and brokenness—broken and petrified trees—broken ground, broken shields, and broken rock. The ground seems to weep muck as if bleeding, and the place smells like blood, terror, and magic.

Cleansing the Battlefield

Removing the two possessed demons around the seat of Barbu, either by killing their hosts or capturing them and moving them away from the desolate battlefield, will stop its corruption, but three Obelisks (one at the entrance, one in the bog, and the other under the temple) must be destroyed to restore this landscape.

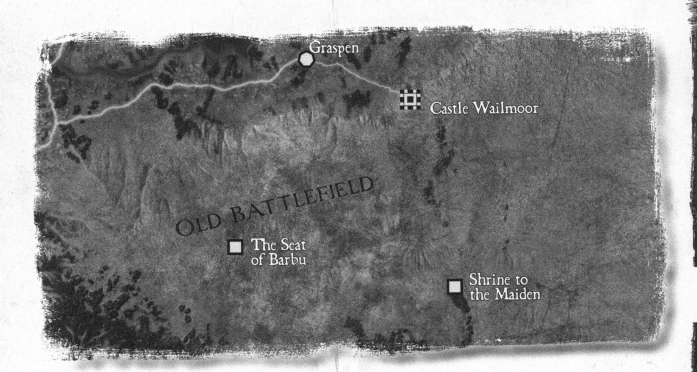

Intro

Lost
at the
Beaux
Seins

**Moortide
Rising**

The Altar
& the
Anvil

Castle
Wailmoor

Appendix

Once the PCs destroy the Obelisks, the area will naturally restore itself over a period of 20 years. Consequently, PCs can simply burn the field in a great wildfire to considerably shorten that time to a few growing seasons—DC 15 Intelligence (Nature) Check to realize fire the best cleansing method. The area will burn like wildfire, as if thankful to be clean of the tainted flora and fauna.

E6.1 THE SEAT OF BARBU

This location triggers a <u>*Lost Memory* at the sight of the Seat of Barbu</u> (if not previously triggered).

This can difficult encounter and if PCs are not careful, could result in PC death or deaths. PCs using Stealth could get the upper hand in this encounter, but even then, success is not certain.

This is the seat where the Demon Barbu conducted his troops and the assault on the Wailmoor. It can be easily seen on a clear night from either of the tors as it glows.

In the middle of the battlefield plain, the seat of command of a demon lord stands, a grotesque throne made of the bones and pieces of armor collected from human victims of the ruthless battle. The throne is surrounded by rusted armors and broken weapons, a sinister testimony of the courageous men who gave their lives to defeat the enemy.

The Seat of Barbu is 18 feet tall, with steps made bones, and can be seen from several miles away in the daytime.

ATTACK OF THE DEMON POSSESSED WARRIORS

Two terrible possessed warriors patrol around the throne. If the PCs are not moving Stealthy and are spotted by the possessed first, those PCs are in for a tough time. The possessed rejoice at the sight of the PCs and will hide among the debris of the siege weapons to try to ambush them. These two possessed are shamed by their defeat and their only objective here is the sheer entertainment of dismembering the PCs and sending their souls to the afterlife.

Protection from evil spells will prevent the warriors from physically attacking the recipient of the ward, but not from the warriors using their effective longbows at the offending PC.

Two human men with grim visages, dressed in worn scale mail and armed with sharp spears, move towards you, seemingly immune to the broken terrain and muck that dogs your every step in this forlorn battlefield.

"More..."

"Souls..."

"For..."

"Orcus," they say, each saying every-other- word as they press the attack.

Martin and Layman aren't immune to the difficult terrain—they just move at a base speed of 40ft.

Martin and Layman the Possessed

Demon Possessed Warrior — Medium demon, chaotic evil
Amor Class 19 (scale mail, shield) — **Hit Points** 90 — **Speed** 40 ft.

Statistics

STR	DEX	CON	INT	WIS	CHA
19 (+4)	16 (+3)	16 (+3)	11 (+0)	12 (+1)	3 (+1)

Saving Throws Str +6, Con +5, Wis +3
Skills Athletics +6, Perception +5, Stealth +5 (Disadvantage from armor worn), Survival +3
Damage Resistances necrotic, cold, fire, lightning, bludgeoning, piercing, and slashing from nonmagical weapons
Damager Vulnerabilities radiant
Damage Immunities poison, disease
Condition Immunities poisoned
Senses darkvision 120 ft., passive Perception 15
Languages Abyssal, common
Challenge 4 (1,100 XP) each

Abilities

Innate Spellcasting. The possessed spellcasting ability is Wisdom (spell save DC 11). It can innately cast the following spells, requiring no material components:
At will: *darkness, dispel magic, fear, heat metal, levitate*

Action Surge. (1/short rest). Can take an extra action on his turn.

Second Wind (1/short rest). Bonus action to heal 1d10+1 hit points.

Actions

Multiattack. The possessed makes two melee attacks.

Spear. Melee or Ranged Weapon Attack: +6 to hit, reach 5 ft. or range 20 ft./60 ft., one target.
Hit: 7 (1d6+4) piercing damage or 8 (1d8+4) piercing damage if used with two hands to make a melee attack.

Longbow. Ranged Weapon Attack: +5 to hit, range 150 ft./600 ft., one target.
Hit: 7 (1d8+3) piercing damage.

Equipment

Scale mail, shield, spear, longbow, 20 arrows, quiver.

Additional Details

On the Possessed Demons can possess any creature with a soul (any playable race). Requiring touch, demons possess people by torture, trickery, coercion, or seduction by battering a person's will until they surrender.

Possessed are thoroughly evil, able to infiltrate societies and conduct espionage and sabotage. They will discard the host for a new one if convenient and have all the hit dice and classes of the person possessed.

To drive out the demon, the possessed must be incapacitated and conscious (non-restrained possessed are exceedingly dangerous) and perform an exorcism.

Exorcism is a simple matter but requires resources and time, all while preventing the possessed from escaping or killing its captors. To drive out a demon, a cleric or other divine agent casts *protection from evil* on the host. The host is then able to make a Wisdom save against the possession, at DC 20. If presented with a silver holy symbol of a good deity, the host receives a +1. *Hollowed* ground is another +1 (in addition to automatically granting a Saving Throw regardless, and if the divine agent sprinkles holy water on the host).

Failure to save requires another cast of the *protection from evil* spell (and more holy water if available). Suffice it to say, the demon does not want to be exorcized and will try everything it can to prevent it with trickery, coercion, seduction, attempted escape and certainly use of its special abilities, making a captured possessed who has not used its special abilities that day exceedingly dangerous.

If exorcized, a demon is destroyed, its essence sent to the Abyss and unable to leave there for 99 years. For this reason, many higher-order demons will not engage in possession. Lower-order demons avoid possession because they lack the nuance to keep their victim alive during the possession process. Succubus and other intelligent demons will engage in possession if they are *gated* to the Welt. They will search out the most powerful host to possess, or, at least, one that will cause the most heartache and destruction.

A person exorcized of his or her demon will have all their levels, except the first, flipped to negative levels which must be *restored* through divine spells. 1 HD or 1 Level PCs or NPCs do not survive the process and die.

ABOUT THE THRONE

If players use *detect magic* around the throne, they will detect a few things. First, the whole area is tainted with a magical curse that seems to radiate from the throne. It is DC 15 Strength (Athletic) Check to push the throne down and dismantle it. Once they've done that, PCs will notice that the magical curse, or at least their perception of it, seems to fade. It will take 2 weeks for it to disappear completely. If PCs manage to remove that curse, award them a 400 XP story bonus award.

Another thing PCs will find using *detect magic* is the broken armor from the *Lost Memory* they might have experienced there. The plate armor lies down in the mud in front of the throne. It has a large hole in the middle of the chest piece, where the heart should be, and all the leather straps tying the armor together have been destroyed by 150-years in this harmful environment. As they might collect the armor (the PC who experienced the *Lost Memory* recognizes the armor), it is currently not usable by them but can be brought to an armorsmith to get it fixed. Once cleaned and repaired, the armor is magnificent with engraved arms of the barony on its chest and silver-inlaid motifs on its shoulder pieces and basinet. It's *+1 plate armor* and with further enchantment, can hold more powerful enchantments.

ABOUT MARTIN AND LAYMAN

The warriors Martin and Layman were formattable combatants during the war 150-years ago but were seduced by succubi and possessed.

As previously possessed go, Martin and Layman are "lucky." They are mountain warriors, hailing from a dwarven town to the northwest. Having traveled to the Barony by traveling the Viscounty, they encountered refugees.

Two of the refugees were possessed succubi, posing as sisters. They begged for help in finding their "little brother," and then seduced and possessed the two men on the way back to the Wailmoor.

It was shortly afterward Barbu was slain. Being made heartier stock than most other possessed, they survived the Demon War, haunting the Old Battlefield while the rest of the survivors avoided it.

When encountering the warriors, allow the PCs to determine their true natures:

- DC 15 Intelligence (Religion): not only are these warriors evil, but they are also possessed by demons.

- DC 15 Wisdom (Perception), after the possessed use one of their spell-like abilities: These warriors are using supernatural abilities. Whatever they are, they are not merely human.

- DC 15 Intelligence (History): the way these two warriors are using spell-like abilities sounds just like battle accounts about fighting demon-possessed people.

Knowledge of possession is esoteric, but a cleric or a paladin would intrinsically know about exorcism. If Martin and Layman are captured, they can be exorcised. Before possession, they were Level 5 fighters.

If the PCs take the two to the village, Dame Walshan will have them chained in the basement and will eventually perform an exorcism on both. However, she will need the PCs to help because of these demons *dispel magic* and *fear* at will—the process will need more than one spell caster.

If brought to the druids, the druids will immediately take them to Dame Walshan.

It is possible for the PCs to perform the exorcism themselves. Time-consuming and dangerous, doing

so is empathic to the plight of the two men and heroic. Reward the PCs with 1000 XP each.

AN EXORCISED MARTIN AND LAYMAN

What happens depends on the PCs actions:

- If delivered to the druids first, Jeremiah takes responsibility for their rehabilitation. Over the course of a month, their former levels are converted to Ranger levels.

- The warriors are from the same dwarven enclave as Vergali the dwarf, one of the guards at the inn. If the PCs recognize this through their history and accent (assuming they dealt with Vergali previously) and then introduces a restored Martin and Layman to the dwarf, over the course of a month, their levels are converted back to Fighter.

- If delivered to the Dame, she specifically seeks out a knowledgeable specialist on demon possession. A cleric of Platine arrives and works with the men. Paladin levels replace their warrior levels, and the two are trained to become righteous demon hunters.

- If the PCs take responsibility for the two after personally exorcizing them, it is obvious they need time to heal their body and minds. Their levels need magical restoration, and afterward, they treat the PCs as their lords, becoming fiercely loyal. It is at this point they can be molded into something more—training them in any class makes them a 1st Level Fighter and 4 Levels in whatever the class the PCs train them in. Award the responsible PCs an additional 1,000 XP.

- If exorcized and left to their own devices, the men have a tough time of it, but eventually encounter Vergali, who takes them under his wing per above.

Possessed will dog PCs until the end of the Campaign. Indeed, the PCs will become primary targets for possession and once possessed, their PC is removed from play and converted to an enemy NPC until exorcized.

E6.2 SHRINE TO THE MAIDEN

At the Shrine of the Maiden, PCs can have the properties of their weapons changed and obtained odd effects from the shrine itself.

The shrine to the Maiden is a construction on the eastern edge of the battlefield that is quite visible from afar as well, and it too glows with a righteous, red luminosity at night. Players who climbed any of the two tors or the path up to Castle Wailmoor should be

Intro

Lost at the Beaux Seins

Moortide Rising

The Altar & the Anvil

Castle Wailmoor

Appendix

able to spot it easily. The Shrine is composed of a 10ft. tall statue of the Maiden (see appendix describing the Maiden in more details) and a small altar in front of it.

Men of the Wailmoor have built an imposing altar to the Maiden, the goddess of war. She is represented wearing a curve-hugging full suit of plate armor with no helm. Her feminine visage, however, has the gaze of a ruthless warrior determined to enter battle at any moment. Her arms are open and point at a small altar in front of her. The base of the statue shows faded marks of vandalism, but it seems nothing was able to damage the statue itself.

The statue is magical and radiates with great and unstoppable divine energy. If PCs pay homage to the goddess or salute the altar, they will be able to get its benefits:

- A non-magical weapon placed on the altar is temporarily made a magical weapon with a +1 bonus. That effect lasts for 1d4 days until renewed at the shrine.

- Any permanently magical weapon placed on the altar temporarily changes is damage type to radiant. That effect lasts for 1d4 days until renewed at the shrine.

- If the PC has a paladin or fighter level, prays at the altar, for the next 24-hours they receive a +1 divine bonus on Attack rolls.

- If the PC is a cleric of the Maiden and prays at the altar, for the next 24-hours they are immune to all combat maneuvers—he or she cannot be grappled, tripped, bull rushed, overrun, etc. Such attempts automatically fail.

Any number of weapons can be placed on the altar at once, but only one weapon per person will receive a bonus. If a person puts multiple weapons on the altar, assign the bonus randomly.

OPTIONAL: OTHER SHRINE PROPERTIES

Optionally, *sleeping* on the altar has interesting results. The PC has a torrid dream of an encounter with a young human barbarian shield maiden. She is playful, enthusiastic, creative, and flexible. In the dream, there is no talking. The encounter is very personal.

- Any PC who sleeps on the altar and does not have fighter, ranger or paladin levels receives a divine kick in the butt (without the pleasant dream). Sometime in the evening they have launched away from the altar and take 3d6 falling damage, no Saving Throw.

- During the night, the PC is immune to the Wailmoor's effect of randomly transporting outdoor sleeping PCs to the Graveyard during the night and for the next night as well. Furthermore, they are *blessed* as the spell for 1d4 hours duration.

Only one PC can sleep on the altar per night, and the dream is repeatable. The altar has no indication of what its magical properties are, other than the statue pointing towards the altar. PCs wanting to use Insight or Religion Checks to further delve into the shrine without experimenting simply receive an understanding that the Maiden is chaotic. A cleric or paladin of the Maiden can tell the PC not to bother. They are all different, and sometimes the magical properties of her shrines change over time.

SHRINES AND TEMPLES TO THE MAIDEN

The Maiden is a chaotic, but good, deity and no temple or shrine are alike. PCs can learn more about this shrine through experimentation and divination (but note that divinations about the PCs *don't* work).

Warriors (in the mindset sense) come to realize that the Maiden is a rebel against law foremost and a foe of an evil second. More of a deity to war than battle, her clerics know that there are many ways to win a war, stabbing lots of people until they die from is simply one way. The Imperial Scholar Seagrin Dominus described the Maiden as "the most deceptive and passive-aggressive bitch in all of eternity, but then again you will find no finer partner to watch your back on the battlefield."

The Maiden is an ally of the PCs as they are built to wage war and war is her purview. Her engagement thus far is limited because in her mind the PCs already have enough power that they don't understand and that is dangerous. When a martial warrior PC sleeps on the altar, she can feel the PCs latent power, and it both entices her and frightens her. Either way, the PCs are exciting, and the Maiden is not too sure she was the seducer or the seduce-e.

The map shows locations including Temple of Dvalin, THE LAKE, Graspen, and Castle Wailmoor.

Intro

Lost at the Beaux Seins

Moortide Rising

The Altar & the Anvil

Castle Wailmoor

Appendix

E7 - THE DEAD TOWN OF GRASPEN

Graspen contains demons, ruins, a *Lost Memory* and two forges, one of which is highly unusual.

THE RUINS OF GRASPEN

The small town—or large village depending on whom you talked to 150-years ago—of Graspen used to be the heart of the barony. It is located on the shores of the lake, and many rotten and charred wooden piers connect the lake to the village with half-sunken canoes and fishing boats hanging at the docks.

Graspen lays at the feet of the tall hill on top of which Castle Wailmoor rises. From the town, it is almost impossible to ignore the squat, but towering fortress and its strange flickering in and out of the Ethereal Plane (see location Castle Wailmoor). Most of the homes in the village still have sturdy walls, but their previously sturdy roofs have either slumped or collapsed in age and disrepair or are gone entirely for the poor homes that had thatched roofs. Vegetation has grown thick through the paved streets of this little town. All villagers left Graspen a long time ago, and the village is totally unpopulated—with people, that is.

To add to the sadness of the place, the few demons that decided to stay behind when Barbu fell are haunting the village, trying to find ways to penetrate Castle Wailmoor by planning to vigorously interrogate anyone who is approaching the castle.

When PCs visit and explore the ruins, DMs should describe the place as destroyed and barren now, but also how it probably once looked a comfortable, healthy, and wealthy town with a lot of shops and large homes, without a defensive wall protecting it.

The ruined town below the castle appears completely abandoned. Obviously, several battles happened here. Based on the overgrown cobblestone streets and the occasional stone building, this town at one time was wealthy.

From your current vantage point, nothing can be heard, except the faint sound of running water.

E7.1 MAIN SQUARE FOUNTAIN

This area contains two demons. Viewing the Dvalin rune on the fountain could trigger a lost memory, M7 - Blessing of Dvalin.

There is a large paved square in the middle of town with a similar fountain than the one PCs might have seen in Harenvale (they were built by the same stone crafter, Rikard Hosman). The differences are this one doesn't spew a shaft of light skyward when the sun sets, it is still working, and the fountain bears the mark of Dvalin's rune.

This large main square has a beautiful, multi-layered granite fountain still spewing great gouts of water into the air, the pleasant roar of water a sharp contrast to the devastation around you. The fountain drains into a granite-constructed channel that runs downhill, north, towards The Lake.

There are two demons patrolling the square. They are noisy and grunting their malcontent and easy to spot before running into them by surprise. Because the demons are not trying to hide and the perpetual sound of rushing water, PCs get Advantage on Stealth while the demons get Disadvantage on Perception.

These two creatures are lounging by the functioning granite fountain. They are willowy and tall, with a doggie-face filled with sharp fangs and hands that end in even sharper claws.

Two Wailmoor Demons

Medium demon, chaotic evil
Armor Class 15 (natural armor) — **Hit Points** 60 — **Speed** 40 ft.

Statistics

STR	DEX	CON	INT	WIS	CHA
17 (+3)	15 (+2)	18 (+4)	8 (-1)	13 (+1)	8 (-1)

Saving Throws Dex +5, Wis +4
Damage Resistances cold, fire, lightning, necrotic, thunder
Damage Vulnerabilities radiant, force
Damage Immunities poison
Condition Immunities poisoned
Senses darkvision 120 ft., passive Perception 11
Languages Abyssal, telepathy 120 ft.
Challenge 3 (700 XP) each

Actions

Multiattack. The Wailmoor demon makes two attacks: one with its jaws and one with its talons.

Jaws. *Melee Weapon Attack:* +4 to hit, reach 5 ft., one target. *Hit:* 10 (2d6+3) piercing damage.

Talons. *Melee Weapon Attack:* +4 to hit, reach 5 ft., one target. *Hit:* 14 (2d10+3) slashing damage.

Sonic bark (1/day). The Wailmoor demon emits a loud bark. Each creature within 15 feet that isn't a demon must succeed on a DC 12 Constitution Saving Throw or be stunned until the end of the demon's next turn.

E7.2 The Town's Smith

This building contains tools, ingots, a hidden magic item, and a clue to the location of the Waterwheel Forge.

150-years ago Holman Bear was the blacksmith of Graspen. Most of his material in the forge is still there and in relatively good shape (some are rusty, and the leather on the bellows has gone bad). Most of the forge equipment is marked with the initials H.B.

It is obvious Bear was a metalsmith, rather than a weaponsmith or an armorer. Many of the tools are for delicate work.

There are crates against the wall that contain ore (copper, silver), 20 bronze ingots, 20 copper ingots and 100 pounds of coal. The forge is located right on the main square so if players were to search through the forge with regular means; they are likely to drag the attention of the two demons patrolling the square.

A DC 20 Intelligence (Investigation) Check allows players to find a full set of *horseshoes of speed*, hidden in a cache under the anvil, imperious to *detect magic* (due to the metal surrounding the cache) until the anvil is moved.

Odd Remodeling

In the smithy is an area that contains a contraption that, if a smith inspects it, would reveal a hammer-press but without anything to power the press. An Intelligence (Arcana) DC 17 Check reveals that hammer would be powered by magic, letting a smith concentrate in holding the hot metal at just the right angle or place while the contraption delivered consistent hammer blows. With the parts are a set of blueprints and another set of blueprints to a hydraulic press, which includes an illustration of the water channel going from the fountain, turning into a creek, and meeting a waterwheel. The creek continues past the waterwheel to The Lake.

E7.4 The Fish Market

This is an open market close from the main square with stalls and large stone tables where fishermen used to bring the catch of their day on the lake and prepare the fishes they would sell in Graspen.

There are other demons in the village: 4 Wailmoor Quasits. These quasits are obsessed with getting inside the Castle "to finish the job." They will use their shapechange ability and follow PCs who decide to climb up the road to the Castle. If the PCs are not able to get inside the castle, they will then ambush them on site, out of mounting frustration.

Four Wailmoor Quasits

Tiny demon, shapechanger, chaotic evil
Armor Class 13 — **Hit Points** 14 — **Speed** 40 ft.

Statistics

STR	DEX	CON	INT	WIS	CHA
5 (-3)	17 (+3)	10 (+0)	7 (-2)	10 (+0)	10 (+0)

Skills Stealth +5
Damage Resistances cold, fire, lightning, necrotic; bludgeoning, piercing, and slashing from nonmagical attacks
Damage Immunities poison
Damage Vulnerability radiant
Condition Immunities poisoned
Senses darkvision 120 ft., passive Perception 10
Languages Abyssal, common
Challenge 1 (200 XP) each

Ability

Shapechanger. The quasit can use its action to polymorph into a beast form that resembles a bat (speed 10 ft. fly 40 ft.), a centipede (40 ft., climb 40 ft.), or a toad (40 ft., swim 40 ft.), or back into its true form. Its statistics are the same in each form, except for the speed changes. Any equipment it is wearing or carrying isn't transformed. It reverts to its true form if it dies.

Actions

Claws (Bite in Beast Form). Melee Weapon Attack: +4 to hit, reach 5 ft., one target.
Hit: 5 (1d4+3) piercing damage. The target must succeed on a DC 10 Constitution Saving Throw or take 5 (2d4) poison damage and become poisoned for 1 minute. The target can repeat the Saving Throw at the end of each of its turns, ending the effect on itself on success.

Spook (1/day). One creature of the quasit's choice within 20 feet of it must succeed on a DC 10 Wisdom Saving Throw or be frightened for 1 minute. The target can repeat the Saving Throw at the end of each of its turns, with Disadvantage if the quasit is within line of sight, ending the effect on itself on success.

E 7.5 THE WATERWHEEL FORGE

Directly north of Graspen, halfway between the ruins and the lake, is a large waterwheel on the powerful stream that starts at the fountain in the middle of town and fed by several small streams as it approaches the wheel.

PCs might think the waterwheel is a granary, but inside is something quite unusual. The wheel powers a hydraulic hammer for metalsmithing, specifically, weapons and ironwork.

This waterwheel house, despite the overgrown weeds and reeds around the water, appears surprisingly well-maintained. While the stream is not wide, the water is quick and deep.

The Waterwheel Forge contains the necessary equipment to create high-quality weapons and armor for enchanting either during or after the smithing process. This is the forge where the clerics of Dvalin did their smith work, and the building was built, maintained, and owned by the Temple of Dvalin.

Indeed, this is where High Priest Oakheart created the pieces for the Temple's iron golem.

Inside this wheelhouse is not a watermill, but a multitude of high-end smithing equipment, some even glowing with the slight tell-tale glow an enchantment.

The waterwheel is powering a hydraulic press and other equipment. The press allows for sustained, hammering on a variety of anvils, allowing a smith to focus only on setting the correct speed and strength of the blow rather than smacking away with a hammer.

That hydraulic press is an engineering marvel, but the magically reinforced forge that is heated by magical flame is the real find. Such will allow the smithing of many magical items, save cold-forged weapons.

PCs might be wondering why the building is un-looted and still standing. The wood is treated with a magical preservative that resists weathering, fire, water damage, and physical damage. More than that, however, the place is permanently *hollowed* and *forbiddance*. Intrusion (physical or planar) by *elementals, fey, demons, possessed,* and *undead* is not possible unless both great spells are *dispelled*. They take 5d10 HP of radiant damage for each attempt.

Within the Waterwheel Forge, people have resistance to fire damage.

E8 - GIANT TOE TOR

Giant Toe is the other tor that rises at the eastern border of the barony. Besides the geological wonder, there is not much happening here in *Curse of the Lost Memories*. PCs can attempt to climb up the Tor to get a view of their surroundings, but it won't trigger any new *Lost Memory*. The tor is easy to climb and does not require a climb check. It should take a couple hours to reach the summit if the PCs can maintain a good pace.

From the summit, PCs gets a full vista of the Barony when looking to the west, but the most interesting and newer view is the one to the east, outside the barony. East of the barony is a wilderness area that starts at the foot of the Giant Toe tor and expands for dozens of miles to the east. When the barony was wealthy, these lands were assumed to be part of the Wailmoor, but they were never technically awarded by the King of Lothmar to the Wailmoor family.

PCs will not be able to see any settlements to the east, because there are none. Most of the population in the Barony of Mendron are on the borders of the Elven Protectorate of Shaeniss and the Barony of Halmana.

The wilderness east of the moor will play a bigger role in the next modules. Right now, it's a no-mans-land and the people to the east view the area, and the Wailmoor, as haunted. On paper, it belongs to the Barony of Mendron.

Intro

Lost at the Beaux Seins

Moortide Rising

The Altar & the Anvil

Castle Wailmoor

Appendix

THE
RESERVOIR

E9 - THE RESERVOIR

The reservoir is the local name given to the large lake south of the barony. Olaf of Wailmoor, the 4th baron, had constructed there a large dam to protect farmlands from flooding but also to provide irrigation in the occasional dry spell. The fifth Baron, his son, and a wizard of no small repute embarked on a magical project and over the years enchanted the whole place. The dam is essentially one massive magical artifact.

The dam is still there and in perfect shape. The reservoir, however, is filled with reeds and branches obstructing its opaque and muddy surface. There are no monsters or demonic creatures haunting the reservoir.

The dam holding back the water here appears imposing, an engineering marvel out of place in the abounded and desolate Barony of Wailmoor. It is made of cement, an Imperial construction technique usually not found this far away from the heart of the Empire.

If the PCs approach the dam, they can see faint runes all along its surface that are more than the absence of light than a glow.

The PCs can walk on the dam. If they do so, they feel a slight thrumming vibration through their boots. They will not be able to get inside of it, nor harm it in any way. *Detecting magic* will reveal a strong aura of Alteration and Enchantment and *stun* the person who cast the spell 1d4 hours. The caster is blown back away from the dam (possibly over a side!), taking 3d6 falling damage (no Saving Throw).

The dam is a key location to the next module *Beneath a Dreary Wave* but at this point in the campaign, does not offer much more content to the PCs.

Its magic is the reason why the wayward wards and magical effects around the Wailmoor act as they do.

If the PCs manage to destroy all three Obelisks, Boo the Owl is here, studying the dam and if the PCs have talked to him, he'll wonder why the leaders of old built the thing. He thinks it's crazy over-engineered and dangerous.

Intro

Lost
at the
Beaux
Seins

**Moortide
Rising**

The Altar
& the
Anvil

Castle
Wailmoor

Appendix

E10 – Decaris Farms

These farmlands were rich and fertile and highly productive (using Imperial farming techniques), overseen by the rural Lord Decaris and his knights. Rock fences denote fields and property lines, but little else remains.

During the war, all the knights protecting the farms and Lord Decaris were slain or possessed, the farm structures burnt to the ground, either by the demonic-led evaders or elven troops from the east trying to contain the demonic hordes by denying their possessed victims' food.

This slash-and-burn tactic worked but resulted in only the occasional foundation remaining. A druid PC or one with an agriculture background will recognize the rich farmland.

South of the farms lies the Duchy of Hardred, although the Duchy maintains a no-mans-land five-miles wide. Many refugees fled to the Duchy, and the Duke, having lost one of his highly-trained mages and operatives, and found several of the refugees were possessed by demons, closed the border and forbade any contact with the no-mans-land, which is still in effect after all this time.

E11 – The Lake

At one point, this lake had a proper elven name, but the human cartographer who visited the Old Elven Tower (now Castle Wailmoor), while smoking a fine pipe crossed out the twenty-three-letter word and replaced it with "The Lake."

The lake is deep, and fish abound. It is beautiful and primal, and home to The Guardian, a divine entity that could be argued *is* the lake.

E12 – The Old Graveyard

Viewing the graveyard triggers one or two *Lost Memories*.

This is a graveyard where the Knights of the Wailmoor are buried, the location of the burial of the first Knight of Wailmoor who died in the line of duty.

The graveyard is large and extensive, serving both as a place of rest and a place of contemplation for the Knights of Wailmoor, a garden retreat of sorts.

This graveyard is surrounded by a circular stone wall, 4-feet tall, with metal bars extending out of the stone for another 4-feet, ending in sharp spikes like a spear.

The trail leads right to an archway serving as a gate of sorts. Beyond the wall is the occasional grave, the landscape appearing as an overgrown garden.

Jackon's grave is easily found, and if dug up will reveal:

- Jackon's bones, although many have deteriorated completely
- A magical *staff*
- *Ring of protection +1*
- *Suit of mithril chainmail*

Digging up the grave and retrieving the items is not a sacrilegious action, although the PCs might not reach that conclusion. Not only is one of the PCs the reincarnation of Jackon, but the staff is an artifact a previous Hierophant incarnation created and Jackon "found."

There is no other loot of worth in The Old Graveyard. Except for Jackon, the last Knight to be buried there, the Knights pass on any magical equipment to others in their order.

The *Lost Memory* M12 – After the Graveyard will dog the PCs every time they sleep outside until they destroy all three Obelisks.

JACKON'S STAFF (STAFF OF ISHTARI)

The staff appears in perfect condition. It is a long quarterstaff, shod in mithril steel infused directly into the woodwork in a somewhat vaguely elvish pattern. The top of the staff is an obsidian claw holding a floating blob of liquid metal that glows sapphire blue.

Until the power of the staff is unlocked, it operates as a *quarterstaff +1* that can cast these arcane spells at will:

- *detect magic*
- *light*
- *mage armor (self-only)*
- *mage hand*

The only clues this staff may be more than a convenient magic item is its unusual construction.

If someone attempts to destroy the staff, it will appear as if destroyed, but, it simply moves back to Jackon's grave to re-await its true owner (the reincarnate of Jackon).

The only way to unlock the full power of the artifact is to progress along the *Chronicles of the Celestial Chains* campaign.

THE DIVINE, MAGICAL GRAVEYARD

Silas didn't pull the idea of linking the Obelisks to the dam out of nowhere — it's been done before.

The dwarves, elves, and men who built the dam also built the wall around the graveyard and several of the shrines within. They then used the power of the damn to provide the wards with permeance, linking the two places through a magical "stream" in the Ethereal Plane.

Where Silas (and Jackon) went wrong is the wards around the graveyard are divine in nature, not arcane. The gods the graveyard builders prayed to deities opposed to demonic influence, and thus these wards here are more powerful and able to resist demon corruption in its totality.

The entire graveyard is *hollowed* and operates as a giant, 300-radius *circle of protection from evil* spell. Not only that, the wards, overpowered by the dam, has a *forbiddance* effect on the entire graveyard, with only Knights of the Wailmoor, or the PCs as reincarnates of the Knights, able to enter without triggering the negative effects of the *forbiddance*.

Absolutely nothing will bother the PCs if they stay in the graveyard. Nothing evil, and certainly evil outsiders, can follow the PCs into the graveyard. Non-evil NPCs that attempt to enter the graveyard have a feeling of danger and find they cannot proceed.

If any trespasser persists in trying to breach the mighty wards, they take the damage a *forbiddance* can cause (5d10 radiant damage) even if they are not a creature normally associated with a *forbiddance* ward.

If the PCs explore the graveyard, they find a vast overgrown garden behind a 300-foot radius, circular wall. Graves dot here and there, and there are shrines to all the good deities of the Welt, along with stone benches and small stone plazas. The mausoleums here contain urns of ashes.

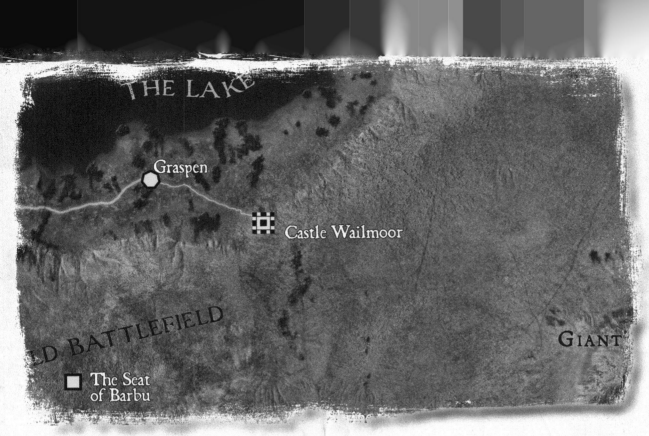

The Lake

Graspen

Castle Wailmoor

...D BATTLEFIELD

GIANT

The Seat
of Barbu

Intro

Lost
at the
Beaux
Seins

Moortide
Rising

The Altar
& the
Anvil

Castle
Wailmoor

Appendix

E12 - Castle Wailmoor

The PCs cannot enter the castle before the three Obelisks are destroyed. They can see the structure, but it is intangible and impenetrable. Attempting to touch the castle results in the air becoming more solid until the PC is unable to move their hand further. So of course, they are going to want inside.

Trapped in the Ethereal

Castle Wailmoor is perched on a hill, towering over the Lake and the destroyed town of Graspen below. A narrow drawbridge connects the road that snakes up the hill with the entrance to the castle. But, there is a problem, the castle is not truly there. If the PCs had not realized it during their visit of Graspen or their climb to the castle, they could see through the fortress as it flickers in and out of the ethereal plane.

You stand in front of a stone bridge that connects the dry parts of this hill-top moor to the castle. The fortress bears the scars of battle and its walls, while still standing strong, are darkened by the marks of a fiery assault. As you observe the castle, it seems to shine with a faint flickering green glow, and to your surprise, you can see the landscape behind it, the hills, and the battlefield below, as if the castle structure itself was translucent.

This area is a dangerous place as the castle is located atop a hill, surrounded by a swamp. It's a beautiful swamp, but a swamp nevertheless. Falling into the water or intentionally going for a wade will attract either 1d12 crocodiles, leeches, or having the PC getting stuck in the muck surrounded by leeches and crocodiles.

E10 - The Temple of Dvalin

The entrance to the Temple of Dvalin is guarded by a witch and her bandit cronies.

The witch coven of Kandra is led by a very old witch, Kavita, the same protagonist who summoned the demon Barbu and ordered him to destroy the barony 150-years ago. These witches are worshippers of the Demon Prince Orcus. Kavita has been jealous all these years of Chrystelle and sees her eternal life as an insult to the prince of Undeath himself. Even though the Barony has been destroyed, Kavita knows Chrystelle is still around, protected in her lair in the Castle, behind the powerful wards that place the fortress on the Ethereal Plane. When word reaches her of the swamp dog attack on the Crossroads Village, Kavita quickly dispatches one of her powerful lieutenants, Haeggra, to the Wailmoor with objectives to deal with the alleged agents of the Viscount and to see if the newly reported incursions of monsters into the Viscounty is an indicator of change.

Haeggra made an incursion into the Wailmoor from the north. She split her forces in two, with one team taking up residence in Harenvale after she verified she could not get into the Castle, and another team, led by herself, to investigate the Temple of Dvalin. Haeggra is convinced the Temple has something to do with the castle's powerful wards.

Haeggra has set camp in front of the Temple, with her two bandit bodyguards. She had more, but the rest of her men-at-arms fell victim to the golem and the magical trap around the well.

She is planning to rest after the first attempt and try to enter the Temple again on the next day. Based on how PCs arrive on the scene, they will either be surprised to find her there, or they surprised her if they manage to approach the site with Stealth and carefulness.

If the PCs have not triggered the Blessings of Dvalin Lost Memory, they now receive it.

The old and faded road climbing to the northern shore of the lake arrives before an old temple of dwarven architecture built on one side of a tall hill. The façade of the temple has seen the assaults of time, and most of its columns and statues are covered with moss and ivy. A large and tall metal set of opened double doors leads inside the temple, one clearly broke. A campfire has been set in front of the building, and you can see some human silhouettes focused on preparing their next meal.

As soon as Haeggra or her men notice the PCs, they initiate combat and will fight to the death. That the PCs are at the Temple is all the confirmation she needs that there is something in there that has to do with Castle Wailmoor.

Haeggra stays silent during the whole fight unless she is trying to *charm* a PC—this is a test of her leadership and retreat is worse than death. She will try at all costs, even her life, to avoid being captured or interrogated. Should the PCs manage to subdue her, she will not reveal anything out of her own will. Her two bandit acolytes do not know more than other bandits based in Harenvale, but should they be interrogated by the PCs, DMs should feel free to have them reveal the same bits of information.

Once the PCs have defeated Haeggra, they will be able to enter the temple (and understand why Haeggra took a break before getting in there herself!) as part of Chapter 3.

Before entering the temple, the PCs should be close to Level 3 and if not, give them a story award to put them at that level now.

HAEGGRA THE WITCH

Haeggra appears young and attractive, but is a thoroughly rotten individual, using her wicked ways to *charm*, seduce and dominate weaker people and torment them whenever it strikes her fancy. In a pinch, she simply blows things up with a *fireball*. Followed by another *fireball*. She really likes *fireballs*.

Haeggra the Witch

Human Warlock 8 — Medium humanoid, chaotic evil
Armor Class 14 (mage armor + Dex — **Hit Points** 55 | **Speed** 30 ft.

Statistics

STR	DEX	CON	INT	WIS	CHA
12 (+1)	12 (+1)	14 (+2)	13 (+1)	14 (+2)	18 (+4)

Saving Throws Wis +5, Cha +7
Skills Arcana +4, Deception +7, Perception +5, Persuasion +7
Senses passive Perception 15
Languages Common, Dwarvish, Elvish, Halfling
Challenge 5 (1,800 XP)

Spells

Spell Save DC: 16 — Spell Attack Bonus: +8 — Slots 2 4th
4th *blight, fire shield*
3rd *fireball, vampiric touch*
2nd *hold person, suggestion*
1st *charm person, protection from evil and good, witch bolt*
Cantrips *animal friendship (book of shadows), eldritch blast, friends, minor illusion, shocking grasp (book of shadows), vicious mockery (book of shadows)*

Abilities

Agonizing Blast. adds +4 damage to *eldritch blas*t on a hit.

Dark One's Blessing. gain 10 temporary hit points when reducing a hostile target to 0 HP

Dark One's Own Luck (1/short rest). contact patron for d10 to ability check or a Saving Throw after seeing the initial roll but before any of the roll's effects occur.

Eldritch Spear. eldritch blast, its range is 300 feet.

Rod of the Pact Keeper +1 (1/long rest). bonus to spell attack rolls and to the Saving Throw DCs of warlock spells. Also, regain one warlock spell slot as an action while holding the rod.

Staff of Charming (10 charges). While holding the staff, expend 1 of its 10 charges to cast *charm person, command,* or *comprehend languages* from DC 16 Spell Save. The staff can also be used as a magic quarterstaff. **(1/day)** turn failed enchantment Saving Throw into succeeded Saving Throw. Expend a charge to turn a spell back upon caster if saved. Staff regains 1d8 + 2 expended charges daily at dawn.

Actions

Dagger. *Melee or Ranged Weapon Attack:* +4 to hit, reach 5 ft. or range 20 ft./60 ft., one target.
Hit: 3 (1d4+1) piercing damage.

Spell Attack. *Ranged Weapon Attack:* +8 to hit, range 0 ft., one target.
Hit: As Spell damage.

Eldritch Blast. (2/Action) *Ranged Weapon Attack:* +8 to hit, range 300 ft., per beam
Hit: 1d10+4 per beam.

Staff of Charming. *Melee Weapon Attack:* +4 to hit, reach 5 ft., one target.
Hit: 4 (1d6+1) bludgeoning damage or 5 (1d8+1) bludgeoning damage if used with two hands to make a melee attack.

Items

Staff of charming, book of shadows, rod of pack keeper +1, philter of love, potion of greater healing, dagger

Tactics: Before Battle

Since it's "free," Haeggra always has *mage armor* on. Haeggra isn't really a combatant, but she is a competent manipulator and thoroughly *charms* everyone in her way if she can get away with it. She will use lies, seduction and all manner of passive-aggressive means to accomplish her goals. If not surprised, she will try to use her *friends* cantrip and *charm person* from her magical staff.

Tactics: During Battle

If it's on suddenly, in her mind, it's on. Haeggra *fireballs* enemies *twice in a row* expends her *rod of the pack keeper* to regain a spell slot, and *fireballs* again. This tactic has never failed her ever since she became powerful enough to cast *fireball*. She gets 10 temporary HP every time someone reaches 0 HP (although each grant of temporary hit points does not stack, she has to pick one or the other), and in her experience, there is a lot of death in *fireballs*.

Once her spells slots are expended (she only has 2, and an additional +1 from the rod), she snipes with the cantrip *eldritch blast* per round, which at her level creates two beams (each requiring a separate to hit roll). She tries to put space between her and her enemy, as she can snipe using the spell from 300 feet away.

Her two bodyguards are completely expendable. She'll *fireball* them if she can get the most PCs in a blast. In a heartbeat.

Stealth is the PC best option when dealing with the Haeggra. She has a low Armor Class and not a lot of Hit Points. Competent PCs can burn her down in a round.

2 Kandra Bandits

Medium humanoid, chaotic neutral
Armor Class 12 (leather armor) | **Hit Points** 20 — **Speed** 30 ft.

Statistics

STR	DEX	CON	INT	WIS	CHA
13 (+1)	12 (+1)	12 (+1)	10 (+0)	9 (-1)	10 (+0)

Senses passive Perception 10
Challenge 1/2 (100 XP) each

Actions

Light Crossbow. *Ranged Weapon Attack:* +4 to hit, range 80 ft./320 ft., one target.
Hit: 5 (1d8+1) piercing damage.

Long Sword. *Melee Weapon Attack:* +4 to hit, reach 5 ft., one target.
Hit: 6 (1d6+2) slashing damage.

AFTERMATH

To bring Castle Wailmoor back into reality from the Ethereal Plane, the PCs must destroy all three Obelisks, and the hardest one to reach, and destroy, is the one under the Temple of Dvalin. Doing so will reset the old Elven Tower's attunement to the dam's spell-engine that Silas and Jackon poked at by mistake. Once the Tower is back into the Welt, the Castle

follows, and the wards around each are as they were before the Demon War.

The PCs should be Level 3 before they attempt to enter the dangerous and far-from-empty temple. If they are not Level 3 and the PCs have destroyed the other two Obelisks, award them a story award to bring them up to a level they can survive in the temple.

It is possible for the PCs to bypass everything and arrive at the temple either through bad luck or scouting (via flight using a familiar) and randomly picking that as an interesting place to visit. If so, Haeggra probably killed them (with *fireballs*), and on the off-chance, she did not, then the PCs are in for a tough time. If they enter the Temple before Level 3, leave a subtle hint that there may be secrets to the Temple of Dvalin that only the moor can reveal.

The PCs are also approaching challenges where the lack of magical gear will be a detriment to their survival.

DM OPTION

The open-world nature of the Wailmoor can be disadvantageous if the PCs fixate on a location before they need to explore it and the worse place to do that is the Temple of Dvalin.

While it's impossible to articulate every permutation, in the case of the Temple of Dvalin, there are several options:

- The Witch Haeggra could simply not be there at the time too-low-of-levels PCs arrive, but she'll show up later

- A helpful ghost of a dwarven monk could flat-out tell the PCs that there is a corrupted obelisk inside, but the PCs need to destroy the other two first, or the temple wards will be too powerful to overcome. He or she could even warn about the witch

- The PCs encounter a singular bandit that talks about the Harenvale bandits and how they know something about the witch guarding the temple

- Boo the Owl could make an appearance, talking about the other two Obelisks and warning that they need to be taken care of first

- Go for it and remove Haeggra's *rod of the pack keeper* and *staff of charming*

LOST MEMORIES

Before leaving the exploration phase of the chapter, review the *Lost Memories* for any memories the PCs may

Intro

Lost at the Beaux Seins

Moortide Rising

The Altar & the Anvil

Castle Wailmoor

Appendix

The Altar & The Anvil

"YOUR MIND IS AN ANVIL WHERE THE RED-HOT THOUGHTS OF RIGHTEOUSNESS ARE POUNDED, SOMETIMES LITERALLY, INTO A PRAGMATIC WORLD-VIEW THAT CAN STILL RETAIN AN EDGE."

—OLD DVALIN

have inadvertently skipped, specifically <u>M6- The Spell</u>. Dvalin is the creator of dwarves and elves, seeded unto The Welt when he alone, outside of the purview of the Gods of Law, decided the Welt should have more life.

This chapter deals with one of his temples, an old structure that predates all other structures in the fallen Barony of Wailmoor. The PCs must brave its traps, run-amok defenses, corrupted monsters, and divine tests to destroy the corrupted obelisk within and obtain access to Castle Wailmoor.

Dvalin is a pragmatic deity, and his religion reflects his practical, realistic, and rational cannon. Consequently, there is no divine mystery on what the PCs must do here at the Temple. They encounter a *Lost Memory* that lists the lengthy, arduous and at times rewarding steps necessary to move forward. The PCs will need to make sacrifices, make difficult choices, and live with the consequences. Possibly for all eternity. Gaining access to the secrets of the Temple could take the PCs *months*, or even a year.

Clever PCs with an exploration streak and analysis of the esoteric hints can learn the true secrets of the place. Dvalin, with his limited, but uniquely powerful view into the future, decided he wanted skin in the game. Rather interfere directly, he took a practical approach and, through his influence and long-term manipulation, decided that one of the PCs will become one of his divine servants, one way or the other.

If a PC is standing at the Warding Glyph and thinking, "this restriction is awfully convenient," he or she would be correct.

Because the Temple also manifests into the Ethereal, *Lost Memories* here are plentiful, seemingly random (they are anything but), and especially vivid. These memories paint a specific story, but they are intentionally not in chronological order.

The PCs either get it or they don't. Either way, Dvalin will have his due.

TEMPLE HISTORY

Temples to Dvalin range from dwarven centers of religious study to engineering schools to frontier outposts and everything in between.

EARLY DAYS

This temple was originally placed here because Dvalin, long ago, asked for it to be constructed, although that detail is lost in time. Over the centuries, it became a scholarly-focused monastery, a place of contemplation for priests wanting focus far from dwarven enclaves or Imperial civilization. As the Wailmoor became wealthier, so did the Temple prosper.

GROWTH

Fortunes changed when the fourth Baron of Wailmoor decided to enact the dam for flood control and to build up a reservoir for advanced irrigation. The construction for such was headed by the Temple and the Baron's son, who went on to become a powerful, Imperial-class wizard and eventual fifth Baron, Olaf of Wailmoor.

Design of the dam and subsequent call for engineers to build it came from the Temple and Olaf the Fifth going so far as to live there during its design.

The process of designing and constructing the dam shuttled enormous amounts of coin to the Temple, and as the Wailmoor became wealthy under the tutelage of its benefactor Chrystelle, the Temple took on an advisory role to the small villages and towns in Wailmoor. It took on far more coin than it could spend, so funds were sent on a regular basis to other Temples.

THE DEMON WAR

At the onset of the Demon War, most of the scholars making use of the Temple did not live on the Temple grounds. The Temple was primarily the home to the dwarven High Priest Beram Oakheart and his elven lover Merisee, a Priestess and Dedicate to Dvalin. The temple had two guardians, Paladins of Dvalin, and two scholar-priests. All but Oakheart and Merisee perished in the Demon War, not defending the Temple but trying to save the Barony from the demonic forces bent on destroying it.

After the war, a despondent Oakheart was served an Imperial Summons for reasons he did not reveal, leaving the Temple to Dedicate Merisee, a powerful divine agent of Dvalin. She assisted Silas and Jackon in their plan to enact wards preventing demons from *teleporting* or opening functional *gates* (amongst other things) into the Wailmoor, stuffed the books and blueprints on the dam into her *bag of holding,* sealed the Temple, and left.

It has lain empty for 150-years.

Intro

Lost at the Beaux Seins

Moortide Rising

The Altar & the Anvil

Castle Wailmoor

Appendix

TEMPLE OF DVALIN

Chapter Three Summary

Area 33 contains a warding Obelisk, but Silas and Jackon used the temple's link to the dam to seal it away into the Ethereal. To manifest the Obelisk to destroy it, the PCs must perform the ritual to unbind it from the dam's magic. The ritual book is locked away in a heavily warded reliquary.

DM Note

This chapter is an example of the difference between a simple dungeon crawl and lore-rich, world-building campaign play. On the one hand, players are literally given a list of tasks to accomplish. On the other hand, that list will take a considerable amount of time, resources, and effort to complete. PCs must pay Dvalin's price to move forward.

"There ain't no such thing as a free lunch" is exactly something a priest of Dvalin would say.

This chapter is in four sections.

Area Descriptions

This section is a room-by-room description of the Temple of Dvalin. The temple is divided up into three sectors, each with their own direct means of egress:

- Areas 1 to 11: The Chapel, Library and supporting rooms, dominated by an Iron Golem and belligerent and vicious dire badgers

- Areas 12-25: The Monastery, where the monk-like priests studied religion, engineering, and philosophy. Animated objects, clockwork, and traps pose challenges to the PCs.

- Areas 26-34: The Crypts, where the Obelisk is hidden away. This area is no longer inside the Temple's wards and is thoroughly corrupted by the Obelisk. Mundane and powerful undead oppose the PCs at every turn.

UNLOCK THE OBELISK

This section describes the over-arching mission of manifesting the Obelisk. The steps necessary could take the PC a substantial length of time. They will need to:

1. Forge and enchant two keys out of mysterious metal, wolfram (tungsten), through a difficult process to raise the magical portcullis in Area 31.

2. Traverse past the warding glyphs—if none of the PCs are a paladin or cleric of Dvalin, one of them must choose to become a Dedicate of Dvalin, a painful transformation that carries with it rewards and obligations.

3. Once obtaining the codebook, PCs will need to not only learn the ancient language it is written in, but transverse the dream realm, which spills into the Ethereal to find its code cipher.

Each of these steps contains sub-steps.

TEMPLE DISPOSITION

The temple has been around for so long that it has achieved a small measure of independence and is more than a connection to the divine. At the end of their shenanigans in the temple, the PCs can have an adversarial, neutral, or friendly disposition with the temple itself, each with its own penalties, obligations, and rewards.

END GAME

As a lore-heavy, campaign-rich chapter, this section lists details for the DM to fit the chapter into an over-arching campaign, instead of simply a linear adventure that restricts PCs agency to advance the plot.

AREA DESCRIPTIONS

This temple is more of a monastery and place of contemplation than an engineering and smithy college. PCs with any modicum of religious skills will note this immediately as the traverse the three main areas of the temple.

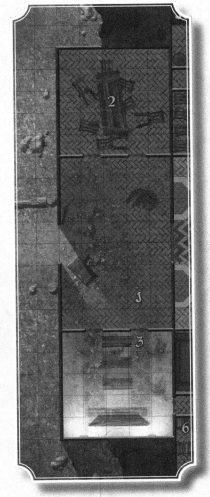

The Temple of Dvalin has three main areas, each with their unique ecosystem (such as it is).

TEMPLE PROPERTIES

WARDS

The temple is thoroughly warded, with permanent *hallow* and *forbiddance* spells that cannot be dispelled in any way, as they are linked to the dam.

Unfortunately, the lower crypts in the temple, near the corrupted Obelisk, are not under these wards. If the PCs do not destroy the Obelisk, in several decades, the corruption will creep up the stairs into the Chapel and defile the Temple for all time.

Until then, the wards have these properties:

- Demons and undead can't enter the Temple, nor can such creatures charm, frighten, or possess creatures within it. Any creature charmed, frightened, or possessed by such a creature is no longer charmed, frightened, or possessed upon entering the Temple

- While undead or demons cannot enter the upper Temple, they can try. Doing so causes them 5d10 radiant damage per round (no Saving Throw)

- The upper temple is thoroughly proofed against planar travel (including *teleportation*) and therefore prevents creatures from accessing the Temple by way of the Astral Sea, Ethereal Plane or any other plane or dimension

DOORS

The doors here are typical iron doors, now rusted but quite formidable. Unless otherwise noted, they are not locked. The doors have an AC of 25, and if locked, it takes 10 + 2d4 minutes to breach the door—with a ram and four PCs with STR 16 or higher.

LIGHTING

Areas do not have light sources unless otherwise noted. Some rooms do have *continual flame* or *continue light* spells that still function.

Intro

Lost at the Beaux Seins

Moortide Rising

The Altar & the Anvil

Castle Wailmoor

Appendix

1 - Entry Room

Almost all the demons during the Demon War were smart enough not to try to breach the Temple's wards, or even come *near* the Temple.

Looters and bandits over the years—not so much. Inside the grand entry room beyond the breached doors is a dwarf-looking iron golem infused with energy from the ever-burning font in the Radiant Chapel. It's standing in a dark corner glowering at the door, hands on its hips.

This grand entry room must have been impressive and a sight to behold, but now one half of an ornate metal double-door, ruble, dead animal carcasses, bones, and three dead bandit bodies litter the floor. The bodies line near the closed, ornate double doors to the east, appearing as if they are squished flat by mighty blows and then splashed with acid.

A large iron statue is in the dim northeast corner hands on its hips, as if glowering at the broken entry. Around its neck is a silver necklace dangling a key.

The lock is a complex and high-quality requiring a DC 20 Dexterity (Thieves' Tools) Check to open without the key.

The iron golem will attack anyone attempting to open the ornate double doors to the east—unless its conditions are met.

As soon as the PCs get within 10ft of it or the doors, it will point to the room to the north, which contains two brooms and two mops and several buckets. If the PCs clean Areas 1, 2 and 3 (which includes rehanging the broken door), the iron golem will hand the PCs its key to the door to the Radiant Chapel and resume its glowering at the entry to the temple.

A crude cleaning job from the PC results in the iron golem pointing out all their deficiencies and then moving back to its corner to glower at them.

It will let any non-undead and non-demon inside the Chapel if the people that desire entry clean up the place.

If anyone tries to pick the lock on the door, steal the key or attack the golem, it immediately attacks and will pursue trespassers anywhere in the Temple (including the lower portions), but will not leave the Temple grounds. If engaged with missile weapons from outside the temple, it will pick up rubble and throw it at attackers outside the door, in addition to launching one of its fists. It will also close the non-broken door half and lean the other door, giving it cover, or simply stand to one side.

The Radiant Iron Golem

Large construct, unaligned
Armor Class 20 (natural armor) — **Hit Points** 230 — **Speed** 30 ft.

Statistics

STR	DEX	CON	INT	WIS	CHA
24 (+7)	20 (+5)	20 (+5)	5 (-3)	11 (+0)	1 (-5)

Damage Immunities necrotic, fire, poison, psychic; bludgeoning, piercing, and slashing from nonmagical attacks that aren't adamantine
Condition Immunities charmed, exhaustion, frightened, paralyzed, petrified, poisoned
Senses darkvision 120 ft., passive Perception 10
Languages Old Dvalin (can understand but not speak)
Challenge 18 (20,000 XP)

Abilities

Fire & Radiant Absorption. Whenever the golem is subjected to fire or radiant damage, it takes no damage and instead regains hit points equal to the damage dealt.

Immutable Form. The golem is immune to any spell or effect that would alter its form.

Magic Resistance. The golem has Advantage on Saving Throws against spells and other magical effects.

Magic Weapons. The golem's weapon attacks are magical.

Actions

Multiattack. The golem makes two melee attacks.

Slam. Melee Weapon Attack: +13 to hit, reach 5 ft., one target. *Hit:* 20 (3d8+7) bludgeoning damage

Poison Breath (Recharge 4-6). The golem exhales poisonous gas in a 15-foot cone. Each creature in that area must make a DC 19 Constitution Saving Throw, taking 45 (10d8) poison damage on a failed save, or half as much damage on a successful one.

Legendary Actions

The radiant iron golem can take 3 legendary actions, choosing from the options below. Only one legendary action option can be used at a time and only at the end of another creature's turn. The iron golem regains spent legendary actions at the start of its turn.

The Backhand of Dvalin (1 action). The golem makes a slam attack, but the damage is typed as radiant.

Fists of the Dawn Dwarves (2 actions). The golem can launch a fist up to 120ft. that hits with a slam attack and then flies back and re-attaches to the golem in the same round

Death from Above (2 actions). The golem launches itself into the air up to 60 feet and lands in a 10ft. by 10ft. square. Everything in the square takes 20 (3d8+7) bludgeoning damage, Save DC 20 Reflex for half.

The iron golem will not communicate and in its present state cannot receive other commands.

Entry After Granting of the Key

Presenting the key to the golem will allow entry for the holder and their party without the iron golem attacking.

If the entry is already clean, those desiring entry *without the key* must spend time polishing the floors, the golem itself, or the doors or making other improvements such as bring in fresh flowers, etc. Those with the key can walk right on in.

The iron golem will attempt to communicate this through a nod at the repaired place but a glance at the floors, door, and itself. A DC 15 Intelligence (Insights) will intuit its desire for more polish.

Assuming the doors are unlocked. If the door is locked, the iron golem can't open the door. The lock may be picked without hassle, but the iron golem will not allow damage to the door.

2 - BANQUET ROOM

Entering this room triggers a *Lost Memory*.

This room used to host large banquets for the people of the Wailmoor. It is now filled with debris and dust. The rotten remains of a wooden table and chairs are gathered on the floor.

> This room is filled with debris and dust, and the rotten remains of an ornate table and chairs fill the middle. This appears to be a former banquet room. In one corner of the room are two brooms, two mops and two buckets with rotted, old cleaning rags draped across the handles.
>
> On the table is a large, yellowed piece of parchment with the corners held down by pewter mugs.

On the table is a geological feature map of the Barony of Wailmoor, detailed and accurate.

LOST MEMORY

In the Demon War, this room was used by Wailmoor defenders after the castle was breached.

> The wizard Silas, the Wailmoor Knights Heleshia and Jackon, several harried soldiers and the remains of the Temple personnel are staring at the map.
>
> "The Baron is dead," Hight Priest Beram Oakheart says flatly.
>
> Nobody says anything, the silence ever creeping around the map.
>
> "it is time to alter our tactics," Jackon says into the quiet. "We've been trying to get to Barbu to cut this off at the head. Without the demon's leader, they will fragment and flee."
>
> "The last time we tried I lost my two paladins," Oakheart points out. "The first time my two priests. He is too heavily defended."
>
> "Then," says Jackon, "we must make him come to us."

That is exactly how Jackon the War Wizard, Knight of the Wailmoor ended the Demon War. The remaining forces drew out the mighty Barbu with false information of an underground passage into the elven tower with wards that would need dispelling, singled him out, prevented him from *teleporting* and slew him with enchanted siege artillery.

The iron golem will not give up his key until this room is clean.

Intro

Lost at the Beaux Seins

Moortide Rising

The Altar & the Anvil

Castle Wailmoor

Appendix

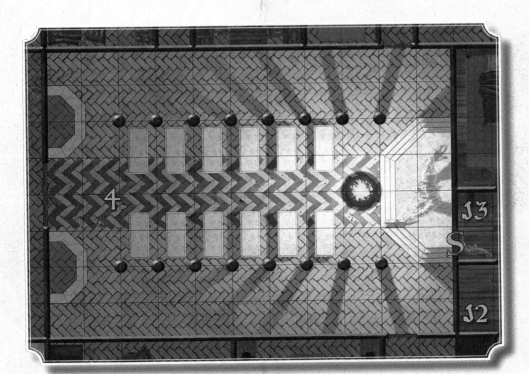

3 - Side-Chapel

The grandiose and awe-inspiring nature of the central Chapel, for the most part, was too intense for many people. Even the well-off, educated middle-class of the later-period Wailmoor found the Radiant Chapel disconcerting.

Thus, this side-chapel saw much use before the Wailmoor downfall.

The two ornate, thick wood doors to the are unlocked, but the iron door to the east is locked, DC 15 Dexterity to open.

This side-chapel is still-well-lit by two *continual flame* light sources to the south. At one time this must have been a beautiful place of worship, but now is empty of even the most basic of reliquaries to Dvalin.
The walls have fading murals of mountains and forest landscapes.

There is nothing hidden in this room, but the iron golem will check to see if it is clean before giving up the key to the main chapel.

Opening the door to the east has the possibility of altering the belligerent dire badgers that nest in the courtyard. If disturbed with the slightest noise, they attack.

4 - The Radiant Chapel

This huge room (40ft. x 55ft. with 30ft. ceilings) is the focal point for all the Temple's power, both latent and obvious. Less of a concentration of a population's devotion, the Radiant Chapel with its radiant energy basin is a focal point of Dvalin's divine power from beyond.

People who are not expecting to be near such a powerful concentration of divine energy find the Temple, and the Radiant Chapel bewildering, especially those familiar with Dvalin—temples to other deities may be similar in architecture, but not in function. The Radiant Chapel and most of the Temple exists simultaneously both in the Welt and the Ethereal Plane.

A large basin in the floor spilling light dominate what would be a dark, large room, the flickering radiance illuminating painted statues of dwarves and serene, mountain landscapes.
The Chapel is built in white granite. Ornate columns with runes at their base outline stone benches facing the altar and statue to the east. Baptismal fonts for holy water ornate the walls to the west.
At the east of the room beyond the basin is a statue of Dvalin on a large dais.

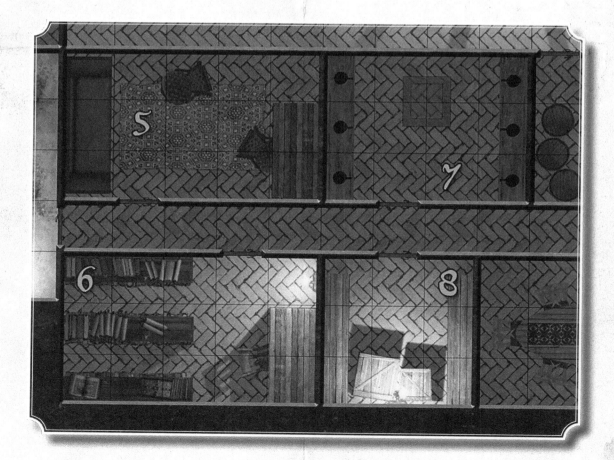

The Water Fonts

The fonts to the west are feed from underground plumbing—water trickles in to replace water evaporating out. They are filled with water, but right now, it's not holy water. Their proximity to the basin spewing radiant energy has changed the water somewhat. If a PC drinks a vial of it like a potion, it cures 1d4 HP of any non-radiant damage.

The Columns

The columns lining the Radiant Chapel have four runes on each compass point with an artistic line from the top of the rune to another, different rune above it, for a total of 8 runes per column.

Anyone with a silver holy symbol of Dvalin will recognize the dwarven runes, although there are many that are not on the symbol.

The Basin

This basin, with its top flush to the floor, is a pure font of radiant energy. While a person can get close to the ever-present flame, touching it causes 1d8 radiant damage per round, no Saving Throw.

The Statue

Holding a hammer, this statue of Dvalin is an impressive sight, lit by the flickering flames of the radiant font before it. Dvalin appears either as a tall dwarf or a stout human with a kind, but resolute expression on his face.

Doors

All the doors to the Chapel, besides the secret door, are made from a steel alloy. They have an AC of 30, almost indestructible, but a day's worth of battering with a quality ram will eventually break one off its hinges.

From the Chapel side, the secret door is found with a DC 18 Intelligence (Investigate) or a DC 20 Wisdom (Perception) Check.

5 - Study

This was a nicely furnished room for quiet reading and discussion. The iron door is unlocked. There is 5 SP of loose change in the couch.

6 - Library

Entering the Library triggers a *Lost Memory*.

This Area is lit by a *continual flame* lantern.

The Glyph

The door is locked, DC 15 Dexterity (Thieves' Tools) to open, and warded with a glyph placed by the Dedicate Merisee as she left. The glyph glows faint blue, and unlike most *glyphs of warding,* the proximity to the radiant font in the Chapel makes it easy to spot. It is a small glyph over the lock and triggers when the lock is touched with or without the key.

When triggered, the glyph erupts with magical energy into the 5′ square before the door and two squares both to the east and the west (for 25′ impacted area total) into the hallway with 5d8 thunder damage (DC 15 Dexterity Saving Throw, save for half).

The Room

This small library had several shelves of books and many scrolls, along with a desk. There are 241 books in the library (some of them necessary to manifest the Crypt Obelisk) and 21 scrolls.

The Books

The scrolls are mainly illustrated notes on books, but they are artistic and written by competent, thoughtful scholars. The whole would fetch at least 800 GP at any Imperial University Library.

This is a mundane library: the books here, while esoteric and scholarly in nature, are mostly found in other places. The rare and expensive books were stored in the Temple's Reliquary in Area 31. The books here are collectively worth as much as the scrolls. These books are used later by the PCs:

- *Tome of Undeath*
- *Dedicates of Dvalin*
- Seven books on the Old Dvalin language
- Books on the religion of Dvalin (prayers, rituals)
- *Dreams of the Ethereal* and other dream books
- Books on rare herbs

Lost Memory

The Wailmoor Knights Heleshia and Jackon are pursuing the books in the library when Merisee the elf Priestess of Dvalin sticks her head in the open door.

"What are you looking for?"

"Books on the dam," Jackon quips.

"Why are you interested in restricted books?"

"Because I am a war wizard and I blow up people who stand in my way," Jackon says without looking up.

"Jackon! Manners!" rebukes Heleshia.

"Ha, ha, ha, ha, ha! Well then. Follow me to the Reliquary," says Merisee. "Be warned though; the Crypts are heavily defended by divine guardians that take exception to explosions and mayhem."

Intro

Lost at the Beaux Seins

Moortide Rising

The Altar & the Anvil

Castle Wailmoor

Appendix

7 - Latrines

There is nothing of note in this room. The water fountain in the middle still runs and drains after all these years, a testament to the engineering of the Temple. These latrines were mainly used by guests, Temple visitors and Temple personnel that did not live in the Temple but worked there.

8 - Storage Room

This room was used for different purposes throughout the Temple's history; sometimes it was an extension of a library, a bedroom with two beds, a storage room, and an armory. Before the High Priest and Merisee abandoned the Temple, the dwarves here used it as a storage room.

Oddly, the boxes contain an alchemist's laboratory carefully packed for travel. The alchemist sent the boxes here for the equipment to be studied by the High Priest—while non-magical, the explorers who found the equipment, in turn, found them in an abandoned dwarven stronghold. The glassware has religious symbols of Dvalin, but before the High Priest could study the mystery, the Demon War broke out.

9 - Pantry

Both the doors here at closed and locked. The door to the north to the Chapel in Area 4 is DC 18 and to the south is DC 15, both Dexterity (Thieves' Tools).

This small kitchen was primarily used by the permanent occupants of the Temple. It was customary for the Temple to receive fresh food from the populous both in tribute to Dvalin and tradition.

Because of the abandonment of the Temple coupled with the permanent font of radiant energy in the chapel, a group of beetles, with access to the stove through the stove pipe, have mutated into giant glow bugs.

This small kitchen served as storage and a place to cook warm meals. From the stove on the east wall, there is a glow coming from the oven.

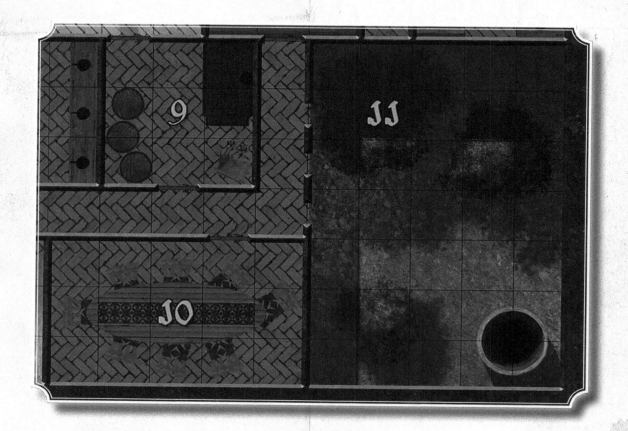

4 Giant Radiant Beetles

Small beast, unaligned
Armor Class 13 (natural armor) — **Hit Points** 4 — **Speed** 30 ft.

Statistics

STR	DEX	CON	INT	WIS	CHA
8 (-1)	10 (+0)	12 (+1)	1 (-5)	1 (-5)	3 (-4)

Senses blindsight 30 ft., passive Perception 8
Damage Immunities radiant, fire
Damage Vulnerabilities necrotic, cold
Languages —
Challenge 0 (10 XP)

Abilities

Illumination. The beetle sheds bright light in a 10-foot radius and dim light for an additional 10 feet.

Actions

Bite. *Melee Weapon Attack:* +1 to hit, reach 5 ft., one target. *Hit:* 2 (1d6-1) piercing damage.

These giant radiant beetles pose little threat to a group of seasoned adventurers, but they can cause mayhem. If the north door is open, then they flee into the Chapel and if the door is open between Area 1 and 4 the Iron Golem in Area 1 takes exception to their presence and chases them around, stomping on them with its foot.

If the southern door is open, and the party has thus far avoided the angry dire badgers, the fire beetles scurry that way and disturb them.

If *both* doors are open, both events can occur simultaneously.

10 - Supper Room

Entering this room triggers a *Lost Memory.*

The door to this room is locked with DC 15 (Dexterity) quality lock.

This room contained a large oval wooden table and chairs and was used for supper.

Lost Memory

Silas, Jackon, Heleshia, the High Priest Oakheart, and Merisee, the elf priestess, sit at this table, staring at a scroll that seems to be made of paper-thin, flexible bronze, the words more etched into the metal than written in ink.

"Is that what I think it is?" Silas asks.

"Aye—it's an Imperial Summon" Beram Oakheart replies. "For me. Specifically."

"Why?" from Jackon. "About the war? Why would the Emperor even care about us way out here?"

"It doesn't say, but I have my theories. I'm leaving for the Capital on the hour. Merisee, you'll need to carry on here."

"Well, so much for our relationship," Merisee says with a sour expression.

11 - Cloister & Courtyard

A covered walk in a colonnade opens to a quadrangle garden with trees and a large well. While difficult to access, this courtyard is open to the outside.

This modest courtyard has three trees, a well, a covered walk allowing access to the Temple to the west and milling, vicious looking giant badgers munching on the severed leg of a bandit.

This area is home to no fewer than seven dire badgers and besides the Iron Golem in Area 1, primarily responsible for preventing the witch's bandits being unable to breach the temple. While they are not corrupted, the Obelisk, through the well, has made them quite angry for no reason. They are thoroughly mean, and if they spot PCs (or anything else), they attack—two per PC—with the remaining growling and hissing from a tree. The seventh will run down the hillside if attacked or approached.

The dire badgers are not even remotely stealthy. Only bumbling or intoxicated PCs will be surprised by the dire badgers.

All the doors to the temple here are closed (note the gaps in the wall to the courtyard have no obstruction). The dire badgers have access to the hallways but are unable to proceed past the doors.

Seven Permanently Angry Dire Badgers

Medium beast, unaligned
Armor Class 11 — **Hit Points** 28 — **Speed** 30 ft., burrow 10 ft.

Statistics

STR	DEX	CON	INT	WIS	CHA
14 (+2)	12 (+1)	15 (+2)	4 (-3)	12 (+1)	5 (-3)

Senses darkvision 30 ft., passive Perception 11
Languages —
Challenge 1 (200 XP) each

Abilities

Keen Smell. The badger has Advantage on Wisdom (Perception) checks that rely on smell.

Actions

Multiattack. The badger makes two attacks: one with its bite and one with its claws.

Bite. *Melee Weapon Attack:* +4 to hit, reach 5 ft., one target. *Hit:* 5 (1d6+2) piercing damage.

Claw. *Melee Weapon Attack:* +4 to hit, reach 5 ft., one target. *Hit:* 7 (2d4+2) slashing damage.

The west-most door to the hallway to Area 13 is locked, DC 20 Dexterity (Thieves' Tools), as is the north-most door to Area 12 (same DC).

Intro

Lost at the Beaux Seins

Moortide Rising

The Altar & the Anvil

Castle Wailmoor

Appendix

THE WELL

The bandit tried to jump into the well to escape the dire badgers. He almost made it, but two of them got his leg as he was falling. The rest of his body fell into the well, triggered the fire trap, and rests as a burnt lump on the grate.

The well at one time was a way to draw water for the kitchen in Area 9 from the underground pond in Area 34, but a security assessment removed that routine. It is 50ft. from the top of the well to the roof of Area 34. 25ft. down is a locked grate with a high-quality lock, DC 20 Dexterity (Thieves' Tools) and a resetting magical fire glyph. It resets every 10 minutes: 5d6 of fire damage, save for half. The trap Saving Throw is DC 20 Dexterity due to the small confine of the well.

The bandit's body sits on the grate. There is nothing of note on his body. He was wearing studded leather, had a dagger and shortsword with a light crossbow and 10 quarrels and a belt-pouch with 12 GP and 23 SP.

12 - VESTIBULE

Entering this room triggers a *Lost Memory*.

The door to the south is locked, DC 15 Dexterity (Thieves' Tools), but the doors to the north and east are not.

This room has polished hardwood floors (now dusty) with an expensive tapestry of a forest valley hanging on the west wall.

LOST MEMORY

Dedicate Merisee is stuffing a pile of books into a sack that does not seem to grow larger or fill as she puts more books than what can obviously fit.

"Don't go," Jackon the War Wizard says. "We need you."

Merisee pauses but then continues stuffing, now adding traveling gear to her seemingly endless bag.

"The Temple can take care of itself. But I'm going to take the blueprints and construction manuals for the dam somewhere else. I don't understand them; you and Silas don't need them anymore. They're dangerous."

"Silas and I can keep them safe."

"Twenty-three."

"Excuse me?"

Merisee, done packing, stands tall. "Twenty-three. That is how many demons and possessed I have killed, half of them before I encountered your little vicious Demon War. I'm a very dangerous person, Jackon—Beram is only alive because of me, but he's safer now, I hope. You and Silas have enough to worry about with your ill-advised scheme to place warding stones. So, for your safety and to prevent you from doing *more* things you shouldn't with the dam, I'm departing. Good-bye, Sir Jackon."

"Merisee..."

"Go to her, Jackon. She loves you."

Jackon turns away. "Never love a War Wizard. That's just as bad as falling in love with a Dedicate."

"Go to her."

13 - HIGH PRIEST OFFICE

Neither the door to the north or south is locked.

This small office contains an ornate desk, a small statue and a shelf filled with books. The small statue is of Dvalin and is moved aside to open the secret door leading behind the altar.

The desk is locked, DC 18 Dexterity (Thieves' Tools), to open. In the drawer is the ceremony book *Trial of the Dedicate,* written in Old Dvalin, a language PCs must learn so they can transverse the Warding Glyph in the Reliquary in the crypt.

Hidden underneath the statue (visible once the statue is moved) in a sealed oilskin pouch along with a small padded pouch containing four potions; two *elixirs of health* and two *potions of poison resistance.*

The books are poems, fiction, and biographies, written both in dwarven, elven and even draconic.

14 - HIGH PRIEST CHAMBERS

Entering this room does not trigger the *Lost Memory* here but lying in bed does. The memory is dangerous to elves.

The door to the south is not locked.

A large and comfortable bed (by Dwarven standards) is here as well as a large cupboard that used to contain the personal clothing and effects of the High Priest; now empty. A rich woven rug covers almost all the room. There are two *continual flame* lanterns on the north wall, but only one is lit.

LOST MEMORY

Jackon and Heleshia are in bed in a passionate embrace.

The memory fades, and the sense of eroticism is replaced by the terrible, terrible ace of unbearable loss.

Any elf experiencing this memory by lying down on the bed suffers a tremendous shock to his or her system for the ache Heleshia felt when she buried Jackon invades this memory like a hammer blow to the head. The elf must make a Constitution DC 16 Saving Throw or be reduced to 0 Hit Points, requiring immediate healing. Those that save are merely knocked unconscious for 2d4 minutes.

Other races are immune to this effect, but half-elves are not. Their Saves are DC 15.

15 - Monk Cells

All the doors to in Area 15 are unlocked.

These four simple and humble cells have simple beds with straw mattresses, latrines, and wooden desks. At the onset of the Demon War, the scholars who used the temple lived at the bottom the hill overlooking The Lake, and this was home to two paladins and two priests, all who perished during the Demon War.

Underneath each bed is a trunk that contains the personal possessions of each of the occupants, faded with time and neglect. Most of it is ceremonial clothing for two paladins and two priests, but there are some coin pouches, with 134 GP and 371 SP total.

One of the chests contains spare armor and weapons; a full suit of plate mail, a silver longsword, and a silver dagger.

16 - Kitchen

Neither door to this room is unlocked.

This large kitchen was used for the dining room in Area 2 but, for security reasons sometime in the past, the door to Area 2 from the hallway serving Area 16 and 17 was removed. Since then, the Kitchen was seldom used by the Temple inhabitants but was popular with the scholars and monks using the Scriptorium in Area 18 who enjoyed its use without disturbing the Temple proper.

There is nothing interesting in this kitchen. The stove contains the broken remains of the two chairs that used to be here, but the fire was never lit.

Unfortunately for the PCs, the magical energy that powers the clockwork in this Temple section has infected some of the mundane items here. Like the stove. As soon as a PC gets within 5ft. of it, it attacks.

Belligerent Animated Stove

Large construct, unaligned
Armor Class 16 (natural armor) — **Hit Points** 39 — **Speed** 40 ft.

Statistics

STR	DEX	CON	INT	WIS	CHA
18 (+4),	18 (-1)	13 (+1)	1 (-5)	3 (-4)	1 (-5)

Damage Immunities poison, psychic, fire
Damage Vulnerabilities electricity, thunder, radiant
Condition Immunities blinded, charmed, deafened, exhaustion, frightened, paralyzed, petrified, poisoned
Senses blindsight 60 ft. (blind beyond this radius), passive Perception 6
Languages —
Challenge 3 (700 XP)

Abilities

Antimagic Susceptibility. The creature is incapacitated while in an antimagic field. If targeted by dispel magic, the creature must succeed on a Constitution Saving Throw against the caster's spell save DC or fall unconscious for 1 minute.

Charge. If the stove moves at least 20 feet straight toward a target and then hits it with a ram attack on the same turn, the target takes an extra 9 (2d8) bludgeoning damage. If the target is a creature, it must succeed on a DC 14 Strength Saving Throw or be knocked prone.

False Appearance. While the animated stove remains motionless, it is indistinguishable from a normal stove.

Actions

Ram. *Melee Weapon Attack:* +6 to hit, reach 5 ft., one target. *Hit:* 13 (2d8+4) bludgeoning damage.

Spit Lid. *Range Weapon Attack:* +6 to hit one target, range 20/240, 4 ammunition. *Hit:* 13 (2d8+4) bludgeoning damage.

17 - Storage

Neither door to this room is locked.

This is a storage room with extra chairs and dining supplies. Like Area 16, the magic powering the clockwork in the Scriptorium has bled into this room. As soon as a PC enters the room, the plates and cups come flying off the shelves and plaster the PC, breaking either on the PC, the walls, or the floor. The PC must make a DC 15 Dexterity Saving Throw or take 1d6 damage (no damage on save).

Once the dinnerware has caused its damage, the animation effect ends.

18 - Scriptorium

None of these doors are locked. However, if a PC listens at the door, they can hear the whirring and tick of gears and small machinery.

This large room with a dozen wooden desks is where monks and scholars worked on calligraphy, maintenance of old and holy tomes, and new books. The room also has tall candelabra candles, once providing lighting.

In the years leading up to the Demon War, the books produced in the Temple were philosophical and commentary of other works, and quite popular with the better educated of the people of Wailmoor and even throughout the Kingdom of Lothmar.

The dust covered book and parchment left out are oddly about green dragons and their preferences for virgin elf maiden and is either a parody or a disturbing insight into bad dragon habits.

In the room, the sound of gears and machinery is louder.

This old scriptorium must have seen heavy use; the tile is worn from feet and the scraping of chairs, the desks heavily used and stained with inks. An abandoned book lies on one desk, empty candelabras, and the occasional

Intro

Lost
at the
Beaux
Seins

Moortide
Rising

**The
Altar &
the Anvil**

Castle
Wailmoor

Appendix

yellow parchment on others. On the walls hangs artistic blueprints to the creation of silver holy symbols of Dvalin.

Oddly, the sound of small machinery and moving gears permeates this room with a hum, along with the sound of tiny electrical discharges.

The sound is from a nearly invisible Scriptorium Automation, a clockwork magical item that is usually stored in the Storage Room in Area 17 when not in use by monks and scholars. It was left here, however, forgotten by all. Over time, exposed to the Ethereal nature of the Temple, it has taken on a semblance of etherealness. Its higher-order magic is also leaking into this Temple area, causing problems for the Kitchen in Area 17 and 18.

Perception and Intelligence

It takes a DC 15 Perception role to finally see the Scriptorium Automation as it sits on a desk. It does not attack the PCs unless attacked, but until the PCs remove a book from its repository, it continues to "leak" from the Temple's latent power reserves and inappropriately animates random objects in the upper half of the Temple.

Using the book repository "resets" its magic, and it functions normally without causing problems in the area around it while maintaining its Ethereal property.

Inside of the book repository is a single volume; *Witch Light in the Viscounty,* a non-fiction book on the rise of witches in the Viscounty as the power of druids waned over the centuries.

The automation only speaks and take commands in Old Dvalin. Anybody wearing a silver holy symbol of Dvalin can give it commands.

Right now, the automation is confused. It doesn't understand why it is partially Ethereal, and if a PC tries to talk to it, it asks for help in Old Dvalin. It points to its repository, to a book, and to its repository again.

It will not leave the Temple unless asked to do so and certainly, will not adventure.

Scriptorium Automaton

Small construct, lawful neutral
Armor Class 13 (natural armor) — **Hit Points** 7 — **Speed** 30 ft.

Statistics

STR	DEX	CON	INT	WIS	CHA
8 (-1)	13 (+1)	10 (+0)	14 (+2)	3 (-4)	8 (-1)

Skills History +4, Investigation +4
Damage Immunities poison, electricity
Damage Vulnerabilities force
Condition Immunities charmed, poisoned
Senses blindsight 60 ft., truesight 10 ft., passive Perception 11
Languages Old Dvalin
Challenge 1 (200 XP)

Abilities

Extra-Dimensional Book Repository. A small door on the chest of the scriptorium automaton opens into an extra-dimensional bookcase. This bookcase functions exactly like a bag of holding except that it can store only written materials such as books, scrolls, tomes, parchment, folders, notebooks, spell books, and the like.

Ethereal Sight. The scriptorium automation sees 60ft. into the Ethereal Plane when it is on the Material Plane, and vice versa.

Incorporeal Movement. The scriptorium automation can move through other creatures and objects as if they were difficult terrain. It takes 5 (1d10) force damage if it ends its turn inside an object.

Actions

Bibliotelekinesis. This ability functions as the cantrip *mage hand* but can be used only on books, scrolls, maps, and other printed or written materials.

Gaze of Confusion. The library automaton chooses one creature it can see within 40 feet. The target must succeed on a DC 12 Intelligence Saving Throw or take 9 (3d4 + 2) psychic damage and have disadvantage on Intelligence-based checks, Saving Throws, and attacks until the end of its next turn. If the Saving Throw succeeds, then the target takes half damage and suffers no other effect.

19 - Treasury

This room is highly dangerous to the incautious PCs. Clockwork guardians and animated objects will attack the PCs if the contents are disturbed without the proper conditions met.

This room also contains the key to the fake sarcophagus located in Area 27.

The Glyph

Both doors to this room are locked, DC 18 Dexterity (Thieves' Tools) to open, and warded with a glyph by the Dedicate Merisee as she left the temple. The glyph glows faint blue, and unlike most *glyphs of warding,* the proximity to the Radiant Chapel makes them easy to spot. It is a small glyph over the lock, and trigger when the lock is touched with or without the key.

Intro

Lost
at the
Beaux
Seins

Moortide
Rising

The
Altar &
the Anvil

Castle
Wailmoor

Appendix

When triggered, the glyph erupts with magical energy into the 5' square before the door and two squares both to the east and the south (for 25' impacted area total) into the hallway with 5d8 thunder damage, DC 15 Dexterity Saving Throw, save for half.

Triggering the glyph alerts the room's inhabitants of an impending door breach.

THE ROOM AT A GLANCE

This is an obvious treasure room.

Five large chests are in this room, with a singular continual flame illuminating expert craftsmanship in the flickering light. There are two chests near the south wall and two chests near the north wall, with one dusty, but beautifully ornate chest in the middle.

Hanging on the east and west walls are decorative swords, two per side, their sharp blades gleaming as if polished yesterday.

Hanging from a small metal peg set in the north wall is a key tied with a purple ribbon.

THE TRIGGERS

If one of the PCs is experienced with Dvalin Temples, they will immediately discern that this room is highly dangerous unless the proper command words are spoken (no DC necessary). Those with a layman's familiarity with Dvalin Temples can make a DC 15 Intelligence (Arcana)—DC 20 with no familiarity—to

note there is a magical ward here linked to the chests. If magic is detected, all five chests have a faint aura of alteration.

To access the chests without triggering the guardians and the magic that activates them, the linkage either needs to be unlinked, DC 25 Intelligence (Arcana) check, or the *Prayer of Passage* spoken aloud while holding forth a silver holy symbol of Dvalin—which is a common prayer—but must be in the language Old Dvalin, which is not.

Touching the swords, attempting to use *dispel magic* (which absolutely will not work due to the link to the dam), opening the chests (which are unlocked) trying to pick the locks (which are not locked) or failing at the Arcana check to unlink the chests to trigger wards results in the defenses activating.

Consequently, if the PCs trigger the glyphs to either the door to the south or the door to the west, the guardians also trigger as soon as a PC steps beyond the first 5ft. square.

Simply taking the key **without disturbing anything** does not trigger the guardians. The key opens the false sarcophagus in Area 27.

COMBAT

If triggered, two Clockwork Hounds burst out of the chests along the north wall, and the 4 swords on the wall animate and attack.

The hounds concentrate on melee combatants while the swords attack ranged or spellcasting enemies.

Two Clockwork Hounds

Medium construct, unaligned
Armor Class 12 — **Hit Points** 71 — **Speed** 50 ft.

Statistics

STR	DEX	CON	INT	WIS	CHA
16 (+3)	15 (+2)	14 (+2)	1 (-5)	10 (+0)	1 (-5)

Saving Throws Dex +4, Con +4
Skills Athletics +7, Perception +4 (Advantage when tracking)
Damage Immunities poison, psychic, electricity
Damage Vulnerabilities force, thunder
Condition Immunities charmed, exhaustion, frightened, paralyzed, petrified, poisoned
Senses passive Perception 14
Languages understands Old Dvalin but doesn't speak it
Challenge 2 (450 XP) each

Abilities

Diligent Tracker. Clockwork hounds are designed to guard areas and track prey. They have Advantage on all Wisdom (Perception), and Wisdom (Survival) checks when tracking.

Immutable Form. The creature is immune to any spell or effect that would alter its form.

Magic Resistance. The Clockwork Hound has Advantage on Saving Throws against spells and other magical effects.

Actions

Bite. Melee Weapon Attack: +5 to hit, reach 5 ft., one target.
Hit: 14 (2d10+3) piercing damage.

Tripping Tongue. Melee Weapon Attack: +5 to hit, reach 15 ft., one target.
Hit: 7 (1d8+3) slashing damage. The target must succeed on a DC 13 Strength Saving Throw or be knocked prone.

Explosive Core. The mechanism that powers the hound explodes when the construct is destroyed. All creatures within 5 feet of the hound take 7 (2d6) fire damage or half damage with a successful DC 12 Dexterity Saving Throw.

Four Flying Swords

Small construct, unaligned
Armor Class 17 (natural armor) — **Hit Point** 17 (5d6)
Speed 0 ft., fly 50 ft. (hover)

Statistics

STR	DEX	CON	INT	WIS	CHA
12 (+1)	15 (+2)	11 (+0)	1 (-5)	5 (-3)	1 (-5)

Saving Throws Dex +4
Damage Immunities poison, psychic, fire
Damage Vulnerabilities force, thunder
Condition Immunities blinded, charmed, deafened, frightened, paralyzed, petrified, poisoned
Senses blindsight 60 ft. (blind beyond this radius), passive Perception 7
Languages —
Challenge 1/4 (50 XP) each

Abilities

Antimagic Susceptibility. The sword is incapacitated while in an antimagic field. If targeted by dispel magic, the sword must succeed on a Constitution Saving Throw against the caster's spell save DC or fall unconscious for 1 minute.

False Appearance. While the sword remains motionless and isn't flying, it is indistinguishable from a normal sword.

Actions

Longsword. Melee Weapon Attack: +3 to hit, reach 5 ft., one target.
Hit: 5 (1d8+1) slashing damage.

The hounds and the swords will chase their prey anywhere, with the hounds particularly adept at tracking. However, if the clockwork hounds or animated objects find themselves in Area 1, the iron golem smashes them to pieces.

THE TREASURE

The chests the Clockwork Hounds sprang from are empty.

The two chests along the southern wall contain a trove of esoteric, but expensive items:

- The chest closest to the scriptorium contains a dozen blank books, two sets of wax sealed ink bottles in a variety of colors, a small box containing expensive, jeweled fountain pens and five scroll tubes filled with thick paper. Another small box contains stoppered vials of various alchemical substances, and another box contains expensive spell components for writing scrolls—the whole being enough supplies to scribe 5 scrolls of 4th Level spells and under (3 spells per page). The whole is worth 1,000 GP.

- The southern chest nearest the east wall contains temple trappings—jeweled silver and gold religious reliquaries, silk cloth with fancy embroidery, ceremonial robes and shoes, and a small wooden gift box containing armor smithing tools, with another gift box containing weapon smithing tools. The whole is worth 3,000 GP (all obviously from a Dvalin temple).

The middle chest contained money, although Oakheart and Merisee took most of the portable treasure with them. Left in the chest is:

- 16 gold bars (500 GP each)

- 20 bars of iron (left over from the creation of the iron golem; they have a slight aura of alteration if magic is detected, although they are useless to anyone except a master smith creating an iron golem)

- 12 thick bars of high-grade steel (for magical weapon creation)

- A bag of diamond dust (also for magical weapon creation) worth 5,000 GP

- 20 silver bars (50 GP each)

- A small box of high-quality lose clockwork worth 800 GP

20 - STORAGE ROOM

The door to this room is unlocked.

This is a storage room supporting the stable. It contains shelving for harnesses and wheels for carriage repair. Old saddles, tack, and harness are here, but the leather is dried and cracked. The spare wheels are in perfect shape.

21 - VESTIBULE

The doors to the west and east are unlocked.

This vestibule is used to connect the stable area with the quiet and precious scriptorium. It has stones benches and hangers on the walls for monks to change before entering the Scriptorium, or for lounging on a break, eating a snack, or drinking water (neither allowed in the Scriptorium).

22 - CRYPT ENTRANCE

This room triggers a *Lost Memory*.

The door here is locked, DC 15 Dexterity (Thieves' Tools), to open. The stairs descend to landings which switch direction, for a total decline of 50ft. until they reach the Crypt in Area 26.

DESCRIPTION

The walls here are painted with scenes of bravery honoring Dvalin and his clergy, the march of time doing little to obscure the great artistry used in their creation.

A stone stairway carved into the rock floor descends in darkness to a room.

If the PCs have not encountered any of the *Lost Memories* (and is viewing the room without stepping into it) about the temple's final inhabitants, a DC 13 Intelligence (Religion) or DC 15 Intelligence (History) check reveals this scene is disturbingly depicting Oakheart, Merisee, the two paladins and two clerics doing battle against demonic forces in the Wailmoor.

The paintings are not dated.

A divine servant of Dvalin painted them after the temple was abandoned, a tribute to Dvalin's brave devotees. If the PCs get the impression a Divine Servant of Dvalin descended from the heavens to paint this mural—they are correct.

LOST MEMORY

This plain room with blank walls has stairs going down into the darkness, but the elf Merisee holds her silver holy symbol of Dvalin aloft and it glows with light at her whispered melodic command.

She turns to Jackon behind her.

"Hey Jackon, where did you get your staff?" she abruptly asks.

"Yeah, where did you get your staff, Jackon?" Heleshia blurts out.

"Indeed, Sir Jackon, thy formidable staff is a mystery," Silas adds.

Jackon doesn't miss a beat. "After Imperial War College, I was assigned to an Imperial Black Ops squad that was clandestinely helping an enclave of orcs in the Wild Lands against a goblin host. Afterward, their king showed me this strange statue of a hooded druid-like figure holding a staff he found on his come-of-age walkabout, saying the statue looked like me. Well, we got drunk, we went to the statue, it looked like me, and it was holding this staff." Jackon takes a measured breath in and lets it out slowly.

"So, I took it," he finishes.

"Well, I don't want to know any more about orcs and Imperial covert-ops shenanigans," says Silas.

"Gods above—orcs," Heleshia whispers.

"Bad. Ass," Merisee says, nodding enthusiastically.

The room description used in the *Lost Memory* is specific. The walls in the lost memory are not painted.

A holy symbol of Dvalin is not necessary to light the way, but the stairs are pitch-black dark.

Intro

Lost at the Beaux Seins

Moortide Rising

The Altar & the Anvil

Castle Wailmoor

Appendix

23 - STABLES

Horse (pony) booths are carved into the rock. Two large doors lead outside of this room that is covered in stone pavement. Old rotten hay litters the floor, home of an odd set of bugs that have mutated from exposure to the Temple's magical auras. They attack anyone disturbing the hay.

This area was most likely a stable for ponies. There is old, rotten hay in the stalls to the south. There are two doors to this room, both to the north. In one of the rotten hay piles, there is an odd, faint glow of rainbow colors.

Swarm, Prismatic Beetles

Prismatic beetles swarm
Medium swarm of Tiny beasts, unaligned
Armor Class 13 — **Hit Points** 38
Speed 20 ft., burrow 5 ft., fly 30 ft.

Statistics

STR	DEX	CON	INT	WIS	CHA
3 (-4)	16 (+3)	12 (+1)	1 (-5)	13 (+1)	2 (-4)

Skills Perception +3, Stealth +5
Damage Resistances bludgeoning, piercing, slashing
Condition Immunities charmed, frightened, paralyzed, petrified, prone, restrained, stunned
Senses blindsight 10 ft., darkvision 30 ft., passive Perception 13
Languages —
Challenge 3 (700 XP)

Abilities

Glittering Carapace. The glossy, iridescent carapaces of the beetles in the swarm scatter and tint light in a dazzling exhibition of colors. In bright light, a creature within 30 feet that looks at the prismatic beetle swarm must make a successful DC 13 Wisdom Saving Throw or be blinded until the end of its next turn. If the Saving Throw fails by 5 or more, the target is also knocked unconscious. Unless it's surprised, a creature can avoid the Saving Throw by choosing to avert its eyes at the start of its turn. A creature that averts its eyes can't see the swarm until the start of its next turn when it can choose to avert its eyes again. If the creature looks at the swarm in the meantime, it must immediately make the Saving Throw. The Saving Throw is made with advantage if the swarm of prismatic beetles is in dim light, and this ability has no effect if the swarm is in darkness.

Swarm. The swarm can occupy another creature's space and vice versa, and the swarm can move through an opening large enough for a Tiny insect. The swarm can't regain hit points.

Actions

Bites. *Melee Weapon Attack:* +5 to hit, reach 0 ft., one creature. *Hit:* 10 (4d4) piercing damage. Or 5 (2d4) piercing damage if the swarm has half of its hit points or fewer. The target also takes 10 (4d4) poison damage and becomes euphoric for 1d4 rounds or takes half as much poison damage and is not euphoric if it makes a successful DC 11 Constitution Saving Throw. A euphoric creature has disadvantage on Saving Throws.

24 - INNER COURTYARD

This courtyard is carved into the mountain with a high ceiling where a magical light provides outdoors-like lighting to the place. Rock pavers cover the floor.

There is nothing interesting here in this area. The door to the stables in Area 23 is unlocked and closed, as is the west-most door.

25 - Tunnel in the Mountain

A long, paved hallway connects the inner courtyard with a secret door to the side of the mountain. This secret door is easy to find with a DC 13 Wisdom (Perception) or Intelligence (Investigate) Check, but the rusted iron door on the south end is locked with a high-quality lock and requires a DC 20 Dexterity (Thieves' Tools) check to open.

Moving south past the secret door places the PCs in the Temple's powerful wards. The entire upper complex of the Temple is permanently *hollowed* and under *forbiddance*, and these effects cannot be dispelled as described in the front of the chapter.

26 - Crypt

Stone stairs here climb back to Area 22. Descending the stairs leaves the Temple's powerful wards (which used to extend to the entire temple complex), consequently, ascending the stairs brings PCs into the wards and none of the creatures encountered, including the cave adders in Area 34, can follow them up the stairs.

The ground in the lower part of the temple is dirt, and the only light sources are the continual flame torch in Reliquary in Area 31 and the soft, green, glow from the transparent Obelisk in Area 33.

The walls are carved into body-sized emplacements for receiving the remains of the local clergy.

It is customary for dwarves to simply place a body on top of another body in a crypt, and this is no exception.

The stairs terminate in a typical dwarven crypt, bones stuffed in alcoves, piled on top of other bones. The air is cold and dry.

Hidden in one of the alcoves for bones is a Frostskull, a dwarf's skull corrupted by the Obelisk in Area 31. It waits until the PCs move north or south, shouts "Losers!" in a squeaky, demonic voice and let's lose with a *sleet storm*.

It then laughs maniacally and flees at its full movement either north or south, depending on where the PCs are. It takes time to cast *shield* and *blur* if it can and then proceeds to attack the PCs from the opposite direction. Each time it attacks, it insults the PCs with squeaky taunts such as "You suck!", "Your mama's butt is so big you need a ranger to find a way around it!" and "I've seen better combat tactics from drunk fornicating pixies!"

If destroyed and reformed, the frostskull will shout "Miss me?" when attacking again with more insults, although it doesn't regain any cast spells until the next day (*frost ray* and it's cantrip are always available).

Regardless, it is trapped in the crypts here and can neither go up the well in Area 34 nor up the stairs.

Frostskull

Tiny undead, neutral evil
Armor Class 13 — **Hit Points** 40 — **Speed** 0 ft., fly 40 ft. (hover)

Statistics

STR	DEX	CON	INT	WIS	CHA
1 (-5)	17 (+3)	14 (+2)	116 (+3)	10 (+0)	11 (+0)

Skills Arcana +5, Perception +2
Damage Resistances lightning, necrotic, piercing
Damage Immunities cold, fire, poison
Damage Vulnerability radiant
Immunities charmed, frightened, paralyzed, poisoned, prone
Senses darkvision 60 ft., passive Perception 12
Challenge 4 (1,100 XP)

Abilities

Illumination. The frostskull sheds either dim blue light in a 15-foot radius or bright blue light in a 15-foot radius and dim light for an additional 15 feet. It can switch between the options as an action.

Magic Resistance. The frostskull has Advantage on Saving Throws against spells and other magical effects.

Rejuvenation. If the frostskull is destroyed, it regains all its hit points in 1 hour unless holy water is sprinkled on its remains or a dispel magic or remove curse spell is cast on them. Reducing the Frostskull to 0 HP with radiant damage also destroys it permanently.

Spellcasting. The frostskull is a 5th-level spell caster. Its spellcasting ability is Intelligence (spell save DC 13, +5 to hit with spell attacks). It requires no somatic or material components to cast its spells. The frostskull has the following wizard spells prepared:
Cantrip (at will): *mage hand*
1st level (3 slots): *magic missile, shield*
2nd level (2 slots): *blur, acid arrow*
3rd level (1 slot): *sleet storm*

Actions

Multiattack. The frostskull uses Frost Ray twice

Frost Ray. Ranged Spell Attack: +5 to hit, range 30 ft., one target. Hit: 13 (3d6+3) cold damage.

Intro

Lost at the Beaux Seins

Moortide Rising

The Altar & the Anvil

Castle Wailmoor

Appendix

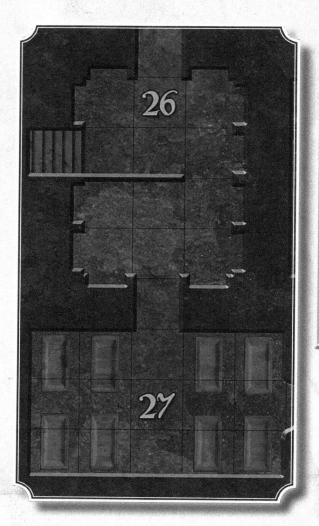

Seven Corrupted Dwarven Skeletons

Skeleton Fighter 1| Medium undead, neutral evil
Armor Class — 13 (armor scraps) — **Hit Points** 22 — **Speed** 30 ft.

Statistics

STR	DEX	CON	INT	WIS	CHA
14 (+2)	14 (+2)	15 (+2)	6 (-2)	8 (-1),	5 (-3)

Saving Throws Str +4, Con +4
Skills Athletics +4, Perception +1
Damage Immunities poison, necrotic
Damage Vulnerabilities bludgeoning, radiant
Condition Immunities exhaustion poisoned
Senses darkvision 60 ft., passive Perception 11
Languages Dwarven (understands but can't speak)
Challenge 1/2 (100 XP) each

Actions

Warhammer. *Melee Weapon Attack:* +4 to hit, reach 5 ft., one target.
Hit: 6 (1d8+2) bludgeoning damage or 7 (1d10+2) bludgeoning damage if used with two hands to make a melee attack.

Light Hammer. *Melee or Ranged Weapon Attack:* +4 to hit, reach 5 ft. or range 20 ft./60 ft., one target.
Hit: 4 (1d4+2) bludgeoning damage.

27 - Burial Vault

Temple priests or other functionaries within the church are buried here, but the sarcophagus in the upper north corner doesn't contain any bodies.

The bodies buried here are thoroughly corrupted by the Obelisk.

This dark room is dominated by eight stone sarcophagi. It is cold, dark, and dusty.

As soon as one PCs attempt to move one of the stone lids, the seven corrupted skeletons attack. They push back their lids and jump into the fray. They are quite enthusiastic about killing the PCs and will pursue them all over the lower temple. They have a warhammer in one hand and a light hammer in the other.

Cautious PC can avoid activating the skeletons, but they must remain quiet enough where the skeletons' Perception does not detect the disturbance.

Unless the PCs burn the bones after defeating the corrupted skeletons, the Obelisk will use them to form a giant skeleton construct when the PCs force it to manifest itself.

Treasure

In the upper-right corner of the burial vault is a fake sarcophagus that has an elaborate locked lid. The key is in the trapped and warded Treasure Room in Area 19 hanging on a hook on the wall with a ribbon on it.

Finding the lock requires a DC 15 Intelligence (Investigate) Check or a DC 20 Wisdom (Perception) check. Picking the lock is a DC 18 Dexterity (Thieves' Tools) Check.

Forcing the lid requires a Party DC 15 Strength (Athletics) Check.

The fake sarcophagus is a hide-in-plain-sight bug-out treasure chest. In it are 6 mithril bars (enough mithril for 6 dedicate ceremonies), *3 potions of greater healing*, 1,000 Imperial gold coins and a pouch of gems worth 5,000 GP, 3 sets of high-quality travel clothing for dwarves, 3 sets of high-quality travel clothing for humans and a *folding boat*.

28 - Tomb of the Temple Warrior

A single stone sarcophagus sits in the middle of the room, and it contains a powerful, corrupted spirit that reacts badly to being disturbed.

A stone sarcophagus, bearing the tale-tell depictions of an important dwarf, dominates this small 15ft. x 10ft. room.

An aura of cold permeates this room, originating from the sarcophagus. The sarcophagus is both closed and sealed—a small glowing rune made of silver seals the lid and base like a wax seal to an important document.

This sarcophagus contains a corrupted temple warrior that moves from its resting place and attacks from a position from behind the PCs (using its Ethereal ability) as soon as someone tries to open its lid. Once a spectral temple warrior, it is now an evil thing bent on destroying all who disturbed it.

This ghost-like dwarven warrior seems to radiate hate and evil in equal measures, holding it longsword and shield with expertise and fell purpose.

Corrupted Temple Warrior

Spectral Fighter 5 — Medium undead, chaotic evil
Armor Class 17 (spectral armor and shield) | **Hit Points** 100
Speed 30 ft.

Statistics

STR	DEX	CON	INT	WIS	CHA
16 (+3)	13 (+1)	16 (+3)	8 (-1)	10 (+0)	15 (+2)

Saving Throws Str +6, Con +6
Skills Acrobatics +4, Athletics +6, Perception +3, Stealth +7
Damage Resistances bludgeoning, piercing, and slashing from nonmagical attacks
Damage Immunities cold, necrotic, poison
Damage Vulnerabilities radiant, force
Condition Immunities charmed, exhaustion, frightened, grappled, paralyzed, petrified, poisoned, prone, restrained
Senses darkvision 60 ft., passive Perception 13
Languages common, dwarven
Challenge Rating 6 (2,300 XP)

Abilities

Ethereal Sight. The corrupted temple warrior can see 60 feet into the Ethereal Plane when it is on the Material Plane, and vice versa.

Incorporeal Movement. The corrupted temple warrior can move through other creatures and objects as if they were difficult terrain. It takes 5 (1d10) force damage if it ends its turn inside an object.

Spectral Armor and Shield. The corrupted warrior's AC reflects its spectral armor and shield.

Actions

Multiattack. The corrupted temple warrior makes two attacks with its spectral longsword.

Spectral Longsword. Melee Weapon Attack: +6 to hit, reach 5 ft., one target. Hit: 9 (1d8+5) force damage.

Etherealness. The corrupted temple warrior magically enters the Ethereal Plane from the Material Plane or vice versa. It is visible on the Material plane when it is on the Border Ethereal, and vice versa, yet it can't affect or be affected by anything on either plane.

Inside of the sarcophagus is an odd *magical copper crucible*, cold to the touch with many dwarven runes on its surface both inside and outside the crucible.

This copper crucible is clearly magical. On the outside, it is painfully cold. Runes cover both the inside and outside, and the whole is of great workmanship. The runes are all dwarven in nature, but one stands out, a depiction of a waterwheel and its wheelhouse.

29 - TOMB OF THE TEMPLE GUARDIAN

Like the tomb in Area 28, this sarcophagus radiates cold. While it's corrupted tomb guardian is not as formidable as the one in Area 28, it is still a challenge for unwary PCs.

A stone sarcophagus, bearing the tale-tell depictions of an important dwarf, dominates this small 15ft. x 10ft. room.

An aura of cold permeates this room, originating from the sarcophagus. The sarcophagus is both closed and sealed—a small glowing rune made of silver seals the lid and base like a wax seal to an important document.

The Corrupted Spectral Guardian within attacks as soon as its sarcophagus is touched.

This translucent form of a dwarf has piercing eyes of glowing purple and hands that end in claws dripping with shadow.

Intro

Lost at the Beaux Seins

Moortide Rising

The Altar & the Anvil

Castle Wailmoor

Appendix

Corrupted Spectral Guardian

Medium undead, neutral evil

Armor Class 13 — **Hit Points** 67 — **Speed** 0 ft., fly 60 ft. (hover)

Statistics

STR	DEX	CON	INT	WIS	CHA
6 (-2)	16 (+3)	16 (+3)	12 (+1)	14 (+2)	15 (+2)

Damage Resistances acid, fire, lightning, thunder; bludgeoning, piercing, and slashing from nonmagical attacks that aren't silvered
Damage Vulnerabilities radiant, force
Damage Immunities necrotic, poison, cold
Condition Immunities charmed, exhaustion, grappled, paralyzed, petrified, poisoned, prone, restrained
Senses darkvision 60 ft., passive Perception 12
Languages common, dwarven
Challenge Rating 5 (1,800 XP)

Abilities

Incorporeal Movement. The corrupted spectral guardian can move through other creatures and objects as if they were difficult terrain. It takes 5 (1d10) force damage if it ends its turn inside an object.

Sunlight Sensitivity. While in sunlight, the corrupted spectral guardian has disadvantage on attack rolls, as well as on Wisdom (Perception) checks that rely on sight.

Actions

Life Drain. *Melee Weapon Attack:* +5 to hit, reach 5 ft., one creature.
Hit: 21 (4d8+3) necrotic damage. The target must succeed on a DC 14 Constitution Saving Throw or its hit point maximum is reduced by an amount equal to the damage taken. This reduction lasts until the target finishes a long rest. The target dies if this effect reduces its hit point maximum to 0.

The spectral guardian also moves to attack the PCs from behind with its incorporeal movement ability, but unlike the occupant of the sarcophagus in Area 28, it isn't interested in stabbing PCs with a spectral sword—it wants to suck the lifeforce out of them until they are husks devoid of warmth. It is a formidable opponent, and quite insane with its corrupted-driven hatred for life and good.

Inside of the sarcophagus is an odd *magical copper key mold,* cold to the touch with many dwarven runes on its surface.

Inside the sarcophagus is an odd key mold made of copper, covered in slightly glowing runes and cold to the touch. It is a hinged copper box that can be opened and laid flat, exposing its contents. While closed, there is a channel to pour molten metal, and the whole is of great workmanship if a bit odd—copper is not a metal molds are usually made from.

The runes on the copper mold are all dwarven in nature, but one stands out, a depiction of a waterwheel and its wheelhouse.

---

30 - TOMB OF THE PALADIN

Like the tomb in Area 28 and 29, this sarcophagus radiates cold, but its occupant is both less and more dangerous. This is the tomb of a former paladin of Dvalin one Sir Gwane Germnise (surname is pronounced GERM-nize), but now has been corrupted in a vile monster and given some semblance of life and unlife—he is now a fledgling vampire, and despite his hunger for blood, he is righteously angry that his spirit is corrupted instead of used to protect the Temple. He feels a great sense of betrayal and despair fueled with an overwhelming sense of fear.

A stone sarcophagus, bearing the tale-tell depictions of an important human, dominates this small 15ft. x 10ft. room.

The sarcophagus is both closed and sealed—a small glowing rune made of silver seals the lid and base like a wax seal to an important document.

Sir Germnise's motivations are to flee the Temple and the PCs. Unlike the occupants of the other tombs, he looks like a human corpse, and simply lies there when the sarcophagus is opened, appearing quite dead. How he reacts depends on the PCs actions, which in turn depend on if the PCs are expecting an attack because they opened the sarcophagi in Areas 28 and-or 29 first.

Unsealing and removing the sarcophagus lid reveals the corpse of a heavily armored human warrior, his emaciated skin taunt in a death pallor. He appears to have died of old age. It seems if you merely touch his corpse it will fall apart. He clutches a sword and shield. At his feet is a wooden box with carved runes and an artistic depiction of a watermill.

Sir Germnise doesn't have to fake death; he *is* dead. The only thing amiss in his fakery is his holy symbol of Dvalin is gone, driven into the Ethereal by the Corrupted Obelisk.

If the PCs merely take the box and close the lid, Sir Germnise waits until the next evening to slowly open the lid and escape through the well in Area 11 that connects to Area 34—the PCs, after all, broke the magical seal. Using his spider climb ability to traverse the well and his regeneration ability to weather the traps, he flees.

Theoretically, the PCs could reseal the sarcophagus, and Sir Germnise is screwed, but such resealing must be done by a priest of Dvalin using a ritual that takes time to learn and cast—the cleric would need to start working on a new seal immediately to be done by the next nightfall.

If the PCs try to take his sword or shield (or armor), the PC doing so gets a sense of resistance as Sir Germnise holds onto them, giving an overall sense that the "corpse" is clutching his equipment so tight in death that to pull further is to defile his corpse.

If the PCs persist, Sir Germnise attacks (see below).

If the PCs sprinkle Sir Germnise with holy water, he screams in pain and attacks (see below).

If the PCs pause and attempt to talk to Sir Germnise (a distinct possibility if the PCs have encountered the other two corrupted temple guardians that merely attacked them), he will slowly rise in a non-threatening manner, pick up the box at his feet and hand it to the PCs. If they do not attack him, he replaces the lid on his sarcophagus himself, giving the illusion that he is simply a helpful spirit. Which, in a sense, at this moment, is true.

If the PCs use divination magic or some type of detect evil spell or ability and then attempt to communicate, Sir Germnise is thoroughly infected by the Crypt Obelisk and is evil as evil ever was, despite his disposition to the PCs for "rescuing" him. While he is a fledgling vampire, he is a veteran warrior and a survivalist, and that is the instinct overrides everything he does.

He will admit that his spirit was supposed to be recalled back to his resting place in the form of a ghost to defend the temple against supernatural forces. But, it seems, something corrupted his resting place, and he himself no longer resides in heavenly Elysia. He can feel no connection to Dvalin at all.

He then challenges the PCs to a duel, practically begging them to put him out of his misery. He suggests fighting them in the middle of the cavern in Area 32 and will propose the PCs fight him all at once, as one-on-one he will kill them all.

Once defeated his body crumbles to dust. And reforms the next evening in his sarcophagus (see below).

ATTACKING SIR GERMNISE

While corrupted, Sir Germnise is an honorable person with motivations of his own. He suffers from a sense of betrayal and abandonment—he lived his life as a paladin to Dvalin and in return, was turned into an undead thing.

Sir Germnise is depressed. He views the PCs as less graverobbers or whatever they are and more of the people who rescued him from his hungry torment. How he reacts to the PCs attacking him depends on when and why they do it.

ATTACKING AT NIGHT

If the PCs attack him while he is in his sarcophagus, they have Advantage for one blow, but Sir Germnise is heavily armored. If this happens at night, he springs out of his resting place with his spider-climb ability, trades the PCs one blow (it is the honorable thing to do) and then flees the temple via through the well in Area 11 that connects to Area 34, simply taking the damage from the fire trap if it is still active. He also takes damage from the undead ward.

Even when armored, his speed is still 30ft. Short of a coordinated and immediate burst of damage from the PCs that punch through his damage resistances, he will escape.

ATTACKING AT DAY

Sir Germnise attempts to flee at per above but is stopped short of the sunlight coming in from the well as soon as he sees it. Resigned to fighting his rescuers, he grimly goes about putting up a good fight, because that's all he knows how to do. He will attempt to take up his last stand in the middle of Area 32. He won't converse, but he will bite a PC at every opportunity to do so.

Intro

Lost at the Beaux Seins

Moortide Rising

The Altar & the Anvil

Castle Wailmoor

Appendix

If defeated, he turns to dust, leaving only his magical sword behind. He reforms, armor, shield and all, in his sarcophagus the next evening and then attempts to flee the temple.

Stake Through the Heart

It is possible but unlikely the PCs can figure out Sir Germnise is a vampire. Staking him in the heart as he is in his sarcophagus will end his torment. His soul goes straight to Purgatory to be purified of his corrupted demon taint.

The Escaped Sir Gwane Germnise

He flees east to the no-mans-land outside of the purview of the Empire. In 1d6 months he goes from a fledgling vampire to a vampire will full capacities.

In another 1d6 months, he regains his paladin levels as a fighter and adds 7 HD of Fighter levels. Finally, after an additional 1d6 months, Sir Germnise pieces together what happened to him. Never one to whine about his lot while alive, he accepts his new condition and quietly goes about opposing demons in his own twisted way, opposing the cult of Orcus in particular.

Sir Germnise can become a tragic anti-hero in the Campaign or a reoccurring villain holding a grudge that the PCs did not put him out of his misery when they had the chance.

Vampiric "Cure"

There is no cure for vampirism, but there is a cure for a broken spirit. If a priest, paladin or dedicate to Dvalin intuit that Sir Germnise doesn't have his heart in the battle, or if they realize he can be conversed with before steel is drawn (see above), then with a DC 20 Charisma (Persuade) Check, Sir Germnise will pause the festivities for the PCs to search for a book to help him in the Library in Area 6.

The book in the Library in Area 6, the *Tome of Undeath*, describes the nature of vampirism is linked to corruption—specifically the Demon Lord Orcus. And like all corrupted things, exposing the lies of unlife to the sun is the only path to redemption. It explains clearly and in detail that the vampire must willingly expose himself to sunlight, but because of the self-defensive nature of the vampire, he or she will need help in doing so. Two people are going to need to help him stay standing on his own feet by holding him up— while he is on fire. And the ceremony needs to be done as soon as possible.

This makes a lot of sense to Sir Germnise, and he'll do it, but there is a lot of trust involved on the PCs part because unless he is using the sunbeam in Area 34 (via a raft made out of a table or some such), he will have to meet them outside the temple to await the dawn, as he is unable to traverse the stairs in Area 26. He needs to wait until evening to leave the Temple via the well.

There is also a trust component that the vampire will not bite the PCs helping him out of hunger.

In any event, Sir Germnise remains committed to this course of action. It takes him 4 rounds to be consumed by sunlight, and the two PCs are holding him up on the start of round 2 starts taking 10 points of damage per round for a total of 30 HP of fire damage each (no Saving Throw).

Sir Germnise keeps his promise and burns away without even a whimper, leaving behind his magical longsword as his tormented, but cleansed soul is free to enter Elysia. The two PCs who helped him receive a permanent Damage Resistance to Fire and becomes immune to a vampire's charm ability. The party should be rewarded with the XP for defeating him.

Sir Gwane Germnise, Fledgling Vampire

Vampire Fighter 1 — Medium undead, lawful evil
Armor Class 21 (plate, shield) — **Hit Point** 93 — **Speed** 30 ft.

Statistics

STR	DEX	CON	INT	WIS	CHA
16 (+3)	16 (+3)	16 (+3)	11 (+0)	10 (+0)	12 (+1)

Saving Throws Str +6, Dex +6, Con +6, Wis +3
Skills Athletics +6, Perception +3, Stealth +6 (Disadvantage from armor worn), Survival +3
Damage Immunities necrotic
Damage Resistances cold; bludgeoning, piercing, and slashing from nonmagical attacks
Damage Vulnerability radiant
Senses darkvision 60 ft., passive Perception 13
Languages common, dwarven, Elvish
Challenge 5 (1,800 XP)

Abilities

Regeneration. The vampire regains 10 hit points at the start of its turn if it has at least 1 hit point and isn't in sunlight or running water. If the vampire takes radiant damage or damage from holy water, this trait doesn't function at the start of the vampire's next turn.

Spider Climb. The vampire can climb difficult surfaces, including upside down on ceilings, without needing to make an ability check.

Vampire Weaknesses. The vampire has the following flaws:
Forbiddance. The vampire can't enter a residence without an invitation from one of the occupants.
Harmed by Running Water. The vampire takes 20 acid damage when it ends its turn in running water.
Stake to the Heart. The vampire is destroyed if a piercing weapon made of wood is driven into its heart while it is incapacitated in its resting place.
Sunlight Hypersensitivity. The vampire takes 20 radiant damage when it starts its turn in sunlight. While in sunlight, it has disadvantage on attack rolls and ability checks.

Actions

Multiattack. The vampire makes two attacks, only one of which can be a bite attack.

Bite. *Melee Weapon Attack:* +6 to hit, reach 5 ft., one target. *Hit:* 6 (1d6+3) piercing plus 7 (2d6) necrotic damage. The target's hit point maximum is reduced by an amount equal to the necrotic damage taken, and the vampire regains hit points equal to that amount. The reduction lasts until the target finishes a long rest. The target dies if this effect reduces its hit point maximum to 0.

Claws. *Melee Weapon Attack:* +6 to hit, reach 5 ft., one creature. *Hit:* 8 (2d4+3) slashing damage. Instead of dealing damage, the vampire can grapple the target (escape DC 16).

Flame Tongue. *Melee Weapon Attack:* +6 to hit, reach 5 ft., one target.
Hit: 7 (1d8+3) slashing plus 2d6 fire when ablaze damage or 8 (1d10+3) slashing plus 2d6 fire when ablaze damage if used with two hands to make a melee attack.

Items

Flame tongue longsword, heavy shield, plate armor

The Box

This wood box with carved runes and an artistic depiction of a watermill opens easily. Inside are smith's tools—tongs, files, two rods, a hammer, etc., all made of copper and featuring runes with a slight blue glow. They are unnaturally cold to the touch, and a quick examination reveals that despite the soft metal they are crafted in, they are harder than steel and far from delicate.

These are smith tools needed to finish the keys after they are removed from their mold (the file is used to file the mold lines, flashing, etc.).

They have Damage Immunity Fire and Cold, and Damage Resistance All except magical blunt damage.

31 - Old Reliquary

Examining the keyholes triggers a *Lost Memory,* either from Jackon's or Heleshia's perspective.

This area of the lower temple is heavily warded with powerful divine magic in addition to engineering that hardens this reliquary into a vault.

A steel portcullis with dim glowing blue runes seals off the room to the west. Immediately beyond the portcullis is a glowing blue glyph with runes that rotate around the glyph's parameter.

The room beyond contains a large, stone desk with three small chests and at least one bookshelf.

On either side of the portcullis is a large, copper lock mechanism, set flush into the stonework. The copper panel has a keyhole and contains numerous glowing, blue runes.

Two master thieves with a high proficiency bonus can attempt to unlock the portcullis. They would need to simultaneously make a DC 30 Dexterity (Thieves' Tools) Check followed by a one DC 30 Intelligence (Arcana) check to bypass the magical ward, and if they

Intro

Lost at the Beaux Seins

Moortide Rising

The Altar & the Anvil

Castle Wailmoor

Appendix

are not using tools made from wolfram, they need to make another DC 30 Intelligence (Arcana) check to bypass the magical heating property of the locks.

Failure in any step causes the material inside the keyholes to be ejected (at the same time) as a high-velocity stream of plasma that does 5d6 fire damage (DC 15 Dexterity Save for half) to the squares in front of the locks and the square between them (the portcullis).

It is also possible to brute-force into the Reliquary, although a PC must make an Intelligence (Arcana) DC 30 check to remove the damage reduction ward that would allow an attack on the stone to occur—the interlocking carved stone of the Reliquary vault has an AC of 20 and a Damage Threshold of 20, but the damage reduction ward, unless dispelled, reduces all attacks against it by 20 HP. It takes 30 hits above the damage threshold (only after damage reduction ward is removed) to break into the vault.

Using spells to bypass (*knock* or *dispel*) the wards are impossible, as the wards preventing the temple from being egressed via spells are powered by a spell-engine in Olaf's Dam.

Closing the portcullis resets the magical locks and the runes on the bar glow blue again.

LOST MEMORY

Heleshia pulls down the portcullis, and the runes on it start to glow blue, and there is an audible click. Jackon hands Merisee the Priestess a metal key, and she puts it in her pocket with another just like it.

"Will you be taking these keys with you to university?"

"Psh. I'm going to melt them down. Someone wants into the Reliquary—they'll need to make their own."

"How will you melt something made of wolfram? I saw you seal away the magical crucible where they were made."

"Gonna feed them to the iron golem," the elf says.

Jackon practically rolls his eyes. "You're so weird," he says.

Merisee snorts, "You have no idea."

She winks at Heleshia, tongue between her teeth in an impish grin.

RELIQUARY CONTENTS

Inside the Reliquary are two bookshelves with Merisee's ritual book that extensively documented the ritual Silas and Jackon used to seal the Obelisk in Area 33 to the Ethereal Plane.

There is a large stone desk, with three small chests. There are numerous items in the room:

- *Scroll of haste* sitting on top of a bookshelf wrapped around a scroll of *raise dead*

- *Scroll of protection from evil* sitting on top of a bookshelf

- *Scroll of daylight* sitting on top of a bookshelf

- A *tome of understanding* amongst the other books

- Small chest on the desk with 500 platinum pieces

- Small chest on the desk with 500 gold pieces

- Small chest on the desk with 500 electrum pieces

- *Candle of invocation* (attuned to Dvalin) inside the desk

- Merisee's ritual book

- While a considerable treasure trove with a powerful Dvalin-focused item (*the candle of invocation*), the 59 books are the real treasure. These are the books that were used to do research on the dam, engineering, and the Ethereal Plane, but the books on the dam itself including the advanced engineering techniques developed (including the formula for the concrete used), the rituals created to tap into the dam's energy, the construction blueprints, and the work history were all taken by the Priestess-Scholar (and Dedicate) Merisee.

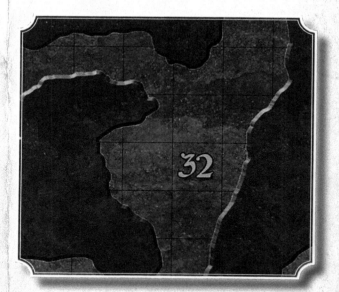

32 - ENTRANCE TO CAVES

At some point in the temple's history, the occupants embarked on a mining operation but discontinued it after a lengthy discussion on creating protentional means of additional egress into the temple's crypts.

The area is now a simple crossroads of tunnels in a set of natural caves. Entering it triggers a *Lost Memory*.

Jackon the War Wizard places a hand on Silas's arm, who now has the appearance of a man slipping from middle-age into decrepitude.

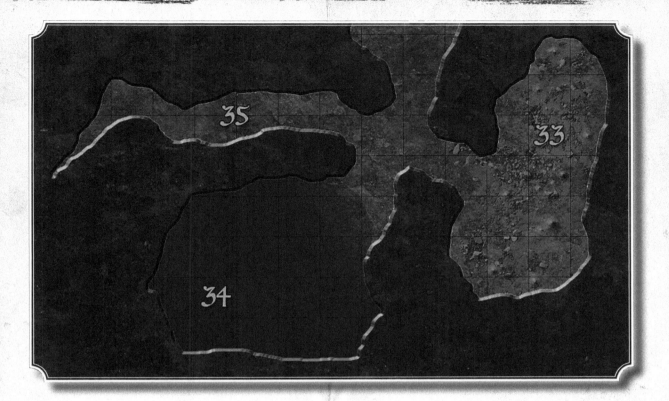

Intro

Lost
at the
Beaux
Seins

Moortide
Rising

**The
Altar &
the Anvil**

Castle
Wailmoor

Appendix

"Silas. I will place the final Obelisk at the edge of the Plateau. You need to rest."

Silas pauses. "It's a shared responsibility, Sir Jackon," he says, formally.

Jackon also pauses. Heleshia looks to one, and then to the other. To her, they both appear as if placing the ward stone took parts of them to complete. Permanently.

"I'm not asking, Lord Silas," the War Wizard eventually replies, just as formally.

Silas nods in reply.

33 - CORRUPTED CAVE

This is the location of the Corrupted Obelisk, and entering it triggers a *Lost Memory*. The memory will trigger over-and-over again until one of the PCs willingly accepts the memory. Old Dvalin himself is sending a message to the PCs, and it isn't cryptic.

This cave is filled with stalagmites and stalactites; the floor is covered by rock debris and slippery.

LOST MEMORY

Heleshia observes as Jackon and Silas complete the ceremony, and the warding Obelisk fades until it is mostly transparent.

"This is so fascinating! Don't see magic like this every day," Merisee the Priestess quips, writing in her ever-present book. She has followed Jackon and Silas around like a puppy, an immature trait from the vastly out-of-

place priestess of Dvalin. Merisee is an elf and a young one at that.

Silas and Jackon turn to her, both appearing worn and frazzled from the powerful magic of the ritual.

"I would like to protest again that it is unwise to write the secrets of the Obelisk down in a book," says Silas.

The young elf maiden simply raises an eyebrow. "My lord, I can assure you this book cannot fall into the wrong hands. First, we'll lock it away behind a portcullis that can only be unlocked via two special keys forged from wolfram, a metal known only to a few esoteric smith-priests of Dvalin. To do so requires special tools, the special mold, and a magical crucible. The metal, tools and the crucible are locked away and guarded separately from all the other temple reliquaries. Then, after unlocking the portcullis, only a cleric, paladin or Dedicate to Dvalin can traverse the warding glyph. And *then*, this book is written in Old Dvalin, which is a language only Dvalin scholars know. But there's more!" She pauses.

"Go on," Jackon says, annoyed.

"I've written it in Dedicate Code. You have to know the cipher to decode it."

"Is there a way to get the code other than from someone like yourself?" Silas asks.

"Ha! No—wait, yes. Theoretically, any worshiper of Dvalin with a proper holy symbol can start putting together the key to the cipher—the key is in the Radiant Chapel, after all, and all they need to do is match the symbol on the columns to the symbol key on a silver holy symbol—but they'll have to traverse the Realm of Dreams to see the correct symbol correlation on the columns!" Merisee says the last with a gleam in her eye.

Both Silas and Jackon exchange glances, and both sigh at the same time.

These steps outlined in the *Lost Memory* are literal, although the exact location or the numerous sub-steps are not articulated by the memory.

PCs don't need to be penalized for not writing down the *Lost Memory* as it occurs. Hand them the appendix with the *Lost Memory* for reference.

THE OBELISK

The Obelisk is currently transparent. It exists on the Ethereal Plane, but it can be seen here, glowing green, a squat, evil thing infecting everything around it with its unholy presence. It has corrupted the entire lower portion of the Temple except for the Reliquary, and its vileness is slowly creeping up the stairs. Several decades from now it will reach the Chapel, desecrating the entire Temple when it snuffs out the Font of Radiance.

See the Unlock the Obelisk section below for the steps the PCs need to undertake to manifest the Obelisk, so it can be destroyed, along with details on what happens when the PCs drag it back to reality.

34 - UNDERMOUNTAIN POND

The underground pond's waters are stagnant and murky. The pond is about twelve feet deep. It is normally drained by an underground stream, but somewhere along the line during the Demon War, a group of miscreants made it past the grate but not the fire trap, and now rusted armor, a shield, weapons, and equipment are blocking the water's normal egress.

The ceiling here is 12ft. high, and well is 50ft. in length. If PCs had not disabled the trap and removed the grate, they are still present.

Normally this pond is not as deep or large as depicted, but the slow drain because the body has interrupted its design as a source of fresh water.

The shield presently blocking the outlet is a *shield +1*. However, 4 cave adders take up residence in the cave and attack anyone entering the water. They are vicious and infected by the corrupted Obelisk.

Four Cave Adders

Small beast, neutral evil
Armor Class 13 — **Hit Points** 26 (4d6+5) — **Speed** 30 ft.

Statistics

STR	DEX	CON	INT	WIS	CHA
6 (-2)	16 (+3)	12 (+1)	2 (-4)	10 (+0)	(-3)

Senses blindsight 10 ft., passive Perception 10
Languages —
Challenge 1/2 (100 XP)

Abilities

Cave Camouflage. The cave adder has Advantage on Dexterity (Stealth) checks while in a cavernous terrain.

Actions

Bite. *Melee Weapon Attack:* +0 to hit, reach 5 ft., one target. *Hit:* 1 piercing damage. The target must make a successful DC 11 Saving Throw or become poisoned. While poisoned this way, the target is paralyzed and takes 3(1d6) poison damage at the start of each of its turns. The target can repeat the Saving Throw at the end of each of its turns, ending the effect on itself with success.

Description

A large, vicious snake with a squat, diamond-shaped head, a puffed neck, and a peculiar yellow band around its body, the cave adder is a stout, somewhat lethargic hunter.

If PCs destroy the Obelisk, the cave adders die from the shock. Cleaning the pound of debris restores its function as a supply of fresh water.

TEMPLE WARDS

The Temple has powerful wards, but the well opening here is a hole of sorts. Both the fledgling vampire in Area 30 and the bone giant (if formed) could traverse the traps and push past the wards to escape into the landscape around the Temple, but only the vampire would choose to do so. He still takes 5d10 radiant damage (in addition to the fire damage), but unless it kills him outright (doubtful as he will likely be regenerated to full health), he can escape the underground complex with his spider climb ability and his strength to simply rip the grate off its hinges.

35 - OLD VEIN

The dwarven scholars of the temple at one time mined some silver here but did not dig very deep, as the pursuit of the vein was to test out a mining technique rather than retrieve the silver itself. Theoretically, the PCs could continue mining the vein (which travels downward and back towards the east.

If a DM wishes to expand on adventuring beneath the temple, this is an area provided for that purpose.

Unlock the Obelisk

The arcane ritual used to send the warding Obelisk to the Ethereal Plane has powerful magic behind it, magically linked to the artifact that it is the dam, both an engineering and magical marvel. Without the *Lost Memory* in Area 33, PCs would have a nearly impossible time undoing the ritual that placed the Obelisk outside of the Welt.

The PCs need to:

- Forge two special keys to unlock the portcullis
- Traverse the powerful warding glyph
- Retrieve and decipher the codebook and reverse the Ethereal ritual
- Fight the desperate Obelisk for control of the Temple

1-Forge and Enchant Two Keys

The PCs must make the keys to unlock and raise the portcullis to Area 31 out of the dense and extremely high melting point wolfram (tungsten). Any other metal or lockpick tools simply melt in the magical locks; they are spit out of the locks as a high-velocity stream of plasma that does 5d6 fire damage (DC 15 Dexterity Save for half) to anyone standing in front or between them.

1.1 Obtain the Copper Crucible from Area 28

Wolfram has a high melting point, much higher than crucibles normally used to make steel objects, armor, and weapons. Long ago the temple experimented with the metal to make enchanted weapons but found the magic required to keep a crucible from melting itself was a wasted effort. Such a magical effort could be used more effectively in other ways.

The crucible works by transferring heat from the outside of the crucible to the inside while keeping the outside cool and the inside from melting. It stores the heat in the runes until it has enough temperature to melt the wolfram, then it releases it to do so.

Any flesh or other objects inside the crucible when it releases its heat is incinerated.

1.2 Obtain the Key Mold from Area 29

This elaborate mold magically operates just like the crucible, although the primary function of the mold is to magically cool the wolfram, which it does over the course of 10 minutes.

1.3 Obtain the Forging Tools from Area 30

The forging tools necessary to handle wolfram are in a wooden box in the sarcophagus in Area 30. There are tongs, two rods to hang the crucible in place while heating, files, and a smith's hammer in the box.

Once forged, wolfram is both heavy and dense. It's possible, but difficult, to use normal smith tools, but a smith has greater difficulty in preventing steel or iron melting on the wolfram, and the heat required to work the metal could burn an unwary smith using standard tools.

1.4 Option: Learn Smithing

If none of the PCs don't know smithing, the will need to learn. There are several illustrated guides to learn smithing in the Library in Area 6. PCs can use the Waterwheel Smithy or the intact smithy in Graspen. Self-tutelage for smithing proficiency normally would take an extensive amount of time, but because of the quality of the books in the library, it will take a PC a maximum of only 28 days. Add both the PCs Strength and Dexterity Modifiers together, and then subtract the total from 28, and that's how long it takes to learn smithing.

There is a multitude of smith tools in both smithies.

1.5 Forge the Keys at the Waterwheel Forge

The Waterwheel Forge outside of Graspen (outlined in Chapter 2) is where the prior two keys were made (along with the iron golem). Merisee the Priestess destroyed the prior two, and the waterwheel stamp that appears in numerous places that point the PCs to the great smithing complex.

Any undefeated demons still skulking around Graspen are attracted by the noise and smoke and attempt to distract the PCs during the forging process (they are still unable to enter the Waterwheel Forge).

A normal forge can never heat the crucible hot enough to melt the wolfram. A smith can only forge the keys at the waterwheel forge, DC 15 Dexterity (Smith's Tools) to complete the forging. There is enough wolfram for several attempts.

1.6 Open the Portcullis to the Reliquary

The two keys the PCs made have an extremely high melting point (as they are made of wolfram) and can survive the great heat from the magical locks. Once inserted into the two keyholes and turned, they form a magical circuit that turns off the portcullis's wards (the runes on the bars stop glowing blue). The portcullis can then be raised with a group DC 12 Strength Check. The PCs then have access to Area 31.

Intro

Lost at the Beaux Seins

Moortide Rising

The Altar & the Anvil

Castle Wailmoor

Appendix

2-Traverse the Warding Glyph

If none of the PCs are a paladin or cleric of Dvalin, one of them must choose to become a Dedicate of Dvalin, a (painful) rite of passage that carries with it rewards and obligations. The book in the Library in Area 6, *Dedicates of Dvalin,* described the process of proving one's devotion to Dvalin outside of becoming a priest or a paladin.

A cleric, paladin or dedicate can traverse the glyph simply by holding a silver holy symbol of Dvalin and walking through the circle ward. The ward repels all other people or things and the magic, powered by Olaf's spell-engine, cannot be *dispelled* nor tinkered with.

If one of the PCs is not a cleric or paladin of Dvalin, then one of them needs to go through (and survive) the Dedicate ceremony—or chose to convert to a Cleric or Paladin of Dvalin.

2.1 Learn About the Dedicates of Dvalin

The book *Dedicates of Dvalin* is in the Library in Area 6. Dedicates of Dvalin are free-roaming inter-organizational agents granted the divine power to oppose the demonic forces of entropy through less than conventional means that a cleric or paladin would employ. They are immune to possession as they have permanent *protection against evil (demons)* supernatural effect on them. In addition, they receive a +1 natural armor bonus to AC and the ability to use *divine sense* like a paladin, but only for demons.

However, becoming a dedicate comes at a price. The Dedicate is infused with holy power, and in addition to their racial type, they also are celestial and thus can be impacted by *protection from good, magic circle* and *dispel good* spells (and the like). The process is also so physically taxing; the Dedicate loses a point of Constitution. Some people do not survive the process. Finally, due to the interaction of the metal in their system, the Dedicate has a Damage Vulnerability to poison.

Dedicates have a loose honor code. Those that have turned down opportunities to root out demons or possessed have found themselves without their Dedicate powers but all the disadvantages until they've atoned. They can also receive resource assistance, albeit limited, from clerics, paladins, and temples of Dvalin. Dedicates are also one of the few people that can craft certain divine magical items and might be called on to aid such at any time.

Dedicate Summary

- Dedicate honor code
- +1 Untyped Armor Class Bonus

- Permanent protection against evil (demons)
- Divine Sense (Demons) 1/day + Charisma Modifier, refreshed after long rest
- Celestial addition to his or her original racial type
- -1 permanent loss of Constitution point
- Damage Vulnerability: poison

PCs studying the book have a full understanding of the benefits and price of becoming a Dedicate. Exactly how they are organized, not so much. A PC with a DC 15 Intelligence (Religion) check will know of the existence of Dvalin Dedicates, but only insofar as they are a legitimate faction within the Dvalin temple organizations.

Dedicates of Dvalin only talks about the ceremony; it doesn't outline *how* to perform one. *Trial of the Dedicate* is found in the Hight Priest Quarters in Area 13.

2.2 Find the Ceremony Book

Demon hunting is a dangerous occupation at best and exceedingly dangerous to everyone around the hunter at worst. Demons are far from stupid, and while going after a Dedicate directly usually does not end well for a demon, attacking the Dedicates support structure, friends and family is a viable tactic and right in the demonic wheelhouse.

A DC 15 Wisdom (Religion) check about Dedicates indicates that while a legitimate faction, the creation of one was highly regulated by the temple hierarchy.

It is for these reasons the book is locked away in the former High Priest's quarters in Area 13.

2.3 Decision Time: Cleric, Paladin or Dedicate

The Dedicate ceremony as outlined in the book is obviously painful and warns not everyone survives the process:

- At the base of the altar in the Radiant Chapel in Area 4, strips of flesh are removed from the PC's arms, legs, and chest
- In the radiant fire basin as the front of the temple, mitral bars are heated to the melting point (any crucible for silver will do)
- The melted mitral is then poured on Dedicate where the flesh was previously removed
- The proper runes are then inscribed into the mithril as it cools
- Holy water is then poured on the mitral strips while saying the *Dedicate Prayer*
- If Dvalin accepts the Dedicate, the mithril then "sinks" into his or her skin, and the flesh is made anew without scaring

The Dedicate ceremony requires all the participants to wear a silver holy symbol of Dvalin.

The book recommends the Dedicate receive healing during this process to stay alive. Any PC going through the ceremony must receive 20 Hit Points of healing or perish during the process. A DC 15 Wisdom (Medicine) Check will give PCs an approximation how much healing is required.

PCs may decide that it is easier to become a cleric or paladin of Dvalin than to go through the Dedicate ceremony or may be forced to go down that path because the party has no healers capable of healing 20 HP over the course of an "encounter"—although there are healing potions hidden throughout the Temple.

Doing so is easier than becoming a Dedicate. The PC merely presents a holy symbol of Dvalin at the altar in Area 4 at dawn, recite the *Cleric* or *Paladin Pledge* (both of which are found in the Library in Area 6), and beseech Dvalin to join his cause in holy purpose. Dvalin will grant such a request to any (and all) of the PCs.

The PCs last level is then converted to cleric or paladin, respectively. They lose all the benefits of the lost level and receive all the benefits of the new level at the same XP total.

WAY OFF IN THE FUTURE

If the players ask, it is possible to go beyond Level 20, thus, giving a paladin or cleric convert the opportunity to reach Level 20 benefits. Don't volunteer this information—it's a meta-answer to a meta question.

2.4 CREATE SILVER HOLY SYMBOLS OF DVALIN

Those participating in the Dedicate Ceremony must wear a *silver* holy symbol of Dvalin. A wooden holy symbol of Dvalin is a depiction of a hammer striking an anvil—the silver version is quite an elaborate affair adding a multitude of runes, 54 in all. Creating the silver symbol is a DC 20 Dexterity (Smith's Tools) Check.

To create silver holy symbols, a blacksmith must have a blueprint to do so, or a pristine symbol to create a wax mold.

2.4.1 FIND THE BLUEPRINTS FOR HOLY SYMBOL CREATION

There are several high-quality blueprints for a silver holy symbol in the Scriptorium in Area 18.

2.42 FIND "NORMAL" SILVER FOR THE HOLY SYMBOL

There are numerous bars of silver to create a multitude in one of the chests in the Treasure Room in Area 19.

2.4.4 MAKE THE HOLY SYMBOLS

The smithy in <u>Graspen</u> or the Waterwheel Smithy just north of the village are places a blacksmith can make the silver holy symbols. One or more PCs needed to learn smithing to create the wolfram keys, <u>detailed in previously in wolfram key mission description</u>.

2.4.5 ENCHANT THE HOLY SYMBOLS

Cleaning and purify the water basins in Area 4, along with saying the proper prayer to Dvalin, creates holy water. When the symbols are placed in the basin, it will enchant them as proper holy symbols.

2.5 OPTION: OBTAIN THE MITHRAL FOR CEREMONY

The precious mithril for the Dedicate ceremony lies hidden in the fake sarcophagus in the <u>Burial Vault in Area 27</u>.

2.6 OPTION: PERFORM THE DEDICATE CEREMONY

The prior Section 2.3 outlines the steps necessary for the Dedicate ceremony.

If *all* PCs decided to become dedicates to Dvalin (using the *healing potions* found within the temple to keep the healer alive during the ceremony), this effectively transfers ownership of the Temple, in a legal and religious sense, to the PCs. The radiant iron golem in Area 1 will take commands (in Old Dvalin) from the PC but will not move far from the Temple grounds. It can wander up to 80' away from the Temple.

Taking ownership of the Temple is a serious responsibility but grants the PCs additional autonomy from within the Dvalin religious organization. The Temple then will need a dedicated cleric of any level.

THE LADY'S
WOODS

The Statue
of the Lady

3 - DECODE THE RITUAL BOOK

Not only will the Player Characters need to learn the ancient language Merisee used when she documented Silas's and Jackon's ritual, but they will also need to decode the cipher.

3.1 LEARN OLD DVALIN

Old Dvalin is a dead language, spoken only by scholars, dedicated historians, and certain factions within the Dvalin religion. It is the root language to both Elvish and Dwarvish and unlike both of those languages, almost absurdly overly complex. Indeed, modern scholars attribute the advancement of the elven and dwarven people to "dumping the shackles of their mother tongue that seemed only to exist to sneer at simpler languages."

All the primers to learn the language are in the Library in Area 6, four books in all, including two exercise books where the students are expected to write sentences and essays on parchment or paper and have them graded by an instructor. Consequently, there is also an instructor's tome.

Learning enough of Old Dvalin to understand the ritual book will take 60 days with the following modifiers:

Days	Modifier
- (INT Mod)	Subtract the PCs Intelligence modifier
-5	PC knows elvish
-5	PC knows dwarvish
-5	PC knows both elvish and dwarvish
-10	PC is a known linguist and speaks 4 or more languages
-3	PC is proficient in Investigation
-10	One or more other PCs is learning Old Dvalin
-5	PC has attendance at an Imperial University in their background

3.2 DECIPHER THE RITUAL BOOK

Simply having the ritual book and learning Old Dvalin is not enough. The PCs need to decipher the code used in the ritual book. The cipher is easy enough to apply but obtaining it—not so much.

All the letters in the code are on the columns in the Chapel in Area 4 and correspond to Old Dvalin phrases (not simply letters). However, they are not arranged properly and must be read from the Realm of Dreams. Matching the code (in the waking world) produces a ritual book of obvious gobbledygook, double gobbledygook if the reader doesn't understand Old Dvalin.

Theoretically, someone versed in code-breaking could break the code. To do so requires a DC 30 Intelligence check and requires the reader to be proficient in the Old Dvalin language, or able to cast a spell to read and understand unknown languages, in addition to having a silver holy symbol of Dvalin. Such spells do not grant the ability to decipher codes, only the ability to use a language the caster isn't proficient with at the time.

Code breaking without the holy symbol of Dvalin is another DC 30 Intelligence check.

3.2.1 Find the Dream Book in the Library

The Library in <u>Area 6</u> has several books on dreaming. One book is a rumination on dream interpretation where the author concludes much non-divine dream interpretation is "crap."

The other book, however, is far more practical. *Dreams of the Ethereal* is a detailed book listing the connection to intense or reoccurring dreams to the Ethereal Plane. The author, one Lord Gregory Kemora, describes an arcane potion called "Dream Tea" that, once ingested, will allow a dreamer to perceive the dreams attached to the ethereal near the dreamer.

Dream tea is an arcane potion, and the recipe is included in the book. Small sips go a long way, with a PCs ability to experience the dreams floating around in the Ethereal for weeks or months at a time. Consequently, Lord Kemora warns against those with weak minds or lacking maturity from using *dream tea,* noting that without a scholarly detachment, the dreams are too intense for an unguarded mind.

3.2.2 Collect the Herbs in the Lady's Wood

PCs will need to go and adventure once more on the moor to collect the necessary herbs to brew the *dream tea*.

At this point, the DM should encourage the PCs to be creative in how they can go and collect herbs around the moor considering that they have limited knowledge of where these herbs can be found. They *should* be wary of running into more demons or witches and wasting resources on unnecessary encounters.

Searching the Library, the PCs can find a book on local rare herbs. PCs will have to collect:

- A piece of bark from a Slippery Elm
- A piece of bark from a Black Walnut
- A piece of bark from a Silver Birch
- A "Cairn Cap" mushroom
- Crowberry
- Wavy hair grass
- Sphagnum moss

Finding the three Barks in the Forest

This should not be too much of a challenge for PCs to figure out that tree bark can be found in a forest, especially the largest forest on the Wailmoor, the Lady's Woods.

Using the book on rare herbs in the temple of Dvalin Library in Area 6, it will take them 3d10 days to do so. If they have an herbalist, it only takes 2d10 days. If they elicit the help of the druids in the Crossroads Village, it only takes 1d10 days.

The Lady's Woods are not inherently dangerous, even though they are wild and not maintained by Wailmoor Rangers as they once were (those rangers being a defunct organization). There is still a probability for PCs to run into random encounters. Assuming the PCs have already traversed the woods prior to Chapter 3, use this encounter table to determine random encounters (scarcity determined by the DM), otherwise use the encounter table in Chapter 2 for The Lady's Woods:

1d12	Encounter	Avg. CR
1	Swarm of Bats	1/4
2	1d4 Giant Spiders	2
3	Swarm of Wasps	1/2
4	4 Boars	1
5	1 Giant Boar	1
6	1 Cave Bear	2
7	1d4 Dire Wolves	2
8	1 Ettercap and 2 giant spiders	4
9	1d6 Giant Wasps	2
10-12	Mathilda the Pixie	1/4

At the DM's discretion, PCs could also run into some Kandra bandits (use the stats from the Harenvale bandits in Chapter 2), depending on how into the scavenger hunt the players are.

Mathilda the Pixie

Mathilda is a member of the fey court from the nation-wide faerie realm that lays far west beyond the borders of the Kingdom of Lothmar. She is not evil and does not mean harm to the players; she is however very mischievous and based on how players treat her, she might be a huge help to them or a total pain in their neck.

Mathilda cares about the forest inhabitants and respectful visitors. She will start to follow the players and see how they behave. If the PCs talk unnecessarily loud in the forest, kill animals outside of self-defense and sustenance and destroy the local flora, Mathilda won't like that.

Intro

Lost at the Beaux Seins

Moortide Rising

The Altar & the Anvil

Castle Wailmoor

Appendix

Once she introduces herself to the PCs, Mathilda is in for some fun. Genuinely the only thing she wants from the PCs is a good time. "You need to entertain me!" should be her main tantrum. PCs can throw some jokes at her, perform some acts or tricks to amuse her or tell her stories. She *loves* romance stories and thinks fancy tiny shoes are the best thing ever.

If PCs are "boooring!" to her and insist on only talking about plants, their locations or try to obtain information from her without taking care of her desires first, she will leave them.

If they can befriend Mathilda, she will offer to collect all the pieces of bark for them (it will take her 2 hours) and can point them at the Cairns and the Bogs as where to look for the rest of the *dream tea* ingredients. She will, however, refuse to leave the Lady's Woods.

If Mathilda is not so inclined to like the PCs, her annoyance can take several forms. She can lure wild animals onto them, set traps in the forest to slow or injure the players, wake them up at night and cancel out their rest periods, collect available food ahead of them so they can't forage, steal their rations while they sleep, etc. But she won't directly attack them and will flee any combat situation with the PCs.

Finding the Cairn Cap

Besides the Herbs, the PCs need a rare mushroom, described in the book as a "Cairn Cap." This mushroom indeed grows in the region of the Wailmoor called the Cairns.

PCs can easily find this mushroom that grows on the slopes of the mountains, where the old barons of Wailmoor and the first settlers of the moor are buried. This simple task triggers one random encounter:

D10	Encounter	Avg. CR
1	Swarm of Bats	¼
2	1 Phase Spider	3
3	1d4 Assassin Vines	5
4	2d12 Loud Crows	0
5	1d2 Otyugh	5
6	1 Shambling Mound	5
7	1d2 Trolls	5
8	1d4 Giant Spiders	2
9	1d4 Dire Wolves	2
10	1 Black Pudding	4

FINDING THE BOG PLANTS

The last ingredients (crowberry, wavy hair grass and sphagnum moss) are found in a swamp.

If the PCs have destroyed the Bog Obelisk, then they should be rewarded with a modified encounter table:

1d20	Encounter	Avg. CR
1-2	4 Crocodiles	3
3	2 Wailmoor Giant Leeches	1
4	2 Wailmoor Giant Leeches in Trees	1
5-12	Creepy sounds	-
13-20	No Encounter	-

If the PCs left the Obelisk in the swamp alone, see Chapter 2 for its modified encounter tables, and difficulties in encountering the fell ward stone. Hopefully, the PCs did the right thing and destroyed the corrupted device before it created even more corrupted swamp creatures.

3.2.3 COLLECT THE SPECIAL WATER FROM THE LAKE GUARDIAN

The book on the *dream tea* is a local book, and the writer makes strange references to The Guardian of the Lake, which is the aforementioned fresh-water divine octopus described in Chapter 2. The book on *dream tea* is clear that the water needed for the tea must come from the Realm of Water, "The Guardian" controls the gate at the bottom of The Lake to it, and that unless the brewer has access to other sources, "asking the thing politely will suffice—it's telepathic. Bring him a bottle, one of the fancy ones where the stopper is connected to the neck with a hinge."

The Guardian of the Lake

This encounter should build a bit of stress for the PCs who do not know of the neutral, but kind nature of the octopus and feel they might have to fight another monster. They might even attack him on sight, just to get an advantage in combat.

From a divine perspective, The Guardian of the Lake *is* The Lake, and The Lake is The Guardian. To communicate with him, all a PC needs to do is stick a foot (or another part) in the water and telepathically call out. Upon doing so, the PC will get a sense of something coming towards them.

In 1d12 minutes, The Guardian will make an appearance. The Guardian glides near the shore and shows his large, strong tentacles, without making threatening moves towards the PCs.

Once face-to-face (so to speak), The Guardian can be communicated with telepathically. The Guardian speaks obtusely about what he is Guarding (leery of the PCs latent power), but clever players will probably guess it is a gate to Oceanna (the Realm/Plane of Water) and it doesn't take a lot of Intelligence modifiers to understand that such a thing is indeed dangerous and should be guarded.

The Guardian can furnish the players with what they seek, but he needs a favor in return, something that has been bothering him for some time now. His cleric

The map shows locations including Temple of Dvalin, THE LAKE, Graspen, and Castle Wailmoor.

Intro

Lost
at the
Beaux
Seins

Moortide
Rising

**The
Altar &
the Anvil**

Castle
Wailmoor

Appendix

died during the Demon War, and she was cremated somewhere near the reservoir, and her ashes buried. He can describe the location in detail. He wants the PCs to bring him the rocks used to cover her grave, a sack full of dirt from the grave itself, and her (intact) holy symbol. Once this simple task is completed, The Guardian will take the bottle and fifteen to twenty minutes later, bring it back filled with water from the Oceanna, the Realm of Water.

With clear instructions from The Guardian, this is not a hard task; the grave lies exactly where the giant octopus said it would be. However, much time has passed since the druid died and the area of the grave—a rocky promontory near the reservoir—is now near the home to three nesting stirges who use the elevation of this location to pray on moor animals below. The stirges will notice PCs who do not make specific precautions approaching the grave and will attack them on sight.

This bird-like creature has a long, needle-like beak and curious eyes, and is large enough to carry off tiny or small game with ease.

Three Wailmoor Stirges

Small beast, unaligned
Armor Class 13, 13 & 14 (natural armor, magic) — **Hit Points** 22
Speed 10 ft. fly 60 ft.

Statistics

STR	DEX	CON	INT	WIS	CHA
8 (-1)	14 (+2)	11 (+0)	6 (-2)	8 (-1	6 (-2)

Senses darkvision 60 ft., passive Perception 9
Languages — possible sign language with humanoids
Challenge 1 (200 XP) each

Actions

Blood Drain. *Melee Weapon Attack:* +4 to hit, reach 5 ft., one creature. *Hit:* 4 (1d4+2) piercing damage. The stirge attaches to the target. While attached, the stirge doesn't attack. Instead, at the start of each of the stirge's turns, the target loses 5 (1d4 + 3) hit points due to blood loss. The stirge can detach itself by spending 5 feet of its movement. It does so after it drains 10 hit points of blood from the target or the target dies. A creature, including the target, can use its action to detach the stirge.

Tactics – During Combat

During combat, a stirges are intelligent enough to use advanced pack tactics. They will attack an unarmored opponent from three different directions simultaneously.

Tactics – Morale

Unless guarding a nest or starving, a stirge will flee when attacked with melee or ranged weapons, recognizing such is dangerous.

Additional Details

Stirges are an intelligent (for a mammal) bird of prey that uses its long beak to pierce its prey and drain in blood. They usually hunt and nest in groups of three, two males and one female.

Highly adaptive and inquisitive, stirges normally do not attack humanoids, horses, or livestock unless such is sickly and alone. They are smart enough to avoid armored characters, ranged weapons and have a rudimentary understanding of the existence of magic. Therefore, a stirge, when faced with such, simply flees unless they are guarding a nest, where they will fight to the death unless faced with overwhelming odds.

Stirges will hold grudges, but also can be befriended. They are highly susceptible to music, and when faced with such, exude a calm that overrides their baser instincts. Some rangers and druids report success in teaching a stirge sign language.

If the PCs manage to becalm the stirges, one of them will give the PC its *ring of protection +1* while the other makes "shoo" motions with its wings after watching the PCs dig up the grave with interest and curiosity.

The ring is also retrievable if the PCs kill the stirges, but if they are defeated and fly away to do battle another day, the ring is lost.

The Bottle

Player Characters can simply make the bottle (anybody with a crafting skill can fashion a bottle with a stopper that is connected to it) or find one from the ruins around Harenvale from one of the burnt-out estates. Doing so, however, will draw attention to any bandits still in Harenvale. The PCs can even use a jar with a screw-on lid, found in Silas Tower.

3.3 MAKE THE DREAM TEA

The water from the Plane of Water is the key ingredient to *dream tea*. A simple mortal, pestle, tea-leaf strainer, and teapot will suffice to make *dream tea*. The tea has a smoky, pleasant taste and can be reheated if allowed to cool and still work.

Diluting the water with normal water invalidates the magical formula used in making the tea, but there are enough doses in the batch to last for months on end— one sip of *dream tea* causes 2d12+12 days of dreams from the ethereal.

But is it not instant lucid dreaming, and there are many charged dreams around the vicinity of the Temple. The dreaming PC could be at this for weeks.

3.4 ENTER THE REALM OF DREAMS

Mortal dreams that are charged with emotion find their way into the Ethereal and sometimes manifest themselves like an illusion to anyone traversing the Ethereal. *Dream tea* lets a dreamer view these dreams, not simply peer around the Ethereal while dreaming.

Drinking *dream tea* gives a PC access to this realm, but unless they are a cleric of Melaina, they will not be able to lucid dream and simply traverse to the Radiant Chapel and read the glyphs on the column within. The PCs must dream, once a night, until they have they can dream themselves into the Temple. Each night, they roll a D100.

D100	Dream Encounter
1	The PC is dreaming about their family, a family possessed by demons and subsequently killed by the Knights of Wailmoor (the dreamer is not a Knight)
2	A dream about a group of elves setting an entire farm compound on fire with magical, flaming arrows and eventually demonic screams are heard from the flames, along with several child-like voices that call out for "mommy" but later curse the elves in a demonic voice
3	A dream about being chased about by a group of demons into the Temple of Dvalin and having the demons stomped by an iron statue into pasty goo
4	A child's dream of a Dragon Knight personally laying waste to an evil cleric and his cohort, the vile spells of the cleric don't affect the Dragon Knight at all
5	A dream from the perspective of some tentacled creature in a lake grasping a demon flying close to the water and yanking it under
6	A pleasant dream of two lovers in a forest glade having passionate intercourse underneath a statue of a noble, beautiful woman
7	A dream about studying a book that is quite disturbing, in sharp contrast with the pleasant outdoor setting around the dreamer
8	A dream about having a picnic lunch above an outlook over the Reservoir Dam
9	A horde of zombies is shuffling after the dreamer. She runs them around and around in circles until they are near each other, and then she takes out her holy symbol, screams the Guardian will have them all, and then the zombies explode in a burst of divine energy
10	A dream about wandering the deserted Wailmoor, while constantly looking up in the sky with an arrow in a longbow ready to be notched at a moment's notice
11-20	Roll a 1d10
21-80	A vivid, personal dream not having to do with the Wailmoor but prior events in the PC's immediate past based on their character history
81-90	**Success! The PC is in the Temple of Dvalin and can find the glyphs on the columns in the chapel and, using their holy symbol, construct the cipher.** Show the PC the Temple of Dvalin depiction at the start of the chapter.
91-100	A lucid dream in which Lady Leighandra Rothcannon, Scion of Hardred, Wizard of the Higher Order, Mistress to Baron Amschel Mayer Carl, Ninth Weaver of Broken Dreams, the Aether Witch (the woman on the cover) is trying to talk to the PCs, but she simply fades away with a sad expression before anything is said

Traversing the realm of dreams in a lucid fashion is a skill any devoted worshiper of Melaina has, not simply her clerics. Such a PC can drink the tea and will their consciousness into the Chapel without hindrance.

Finding the Code

Once in the Chapel in the dream state, the PC notes which symbols on the Chapel's columns correspond to the symbols on his or her silver holy symbol.

The Radiant Chapel, a grand affair in the Welt, is an awesome sight to behold in the Ethereal. You have seen nothing like it, and the sight threatens to eject you from the dream in its grandiose awe.

But the glowing symbols on the column and your holy symbol beckon you—the symbols here in the Ethereal are different than what's in the waking world, and as you look at each one, its corresponding symbol burns into your mind.

Your holy symbol, here, is different too. The correct column symbol matches one on the back of your holy symbol, which, in turn, has a letter from the Old Dvalin language above it.

You realize you have the cipher. You've learned the Dedicate Code.

Upon waking, the PC can translate the ritual book and no further checks, or special effort is needed, all that remains is time. The process takes 2d8 days and requires ink, a quill, and a blank book, all which PCs can find in the Temple or Silas Tower.

Beram Oakheart's Warhammer

Oakheart was always more of divine spell caster rather than an artisan, but when he set his mind to creation, the iron golem and his hammer was the result. Serving him well in battle in the Demon War, he left it at the feet of the statue, and there it sits after all this time—in the Ethereal Plane.

Dream walkers in the Chapel can see the hammer easily—a shaft of pure light highlights it and stretches to the ceiling.

As the symbols of the Dedicate Code scorches your dreamy thoughts, the waking world pulls at you. But here, in the Ethereal, you see the great statue of Dvalin, and at his feet is a mighty hammer, a shaft of radiance ascending to the heavens from its runes.

You wake with the Dedicate Code, and the odd memory that the statue winked at you.

The hammer is not obtainable in *Curse of the Lost Memories* but is in the next adventure, *Beneath a Dreary Wave*. If the PCs try to obtain it by dreaming of the Radiant Temple again, they are unable to grasp it from the Ethereal. After all, only their conscious is in the Ethereal. If they want that awesome hammer, they're going to have to traverse the Ethereal Plane to get it.

3.5 PERFORM THE RITUAL

When the PCs have a decoded ritual book, the arcane ritual takes 1d4 hours to complete with a 100% chance of success if the translated ritual book is in Old Dvalin and not further translated into another language.

If the PC applying the code to the new book decided to use a modern language, this produces errors and the ritual has a 50% chance of failure and wounds the caster with 2d10 points of force damage (much like a magic missile), no Saving Throw. The caster must wait until the next day to try again.

Once the PCs manifest the Obelisk, they can destroy it. It is an evil and corrupted thing, once a tool of good, now a mockery of everything it was built for, slowly chewing away at the Temple of Dvalin like some cancerous growth feeding off everything bad in the Welt.

This Obelisk is highly dangerous in its manifested state.

4- FIGHT THE DESPERATE OBELISK

As soon as the Crypt Obelisk is yanked into the real world, it loses its transparency, appears in the middle of the cavern, and turns into a trap: PCs must make a DC 15 Constitution Save any time they are in Area 33 or take 1d6 necrotic (negative) energy damage *per round* as an aura effect. They must make the DC Save each round.

The Obelisk then summons any remaining skeletal warriors from Area 27, but not simply as individual combatants. They push back their sarcophagus lids and then form into a giant skeleton, and it proceeds to Area 33 at a double move (the NW sarcophagus is a storage container and does not contain a corrupted warrior).

The Obelisk can also reconstruct the bones of the warriors if the PC open the lids and destroyed the skeletons but did not dispose of their bones by burying them away from, the temple or burning them. Failing that it will construct the bone golem from the bones in Area 26, but it will take an additional round to arrive.

If the PCs burned both sets of bones or reburied them outside of the corruptive influence of the Obelisk for both rooms, its only defense is its evil aura.

The Obelisk is a 3ft. slab of granite-like material—it has AC17, 220 HP and Damage Resistance: All (except Bludgeoning, Radiant, and Force) and Damage Vulnerability: Bludgeoning, Radiant, and Force.

Intro

Lost at the Beaux Seins

Moortide Rising

The Altar & the Anvil

Castle Wailmoor

Appendix

Corrupted Crypt Obelisk

Demonic Ward Stone
Armor Class 17 (natural armor) — **Hit Points** 220 — **Speed** 0 ft.

Statistics

STR	DEX	CON	INT	WIS	CHA
-	-	20 (+5)	-	-	-

Damage Immunities poison, disease, necrotic
Damage Resistance All except bludgeoning, radiant, force
Damage Vulnerabilities bludgeoning, radiant, force
Condition Immunities blinded, charmed, deafened, exhaustion, frightened, paralyzed, petrified, poisoned
Senses —
Languages —
Challenge Rating 4 (3,900)

Abilities

Bone Giant Construction. When removed from the Ethereal Plane, the corrupted obelisk constructs a bone giant if there are bones available to do so within its reach (200ft.-radius).

Anchored in Place. The corrupted obelisk cannot move, and automatically fails all Saving Throws except Constitution based saves.

Terrible Aura. Any creature in Area 33 takes 1d6 necrotic damage at the start of their turn (DC 15 Constitution Saving Throw for no damage).

Obelisk Regeneration The bone giant constructed by the Obelisk regenerates 10 Hit Points at the start of its turn whenever it is in the cave in Area 33.

Obelisk Fate If the Obelisk is destroyed, so too is the bone giant constructed by the Obelisk. The Giant explodes, doing 3d6 piercing damage to anyone within 30ft. (DC 15 Dexterity Save for half), and then the shards crumble to dust.

Obelisk Resurrection If the bone giant constructed by the Obelisk is destroyed before the Obelisk, it reforms at the beginning of its next turn with 10 Hit Points and immediately *multiattacks*.

As soon as the Obelisk appears solid, there is a clatter of odd sounds from the west. Stomping towards you is something that can only be described as a giant skeleton made from twisted and broken dwarf bones, complete with a large warhammer also constructed entirely of bones. Its red eyes gleam with fell purpose, and it hisses a challenge through its bony jaw, the hiss more of an escape of evil from the pits of the Abyss rather than the movement of air through a respiratory system.

Bone Giant Made of Dwarf Bones

Huge undead, neutral evil
Armor Class 17 (natural armor) — **Hit Points** 115 — **Speed** 30 ft.

Statistics

STR	DEX	CON	INT	WIS	CHA
21 (+5)	10 (+0)	20 (+5)	4 (-3)	6 (-2)	6 (-2)

Damage Immunities poison, necrotic, psychic
Damage Vulnerabilities bludgeoning, radiant, force, thunder
Condition Immunities exhaustion poisoned
Senses darkvision 60 ft., passive Perception 8
Languages understands dwarven but doesn't speak it
Challenge Rating 8 (3,900)

Abilities

Evasion. If the bone giant is subjected to an effect that allows it to make a Dexterity Saving Throw to take only half damage, the skeleton instead takes no damage if it succeeds on the Saving Throw, and only half damage if it fails.

Magic Resistance. The bone giant has Advantage on Saving Throws against spells and other magical effects.

Turn Immunity. The bone giant is immune to effects that turn undead.

Obelisk Regeneration The bone giant regenerates 10 Hit Points at the start of its turn whenever it is in the cave in Area 33.

Obelisk Fate If the Obelisk is destroyed, so too is the bone giant. The Giant explodes, doing 3d6 piercing damage to anyone within 30ft. (DC 15 Dexterity save for half), and then the shards crumble to dust.

Obelisk Resurrection If the bone giant is destroyed before the Obelisk, it reforms at the beginning of its next turn with 10 Hit Points and immediately *multiattacks*.

Tactics: During Combat

The bone giant targets clerics, then paladins and then combatants using blunt weapons, in that order.

Actions

Multiattack. The bone giant makes two bone thrower warhammer attacks, any combination of ranged or melee.

Bone Thrower Warhammer (ranged). *Ranged Weapon Attack:* +8 to hit, range 20 ft./60 ft., one target. The weapon immediately returns to the bone giant.
Hit: 18 (3d8+5) bludgeoning damage.

Bone Thrower Warhammer (melee). Melee Weapon Attack: +8 to hit, reach 10ft.., one target.
Hit: 18 (3d8+5) bludgeoning damage.

The monstrosity will pursue its attackers all through the lower areas but takes every opportunity to chuck its returning bone thrower warhammer. It cannot traverse the stairs in Area 26 that lead to Area 22. Theoretically, it can push past the weakened Temple wards in the well in Area 34 that leads to Area 11, but that route never occurs to the bone giant.

If the PCs destroyed all the bones in Area 26 *and* 27, then the Bone Giant does not appear. Well-played!

If the PCs destroy the Crypt Obelisk before the Bone Giant, the Giant explodes, doing 3d6 piercing damage to anyone within 30ft. (DC 15 Dexterity Save for half), and then the shards crumble to dust.

TEMPLE DISPOSITION

Once the PCs have destroyed all three Obelisks, the effect that dragged the Old Elven Tower, and then Castle Wailmoor into the Ethereal ends and the Castle manifests.

Enterprising PCs may want to use the Temple as a base of operations. Like the Graveyard, it's heavily warded and not susceptible to supernatural monkey business. It also has beds, latrines, and kitchens (well, probably one kitchen now).

This is an old Temple. It is a literal font of radiant energy, a focus point in the Welt for life and creation. It is also linked to the gigantic, and powerful artifact that is the dam. For 150-years, no High Priest has tended the temple.

Thus, the temple has a limited amount of sentience. What it does depends on how the PCs conducted themselves.

HOSTILE

The Temple "considers" the upper portion as part of itself, and the crypt's lost to the corruption from the Obelisk, not in its purview. If PCs defile, vandalize or commit overt evil acts in the upper Temple (Areas 1 to 25) it will respond by trying to burn them if they approach the font in the Radiant Chapel in Area 4. It surges with radiant energy, doing 12d6 radiant damage to anyone within 30ft. of it, (DC 15 Dexterity Save for half damage).

That is not the worst of it—if the PCs continue their wicked, wicked ways, sometime during the night when the PCs are sleeping, the radiant iron golem will awaken and rampage throughout the Temple, killing any trespassers it finds. It will not leave the Temple, but it will traverse the stairs to the lower Crypts. It stays an active guardian until destroyed or a High Priest of Dvalin changes its orders via commands in Old Dvalin.

INDIFFERENT

It is possible to manifest the Obelisk and leave the Temple more-or-less how the PCs find it. This is especially true if the PCs by-pass the Iron Golem's "request" to clean up Areas 1-3.

In this instance, the Temple appears as any abandoned structure built by dwarves—a strong "roof" over their heads, fresh water and lots of iron doors

that can be closed to keep out the local fauna and wandering monsters.

FRIENDLY

PCs who clean out the Temple and repair it receive its limited help. They will need to:

- Complete the Iron Golem request to clean up Areas 1 to 3
- Destroy the corrupted Obelisk in Area 33
- Destroy the Frostskull in Area 26
- Destroy the corrupted guardians and skeletons in Areas 27 to 29
- Drive Sir Gwane Germnise in Area 30 from the Temple or set his spirit free
- Clean Area 34 to restore the fresh water supply
- Kill the angry badgers in Area 11
- Destroy the Radiant Beetles in Area 9
- Destroy the Prismatic Beetles in Area 23
- Place a book into the Scriptorium Automation in Area 18 to stop it from leaking
- Pray at the great statue of Dvalin

With a Friendly Attitude, all healing spells the PCs cast in the temple will heal their maximum amount. For 24-hours after sleeping in the temple, PCs that are a target of a *bless* spell need not roll a d4, they are able to always apply the maximum amount (4) to attack rolls and Saving Throws (this effect ends with the bless spell duration, but if receiving another *bless* spell, the result is the same, +4, until 24-hours has lapsed).

Cleaning out and Restoring the temple will let its wards, that used to cover the lower portions of the temple, reassert itself over the course of 2d4 months.

PCs are obligated to keep the Temple clean and tidy. If they let it go, in 1d4 weeks of a mess, the PCs receive no rewards for staying there.

OWNERSHIP

The religion of Dvalin may be diverse, but it has a distinctive hierarchy, and the Temple is still owned by the Church.

If all the PCs decide to become Dedicates of Dvalin, this essentially passes ownership of the Temple to them by Divine Edict. The PCs are afforded a great deal of independence in the church hierarchy and can receive assistance as requested and required.

Consequently, the PCs can give the Iron Golem commands in Old Dvalin, but it still cannot leave the Temple grounds.

Intro

Lost at the Beaux Seins

Moortide Rising

The Altar & the Anvil

Castle Wailmoor

Appendix

End Game

At the end of Chapter 3, the PCs should be at Level 4, and if using Milestone Advancement, award them the level now. If not, award them enough Story Awards XP to advance them to the new level.

There are various campaign aspects to the Temple that carry forth into the campaign.

Jackon's Staff

The *Lost Memory* in Area 22 is the **last** hint that Jackon's Staff—the *Staff of Ishtari*—is a powerful item and linked to the PCs via the Hierophant's ill-fated reincarnation ritual. Since it was created by the power archmage Aggerman, it has followed the reincarnates of the Hierophants throughout history, serving whichever one was a wizard at the time. Jackon, as an Imperial War Wizard, not simply a Knight of the Wailmoor, up to that point been the closest representation of whom Aggerman was. He had access to powers of the staff that the PCs presently do not.

The *Lost Memory* in Area 22 is also a hint that Jackon himself might be a reincarnation of a previous life. PCs have enough to deal with coming to grips that they used to be Knights of the Wailmoor 150-years ago, no need to pile onto the confusion by dropping other hints, unless as the DM, you want to tell the PCs it seems Castle Wailmoor probably has some of the answers to the questions they seek.

Oakheart & His Warhammer

The hammer, visible when using *dream tea* and traversing to the Chapel in Area 4 is not obtainable in *Curse of the Lost Memories,* but is in the next adventure, *Beneath a Dreary Wave.*

Oakheart is still alive. Jackon was correct. The Emperor didn't care anything about the Demon War on the edges of the Empire (the Wailmoor was technically a vassal state of Lothmar, rather than an Imperial Realm).

However, the Emperor summoned Oakheart because of both his battle experience and his ties to the dwarven enclaves at the edge of the Empire, yet another long-term machination of the Empire to extend its borders without belligerent military action. Councilor Beram Oakheart is currently one of the Emperor's most trusted advisors (DC 15 Intelligence to recall, DC 12 to anybody familiar about the Imperial Court).

PCs who rampage in the temple will find themselves on the wrong end of the Imperial Bureaucracy if word reaches Oakheart. On the flip side, when PCs eventually wind up in the audience of the Emperor himself, if they have resorted the Temple, Oakheart is extremely grateful.

Professor Merisee the Elf

The Dedicate-Priestess, while young during the Demon War, was a formidable warrior, far more powerful than her cheerful, nubile disposition let on. Indeed, any of the PCs going through the Trial of the Dedicate will understand just how resolute she must be.

If any of the PCs have an academic background in Lothmar, and the Viscounty they may recognize her name or even have met Merisee herself. She is currently a tenured professor at the Imperial University of Darathole in the northern Kandra, the most remote Imperial University in the Empire. She teaches courses on religion and Lothmar history, but any PC familiar with her will be quite surprised to hear she is a Dedicate of Dvalin, a professional demon hunter.

Professor Merisee currently looks exactly like she did in the *Lost Memory* visions. She plays a key role in the next module, *Beneath a Dreary Wave,* becoming one of the PCs most staunch and powerful allies—for a price.

There's always a price.

The Dam - Olaf's Spell-Engine

There are many hints both subtle and not-so-subtle that the dam is a powerful artifact and that Dedicate Merisee took the books that explain it all with her.

In *Beneath a Dreary Wave,* PCs will need those books. Without taking control of the dam, it will kill them from afar in a way they cannot recover from, ending their long reign as reincarnated Hierophants.

Castle Wailmoor

Destroying the Obelisk in Area 33 drags the Old Elven Tower out of the Ethereal Plane and it, in turn, drags Castle Wailmoor with it. Any demons in Graspen gleefully enter the castle but are immediately thwarted with being unable to enter the Old Elf Tower. They become extremely agitated and patrol around Castle Wailmoor in hopes of finding whoever brought the Castle back and eating them as painfully as possible.

The Temple has given up all the secrets it has to give. Like Dvalin, it's a place of doing and the now, rather than an ancient edifice of secrets. Indeed, its most secret-secret was written in a book! A heavily warded book, but a book never the less.

By now the PCs have fought demons, corruption, and a witch—Castle Wailmoor, by this time, is an enigma wrapped up in mystery. After all, Silas was the Wailmoor Court Wizard, and he wasn't privy to what the Knights were really guarding. If the PCs want answers to questions they pose (and questions they come up on their own are infinitely more delicious than anything we can come up with), they need to clean out the Castle and confront Chrystelle the Enchantress, the tragic and lonely figure trapped in the Old Elven Tower.

CASTLE WAILMOOR

"THIS IS NOT GOOD."

HE CAME TO INVESTIGATE THE TOWER DISAPPEARING, AND AS SOON AS HE TRIED TO SUMMON HIS MAGICAL CHEST TO RETRIEVE A RITUAL BOOK, THE CASTLE DISAPPEARED. WITH HIM IN IT!

"WHAT DID YOU DO, MAGE!?" SILAS TURNED AROUND. TWO DEMONS. VERY ANGRY.

"TRAPPED ME IN HERE WITH YOU, I THINK," SAID SILAS.

"YOU WILL PAY FOR..."

THE DEMON STOPPED TALKING AS THE BALLISTA BOLT THAT SILAS HAD ANIMATED SLAMMED INTO ITS BACK.

"DEMONS TALK TOO MUCH. YOU NEVER SHUT UP," SILAS SIGHED.

Castle Wailmoor is not a beautiful castle. The Elven Tower, previously hidden from view, *is* a spectacular, almost unearthly construction. Castle Wailmoor, while having conservable magical defenses, was built long before the time where grandiose, Imperial Renaissance architecture was all the rage.

But the small, old castle is by design. Large, comfortable places attracted attention. And Chrystelle the Enchantress wanted anything but.

The Baron's primary place of residence, along with anybody in the Barony that had any modicum of power, was in Graspen, in beautiful and functional estates with generous manorial grounds extending to the Lake, or at least a Lake view.

Castle Wailmoor and the Elven Tower had always been a place of mystery for the people of the Wailmoor. Visiting left one with a sense of latent power, of quietness and an aura of—sadness.

Now that the PCs have access to it, their world condenses to a small, abandoned corner of the Kingdom of Lothmar. Castle Wailmoor is where the PCs stop wandering around and start asserting themselves in The Welt.

Chapter RPG Style

As the DM, you need to know up-front that while it is possible to have the end of the chapter be a PC-only confrontation with the Big Bad Evil Guy, the objective of this chapter is the PCs meeting Chrystelle.

Wherein Chapter 3 relied completely on the PCs to stomp everything in their path, Chrystelle in Chapter 4 has limited control over parts of the Castle, but that control is absolute. She's been watching the Dead-Knight that invaded the castle suspiciously after it manifested itself into the Welt. But then he went about preparing for someone *else* to arrive with guile and deception.

She is perfectly capable of dealing with the Dead-Knight, but she has a limited understanding of the PCs. So, she waits for them to arrive. And how they deal with the Dead-Knight is a measurement of both their capabilities but also of their character.

Player Agency

Player Agency, the ability for the *players* to make choices for their characters without coercion or railroading, is the mechanic behind Chapter 4 and is why the BBEG is only a means to this end.

At the heart of agency is the power dynamic. Agency is power. Can the players impact the game, and thus NPC interactions, the plot, the narrative? One doesn't need a complete sandbox to have Player Agency, but

the world presented needs rules and a few boundaries for the DM—the difference between a sandbox and an open-world, so to speak.

In this chapter, the PCs should be Level 4, and the Dead-Knight is medium difficulty encounter at Challenge Rating 8 for six players—and deadly for four.

But the PCs actions can cause the encounter to be a CR 6, or if they are damaged too much by the Dead-Knight's minions without resting, a TPK.

The players can even maneuver their PCs to get the Dead-Knight into a location where Chrystelle simply blasts him with so much radiant energy, that he explodes, going from BBEG to chump in the space of ten minutes at the game table.

Turning the BBEG into a chump could be just as satisfying as beating him with melee weapons until he dies from it. Chumpification is power.

We designed the end-chapter to preserve the power of the player's choices while giving the DM tools to advance the game. The PCs are being fed information and misinformation—but they need to make dynamic decisions based on their performance all the way back to their character class selection. As DMs in a hard fantasy setting, all we can really do is preserve the rules of the world—therefore the final encounter with the Dead-Knight can be satisfyingly easy or tragically hard.

See "<u>Running with Harakan</u>" for suggestions on the end-battle of the module.

Section Summaries

This chapter is divided up into four sections.

Chapter Objectives

This section outlines the overall objectives the PCs should embark upon, objectives that need DM input to link their adventuring to the overall campaign setting and plot in the *Chronicles of the Celestial Chains* campaign.

While powerful, scary, and tragic, Chrystelle is a person. She still has hopes, dreams, and motivations. And while she is a larger-than-life figure, her story pales in comparison to the PCs, trapped in a loop of reincarnation and life-by-life getting closer-and-closer to their objective of storming the celestial Gates of Elysia.

Chrystelle views herself as a possible patron of the PCs, even if they misguidedly keep her at arm's length. But, she is more than that. She is either their Salvation or the Impetus of their Destruction.

Intro

Lost at the Beaux Seins

Moortide Rising

The Altar & the Anvil

Castle Wailmoor

Appendix

Area Descriptions

This section outlines Castle Wailmoor area-by-area, and the fell inhabitants that have taken residence there. Even if the PCs make a bee-line for the Castle as soon as it manifests, there are new players in town and the PCs will need to use their wits, and the Castle itself, to stay alive.

Many areas have *Lost Memories*. Separate they are seemingly innocuous. Strung together in the proper order (outside the order the PCs manifest them), they give the PCs a window on the Knights, Baron Mark of Wailmoor, his family, and the terrible decisions people are forced to make in war.

Running with Harakan

One way or the other, PCs will need to deal with Harakan the Dead-Knight. Although initially found in a specific location, he's not a static, chained-in-place individual. What the PCs do, when they do it, what Chrystelle does in return; all these things impact the final confrontation with the Witches' hit man. This section lists his likely actions to overcome the battle-hardened PCs.

End Game

At the end of the adventure, PCs will need to make choices, and this section places the adventure in an over-all campaign context.

The ability of the PCs to make decisions on what to do with the Castle, and the Wailmoor, is a major decision that impacts the next adventure, *Beneath a Dreary Wave*, as the consequences of their choices come home to roost—while at the same time, dealing with the run-away magics of the dam to the south. As their *Lost Visions* allude to in Chapter 3, they're going to have to contend with it.

Chapter Objectives

Wherein Chapter 1 was the PCs realizing they are drawn together by visions that haunt their waking moments, Chapter 2 was where they explored the Wailmoor's beautiful and sometimes deadly landscape, Chapter 3 where the PCs rolled up their sleeves and got down to brass-tacks—Chapter 4 is where their overall object is to stab, bludgeon, scorch and generally discuss with extreme prejudice everything that stands in their way. Castle Wailmoor is where a bunch of demons and angry wizards and sorcerers went to war, and the PCs are the cleanup crew.

Another way to look at it—everyone tried to do their best, their best wasn't good enough, and it's up to the PCs to fix it.

Objective: Meet with Chrystelle

Meeting with Chrystelle and getting answers from her to their questions is the big event of this chapter and the conclusion of this first module in the *Chronicles of the Celestial Chains* Campaign.

Chrystelle, once she trusts the PCs, can provide them with not only the big picture about the Demon War but also her role in the Barony's former glory.

The PCs *Lost Memory* curse? Not so much. Finding out the PCs are having former memories of her elite warriors, the Knights of Wailmoor rocks her little world. Rightly paranoid about the people who know of her existence, only the Baron (and sometimes his spouse) and the Knights of Wailmoor knew her true story throughout the years. Purposely spread rumors about the Barons' patron abounded. A magic mirror, a genie in a bottle, a dragon—all these rumors and more were used to conceal her true nature. And when the Witches of Kandra found her out, a Demon War ensued.

Necessary Meeting

Chrystelle and the PCs are a match made in heaven (pun intended) and from their alliance will rise a cascade of events that will shake down the Celestial Hierarchy forever. But for now, both parties do not know what to expect of each other.

Chrystelle worries if the PCs are another threat to her survival and a new trick from her enemies to bring her down. She has been able to survive all this time by selecting who would get access to her inner-sanctum in the Castle.

From the PCs perspective, they will have learned by now about the mysterious figure "haunting" the moor (they might even conclude *she* killed Silas). They should rightfully worry about her nature and her intentions. Chrystelle's enemies have done a good job at depicting her influence as evil and nefarious, and even if they decide she is otherwise, the PCs should wonder about what kind of creature has been around the moor for so long. The false rumors that Harakan (see below) will spread about her undead nature will add to that.

Chrystelle is not exactly undead; she is immortal. But even if she has access to great arcane powers, because she has been so long without being in the presence of Narakata, she's now—skeletal-like. She looks like a lich out of legend. Gone is her physical beauty. She looks like a monster.

DMs should play with this tension throughout the chapter. As they explore the castle and get closer to Chrystelle, PCs should come up with their own conclusions about Chrystelle. She will adjust her actions based on what the PCs say and do with her limited ability to visually see the PCs from the top of her tower as they traverse the visible parts of the Castle.

CHRYSTELLE'S MOTIVATIONS

Chrystelle's overarching motivation has little to do with the Wailmoor itself—one could say thoughts of revenge against her former angelic husband keeps her warm at night.

For hundreds of years, Chrystelle has been trapped inside the tower. She knows that getting out of the tower means certain death, and she does not want to die. She loves life, she loves studying and learning, and she loves human interaction.

But she is consumed by the desire of vengeance. She seeks vengeance from the Celestial Prince who condemned her to this state. She seeks vengeance from the Witches of Kandra who called the demons over the moor and, by jealousy, destroyed the barony she had built carefully, step-by-step, into a peaceful and wealthy place.

In the immediate, however, Chrystelle wants her agents back, the Castle cleaned out of every shred of demon taint, and then she will set about rebuilding the Wailmoor by proxy once again.

When the demon Barbu fell, and the last baron of Wailmoor died, Chrystelle knew she'd have to start anew and call to her a new Baron of Wailmoor. She did not anticipate that Silas and Jackon would drag first the Tower, and then the Castle, into the Ethereal Plane. When it faded, it cut Chrystelle from the outside world. She knew she would never be able to go out in the world and find the new Baron, but now no one was able to get to her either!

She has spent the last 150-years planning for her next move but also found herself depressed and terribly lonely.

Thus, she is depressed, lonely, burring for vengeance and now angry that the Castle was just invaded by a Dead-Knight. She's going to blow something up until it dies from it, and it is up to the PCs to make sure it's not them.

OBJECTIVE: DEFEAT THE DEAD-KNIGHT HARAKAN

When Haeggra the witch dies at the hands of the PCs, the Witch Kavita, who was scrying her protegee, knew she needs to act before some else besides her agents reached Chrystelle.

But Haeggra's death was a serious blow to the Kandra Witch Covens, and, to a smaller extent, the

Viscount becoming involved with the PCs—no matter how tenuous—is an unfolding political disaster for the Witches.

Furthermore, Kavita suspects that it was the rumored group that caused minor trouble in the Crossroads Village that departed for the Wailmoor that did in her sister witch, but she's not sure. During Haeggra's fight, Kavita was unable to see who was slaughtering the bandits and then Haeggra. And that gives her a big pause and is the primary reason she did not simply go to the Wailmoor to personally deal with the matter.

The true villains of the fallen Barony of Wailmoor, the Witches of Kandra, were thwarted at every turn. Even summoning a demonic host to assail Castle Wailmoor ultimately did not work. Now a grim and purposed group rampaged around the Wailmoor and slew her agent as if they were some holy resurrection of the Knights of Wailmoor. And there was something seriously wrong in the Wailmoor—ward stones placed by the accursed Silas and Jackon, long preventing *teleportation* and *gating* into the Wailmoor, went sour in a bad way. When Haeggra tried to examine one, the seeping corruption was powerful enough to make everyone linked to Haeggra sick. It took weeks to recover.

WHAT WITCHES ALWAYS DO

Kavita decides to spend considerable resources to strike a bargain with another fell agent against the Wailmoor. Summoning the demon, Barbu has cost the very old witch a great deal (and in many ways, she is still recovering), and she is not able to call upon another demon. She risks the wrath of Orcus and strikes a bargain with another of his servants, a powerful undead—the Dead-Knight called Harakan. He was once a dragon paladin and now a festering marital blight upon the Kingdom of Lothmar.

Less powerful than Barbu, but nonetheless terrible and ruthless, Harakan flies to the Wailmoor on his Nightmare steed from his hidden redoubt in the remote northern reaches. He watches the Castle from afar, and when it manifests itself, he immediately enters, either hours or days ahead of the PCs. He knows that someone killed a Witch before a Temple of Dvalin, and has assumed, rightly, that everyone is after what everyone else is after—getting in the Castle.

So, when it manifests itself, he simply flies in stables his horse and waits to see who comes knocking.

HARAKAN'S MOTIVATIONS

While granted a great deal of independence, the Dead-Knight Harakan is a servant of the Demon Lord Orcus. He is motivated by a sense of loyalty and duty, but

Intro

Lost at the Beaux Seins

Moortide Rising

The Altar & the Anvil

Castle Wailmoor

Appendix

also by compulsion. He traded life for immortality, his humanity for power. Thus, Orcus's motivations are his own.

Kill the PCs & Secure the Castle

Like a demon, Harakan frequently takes the path of, why directly confront your enemy when they can do your dirty work for you? This conflict philosophy has served him well over the decades. He would vastly prefer if Chrystelle and the unknown assailants went at it, and no matter whom the victor, he would be facing a weakened survivor. Right now, he's betting these attackers will weaken the Enchantress, give him time to secure the Castle with a multitude of summoned demonic allies. He may even be able to get into the tower itself. He would love nothing more than to show up on Orcus's throne room, something he can do, and the Witches cannot, with this Chrystelle in *iron bands* and *dimensional shackles*.

The Dead-Knight realizes he needs to tread carefully—in a game of summoning critters to do thy bidding; he suspects Chrystelle can outperform him. So, he's been skulking about the Castle, knowing full well that his plan is "winging it" but relishing the challenge nevertheless.

The Motivation of the Prince of Undeath, Orcus

Orcus is not embarking on some grand conquest of The Welt using some fell machination that uses Chrystelle at its heart.

He's just mad that she's immortal. So, he has his pride. And then there is the Archangel Narakata. Capturing his former love—that he abandoned—would shake the foundations of the Celestial Hierarchy as the powerful Narakata raged and raged. So, there's that, too. Narakata could simply do all the damage Orcus wanted to do to the other Angels, and by proxy, the gods, *for him*. It would be *hysterical*.

But, Chrystelle also fascinates him. She is alive yet not. Her once astonishingly beautiful body has emaciated with age and is a walking skeleton with paper-thin skin stretched over its frame, but she is an Enchantress supreme, mainly because of her immortality. He even sympathizes with her a little bit—what else does she have to do but study? Is this what happens when you turn wizards into thinking undead? Do they become better wizards? That once they shirk all vanity, it frees their minds to embrace true power?

What if he could *duplicate* the effect but not have it tied to a location? What if he could somehow have powerful wizards trade their mortality for immortality for the price of undeath? They'd have free will, but they'd be corrupted, and the long-term damage they could do to the gods' little soul factory that is the Welt would be amusing and delicious.

Orcus wants to play with Chrystelle. He wants to make liches and use her as the blueprint.

Thus, he sent Harakan a specific omen—complete his mission of securing Castle Wailmoor or be destroyed.

Orcus is not the main villain in this story. There is one entity responsible for the Hierophants casting their terrible reincarnation spells, and he's not a demon. The Hierophant's prophecy said nothing about storming the Abyss.

Objective: Make Necessary Choices to Advance the Campaign

The Dead-Knight Harakan is dead. The witch Kavita's pet agent is dead. The PCs destroyed the three Corrupt Obelisks and dealt with everything in their path. They've discovered impressive enchanted items.

The real reward was information. The PCs wanted to know why they were receiving these *Lost Memories*, and now they understand part of the picture—they are reincarnated Knights of the Wailmoor, but that's only a small portion of the overall conflict that embroils them.

Chrystelle the Enchantress has the capability to find the information they seek and can help them. PCs must choose how they help her, where they establish their home, and what their relationship with the Enchantress on the Moor is.

They can become more than wandering vagabonds. They've cleaned out the Wailmoor—it is theirs.

What do they plan to do with it?

CASTLE WAILMOOR

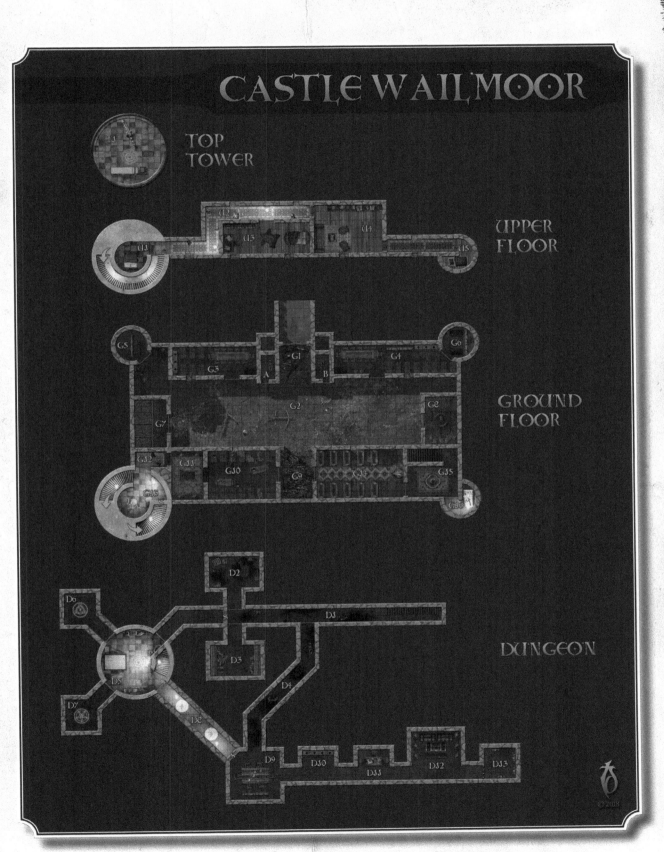

TOP
TOWER

UPPER
FLOOR

GROUND
FLOOR

DUNGEON

Area Descriptions

Harakan orders are simple: kill the other agents rampaging in the Wailmoor and secure Castle Wailmoor to await reinforcements. When he arrives at the castle, there was nobody there, but it's in the Ethereal. He correctly assumes that whomever these other power-players are, they want the same thing. So, he simply waits.

And when a magnificent green granite elven tower appeared and then the castle, he simply flew into the courtyard on his flying steed.

What he couldn't do was enter the tower. And he tried every which way to do so, but the multiple layers of wards are specifically tailored against undead. And given what little he knows about Chrystelle, he's not sure he wants to make a frontal assault. Having PCs do his dirty work for him is in the Dead-Knight's bailiwick. Heck, they might even be able to drag her out of the tower!

Harakan is a formidable combatant but also a master of disguise and intrigue. He will send monsters after the PCs and will try to trick them into killing the "Lich in the Tower" at the same time, assuming the appearance of the innocent daughter of the Baron.

With the ward stones destroyed, Harakan can summon monsters and does so, but he will do it in such a way as to make it seem as if *Chrystelle* did so.

If the PCs enter the Tower and then come hunting for him, or if they see through his trickery (likely as not), he resigns himself to battle, as described in <u>Running with Harakan</u>.

General Castle Features

Right now, Castle Wailmoor appears as if a demonic host assaulted an old castle that was defended by a few melee combatants manning ballista, wizards, and sorcerers. There is evidence of furious, running battles everywhere and when the dust settled, there wasn't anything left in the Castle aside from the Enchantress holed up in her Tower—other than two lingering demons, both whom Silas took with him.

Anyone with historical or architectural knowledge can date Castle Wailmoor to the early Lothmar formation years. It's an obviously defensive location. The castle sits on rock outcroppings surrounded by marshes and swampy parts of the moor, even at its elevation which lets it overlook what used to be Graspen and the Lake.

The ceilings are only 10ft. tall, except in the Elven Tower, where they are 11ft. The place is dark, with the occasional magical illumination.

All the doors are intact, but most are not locked or barred. They are made of reinforced wood. The windows are hinged on the inside and can be bared. They open into a room and lie flat against a wall.

Magical Castle & Tower Features

The Elven tower is warded by a powerful Celestial as nothing has been warded before; literally, The Welt has seen nothing like it, and it may see nothing like it again.

But the wards powered by the dam come close.

The 5th Baron of Wailmoor was (at the time), Chrystelle's equal. His father built the dam and then when he was Baron, he linked several wards to the Tower and the Castle through a mighty spell engine he installed in it.

- The outside Tower and Castle walls cannot take any structural damage. The surfaces can be marred (and are), but actual damage is absorbed by the dam. Inside the castle is another matter. The wards do provide some minor reinforcement to inside walls, but it's not nearly as strong as the wards on the outside.

- It is not possible to *teleport, blink, dimension door,* or use any other magical means of locomotion *into* the Castle, short of the spell *gate,* which will function, and summoning spells, which operate differently than teleportation magic.

- *Gating* into the Tower does not work.

- Now that they are back in the Welt, neither the Tower nor Castle can be traversed through from the Ethereal. This is the powerful ward that Silas and Jackon inadvertently caused to malfunction, first pulling the Tower into the Ethereal and then the Castle. When the PCs destroyed the Obelisk stones, Olaf's wards reset, bringing the Castle back to the Welt.

Wards Specific to the Elven Tower

The Old Elven Tower, with its distinctive, green-tinged granite, is warded against intrusion from demons, undead, fey, shadow creatures, elementals and summoned creatures by wards installed by none other than Erebus, a hebdomad archangel, one of the most powerful celestials in existence. These wards also prevent Chrystelle from leaving the tower or the former tower grounds without having her advanced age catch up with her, all at once.

Erebus's original edict extended to the Tower's garden, long buried and now <u>Areas D1</u> to <u>D13</u>. Chrystelle can move anywhere in the dungeon, but since it makes her remember things she would rather forget, she rarely does so.

Approaching the Castle

While she cannot scry the PCs unless they are standing in front of The Lady's Statue (in Lady's Woods), Chrystelle spots the PC using her normal vision as they approach, with her greater ability in Wisdom (Perception) as compared to the PCs ability to remain in Dexterity (Stealth).

It is unlikely that Chrystelle has seen the PCs through her statue in the Lady's Woods as it is doubtful they went there after destroying the last Obelisk. But, if she saw or heard the PCs at her statue, Chrystelle may be "somewhat leery" of the PCs or "highly leery" of the PCs. She can't scry them, and this gives her pause, but she knows, through her limited divination magic and examination of the Temple, someone or something killed a Kandra Witch. Someone did "something" to push the Castle and Tower back to reality. She is sure it's not the Dead-Knight, and she can guess it was a different group, probably a group allied against the Witches of Kandra—and it is her hope the group is led by the elven knight Heleshia, a former Knight of the Wailmoor, whom, as far as Chrystelle knows, is still alive.

Chrystelle watches the PCs like a hawk from the top of her transparent tower, a top not visible to the PCs or Harakan. As soon as the PCs enter the Castle's rooms, she is not able to see them unless they step in front of a window that she has line-of-sight.

Gone is the translucency of the Castle, but the outer walls still glow slight green.

Strikingly different, however, is a slender, subtlety green-stoned tower rising over the castle, obviously of elven architecture and noticeably different than the architecture of the Temple of Dvalin and even the rest of Castle Wailmoor.

The gate is closed but unlocked, and it creaks when opened.

Graspen Demons

If there are any demons in Graspen, they attack the PCs from underneath the arched stone bridge leading from the gates of the castle, infuriated beyond communication. They operate separately from Harakan, beyond his control.

Chrystelle views this battle and uses it to form her opinion on the PCs.

Ground Floor

The Ground Floor is where most of the action happened. While the defenders were versed in and equipped to shoot flying invaders, there were simply too many of them, and it did not help that most were resistant to magic.

Intro

Lost at the Beaux Seins

Moortide Rising

The Altar & the Anvil

Castle Wailmoor

Appendix

G1 – The Gatehouse

The first 20ft. x 20ft. to the south of the gate is difficult terrain. Movement speed is cut in half.

A fortified gatehouse reduces the entrance to the castle to a narrow corridor with arrow slits on its sides. This could have been an impenetrable defense if the courtyard ahead did not show the scene of a large battle with war machines, debris, and skeletons lying about. From inside the courtyard, low doors lead inside the emptied gatehouse.

Immediately south of the gate, is charred rubble and broken ground, as if someone built a fire before the gate out of broken siege artillery, or, more than likely, the remnants of some magical explosion. A soot-covered skeleton in tattered robes lines there, 15ft. south of the gate.

Just east of Gatehouse A lies the skeleton of Silas, covered in soot. The identity of the mage is hard to figure out unless the players are familiar with his sigil that is still somewhat recognizable on the rags of his robe. A DC 20 Wisdom (Medicine) check will reveal Silas was killed by claws and bite and most likely bled to death from his wounds. In the charred rubble, there are several broken potion bottles, healing potions that Silas used, which kept him in the fight, but, unfortunately, was not enough to save him in the end.

Silas's magical items are still on him and detect as such with the appropriate cantrip or spell, but the Dead-Knight has trapped his skeleton with a magical trap he brought along with him. If touched, Silas's skeleton explodes in a thunderous noise, causing 3d6 thunder damage (Constitution DC 14 Save for half) and the person who touched the corpse is bathed in *faerie fire* for one minute.

On Silas's skeleton is a *cloak of protection +1*, a *ring of protection +1*, a *wand of lightning* (now fully recharged) and a *pearl of power*.

There is nothing in the gatehouse except two skeletons. Since a lot of the demons assaulting the castle were flying, the gatehouse had not been useful in defending the place. All the charred damage was caused by Silas cutting lose.

If the thunder trap goes off, the 4 demon hounds in the Courtyard, Area G2 come running and attack, heading for the looter bathed in *faerie fire*.

G2 – THE COURTYARD

The courtyard is littered with skeletons of both demons (mostly demon dogs) and courageous soldiers of Wailmoor.

The inside of the courtyard still shows a castle at war: broken weapons, scattered parts of siege machinery and shattered ballista bolts litter the paved courtyard. The skeletons of brave Wailmoor soldiers can be seen left and right, some still wearing armor dented by the assault of demonic creatures.

When the PCs enter the castle, Harakan summoned 4 demon dogs in the courtyard with hope to test the party. Should they manage to defeat the hounds, Harakan will be pleased he has found puppets with enough muscle he could drive against Chrystelle. It will also let him see the PCs for the first time.

Harakan is having a grand old time. He found a dog sweater upstairs in Area U3 and thinks it's hilarious as he put it on one of the demon dogs.

If the PCs avoid the trap on Silas's skeleton, the demon hounds need to detect the PCs before attacking. While the demon hounds have good Perception, the PCs at this point are 4th Level and may have considerable experience in avoiding conflict until they've prepared for it. It is possible that the PCs see the demon dogs first.

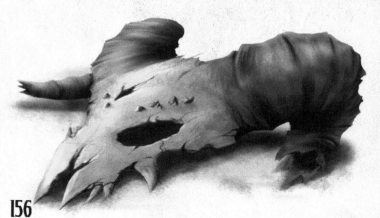

PCs Spot the Hounds First

Sniffing along the edges of the courtyard are large dogs that seem to glow with a sickly orange light, large jaws dripping in saliva that hisses when it touches the ground, smoke rising from their nostrils.

Oddly enough, one of the demon dogs is wearing a doggie sweater that sports the Wailmoor coat of arms.

They don't see you yet, but if you move out of stealth or are noisy, they sure will.

The Demon Hounds Spot the PCs First

From the corners of the courtyard, four demonic hounds come gleefully running. These large dogs seem to glow with a sickly orange light, large draws dripping in saliva that hisses when it touches the ground, smoke rising from their nostrils.

Oddly enough, one of the demon dogs is wearing a doggie sweater that sports the Wailmoor coat of arms.

Four Summoned Demon Hounds

Medium demon, chaotic evil
Armor Class 15 (natural armor) — **Hit Points** 45 — **Speed** 50 ft.

Statistics

STR	DEX	CON	INT	WIS	CHA
17 (+3)	12 (+1)	14 (+2)	6 (-2)	13 (+1)	6 (-2)

Skills Perception +5
Damage Immunities fire
Damage Vulnerability cold
Senses darkvision 60 ft., passive Perception 15
Languages understands abyssal but doesn't speak it
Challenge 3 (700 XP) each

Abilities

Keen Hearing and Smell. The hound has Advantage on Wisdom (Perception) checks that rely on hearing or smell.

Pack Tactics. The hound has Advantage on an attack roll against a creature if at least one of the hound's allies is within 5 feet of the creature and the ally isn't incapacitated.

Summoned. These demon hounds are summoned.

Actions

Bite. *Melee Weapon Attack:* +5 to hit, reach 5 ft., one target. *Hit:* 7 (1d8+3) piercing plus 7 (2d6) fire damage.

Fire Breath (Recharge 5-6). The demon hound exhales fire in a 15-foot cone. Each creature in that area must make a DC 12 Dexterity Saving Throw, taking 21 (6d6) fire damage on a failed save, or half as much damage on a successful one.

G3 – SERVANTS' QUARTERS

Entering this room triggers a *Lost Memory*.

In keeping with the tradition of the fewer people living in Castle Wailmoor, the better, this room used to

G3

be the extent of the servant's quarters and the castle's kitchen. Four servants lived here—two fulltime cooks, one part-time cook/part-time chambermaid and a dedicated chambermaid. It also has a *permanent unseen servant*, waiting for commands in elvish.

The quarters were richly furnished, and the Baron and his family frequently ate here rather than having the servants bring the food across the courtyard to the formal dining room.

That changed during the Demon War when the room was converted to barracks.

This large room seemed to have been an extensive kitchen and the living quarters for perhaps servants but was turned into a hasty barracks before being abandoned. Everything except the stove seems out of place, including the latrines on the west wall.

There is nothing left of much value in these quarters except a chamber pot that glows with faint Alteration magic—body fluids and waste paper entering the *chamber pot* simply fade away after five minutes, leaving behind a light scent of lavender and roses. There were 12 soldiers here (the six beds were always used), and since the *magical chamber pot* couldn't keep up, they built the latrines on the west wall.

PCs who explore here can find the *magical chamber pot*, some broken clay pots, and a few children toys.

LOST MEMORY

An unseen servant goes to pour you another glass of wine. You put your hand over the cup. "No thanks," you say in Elvish. The pitcher floats to Mark, Baron of Wailmoor and tops his glass off.

"For such a hardened warrior, you sure stay sober a lot," says Madeline. She is holding the baby in one hand, her wine glass in her other.

"That's so he can punch people in the face super hard while the rest of us are drunk," Mark says, tipping his cup at you.

Madeline looks at Mark. Then you. Then back to Mark, then you again.

"What?" you both ask at the same time.

"I just love you two so much." She starts to cry.

"No, not tears!" Mark says, laughing, rubbing his eyes in exaggeration.

The Baron of Wailmoor looks so ridiculous you start laughing, too.

Madeline throws a bread roll at your face. It bonks off your nose.

G4 - THE BARRACKS

Much like G3, this room was modified to hold more soldiers. Before the onset of the Demon War, two Knights of the Wailmoor and four guards made this their home, enjoying the space and rich furnishings as a tight-knit, elite group. It was reconfigured to hold sixteen soldiers.

Like Area G3, the guards had to build a latrine, as the *magical chamber pot* could not keep up with the increased personnel.

This is a large and dusty room. The stone floor shows no marks or tracks of visitors in a long time. On the left side of the entrance double doors, are barrels and a stove, to the north a large table and a weapon rack, to the northeast a hastily assembled latrine, and the south wall contains beds—eight in all. A thick layer of dust covers everything.

Perceptive PCs will note that this room underwent a quick reconfiguration.

The weapon racks are empty, but there is a *magical chamber pot* (described in Area G3) by one of the beds. Under the bed are two small trunks (an indication two soldiers alternated sleeping in a single bed), each containing personal effects, indicating that the soldiers here hot bunked. PC can find 234 GPs and 449 SPs if they search all the trunks.

G4

G6

Intro

Lost at the Beaux Seins

Moortide Rising

The Altar & the Anvil

Castle Wailmoor

Appendix

G5 - The Guard's Tower

On the other side of the crossbow rack is the skeleton of Francis, the master of the watch. His full-plate armor has rusted and is pierced in many parts but could be used again after some expensive repair. His *silvered warhammer* still lies in the hand of his skeleton.

The tower floor is empty, its floor covered with a thick layer of black ash-charged dust. A rack for crossbows is in the middle of this room. Murder holes once used by the castle guards to shoot at outside invaders line the circular walls.

A skeletal leg pokes out from behind the crossbow rack.

G6 - The Armory

This room is devoid of treasure.

This room must have been an armory. A weapon wrack is to the east, and two large, open chests probably contained armor suits.

G7 - Stables

A slight nickering can be heard as the PCs approach the closed door to Area G7

The door to this area has a carving depicting several horses running on a windswept moor. From inside, neighing and the occasional sound of a hoof clomp carry faintly from the door.

Inside the stable is Murder Black, the Dead-Knight's evil mount. This is another ruse that Harakan hastily put together. If the PCs open the door, they are greeted by the nightmare.

In the stall facing a door is a large, black horse, hooves glowing with flame, eyes glowing red and hateful. It is saddled and ready to go, a saddle cloth embroidered with heraldic colors and arms of the Barony of Wailmoor. He stares at you as if you were his next meal, but after a moment just snorts in disdain in your direction.

If attacked Murder Black doesn't retaliate and bolts for the Courtyard to fly away, and then goes Ethereal (although he's reluctant to flee from a fight or potential fight).

Harakan found the fancy horse tabard, so he saddled his mount with it, and instructed his trusty steed to leave the PCs alone no matter how much it wanted to murder them.

Murder Black, the Nightmare

Large outerplanar horse, neutral evil
Armor Class 13 (natural armor) — **Hit Points** 80
Speed 60 ft./fly 90 ft.

Statistics

STR	DEX	CON	INT	WIS	CHA
18 (+4)	15 (+2)	16 (+3)	10 (+0)	13 (+1)	15 (+2)

Damage Immunities fire
Damage Resistance necrotic
Damage Vulnerability radiant
Senses passive Perception 11
Languages understands Abyssal, Common, but doesn't speak
Challenge 5 (1,800 XP)

Abilities

Confer Fire Resistance. The nightmare can grant resistance to fire damage to anyone riding it.

Illumination. The nightmare sheds bright light in a 10-foot radius and dim light for an additional 10 feet.

Actions

Hooves. Melee Weapon Attack: +7 to hit, reach 5 ft., one target. Hit: 13 (2d8+4) bludgeoning plus 7 (2d6) fire damage.

Ethereal Stride. The nightmare and up to three willing creatures within 5 feet of it magically enter the Ethereal Plane from the Material Plane or vice versa.

Intro

Lost at the Beaux Seins

Moortide Rising

The Altar & the Anvil

Castle Wailmoor

Appendix

G8 – The Granary

Nothing is usable there. For players interested in rebuilding the barony and the castle, the millstone is an asset of important value.

This room was obviously used as a granary to store hay and grain for the wet winters on the moor. It is now filled with cobwebs and hay dust. A large millstone occupies the room.

G9 – The Foyer

The entire G9 Area is difficult terrain.

Two phase spiders have wandered from the Ethereal Plane while the castle was stuck there (they simply walked in by climbing the walls) and have elected this devastated vestibule as their lair. Chrystelle was toying with the idea of permanently charming them but lacked some necessary spell components to do so. So, she was in the process of researching a *charm monster* variation when other things got her attention.

The roof of the castle's foyer was blasted by a brutal explosion. Shrapnel pieces from a massive grenade-like weapon are still splintered in the walls, and the once tiled floor is now charred and devastated. Broken pieces of burnt furniture, or worse, make moving through the vestibule an odious task.

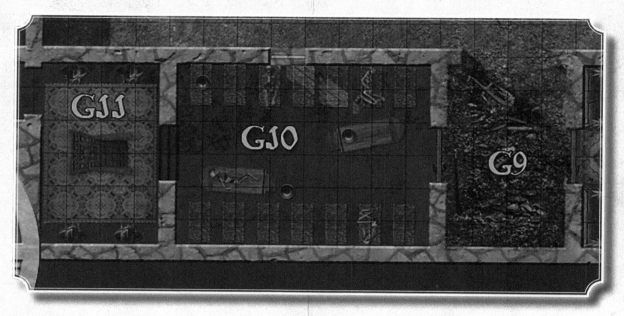

The doors to the east and west are closed and blasted, but as reinforced solid oak, weathered whatever terrible spell occurred here.

They phase spiders attack from Stealth when a PC tries either door to the west or the east. They are unaffected by the difficult terrain. Their Ethereal Jaunt ability only works outside the castle.

Two Phase Spiders

Large monstrosity, unaligned
Armor Class 13 (natural armor) — **Hit Points** 32
Speed 30 ft./climb 30 ft.

Statistics

STR	DEX	CON	INT	WIS	CHA
15 (+2)	15 (+2)	12 (+1)	6 (-2)	10 (+0)	6 (-2)

Skills Stealth +6
Senses darkvision 60 ft., passive Perception 10
Languages —
Challenge 3 (700 XP) each

Abilities

Ethereal Jaunt. As a bonus action, the spider can magically shift from the Material Plane to the Ethereal Plane or vice versa.

Spider Climb. The spider can climb difficult surfaces, including upside down on ceilings, without needing to make an ability check.

Web Walker. The spider ignores movement restrictions caused by webbing.

Actions

Bite. Melee Weapon Attack: +4 to hit, reach 5 ft., one creature. *Hit:* 7 (1d10+2) piercing damage. The target must make a DC 11 Constitution Saving Throw, taking 18 (4d8) poison damage on a failed save, or half as much damage on a successful one. If the poison damage reduces the target to 0 hit points, the target is stable but poisoned for 1 hour, even after regaining hit points, and is paralyzed while poisoned in this way.

G10 – The Great Hall

There is nothing of value anymore in this sad, depressing room. Even the sun shafts from the window appear forlorn.

The once great hall of the Barons of Wailmoor has seen better days. While the opulent wooden frames covering the walls still hint at the wealth of the barony, the formal seat of power was converted into a hospital. Cots, basins, and operating tables are covered with skeletal bodies and black stains on the floor hint at the desperate times the people of Wailmoor experienced during the last days of the Barony.

Meanwhile...

Around the time the PCs enter the great hall, Harakan decides to bump it up a notch by summoning a vrock at the entrance of the Castle by the Gatehouse in Area G1. This demon is not meant to go after the players at this time—at least that is what Harakan wanted.

The demon is going to make some noise (snorts, grunts, cackles) and might draw the attention of the PCs. Noisy PCs also have a chance to draw the attention of the vrock depending on where the PCs are.

Summoned Gatehouse Vrock

Large demon, chaotic evil
Armor Class 15 (natural armor) — **Hit Points** 104
Speed 40 ft./fly 60 ft.

Statistics

STR	DEX	CON	INT	WIS	CHA
17 (+3)	15 (+2)	18 (+4)	8 (-1)	13 (+1)	8 (-1)

Saving Throws Dex +5, Wis +4, Cha +2
Damage Resistances necrotic, cold, fire, lightning; bludgeoning, piercing, and slashing from nonmagical attacks
Damage Vulnerabilities radiant
Damage Immunities poison
Condition Immunities poisoned
Senses darkvision 120 ft., passive Perception 11
Languages Abyssal, telepathy 120 ft.
Challenge 6 (2,300 XP)

Abilities

Magic Resistance. The vrock has Advantage on Saving Throws against spells and other magical effects.

Summoned. The vrock is a summoned demon.

Actions

Multiattack. The vrock makes two attacks: one with its beak and one with its talons.

Beak. Melee Weapon Attack: +6 to hit, reach 5 ft., one target.
Hit: 10 (2d6+3) piercing damage.

Talons. Melee Weapon Attack: +6 to hit, reach 5 ft., one target.
Hit: 14 (2d10+3) slashing damage.

Spores (Recharge 6). A 15-foot-radius cloud of toxic spores extends out from the vrock. The spores spread around corners. Each creature in that area must succeed on a DC 14 Constitution Saving Throw or become poisoned. While poisoned in this way, a target takes 5 (1d10) poison damage at the start of each of its turns. A target can repeat the Saving Throw at the end of each of its turns, ending the effect on itself on a success. Emptying a vial of holy water on the target also ends the effect on it.

Stunning Screech (1/day). The vrock emits a horrific screech. Each creature within 20 feet of it that can hear it and that isn't a demon must succeed on a DC 14 Constitution Saving Throw or be stunned until the end of the vrock's next turn.

Tactics: Combat

Unless summon to the side of the Dead-Knight Harakan through a *signal bomb,* the summoned gatehouse vrock will trade a blow or two with PCs and then fly away, out of sight of vision and missile weapons.

G11 - The Dais

An elevated dais with four decorative, ceremonial, but highly functional, suits of plate armor surround the Baron's chair where he would hold court.

An elevated dais in the great hall was used for the Barons to preside from. It has a massive wooden chair where thick, once comfortable furs are now rotted rags.

A powerful magical item, *a ring of psychic resistance,* is hidden under the rags piled onto the baron's chair.

The suits of armor, with their distinctive Barony of Wailmoor motif, are worth 3,000 GP each.

G12 - Cloak Room

There is nothing remarkable about this cloakroom other than the expensive carpet. On the pegs on the wall, two expensive fur-lined short capes with silver embroidery, worth 200 GP each.

G13 - The Old Elven Tower

Portions of the Elven Tower are accessible to people who may not know of Chrystelle's existence. The stairs here go up to Area U1, while the stairs behind the secret door go to Area D5.

This vestibule-like area with a statue has stairs going up. The architecture here in this tower is completely different than the rest of the castle. While Castle Wailmoor was clearly built by humans, this tower shows very distinct features of old elven architecture. The tower's floor is covered with green tiles and magically illuminated with lanterns along a narrow stairwell going up. At the base of the stairs, a tall statue of Ishtari, the goddess of magic users, gazes in the direction of the cloakroom menacingly.

Anytime someone damages the statue or tries to move past the secret door in Area G13 without wearing the ring found in Area G11 or wearing Knights of the Wailmoor livery, the statue animates and attacks.

Intro

Lost at the Beaux Seins

Moortide Rising

The Altar & the Anvil

Castle Wailmoor

Appendix

Sticky Statue

Possessed statue — Large construct, unaligned
Armor Class 14 (natural armor) — **Hit Points** 96 — **Speed** 20 ft.

Statistics

STR	DEX	CON	INT	WIS	CHA
20 (+5)	8 (-1)	19 (+4)	3 (-4)	11 (+0)	1 (-5)

Damage Immunities poison, psychic, piercing and slashing from nonmagical weapons that aren't adamantine
Damage Resistance bludgeoning from nonmagical weapons that aren't adamantine
Damage Vulnerabilities force
Condition Immunities charmed, exhaustion, frightened, paralyzed, petrified, poisoned
Senses darkvision 120 ft., passive Perception 10
Languages Common (understands but cannot speak)
Challenge 7 (2,900 XP)

Abilities

False Appearance. While the statue remains motionless, it is indistinguishable from a statue or a carved column.

Immutable Form. The statue is immune to any spell or effect that would alter its form.

Magic Resistance. The statue has Advantage on Saving Throws against spells and other magical effects except those that deal force damage

Magic Weapons. The statue's weapon attacks are magical.

Steal Weapons. The eldritch magic that powers the pillar produces a magnetic power that seizes metal objects that touch it, including metal weapons. When a creature successfully strikes the pillar with a metal melee weapon, the attacker must make a successful DC 16 Strength or Dexterity Saving Throw, or the weapon becomes stuck to the pillar until the pillar releases it or is destroyed. The Saving Throw uses the same ability as the attack used. The pillar can release all metal weapons stuck to it whenever it wants. A pillar always drops all weapons stuck to it when it believes it's no longer threatened. This ability affects armor only during a grapple.

Actions

Multiattack. The pillar makes two slam attacks.

Slam. *Melee Weapon Attack:* +8 to hit, reach 5 ft., one target. *Hit:* 18 (3d8+5) bludgeoning damage.

G14 - Chapel of the Three

Traversing past the middle of the Chapel triggers a *Lost Memory*.

The door to the Chapel is closed and blocked by debris from the foyer. PCs will have to remove the debris (and contend with the phase spiders if not already encountered) to move the door and get into the Chapel (party Strength Check, DC 12, or singular Strength Check, at DC 16).

The entire Chapel, Area G14, is under a permanent *hollow* spell. Elementals, fey, demons, and undead can't enter the area, nor can such creatures charm, frighten, or possess creatures within it. Any creature charmed, frightened, or possessed by such a creature is no longer charmed, frightened, or possessed upon entering the Chapel. Furthermore, nothing can move or travel using *teleportation* or by extradimensional or interplanar means within the Chapel.

This large chapel is bathed in an eerie green glow projected by three jade statues sitting in alcoves, along with a glowing green larger dragon statue, on a dais.

Represented on the walls with artistic and detailed painting are the three Dragons of Law, Platine, Tiamat and Sheresha, powerful divinities of the Empire and certainly the Kingdom of Lothmar.

Unlike most of the ground floor of Castle Wailmoor, this area is untouched by battle and is only dusty. A quiet sense of resolution and certainty fills the air. There is a door in the lower part of the east wall.

On Dragons

The green dragon may be recognizable by a historian, DC 15 Intelligence (History) or Religion Scholar, DC 15 Intelligence (Religion), as Cirmussoss, Lady of The Green, a powerful dragon that the Paladin Lothmar rode to do battle with the fell sorcerers of the lizardfolk so long ago during the Lothmar Crusades.

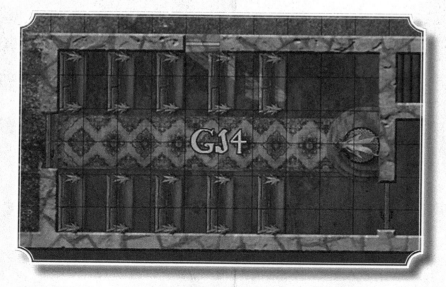

Worshiping dragons is a human oddity, only shared by orcs. Many humans and orcs hold the belief that worshiping a dragon in the Welt is akin to worshiping the Three Dragons of Law. That dragons are not technically immortal, or divine entities that answer prayers is inconsequential to this belief. That the Emperor himself has not weighed in on the veracity of this religious oddity (to reassure the elves, dwarves, halflings, and gnomes) has many concluding this dogma is correct.

The dragons themselves do nothing to discourage these cults—when three cows, a chest of gold and a tasty virgin comes to you; it saves a lot of work!

DRACONIC RELICS

The three statues are resting each in its own alcove, in a wall where the divinity they represent is depicted in a much larger form. They all radiate powerful divine magic but will resist all identification spells. Each statue is about 12 inches tall and weighs 10 pounds. They are carved from a single block of jade and cast a green halo around them (the halo can get hidden under a cloak or inside a bag). They represent a dragon resting on its back legs and roaring at the sky. Each statue if tested for alignment radiates with the alignment corresponding to the dragon god (LG for Platine, LN for Sheresha and LE for Tiamat).

The statues are powerful relics brought to the Wailmoor by the clergy of each dragon divinity. While most of the other baronies in the kingdom of Lothmar are sworn to a specific faith, Wailmoor always maintained a more neutral status, welcoming the faith of Dvalin, the dragon cults of The Three and the rest of the pantheon to a smaller extent.

The Power of the Relics

- All three statues are relics and are unidentifiable for their properties. However, these properties will reveal themselves to PCs as they manipulate and use the statues.

- Created by draconic magic, these relics cannot be located or scryed. While Wailmoor fell, forgotten by most, the clergy of these dragon faiths still looking for the statues.

- The statues radiate with a permanent *magic circle*, a 10-foot-radius, 20-foot-tall cylinder of magical energy centered on the statue. The Statue of Sheresha radiates with *protection from fey*, the statue of Tiamat *protection from demons*, and the statue of Platine *protection from undead*.

- When held in the hands of a living creature, the statues provide the following spell-like abilities to their wielder (each ability is usable once/day, and the wielder needs to have both hands free to hold the statues and cannot wield weapons while so): *divination* (to the matching Dragon of Law), *tongues*, and *bless* (10-minute duration).

The Relic Quests

How PCs will handle these relics (if at all) will have significance in the events unfolding in the next module, and possibly beyond.

When a PC first touches a statue, a low, commanding voice echoes in their head, ordering them to fulfill the destiny of each relic:

- The statue of Tiamat complains she has been in here for too long and wants to be brought to the Bishop of Tiamat in Hardred.

- The statue of Platine wants the wielder to slay a powerful undead (CR 8 or higher).

- The statue of Sheresha orders the PC to visit the court of the King of Lothmar and reinstate Wailmoor as a formal Barony. This is motivated by the lawful nature of the deity.

Completing any of these asks will grant the PC an amount of experience equivalent to 50% of the remaining amount they need to level (or any other amount at the DM discretion).

Should PCs refuse to comply with these instructions and deprioritize them when they have the availability to carry out the tasks, they will be blocked from using the statues powers and abilities.

To move these relics and still use their power requires Attunement. If left on a shelf or altar, they function without the need for commands.

LOST MEMORY

Elayne, the Baron's precious daughter, is sitting alone in the Chapel on a pew, peering at the small statue of Platine, appearing forlorn. You sit next to her.

"Everyone is so, so sad. Mother won't stop crying. It hurts too much!" She leans on you, grabbing your hand.

"I know, Sweetling. I know."

"I would have loved my Baby Brother forever. I would have. My brother is dead! My brother is dead..."

"I would have loved him forever, too."

G15 - VESTIBULE

This Area contains a trap of sorts. Any person not speaking one of the three Dragon of Law's name while walking on the rug is attacked by the rug itself. The rug will not attack anyone in the presence of a cleric of any of the Three, nor anyone in the presence of someone wearing a holy symbol to the Three Deities of Law. It will attack demons and undead.

Intro

Lost at the Beaux Seins

Moortide Rising

The Altar & the Anvil

Castle Wailmoor

Appendix

An empty vestibule connects the temple with private rooms. A richly decorated rug decorates the floor. On the north wall, stairs lead down. There is a doorway to the south.

Rug of Smothering

Large construct, unaligned
Armor Class 12 — **Hit Points** 33 — **Speed** 10 ft.

Statistics

STR	DEX	CON	INT	WIS	CHA
17 (+3)	14 (+2)	10 (+0)	1 (-5)	3 (-4)	1 (-5)

Damage Immunities poison, psychic
Condition Immunities blinded, charmed, deafened, frightened, paralyzed, petrified, poisoned
Senses blindsight 60 ft. (blind beyond this radius), passive Perception 6
Languages —
Challenge 2 (450 XP)

Abilities

Antimagic Susceptibility. The rug is incapacitated while in an antimagic field. If targeted by dispel magic, the rug must succeed on a Constitution Saving Throw against the caster's spell save DC or fall unconscious for 1 minute.

Damage Transfer. While it is grappling a creature, the rug takes only half the damage dealt, and the creature grappled by the rug takes the other half.

False Appearance. While the rug remains motionless, it is indistinguishable from a normal rug.

Actions

Smother. *Melee Weapon Attack:* +5 to hit, reach 5 ft., one Medium or smaller creature.
Hit: The creature is grappled (escape DC 13). Until this grapple ends, the target is restrained, blinded, and at risk of suffocating, and the rug can't smother another target. In addition, at the start of each of the target's turns, the target takes 10 (2d6 + 3) bludgeoning damage.

G16 - THE PRIEST CHAMBERS

The door to this room is open

This room contains a sad task for any PC with a sense of justice for the defenseless.

This small bedchamber is richly decorated and bathed in a permanent light, giving the room an aura filled with divine presence. The walls are covered with draconic symbols, and a thick white-down, dragon-scale decorated blanket rests on the bed.

Drakkon was one of the first citizens of the moor to flee the castle when the demons invaded the Barony. For someone so attuned to Law, the sight of the creatures of chaos was too much for him to bear—and he was not very courageous to start with. He packed most of his personal belongings and fled for the capital where he died 50 years later, writing numerous books about the three draconic relics he left behind on the

moor and how intrepid adventurers should explore the moor and retrieve them. Scholar PCs or PCs with a religious education may have heard about this story, DC 18 Intelligence (Religion). Unbeknownst to all, Drakkon *did* try to take the statues with him—but they would not budge out of their alcoves.

A forgotten *raise dead* scroll can be found in a cedar box under his bed.

But that's not the only thing under the bed—the bones of a dog, collar still around his neck with a cracked-with-time leather leash, are also under the bed. The bone-shaped tag reads "Burko of Wailmoor/My Friend Forever" on one side and "Lady Elayne of Wailmoor" on the other. It is made of bronze and obvious expert craftsmanship, although the leather collar is cracked and stiff.

This was Elayne of Wailmoor's dog, the daughter of the Baron, who was spirited to the Castle from Graspen in hopes of being protected by Chrystelle in a desperate bid to save some part of the Wailmoor. She didn't make it, killed by poison gas in the storage room in Area D2. Her bones are still there to this day.

Her dog, Burko, managed to make it all the way here but then died, alone and afraid, sick, and hungry and cold, whimpering under the bed.

THE QUEST

If the PCs bury poor Burko's bones, the PC who did so finds a Figurine of Wondrous Power, Onyx Dog in his or her pocket the next morning.

Figurine of Wondrous Power Burko the Onyx Dog
This *figurine of wondrous power* is a statuette of a dog, small enough to fit in a pocket. If you use an action to speak the command word (Burko!) and throw the figurine to a point on the ground within 60 feet, the figurine becomes a living dog—a mastiff. If the space where Burko would appear is occupied by other creatures or objects, or if there isn't enough space for the creature, the figurine doesn't become a dog.

The dog is friendly to you and your companions. It understands you and obeys your spoken commands. If you issue no commands, the dog defends itself but takes no other actions other than displays of affection and loyalty. Occasionally it will chase its tail and bark at squirrels.

Once activated, Burko lasts for 24-hours. Burko has an Intelligence of 8 and can speak Common. He also has darkvision out to a range of 60 feet and can see *invisible* creatures and objects within that range. Once it has been used, it can't be used again until 3 days have passed.

Alternate Quest Resolution
If Burko is buried with Elayne, whose bones are in Area D2, then Burko can be summoned and pocketed at will with no restrictions other than if he is reduced to 0 HP, it will take at least 3 days before he can manifest from a figurine again.

Burko the Best Dog Ever

Male Mastiff — Medium beast, unaligned
Armor Class 14 — **Hit Points** 23 — **Speed** 40 ft.

Statistics

STR	DEX	CON	INT	WIS	CHA
14 (+2),	14 (+2),	12 (+1)	8 (-1)	12 (+1)	8 (-1)

Skills Perception +3, Stealth +4, Survival +3
Senses passive Perception 13, darkvision, detect invisibility
Languages Common
Challenge 1/2 (100 XP)

Abilities

Keen Hearing and Smell. The mastiff has Advantage on Wisdom (Perception) checks that rely on hearing or smell.

Figurine of Wonderous Power. If reduced to 0 or fewer hit points, Burko reverts to his figurine form. At least 3 days must past before recalled again, where he will manifest at full hit points.

Actions

Bite. Melee Weapon Attack: +4 to hit, reach 5 ft., one target. *Hit:* 5 (1d6+2) piercing damage. If the target is a creature, it must succeed on a DC 12 Strength Saving Throw or be knocked prone.

See Invisibility. Burko can detect invisible creatures as per the spell within 60ft.

Darkvision. Burko has darkvision up to 60ft.

UPPER FLOOR

The upper floor is in vast contrast to the carnage below. When the Castle was finally breached, nobody escaped in this direction, so none of the attackers came here

to wreak havoc. The attacker's aim was to breach the Tower and eat the inhabitants of the Castle.

Thus, it's the perfect location for Harakan to assert his ruse. Starting in Area U1, PCs have a slight chance (DC 25 Wisdom (Perception) Check) to hear the demon pounding on the door to Area U5 along with the screeches of "Go away!" and the shrill piercing of a little girl screaming. This chance gets better the farther east the PCs travel.

MAGICAL PROPERTIES OF THE UPPER FLOOR

There are some magical properties of the upper floor, but they are subtle.

TEMPERATURE CONTROL

It is a constant 70 degrees F with a comfy humidity no matter what the temperature is like either outside or in other parts of the Castle.

UNSEEN SERVANTS

All five rooms have a permanent *unseen servant*. It can be commanded to do anything the spell attributes to the magical construct. All one must do to command one is to say "Servant" in elvish and then give it a command (either in common or elvish).

Clean & Polish

In any of the rooms, if someone says, "clean and polish," in elvish, the clothes they are wearing instantly become clean, and their shoe, boots, jewelry, and any leather become polished, their weapons sharpened (if a blade) and polished.

U1 - THE GUEST ROOM

Stepping into this room triggers a *Lost Memory*.

This guest room has a certain serenity to it, and guests not familiar with elven architecture may be surprised at how different it is compared to traditional, Lothmarian bedrooms. The Tower is of much older construction than the Castle.

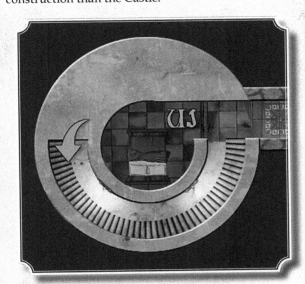

Intro

Lost at the Beaux Seins

Moortide Rising

The Altar & the Anvil

Castle Wailmoor

Appendix

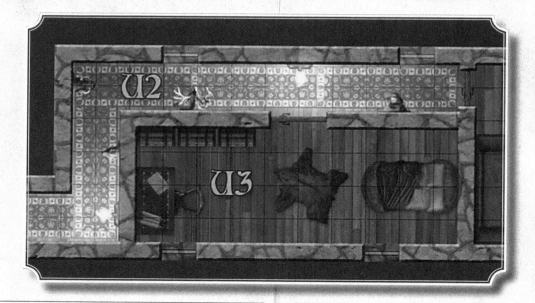

A comfortable bedroom is nested here at the center of the Elven Tower. A large bed occupies the center of the room that has little furniture but the minimum necessary to host one or two guests for a few nights. On the walls, paintings and engravings depict hunting scenes all over the Wailmoor. The ground is covered with lavish green tiles of which look brand new while probably quite old.

There is a guest safe hidden behind one of the paintings. The safe is open and only contains 2 potions (one *potion of greater healing* and one *potion of speed*).

Underneath the bed is a *chamber pot*, like the *magical chamber pot* found Area G3.

The door into the chamber creaks a bit.

LOST MEMORY

Madeline of Wailmoor, the Baroness, climbs naked into your bed.

"Madeline! The servants will know."

"Sir Garret—they know already, Sir Jackon scares the crap out of them, shut up and give me another baby."

U2 - THE HALLWAY

The window to this hallway that overlooks the courtyard is cracked open. PCs will not notice this unless they specifically say they are checking the windows. If discovered, the can close the window if they wish.

The thick rugs into the hallway do not make it particularly loud to move through, and quiet PCs will enjoy Advantage on any Stealth Checks. The hallway ends in a door, and listening PCs have a better chance to hear any of the deceptive shenanigans at the door before Area U5, Elayne of Wailmoor's bedroom.

A well-lit hallway connects the rooms on the upper floor of the castle. A thick, decorative red rug runs on the hardwood floor, most likely crafted in the southern regions of the Kingdom. Large hunting trophies ornate the walls, the most impressive one being a ten-feet wide massacre of a dire stag with dangerously pointy antlers.

U3 - THE MASTER BEDROOM

Looking at the bed in this room triggers a *Lost Memory*.

The Baron and the Baroness stayed here when the Baron wanted a respite from the politics and a thriving throng of upper-class merchants and nobles that had manorial estates in Graspen. The door is unlocked but closed.

This large bedroom must be the Baron's own. A large and comfortable bed, covered with warm furs lies next to the east wall, under a large painting of the moor wilderness around Belver Tor. In the middle of the room, a magnificent pelt of a dire bear covers the floor while the opposite side of the room has the Baron's desk, littered with three scrolls and letters, as well as three closed chests on the north wall.

There is not much to see in the bed or the bearskin rug. Under the bed is the ever-present *magical chamber pot* as found Area G3.

Most of the interesting things to the PCs in this room are from the papers laying on the Baron's desk and the three chests next to it—and some secret, highly political missives.

THE BARON'S DESK

There is a secret compartment in this desk.

PCs searching through the pile of papers and scrolls on the desk will find mostly letters of debt from Hardred and the eastern Barony of Halmana.

Both these provinces owed money to the Barony and recognized these debts through these letters.

The Hardred debt is about 10,000 gold crowns from 3 different letters signed by the Duke of Hardred (the direct descendant of today's duke) and 5,000 gold crowns owned by Halmana.

There is also a well-used, not-so-secret compartment in the desk, revealed by a DC 12 Intelligence (Investigation) Check, or a DC 13 Wisdom (Perception) Check, filled with more papers. Two sets of the papers are highly political.

Wailmoor Charter

The first set of papers establishes a legal authority over the Barony, and the title of Baron, in exchange for:

- The establishment of a feudal authority with a judicial system using an Imperial University Graduated Inquisitor (Judge).

- A pledge of modest taxes once net income, as defined by the Imperial Rules for Commerce is established by the Barony.

- The Appointment of no fewer than three Lords, with each Lord granted the authority to appoint Knights via a grant of land in the Lord's domain.

- The Pledge of Fidelity to the King of Lothmar which includes the movement of no less than 5000 able-bodied men in times of "strife and war" or "sum equivalents in coin thereof.".

- A Pledge to uphold the Dictates and Graces of the Emperor for the Glory of the Empire.

- A Pledge of Protection for the "Monastery of Dvalin northwest of a lake body of water, which is in turn north of a haunted elven tower."

The oddity of this document it is signed by Argenan (ARG-a-nan), King of Lothmar, Paladin of Platine, but it addressed to "Whoever braves the wilds of the Wailmoor lands, bringing safety for the future inhabitants of the Kingdom and the Empire."

An Imperial University-trained legal scholar can explain the dangerous nature of the frontier lands at the time the document was written. It is highly probable that the King (at the time) did not expect the recipient of the document to live through the taming of the moor, and thus did not address it to a specific person.

Imperial Charter

The second scroll once pulled out of its tube, is of bronze so thin and mailable it is like thick paper. This is a letter from the Emperor himself, dated 152-years ago (IY 4859), right before the onset of the Demon War.

Salutations, Baron of Wailmoor, herein the Kingdom of Lothmar and Protectorate of the Divine Empire.

The Imperial Road Authority has noted your linkage of a paved road to the Imperial Road System and your plans to extend the road into the Lothmar Barony of Mendron.

If this is in preparation for an Appeal for Entry into the Empire, you have my enthusiastic support. Long has the Barony of Wailmoor, a "mere" Protectorate, have furnished the Empire with educated citizens, War Wizards and cultural wealth and prosperity. According to my advisors, the Imperial War Wizard Jackon, Knight of the Wailmoor, obliged his term in the Imperial Armed Services with distinction, valor, and courage. If this is the caliber of the young men and women of the Wailmoor, then the Empire would be a better place for your formal entry into our family of jurisprudence and government.

Best Regards,
Emperor, the Divine Provost

Clever players will note that this document is not formally titled to a named baron, either, and that was certainly by design. It is a request by the Emperor himself for the Baron of Wailmoor to move from an Imperial Protectorate to an Imperial Realm, leaving no mention if that would be under the banner of Lothmar (an early Imperial Realm) or independent, or perhaps some other alliance. The letter is the equivalent of a political nuclear-hot potato, and if found, should be a hint of what the players will go through in the next installment in the *Chronicles of the Celestial Chains* campaign. Demons are going to be the least of their problems.

The Emperor is immortal and doesn't forget anything important—he's still waiting for a formal reply.

THE THREE CHESTS

These three chests are identical in appearance, large wooden chests with a metal lock, wide and low, probably used to store expensive clothes more than objects. They are all locked, DC 18 Dexterity (Thieves 'Tools) to pick, and not trapped.

Chest 1

The first chest contains the livery and parade clothes of the Baron. The color of the clothing has faded with time but can be magically restored by a simple spell. It contains a thick linen shirt with the arms of Wailmoor on the chest, a clerical robe with both the symbols of Platine and the Barony as well as an ebony box (not locked) that contains a silver amulet engraved with the arms of Wailmoor.

At the bottom of the chest underneath the clothing are three books tied together with a faded, but still fancy and feminine, pink ribbon with a yellowed note attached:

Intro

Lost at the Beaux Seins

Moortide Rising

The Altar & the Anvil

Castle Wailmoor

Appendix

"For Elayne, should she want to expand her mind. With Love to your beautiful family, C."

These are spell books, with small, perfect writing and illustrations. Between the three books, they have all the 1st Level Wizard spells, serving as an extensive (and expensive) gift for any new wizard wanting to build up his or her own spellbook (see "Your Spellbook" on p. 114 of the 5E PHB).

Chest 2

The second chest contains the Baron's ceremonial, but functional weapons and armor should he be called to battle by his liege, the King of Lothmar:

- A suit of plate armor is bearing the engraved heraldry of both the Kingdom of Lothmar and Barony of Wailmoor (worth 4,000 GP).
- A +1 *shield* engraved with the coat of arms of the kingdom of Lothmar.
- A +1 *silver longsword* engraved with the Wailmoor arms and comes with a scabbard at the colors of the barony.

Chest 3

The third chest contains the Baron's personal treasure stored here instead of his (now destroyed) estate in Graspen.

- 3 gold ingots of a value of 500 gold each
- 2 platinum bars (1,000 gold value each)
- Gold and platinum miniature of the dragon-god Platine (worth 1,000 gold coins)
- 3 luxurious furs (worth 100 gold each)
- An ivory scroll-case with a high-quality map of the barony, showing clear borders of the domain, the map is stamped with the sigil of the King of Lothmar's Imperial Librarian, giving it a strong political value

LOST MEMORY

The Baroness stands at the southern window, overlooking the beautiful landscape that is the Wailmoor. She is dressed in a beautiful elven-style maiden's gown, diaphanous blue-green silk hugging her skin, delicate metal jewelry intertwined up her arms and legs like flowering vines crawling along tree branches.

"Mark is as a brother to me..."

She turns around. "It's happened before. There isn't a drop of original Wailmoor blood in the tree."

"Excuse me?" Out of all the things you expected her to say, this was not it.

"Sometimes, if someone spends too long in the tower, it does things to them. If it was me, my womb could never be with child. But it is not me. And it *shames* him. Please. Help us."

U4 - THE RECREATION ROOM

Traversing the middle of this room triggers a *Lost Memory*.

The door to this room is closed. By now there are only two doors between the PCs and Harakan's demon which is scratching and giggling at the door to Area U5 while "Elayne" is screeching in terror.

This opulent room looks comfortable and welcoming. It has a chessboard and a target for darts as well as a host of liquor bottles proudly displayed in a bookshelf with a multitude of books. The room has not been used for a long time; everything is dusty. Some melee weapons—a large claymore, and two halberds and a crossbow—are decorating the walls, tarnished with age.

What is more obvious, however, is hollow, reverberating high-pitched giggles and cackles coming from beyond the door in the lower-east wall and the pounding on a door, both interrupted by the terrified screams of a young female child.

The weapons on the wall are silvered, albeit non-magical. They are still sharp and functional, simply needing some polish and care.

If players inspect the chessboard, they see that pawns are placed in a way that suggests a game is in play.

The library shelves contain a few books about the history of the Wailmoor and the kingdom of Lothmar, as well as some folktales and children stories. Some of the books are illustrated books suitable for children.

THE SPIKE DEMON

Harakan summoned the Spike Demon just west of the door in Area U5 in the long hallway between Area U4 and U5. Playing the part, he neither told the demon what-was-what or who-was-who, he simply screamed (as a little girl), and slammed the door shut and barded it. The demon has been pounding away at the door, but since it is a reinforced, riveted iron-shod door of hard-oak, it has been slow going.

Spike Demon

Female medium demon, chaotic evil
AC 15 — **HP** 110 — **Speed** 30 ft.

Statistics

STR	DEX	CON	INT	WIS	CHA
16 (+3)	17 (+3)	18 (+4)	12 (+1)	14 (+2)	14 (+2)

Saving Throws Str +6, Con +7, Wis +5, Cha +5
Skills Deception +5, Insight +5, Perception +8
Damage Immunities cold, poison
Damage Resistances necrotic; bludgeoning, piercing, and slashing from nonmagical attacks that aren't silvered
Damage Vulnerabilities radiant
Condition Immunities poisoned
Senses darkvision 120 ft., passive Perception 18
Languages Abyssal, telepathy 120 ft.
Challenge 5 (1,800 XP)

Abilities

Shrike Hide. At the start of each of its turns, the spike demon deals 5 (1d10) piercing damage to any creature grappling it.

Demon Sight. Magical darkness doesn't impede this demon's darkvision.

Magic Resistance. The demon has Advantage on Saving Throws against spells and other magical effects.

Summoned. This demon was summoned.

Actions

Multiattack. The spike demon makes three melee attacks: one with its tail and two with its claws. Alternatively, it can use *hurl frost* twice.

Claw. *Melee Weapon Attack:* +6 to hit, reach 5 ft., one target. *Hit:* 6 (1d6+3) slashing damage.

Tail. *Melee Weapon Attack:* +6 to hit, reach 5 ft., one target. *Hit:* 10 (2d6+3) piercing damage.

Hurl Frost. *Ranged Spell Attack:* +5 to hit, range 150 ft., one target. *Hit:* 10 (3d6) cold damage.

As the hallway in Area U2, the thick carpet with its now disturbed dust affords the PC Advantage in any Stealth checks. It is highly probable that Stealthy PCs will surprise the demon. It turns and gleefully fights them in the narrow hallway, using its ranged attacks, as necessary.

While the demon does not have a vulnerability to fire, neither does it have resistance to it. She is infuriated by fire-based attacks, focusing on whoever dared to put flame to her person to the exclusion of any of the other combatants, even if tactically detrimental.

This 7ft. tall demon is covered in hoarfrost, spikes and a malignant aura of corruption and awfulness—its naked body appearing as if some fell demon lord took a succubus, ripped off her wings, and stabbed her with a multitude of frozen, oversized needles.

Once the PCs have dealt with the Spike demon, they can converse with the "child" in the room to have her open the door to U5. After some tearful negotiation, Elayne does so and runs under the bed before PCs can open the door.

If the PCs simply start battering the door, she takes up her screaming and wailing.

LOST MEMORY

You stride across the room and peer into the bassinet, where little Elayne, all six-months of her, lies sleeping.

"At least she doesn't look like me."

The Baroness comes up behind you and smacks you on the butt. "You ass. See her for the first time, and that's what you have to say? Brute."

You continue to stare. She's quite the beautiful baby. "I thought that's why you liked me?"

Madeline turns you around, and steps closer. "I'll show you why I like you."

Intro

Lost at the Beaux Seins

Moortide Rising

The Altar & the Anvil

Castle Wailmoor

Appendix

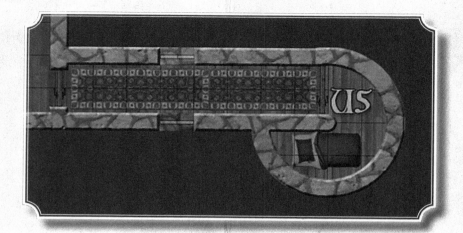

U5 - The Child's Room

Entering this room triggers a Lost Memory

This is the bedroom of Elayne, daughter to the Baron Mark of Wailmoor. Elayne and others who tried to escape the sudden assault died from a high-level slotted *cloudkill* spell that was sent into the lower levels by a possessed witch. Her body is currently located in the dungeons below the castle in Area D2, where she tried to retreat and hide.

A cozy room rests here at the end of a narrow hallway, connecting to the southeast tower. The room was decorated with taste, including tapestries and rich rugs, coming probably from the Southlands of Ghon. A single bed occupies most of the room. Wine-colored bed blankets and drapery hint that this is the bedroom of a noble lady, perhaps the Baron's daughter.
Peeking from underneath the bed are two wide, frightened eyes of a little human girl wearing a purple nightgown, looking at you all with trepidation.

A small chest is hidden under the bed and contains Elayne's favorite gown, a purple linen robe with the arms of Wailmoor embroidered on a silk cape on its back (the robe can still be used, by small-sized PCs), as well a plush bear and the wooden figurine of a stag (non-magical but a nice piece of art that can be appraised in the 250 GPs). Also, under the bed is the ever-present *magical chamber pot*.

Lost Memory

"Sir Garret!"
You pick Elayne and spin her around as she giggles. She then gives you a big hug around your neck.
"What did you get me for my birthday?" she asks breathlessly.
You laugh. "Is not my smiling face enough?"
"Is it chocolate?" She starts rooting around your vest.
"Better."
"A moor starflower?"
"Better."
"What is it!"
A puppy runs into the room.
"Ah! A puppy! Put me down! Put me down!"
You put her down, and the puppy jumps on her, licking her face as Elayne giggles.
"He'll need a name."
"I will call him Burko, and he will be the Best Dog Ever! Thank you so much, Sir Garret."

Harakan's Dual-Layered Deception

Harakan's plan is to pose as Elayne of Wailmoor and have the PCs enter the tower and do battle with Chrystelle, softening her up and biding time for him to figure out a way to get in it. It's not much of a plan, but it amuses him, so he's going for it. He's hoping the dog sweater on a demon hound, and Wailmoor equine livery on his nightmare has set the stage properly for either of his deceptions.

Harakan is eager to secure the Castle, something the Witches were never able to do. Once he's settled in, they can bring their fell power to bear on the situation. And if he can get to Chrystelle first, so much the better.

As soon as the PCs "console" Elayne, she will blurt out:

Did you kill the witch in the tower? She summons demons!

Harakan will attempt to keep up the ruse if possible, answering obvious questions when he can, act like a scared little girl that has trouble talking when he can't. "I want my Mommy!" and "I don't know!" etc., etc.
Who are you?

I'm Elayne, daughter to the Baron Mark of Wailmoor.

What are you doing here?

I ran here to try to find my father, but everyone in the castle seems to be dead! Where is my dad? Where's Mommy?

The baron died 150-years ago!

That cannot be true, my dad kissed me good night yesterday, and I woke up in an empty, destroyed Castle. I'm sure the evil lady in the tower is behind this! You need to protect me from her!

Who is the evil lady?

She is a bad skeleton woman in the old tower! Nobody believed me when I told them she was bad! She is behind everything bad happening here. Will you please find her and kill her?

Are you talking about the lady figure? The statue in the woods?

Yes! Don't be fooled though. She tricks everyone around them and is a conniving witch!

How do you know of her?

When I was playing near the tower, I found this secret door. I saw her summoning demons to the moor and performing nefarious rituals! Did she kill my father?

THE SECOND LAYER

Its possible PCs will see through this ruse. They could have intuited that Chrystelle is not the evil party in the moor. If they searched the priest's quarters, they could ask the fake Elayne about her dog, Burko, and any waffling here would not add up. They could ask her about Garret, or several things they know that she ought to know. They could also *detect evil* or alignment. It would be extremely unusual for a human child to display the terrible aura of chaos and evil that surrounds the Dead-Knight.

PCs caught in a *Lost Memory* will make Harakan pause, and a high Wisdom (Insight) roll (conducted by the DM in secret) with a DC 25 Check will reveal that the little girl had something more in her eyes during the *Lost Memory* than confusion. If asked about it, a fast-thinking Harakan will blurt out "My daddy used to look that way sometimes."

In any event, if the jig is up, Harakan drops his magical disguise. However, if the PCs go so far as to start whacking on him in his Elayne form, simply proceed with the battle. See <u>Running with Harakan</u>.

Standing before you is a vastly different figure than the little girl. A skeletal corpse of a man is encased in regalia of a Dragon-Knight, his mithril plate armor foreboding, the hilt of his weapons somewhat translucent, his dragon helm almost a part of his skull, a green eldritch glow haloing his form.

He bows his head. "Obviously, my lies did not work. Look how low I have fallen." He holds out his arms as if inviting you to take a good look at his undead form.

Harakan at this point pauses, waiting for the PCs to say something or do something. His experience as a subversive agent of chaos is that whatever story people make up in their minds is going to better than what he can come out with.

He's banking on this—his historical knowledge about the Wailmoor is limited.

Who are you, really?

I *was* Jordan Relkan, Dragon-Knight of the Three. Now? I do not know. I am forsaken. I should be dead. But I am not.

Why the deception?

My desire to complete my mission overrode my sense of judgment. You defeated the Witch's demon dogs and the spike demon, so I know you're not in league with her. But I don't know who you are—if I was in your place, I would take one look at my form and try to kill me. I would rather you spend that effort defeating the impetus of my downfall.

What happened to you?

The priest of the Dragon Chapel began to suspect that the Enchantress of the Tower was, in fact, an undead witch in league with Orcus. I was dispatched to investigate. And as near as I can tell, I was the incentive of all the destruction you see here. During my investigation, I partook in communion in the Chapel. The wine was poisoned. I died, right on the Dragon Chapel floor. But when I died, I found myself floating above my body. I could move, but nobody could see me, and I watched helplessly as the Demon War unfolded, caused by the very thing that was supposed to be "protecting" the castle.

I have been haunting the Castle since, but just recently, something drastic has happened, and I found myself back in my body as you see here. I've been avoiding the Witch's fell minions and trying to get into the Tower ever since.

HARAKAN'S FINAL PLEA

I am a'cursed. My failure led to *everything* that has transpired. All this destruction, all this heartache is by my

Intro

Lost at the Beaux Seins

Moortide Rising

The Altar & the Anvil

Castle Wailmoor

Appendix

personal failure. And so, I believe the Gods of Law saw fit to either give me another chance, or punish me, or both.

Please, take these magical bands and shackles. I do not think you can kill the Witch, but they will incapacitate her. I cannot enter the tower in my Cursed Form. You must complete my mission and if you die trying, be warned you could end up just like me. Forsaken. Give it all you have and beware she can charm you with her voice and a glance. If you have spells to protect you from evil, use them early!

THE HOLES IN HARAKAN'S STORY

Harakan spun a good tale and given the events, actually fits within what the PCs may know from their own experiences in the Wailmoor—the corrupted guardians they encountered in the Temple (specifically, the vampire paladin Sir Gwane Germnise) about the gods giving their divine servants a final chance at redemption, various oddities with the Ethereal Plane and finally, the fact that Jackon's and Silas's Obelisks that worked so well, in the beginning, became focal points from spewing corruption. The Obelisks, while preventing further demonic intrusion, trapped what was there from dissipating. And that there were still actual demons loose on the Wailmoor.

But there are several serious holes in his story. Hand the player who falls under the below categories a personal note if they intrinsically pierce his veil. What they say about their revelations, in Harakan's presence, has tactical significance.

Imperial University Scholars

PCs with an Imperial academic background recognize the undead thing before him or her. Not only do they know about him, but they also take a *test* on his history! He's used as an example of what happens when paladins are seduced by the subversive forces of Chaos and Evil.

A graduate of any Imperial University is going to see right through this deception and recognize whom, and what, he is, right down to his mithril dragon armor.

Servants of the Gods of Law Can't Even

A Cleric or Paladin of either of the Three Gods of Law doesn't even need to play this game. They don't need to make a Difficulty Challenge check. Like an Imperial University Scholar, they know a Dead-Knight when they see one. For example, in no circumstance would a dead paladin be grated shape-changing abilities.

Harakan is an affront to all that the Gods of Law stand for, and this classification of PC must destroy him or die trying. It's as if they've just met the absolute worst thing they could meet.

Harakan Loves a Good Fight

The Dead-Knight may be an evil thing, honor-less and corrupted, but he's prideful. He also can make a high Charisma (Deception) Check.

Don't volunteer a roll, but if a PC asks, a successful Wisdom (Insight) Check vs. Harakan's roll with a +6 Charisma (Deception) reveals that even though he doesn't have a living face, "Relkan, Dragon-Knight of the Three" comes across as a bit—gleeful. That is completely different than what his words convey.

If the PC won the Wisdom (Insight) check by 5 or more, not only does it seem he might be spoiling for a good fight, Harakan is conflicted about the PCs entering the Tower.

WHEN IT'S ON, IT'S ON

Harakan must be dealt with one way or the other, and there are many variables to doing battle with him but battle they must. In the grand scheme of things, it's easier on the PCs to confront the "Witch" now and *then* do battle with Harakan.

This situation is an example of where the DM should lean to Player Agency rather than maneuvering PCs one way or the other based on their performance in the module thus far. If the PCs are snookered, that's a great plot device on the DMs part. If they see through Harakan's convincing story, then well-played (but now a dangerous situation). If the PCs happened to have someone with a background that instantly negates Harakan's final ruse, they then reap the rewards of their chosen background and character history.

In any event, either before or after the PCs meet/ confront Chrystelle and doing battle with the Dead-Knight, proceed with <u>Running with Harakan</u> later in the chapter.

"ELAYNE"

The Dead-Knight's Saving Throws and damage reflect his auras and any Proficiency modifiers.

The Dead-Knight Harakan

Male Dead-knight — Medium undead, chaotic evil
Armor Class 19 (Mithral Plate) — **Hit Points** 81 — **Speed** 30 ft.

Statistics

STR	DEX	CON	INT	WIS	CHA
16 (+3)	14 (+2)	16 (+3)	14 (+2)	12 (+1)	16 (+3)

Saving Throws Wis +8, Cha +10, Str +6, Con +6, Int +5, Dex +5
Skills Deception +6, Insight +4, Intimidation +6, Stealth +5
Damage Resistance bludgeoning, piercing and slashing damage that from non-magical weapons
Damage Immunities necrotic, poison
Damage Vulnerabilities radiant
Condition Immunities exhaustion, poisoned, diseased
Senses darkvision 60 ft., passive Perception 11
Languages common, elvish, abyssal
Challenge 8 (3,900 XP)

Abilities

Summon Fell Allies. Summon Vrock (1/day), 4 Hell Hounds (1/day) or Spike Demon (1/day)

Dead-Knight Alteration. A dead-knight can use *alter self* to change to any small, medium, or large human, demi-human or humanoid creature at will.

Aura of Hate (+3, 10 feet). Demons and undead within 10 feet of the dead-knight, gains a bonus to melee weapon damage rolls equal to the dead-knight's Charisma modifier. A creature can benefit from this feature from only one dead-knight at a time.

Aura of Protection (+3, 10 feet). Whenever a dead-knight or a friendly creature within 10 feet of the dead-knight must make a Saving Throw, the creature gains a bonus

Control Undead (DC 14 Wis). As an action, the dead-knight targets one undead creature he or she can see within 30 feet of him or her. The target must make a Wisdom Saving Throw. On a failed save, the target must obey the dead-knight's commands for the next 24 hours, or until the dead-knight uses this Channel Divinity option again. An undead whose challenge rating is equal to or greater than the dead-knight's level is immune to this effect.

Channel Divinity: Dreadful Aspect (DC 14 Wis). As an action, the dead-knight channels the darkest emotions and focuses them into a burst of magical menace. Each creature of the dead-knight's choice within 30 feet of the dead-knight must make a Wisdom Saving Throw if it can see the dead-knight. On a failed save, the target is frightened of the dead-knight for 1d6 rounds. If a creature frightened by this effect ends its turn more than 30 feet away from the dead-knight, it can attempt another Wisdom Saving Throw to end the effect on it.

Divine Sense (4/long rest). As an action, the dead-knight can open his awareness to detect such forces. Until the end of his next turn, the dead-knight can know the location of any celestial, demon, or undead within 60 feet of the dead-knight that is not behind total cover. He can know the type (celestial, demon, or undead) of any being whose presence he senses, but not its identity. Within the same radius, he can also detect the presence of any place or object that has been consecrated or desecrated, as with the hallow spell.

Signal Bomb. When thrown on the ground, this small circular alchemical device lets out a piercing whistle while spinning on the ground, sparking. The shrill whistle can be heard a mile away.

Iron Bands of Binding. The dead knight can take an action to apply iron bands of binding on an incapacitated or grappled combatant.

Actions

Multiattack. The dead-knight makes two melee attacks.

Vicious Longsword. *Melee Weapon Attack:* +9 to hit, reach 5 ft., one target.
Hit: 10 (1d8+6) slashing damage or 11 (1d10+6) slashing damage if used with two hands to make a melee attack. When Harakan rolls a 20 on his attack roll with this magic weapon, his critical hit deals an extra 2d6 slashing damage.

Iron Bands of Binding. Ranged Weapon Attack: +6 to hit, range 60 ft., one target.

Lay on Hands (35 damage pool) (1/long rest). Open Hand as a Melee Weapon Attack, +9 to hit, reach 5 ft.
Hit: up to 35 necrotic damage

Dimensional Shackles. The dead knight can take an action to apply dimensional shackles to an incapacitated or grappled combatant.

Items

Dimensional shackles, iron bands of binding, mitral plate, vicious longsword, signal bomb x3

Intro

Lost at the Beaux Seins

Moortide Rising

The Altar & the Anvil

Castle Wailmoor

Appendix

The Dungeon

While there are obvious indications of battle in the upper portions of the Castle above this lower level, the carnage here is almost never-ending. The demons, with the help of a newly-arrived possessed witch, were finally able to penetrate the Castle. The defenders, trying desperately to keep the Baron's daughter Elayne alive as she fled to the lower level (after her dog), made their last stand here. Their initial plan was to find Elayne and rally, counting on the fact that demons and undead could not move through the Dragon Chapel.

But this plan, such as it was, went quickly awry—the possessed witch created an ethereal tunnel between the courtyard and the dungeon, and the resultant quick assault slammed into the defenders. The brave wardens were wizards, sorcerers and heavily armed and armored soldiers, but they died in the furious assault while giving as good as they got.

The assault ended when Chrystelle physically yanked the possessed witch into her Tower after opening the secret door at the west end of the Area D1 Hallway (and then blowing her into the Deep Ethereal). Shortly after, the Knights of Wailmoor's ploy to kill Barbu succeeded. What few demons left fled in complete disarray, as Jackon predicted.

D1 Hallway

Over a dozen defenders died in this hallway. The few skeletons here are intact only because they had magical protections during the great confabulations from both invader and defender alike.

The narrow stone staircase leads to a long, 10 ft.-wide hallway under the castle, with a low-lying mist covering the floor. There is an open door on the south wall of the hallway, and where the hallway ends, a closed door to the north and an open door to the south.

The walls are scarred with battle marks and the floor littered with bones of defenders scattered this way and that, as if subject to numerous explosions. There are two intact skeletons here, but it's a wonder that they are recognizable as such given the carnage around you.

It is somewhat chilly here, colder than it should be—which would explain the mist.

One of the skeletons is holding a *wand of magic missiles*, currently with 7 charges.

The other has clutched a charred child's doll. She was going to use it to lure Elayne out from where she was hiding.

The secret door requires a DC 18 Intelligence (Investigation) to discover. It is hidden well. A DC 17 Wisdom (Perception) check will also reveal the low-level mist on the floor swirls differently around the end of the hallway. It takes a DC 15 Dexterity (Thieves' Tools) Check to pick the hidden lock.

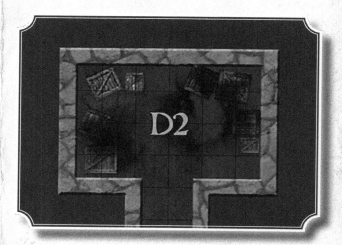

D2 - Storage Room

This room contains a *Lost Memory* triggered when viewing Elayne's skeletal remains.

The door to this room is closed.

The storage room for the castle is located here at the end of the dungeon hallway. All around you, are damaged and empty crates that partially took on fire. The floor itself is charged with marks from intense heat and possibly blast halos of a fire spell, and the crates here seem as if they were lifted off the ground, spun around and tossed in the air, landing as you see them before you. At a first look, none of the stored goods are still in usable shape.

Searching this room reveals Elayne's child-like skeleton, partially in a crate that was tipped over.

Elayne died badly. She was warded against fire and

electricity, escaped the confabulation that terrified her mightily and was injured here from the crates thrown about with *telekinesis*. A defender closed the door, but she died by poison from the possessed witch's massive *cloudkill* spell, which leaked into the room through the gap under the door.

See <u>Alternate Quest Resolution</u> on an option for putting Elayne's bones to rest.

LOST MEMORY

You are sitting on a picnic blanket with Mark and Madeline of Wailmoor, passing a wineskin, nibbling on cheese, and watching Elayne, laughing without a care in the world, running around the wind-swept moor flowers with her dog in a game of human-dog tag.

"Garret, that silly dog might be the best thing you have ever done in your life," Mark says, smiling at you.

Madeline grasps your hand, then Mark's.

"Second best," she says.

If Garret, the former Knight of Wailmoor and reincarnate of a Hierophant, could say what was the moment he was happiest, this memory here would be it. It was that one instant in time where he transcended all his previous lives into one snippet of acceptance and contentment.

Then demons killed everything that he ever loved.

D3 - COLD ROOM

This room's door is open, and a slight cold breeze can be felt as the cold air is drawn out of the room and into the hallway. Closing the door prevents the mist in the hallway from reforming and lowers the temperate in the room to several degrees above freezing.

This is another storage room filled with broken crates and shattered clay pots which fell from thick wooden shelves on the walls. The floor is littered with sharp fragments of clay and pointy shards of wood. It is cold in this room, colder than it is in the hallway.

In the pile of broken junk is an intact, expertly crafted 3ft. x 3ft. x 2ft. box that glows with Alteration magic if detected. Anything placed in this box is frozen solid in several hours.

The littered floor is difficult terrain. The cold effect is permanent but can be dispelled. The spell was cast by an 18th Level Wizard.

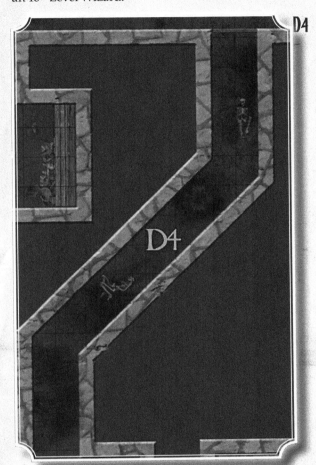

HALLWAY

The door to this hallway is open. The ever-present mist from Area D3 extends here, but it dissipates in 40ft.

This hallway shows similar signs of battle, complete with bones, bone fragments and the occasional intact skeleton.

The hallway goes south, then southwest and then at the edge of your light source or darkvision turns south again.

The low-lying mist ends about 40ft. after the door.

D5 - CHRYSTELLE'S APARTMENTS

Entering this room Triggers a *Lost Memory*.

Making it past the secret door reveals the lower half to Chrystelle's Elven Tower.

Intro

Lost at the Beaux Seins

Moortide Rising

The Altar & the Anvil

Castle Wailmoor

Appendix

Chrystelle has access to the entire lower part of the Dungeon—it used to be the Tower's garden, and she could be there without negating Erebus's conditions to her confinement.

She contemplated doing something with the skeletons down here but can't give them a proper burial. She hopes one day she can trust someone to do the task properly. She opened the secret door and spent a long, long time staring at the carnage in the hallway.

She does not know Elayne's skeleton is in Area D2.

A comfortable bedroom is nested here at the center of the Elven tower. A large double bed occupies the some of the room, but there is little other furniture. On the walls, paintings and engravings depict hunting scenes all over the Wailmoor. The ground is covered with lavish green tiles. The middle of the room, a pink 12' diameter rune circle, glows with magical light.

A circular staircase out of green-hued granite goes up. There are four doors in the room, to the northwest, southwest, northeast, and southeast.

All but the secret door is unlocked.

Below are a few things PCs can figure out about Chrystelle observing this room through perception checks (each bullet below requires a successful check from one party member):

WISDOM (PERCEPTION) DC 15

- Unlike the rest of the castle, there is someone living here (a slightly warm, cup of tea on the side of the daybed, half glass of wine on the table, etc..). it is dust free and does not have the aura of abandonment.

- The person living here is a powerful magician. The whole room is enhanced with arcane wonders, a magic fountain, globes of light floating in the air, a book with pages turning by themselves.

- A bookshelf by the wall has small portraits of many different men. They all represent a Baron of Wailmoor. A Wisdom (Insight) DC 15 check reveals they are displayed like a proud mother displays portraits of her cherished children.

WIS (PERCEPTION) DC 20 OR INT (ARCANA) DC 15

- The rune-circle on the floor is active and not for show: it shines and hums with magical energy. This is a permanent *teleportation* glyph.

WIS (PERCEPTION) DC 25 OR INT (INVESTIGATION) DC 20

- The teleportation circle is frequently used.

If PCs step into the teleportation circle in the middle of the room, they are moved to the room at the top of the tower, otherwise not physically accessible without some epic exploration (See Area T1). This is where Chrystelle waits for the PCs.

LOST MEMORY

"Come on Heleshia. Step into the circle," Jackon says.

"That would be a nope." Heleshia plants her feet.

"Don't be such a scare-dee-elf," Garret quips.

"Maybe we elves live longer because we don't invent stupid magics that discombobulates a perfectly healthy body and then *maybe* reforms it somewhere else."

"I'm ah gonna push ya!" Jackon crows, but as he goes to push on Heleshia's butt, she sidesteps neatly, and Jackon and his staff clatter into the circle and with a *bamf*, disappears.

"Well, Jackon's dead. Can I have his stuff?" asks Heleshia.

Garret laughs.

D6 - SCRYING CHAMBER

This area practically hums with arcane energy.

A small and narrow chamber is built within the walls of the old Elven tower. On the tiled floor, a summoning triangle in a circle has been chiseled, still radiating with magical energy. Four large mirrors surround the arcane circle, each placed at the north, west and south and east of it.

This is the chamber used by Chrystelle to scry on the places and people of interest in the Barony. While outside of the rune-circle, the mirrors look mundane and will reflect their surroundings. When observed from inside the pentagram, they, however, show a place of interest to Chrystelle. Note that the mirrors not only show an image but will reveal sounds and even smell at the target location. With concentration, a DC 15 Intelligence (Arcana Check), the image is movable.

NORTH MIRROR
This mirror looks at the main room at the Inn at the Crossroads.

WEST MIRROR
This mirror looks at the Great Hall in Castle Wailmoor.

SOUTH MIRROR
This mirror looks at the nave of the Temple of Dvalin. If the PCs have cleaned the nave or left other traces of their passing in the Temple, Chrystelle will know because of her recent scrying in this mirror. She can move the image around, but she (or anyone else) is unable to scry into the Radiant Chapel.

EAST MIRROR
This mirror overlooks the charred remains of a manor room. PCs with a DC 15 Wisdom (Perception) Check can intuit this it as a location in Graspen. This used to be the Baron's Graspen manorial estate Council Chambers.

D7 - TELEPORTATION CHAMBER

When this door is open, the air coming from the short hallway is stale.

A small chamber is at the end of this dim hallway. On the tiled floor, a powerful ward in the shape of a pentagram has been drawn, still radiating with magical energy. Dust is covering the floor. No one has entered this room in a long, long time.

This is the room that Narakata used to *gate* to the tower and meet with Chrystelle. He has not used this one-way gate from the Celestial Elysia in a thousand years. Chrystelle has decided to not condemn access to the room as a reminder of her folly and his betrayal.

The circle radiates with strong, strong conjuration magic. PCs may not know that a pentagram in ancient times was a symbol of dedication—DC 25 Intelligence (History)—to Elysia before it was used as a symbol of demon summoning and other nefarious uses.

Regardless, it takes a pass-phrase to activate its magic, and any PC foolish enough to enter the pentagram merely stands there looking like a dork. Activating it without the pass-phrase requires a DC 30 Intelligence (Arcana) Check. PCs managing this herculean task find themselves in Elysia in Narakata's palace and attacked by hound archons until slain—if discovered. The *Curse of the Lost Memory* Death Mechanic still operates in the celestial kingdoms. The Welt will not be denied its due.

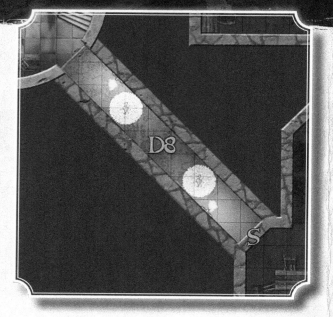

D8 - Peaceful Hallway

This hallway used to be a covered walkway leading to a beautiful pond in Chrystelle's garden. For sentimental reasons and to remind herself of the past, she casts the spells to light the chandeliers each day.

From its characteristic architecture and materials, you can guess that this long hallway extends out of the tower back to the Castle's dungeon. It has not, however, been invaded by demons and its pristine decor remains untouched. It is well lit with magically powered crystal chandeliers and large mirrors on its walls.

Inquiring characters can intuit that the light spells on the chandeliers are not permanent and have been recently cast for the day—DC 17 Intelligence (Arcana).

The door leading into the guard room is not concealed on this side, and the stone panel can be easily pushed open to access the guard room and the outside of the tower.

D9 - Guard's Room

On a hook on the wall, PCs can find the key to the prison cell at the end of the hallway.

The secret door requires a DC 18 Investigate to discover. It is hidden well. A DC 18 Perception check will also reveal the low-level mist on the floor swirls differently around the end of the hallway. It takes a DC 15 Dexterity Check to pick the hidden lock.

A large wooden table with 6 chairs sits at the center of this room. On the walls, empty racks used to carry swords and lances but are gathering dust. The walls are not decorated or showing any paintings or tapestries. This operational look hints at the room being used by soldiers as a guarding outpost in the dungeons. A narrow hallway leaves east, and this room's purpose was to guard its access.

D10 - Latrines

These latrines were placed here so that Wailmoor soldiers could guard the treasure room and access to the Elven tower without leaving their watch for too long. They have not been used in 150-years.

D11 - The Bunker

Examining the map triggers *a Lost Memory*.

This room looks like a 'panic room' of some sorts. Maps of the Wailmoor, marked with locations of demon armies, are covering a thick wooden table. On each wall are a sword and shield, you do not think they were meant to be used but rather saved in case of an emergency. A large open chest by the table contains blankets and woolen capes.

On the map, a big red cross marks the seat of Barbu on the battlefield and wooden miniatures representing the knights of the Wailmoor moving towards it.

Lost Memory

Baron Mark of Wailmoor places a hand on your arm.
"Garret. More reinforcements from our neighbors aren't forthcoming. We've more reports of possessed in the refugees. They're now wreaking considerable havoc. Everywhere."

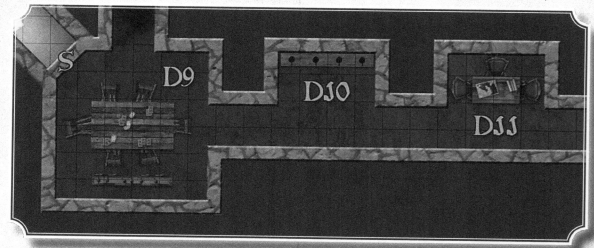

You stare at the map. It's all down to Barbu. Without him, the demon host would collapse. "Then I will receive what magical assistance Chrystelle can give me and make a push to cut off the head of the snake."

"Will you wait for Jackon?"

"No, and we can't send word to him either, or he'll turn back and what is left of Harenvale and everyone still there will be lost."

Mark starts putting on his gauntlets. "That *we'll* make a push. This is it."

"If we fail…"

Mark now puts a hand on your shoulder. "We won't. But if we do, let's give Jackon enough time. He can do this. He just needs more time."

D12 - The Baron's Treasure Room

The treasure chests are linked to the suits of armor (except for one that is just a suit of armor). If they are opened without a key either by breaking the chest or picking the lock, a suit of armor animates and attacks. Each set of armor will also attack if it is disturbed, but the others remain inactive. Nothing untold happens if the normal suit of armor is examined or even removed.

During the Demon War, Wailmoor Manor (the Baron's Graspen manor) treasure was placed here as more and more areas of the Wailmoor became abandoned. Now it is forgotten by all.

This 20ft. x 30ft. room is completely open to the hallway to the south and contains chest and six full suits of plate armor, each expertly etched with the livery of the Barony of Wailmoor and holding a halberd. They are racked on the east and west walls. The chests all closed, aligned on the floor of the dungeon, methodically placed next to each other.

Each suit of full plate armor is worth 3,000 GP, but a suit animated and reduced to 0 HP needs repairing before realizing its full functionality and value.

PCs can disable the magical link from a singular

chest to each animated suit of armor with a DC 16 Intelligence Arcana) Check. Doing so permanently breaks the link, but the armor (except the non-animated suit) will still animate and attack if touched. Failing the Arcana check also activates the armor, and it attacks the person who tried to disable it.

Opening the locked chest requires a DC 16 Dexterity (Thieves' Tools) Check.

Five Advanced Animated Armors

Animated armor — Medium construct, unaligned
Armor Class 18 — **Hit Points** 45 — **Speed** 30 ft.

Statistics

STR	DEX	CON	INT	WIS	CHA
14 (+2)	11 (+0)	13 (+1)	1 (-5)	3 (-4)	1 (-5)

Saving Throws Str +4, Con +3
Skills Acrobatics +2, Perception -2
Damage Immunities poison, psychic
Damage Resistance piercing
Damage Vulnerabilities force
Condition Immunities blinded, charmed, deafened, exhaustion, frightened, paralyzed, petrified, poisoned
Senses blindsight 60 ft. (blind beyond this radius), passive Perception 8
Languages —
Challenge 2 (450 XP)

Abilities

Action Surge (1/short rest). Once per short rest on its turn, the advanced animated armor can take one additional action on top of its regular action and a possible bonus action

Long Rest (1/day). If left alone after a battle, the Advanced Animated Armor will regenerate over the course of 24-hours to full HP value (if reduced to 0 HP, the suit is destroyed and will not regenerate).

Great Weapon Fighting. When the advanced animated armor rolls a 1 or 2 on a damage die for an attack it makes with a melee weapon that it is wielding with two hands, it can reroll the die and must use the new roll, even if the new roll is a 1 or a 2.

Antimagic Susceptibility. The armor is incapacitated while in an antimagic field. If targeted by dispel magic, the armor must succeed on a Constitution Saving Throw against the caster's spell save DC or fall unconscious for 1 minute.

Second Wind (recover 1d10+2 hp, 1/short rest). The advanced animated armor has a limited well of stamina that it can draw on to protect yourself from harm. On its turn, it can use a bonus action to regain hit points equal to 1d10 + 2 HP.

False Appearance. While the armor remains motionless, it is indistinguishable from a normal suit of armor.

Actions

Multiattack. The armor makes two melee attacks.

Halberd. Melee Weapon Attack: +4 to hit, reach 10 ft., one target. Hit: 7 (1d10+2) slashing damage. 1s and 2s are rerolled, taking the newly rolled number instead.

Fist-Slam. Melee Weapon Attack: +4 to hit, reach 5 ft., one target. Hit: 5 (1d6+2) bludgeoning damage.

Intro

Lost at the Beaux Seins

Moortide Rising

The Altar & the Anvil

Castle Wailmoor

Appendix

CHEST 1

This chest contains livery of Wailmoor nobles including velvet breeches, a ferret fur cloak, and black leather boots. The value of these expensive clothing adds up to 200 GP, and the accompany silver jewelry (necklaces, bracers, amulets) are worth 2,000 GP.

There is also a matching jewelry box, dress box, hat box and shoe box holding a noble lady's formalwear. The dress, hat, and shoes are quite fetching and border on somewhat scandalous, embroidered with silver thread and pears. The combined outfit is worth 2,000 GP, and the lady's jewelry, diamond, and platinum come in at a staggering 10,000 GP.

CHEST 2

A metal chest engraved with the Wailmoor crest. This chest contains some antiques of Wailmoor and belongings to former barons. The non-magical weapons (about 7 swords of different sizes) have historical value and are all engraved with the Wailmoor coat of arms. Also, in the chest is a forgotten, but highly magical *frost brand rapier*.

CHEST 3

A wooden chest painted with the symbols and scales of Platine, the good dragon of Law and contains a set of priests of Platine robes, inlaid with platinum, gold, and jade (appraised at 650 GP). The chest also contains 2 *potions of greater healing*.

CHEST 4

This chest contains a whole suit of actual *black dragon scale armor*, etched, and decorated with expert metalsmithing in an odd combination of the Knights of Wailmoor livery and a dark griffon motif, of the like that has never been seen thus far in all the PCs wanderings.

There is also a cloak and boots, both magical: a *cloak of elvenkind* and *boots of elvenkind*. The cloak is wrapped around a *+1 hand crossbow*.

At the bottom of the chest is a saddle, but it isn't a horse saddle, rather designed to keep the rider strapped in at all costs.

Finally, there is a folded piece of paper, yellow with age, with a broken brittle wax seal of a dragon. It is a letter written in draconic.

My Dear Olaf,

Leaving you was the hardest thing I have ever done (so far), but you have a barony to go back to, and when it comes down to it, I know that in an eye-blink you will be dead, and its selfish as selfish is, but I cannot stand the thought of you growing old. I must remember you as you are now, all handsome and cute and charming and all Imperial Griffon Rider.

I made this armor for you. If some other wyrm gives you flack tell them I will fucking bite off their tail of and melt their face. I need to stop writing now before I start blubbering.

Love you forever,
Dee Draco

PS. Glance sideways at another wyrmette, and I swear to Tiamat I will eat everyone in your barony.

CHEST 5

A wooden chest with a simple metal lock. It contains the collection of boots from a long-ago baroness, Baroness Erika of Wailmoor. The collection itself has about 25 pairs of boots and is worth 1,000 GP, not including one magic pair of quite fashionable *boots of striding and springing*—black and with 3' heels, ending slightly below the knee. Inside each magical boot is a hidden sheath, both containing stilettos, two *+1 daggers*.

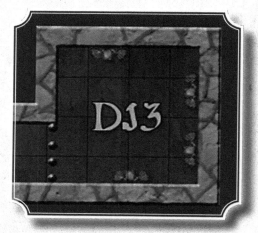

D13 - IMPROMPTU PRISON

The prison bars here have a simple padlock, DC 12 Dexterity (Thieves' Tools). Hastily constructed, it can also be opened with a DC 18 Strength (Athletics) Check.

This used to be a storage room but was turned into a prison during the Demon War.

As the war dragged almost impossibly long, the defenders of Wailmoor were becoming very wary of possessed. Thus, strangers were treated unkindly, and often jailed temporarily until a Cleric or a Paladin could ascertain their condition. These two couples were chained here, and the defenders were going to kill them when they could not reach the divine agents in the Temple of Dvalin. When the Castle was breached and defender and invader alike slain, the prisoners perished from lack of food and water.

These poor souls were simply in the wrong place at the wrong time when they were captured and deserved a proper burial.

Unlike the simple, but the functional architecture of the Castle and the elegance of the Elven Tower, this jail cell seems a crude affair, with rusted iron bars appearing as if they were installed by a drunken dwarf.

Four skeletons are chained to the walls, flesh long since rotted away, appearing as if they were touched the flimsy hand bones would fall through the shackles and collapse the entire bone structure.

THE TOP TOWER

Chrystelle de Valois is waiting for the PCs in this room.

This is both a place of relaxation and an observatory. Even before the Tower was dragged into the Ethereal, this Tower Top was invisible to anyone looking at the tower from the outside.

The walls and ceiling here are transparent, and there are eight windows at each compass point, each 5ft. wide and opening or closing them do not reveal the top of the Tower in any way, or the windows themselves. They are there to let fresh air in and cast spells out.

T1 - CHRYSTELLE'S PARLOR

Chrystelle de Valois is waiting for the PCs in this room.

The walls to this generously large parlor are transparent and offer a panoramic view of the whole Wailmoor below, with its jagged granite hills, its rushing streams, and the barren moor and its many tones of green. A large telescope rests in the north part of this room, pointed in the direction of the Temple of Dvalin. South of the teleportation circle is a delicate daybed covered with plush cushions. A few leather-bound books rest on a small table.

Standing next to the telescope is a serene woman in a noble's regalia. She is extraordinarily beautiful, if somewhat short, and as you stare you realize she is a half-elf.

She is holding a magical wooden staff with a glowing green ball of energy wrapped around brambles at its top. it hums with energy.

WHAT CHRYSTELLE KNOWS ABOUT THE PCs

If the PCs conversed and lounged before her statue in the Lady's Woods, Chrystelle heard and saw everything they said and did, the PCs innate anti-scrying ability not effective with the link Chrystelle has with the statue, which is technically not scrying but a projection of her senses. Such is doubtful given that the PCs needed to bring the Tower and Castle

back from the Ethereal before she could make use of the statue.

If the PCs cleaned up the three western rooms in the Temple of Dvalin, from her recent scrying, she knows someone fixed the Temple but doesn't know exactly when. But given the lack of dust, she suspects it was recent.

She also visually watched the PCs approach the castle and everything the PCs did in the Courtyard, which included doing battle with the demon dogs and possibly the vrock Harakan summoned later.

WHAT CHRYSTELLE KNOWS ABOUT HARAKAN

Unlike the PCs, she can scry Harakan and knows exactly what he is the moment he summoned the demon hounds in the courtyard. She has refrained from roasting him from the tower, mainly because he stopped moving, but also because he started making obvious preparations for deceiving new arrivals.

She knows he's trying to trick someone by morphing into a parody of Elayne (after seeing a dated portrait of her on a wall), and this infuriates her. When the PCs arrived, she put two-and-two together. The PCs may be a big unknown, but this Dead-Knight is laying a trap for them.

How she deals with Harakan specifically depends on how the PCs deal with him. See Running with Harakan.

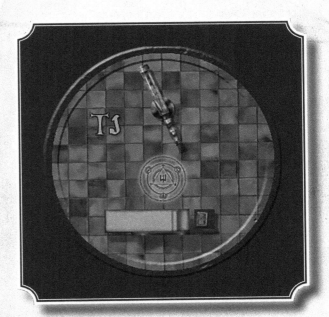

CHRYSTELLE CONDITIONS OF TRUST FOR THE PCs

This is largely dependent on what the PCs have done or said that she knows about thus far. She also will judge the PCs by whom they are. Are they paladins and clerics?

Intro

Lost at the Beaux Seins

Moortide Rising

The Altar & the Anvil

Castle Wailmoor

Appendix

She is confident in her abilities to defend herself, and right now, is simply peering at them, waiting for them to make the first move. Total up her Trust Threshold based on the below to see what actions she takes with the PCs when Harakan is still alive:

Is a PC a Dedicate of Dvalin?

If one of the PCs is a Dedicate of Dvalin, she will greet him or her in Old Dvalin and pre-predisposed to being helpful to the PCs right from the start. She hates demons, now. She hates them more than Narakata, and that's a lot of hate.

Add 1 to her Trust Threshold for each Dedicate of Dvalin in the party.

Is one of the PCs a Cleric or Paladin?

All the gods and their servants oppose demonically corrupted abominations such as the Dead-Knight Harakan. That won't instantly gain her full trust as seeing a Dedicate, but it goes a long way.

Add 1 to her Trust Threshold for each cleric or paladin in the party

Does one of the PCs have Jackon's Staff?

Seeing Jackon's Staff rocks her world (and she's seen it all). She is fully aware that it is a latent artifact only useable by powerful, martial arcane spellcasters such as a War Wizard. At this point, she is super-curious on whom the PCs really are. Obviously, they are no demonic allies no matter how they are presently conducting themselves.

Add 1 to her Trust Threshold for having Jackon's Staff.

Are the PCs holding one or more of the dragon statues found in the Chapel?

Chrystelle knows that the PCs could not retrieve those statues if the Gods of Law didn't want them to have it.

Add 1 to her Trust Threshold for having one or more dragon statues.

Did players figure out the role of the Kandra witches?

And, of course, mention this early while she is assessing the PCs. While the demons infested the moor, the jealous witch Kavita of Kandra is the villain behind all this. She called the demons on the moor to precipitate the fall of Chrystelle and the Barony, and she sends her minions to the moor after the PCs even when she doesn't know whom they are (or what they even look like). She's both an old and a current threat. If the PCs realize that (from interrogating bandits, etc.) and share their thoughts with Chrystelle, it will greatly increase her trust in the players.   Add 1 to her Trust Threshold for talking about Witches as a Common Enemy.

PC Damage

Her tower is her home. Subtract 1 to her Trust Threshold if the PCs damaged anything in her Tower while exploring it, including the Sticky Statue guarding the secret entrance on the Ground Floor in Area G13.

PC Witches and Warlocks

She's not a fan.

Subtract 1 to her Trust Threshold for each witch or warlock in the party.

Is Harakan Dead?

PCs might be able to get to Chrystelle without defeating Harakan first if they:

- side with him, are successfully manipulated in believing Chrystelle is a threat

- are sneaky and avoided any confrontation in a desire to explore all the Castle first

- found the inner Tower first by going downstairs, and then finding the secret door

- found the inner Tower first by defeating the Sticky Statue guardian

- climbed the tower, discovered the invisible top, and got in through an open window.

If Harakan is still alive and her Trust Threshold is 1 or less, she doesn't fully trust them. She will tell them to go kill Harakan and she will buff the party, but only with the conditional *protection from evil* buff that can't be used against her. She'll cast it on every party member.

If two or more of Chrystelle's conditions of trust are met, and the Dead-Knight is still alive, well, he's screwed. She buffs the PCs as no low-level PCs have been buffed before:

- *Haste* on the melee PCs

- *Protection from evil* on each party member

- *Stoneskin* and *mage armor* on any of the non-armor wearing PCs

- *Longstrider* on the entire party

- *Magic weapon* on any PC without a magic weapon

- *Foresight* on one PC, favoring in order: Dedicate of Dvalin, Paladin, Cleric, Fighter, Ranger, Barbarian, Rogue

Proceed with the Running with Harakan scenario.

Lying to Chrystelle

Chrystelle has an Insight Skill of +10. It is difficult, but not impossible, to lie to her. If she catches PC in a lie, what she does depends on the lie itself.

Her Safety

If the lie is a prelude to attacking, Chrystelle preemptively goes on the offensive. Things do not turn out well for the PCs, but if she thinks the PCs are being deceptive because they were deceived by the Dead-Knight, she adjusts her actions accordingly. She uses her charming abilities instead of her death-dealing spells and fell magical staff.

Other Lies

If the lie she detects is about the Obelisks or recent events, she caulks it up to security cautious PCs, immaturity, or a combination of both.

If the PCs Attack Chrystelle

Chrystelle de Valois is a 20th Level Enchanter with a CR of 23 and Legendary and Lair Actions, who's had centuries to perfect her craft, battle-hardened and highly educated, holding *a staff of absorption*. She can hypnotize people at a glance and melee combats who try to hit her usually wind up hitting someone else.

The DM can access her character sheet in the Appendix and play it out, but really, she either charms and suggests the PCs refrain from attacking her further or waffle-stomps the PCs into unconsciousness using spells like *power word stun* (which as an Enchanter she can split between two PCs!) and the PCs wake up in an extra-dimensional space being fed milk and cookies (still with their gear) from a djinni named Mimi.

At that point, Chrystelle will start over. Once Mimi shows them the door back to the tower, Chrystelle will start by telling what she knows about the PCs, says she doesn't think they are bad people, and can they start over again and converse in a civilized manner? Harakan is their enemy, not her.

In any event, she still will buff the PCs with *protection from evil,* but her <u>conditions of trust</u> threshold for the other buffs increase to 3 before she gives them the juice.

Chrystelle is a very benevolent person, but she is experienced enough to be utterly ruthless in combat. She is not above using a *power word kill,* on a PC to then tell the other PCs to stop and listen to her side of the story or she will do it again.

If the PCs attack her again, she kills them all, and the *Curse of the Lost Memories* death mechanic takes over. They wake up in the great tree at the Crossroads Village, -1 to all their stats and hopefully feeling foolish.

Questions to Chrystelle

PCs are going to have questions, and Chrystelle will answer if the PCs answer a question in return, in a tit-for-tat Q&A.

Who are you?

I am Chrystelle, the benefactor of Wailmoor. I have been living in this tower for countless years. Very few are those who know I exist, besides, of course, the Wailmoor Barons, the occasional Baronesses and their elite warriors, the Knights of Wailmoor.

What are you doing here?

An ancient curse binds me to this tower. I cannot leave it. My sanity then relies on the visits I get and my work building up the Wailmoor dynasty and the Barony.

However, I believe Jackon and Silas tapped into magic they did not fully understand. First the Tower, and then the Castle was pulled to the Ethereal for the last 150-years. I have so many questions for you because I do not know what was going on since being locked away. If you are responsible for bringing back the Tower and Castle, then I thank you. I am in your debt.

What is this curse about?

It is an old story I might share with you once we know each other better. Let's just say that I was given eternal life by a former lover, but this gift was restricted to this tower. Orcus, the demon prince who oversees the Undead, takes great ire of this status of mine and his demonic troops have looked for my fall for many years.

Why are demons attacking the moor?

Demons were called to the moor upon the summoning of a nefarious witch, Kavita. She is the leader of the coven influencing the neighboring Barony of Kandra. Kavita discovered my existence and my influence on the wealth of the Wailmoor. Since then she swore to bring me down. A hundred and fifty years ago, she called the great demon Barbu upon the moor and devastated the Barony. Now that the Castle is back, she has called another minion, a Dead-Knight to secure the castle so the Witches can find someone to access the tower and drag me to Orcus himself.

If you are so powerful, how did the demons breach the castle in the Demon War?

The demons breached the castle because they brought in a powerful ally, a possessed witch previously not encountered.

You must understand by that time the defenders of the Barony were stretched thin—the Baron was dead and so too where most of the Knights of Wailmoor.

The invaders kept this witch in reserve. We had no reserves of our own. She made many attackers immune to my scrying, and they flew into the Courtyard. I am always limited in what I could do when I don't have time to prepare—I tried to summon defenders, but I could not do so fast enough. In the end, I banished her from the Welt.

Why do we have these *Lost Memories*?

I can tell you right now, the Knights of the Wailmoor did not do anything that would cause their memories to—be experienced by someone else. Give me a few days, and I can have some information for you, I am sure. I can use some investigative magic at my disposal.

These memories are another piece of a puzzle I still struggle to put together. Based on what you described, I believe you are reincarnates of the Knights of Wailmoor—souls that neither went to Purgatory or Elysia on death but were reborn. Beyond that, I need to start actively researching who you are and who you were.

I can see it in your eyes: you came all this way for answers, and it disappoints you I have little to give right now, but I can say this for certainty—I can practically *feel* your latent power. That I am not able to scry you, yet you do not have the spells nor the items to shield yourself is an indication that, unlike almost everyone else under the purview of the gods, you were born for a specific reason.

I swear unto you that we will find these answers you seek. Suspiciously, I may be the one of the best in the Empire to answer your questions, and that should give you, as it does me, pause. Are you simply reincarnated Knights of the Wailmoor—or are you something *else*?

What are your plans now?

In the immediate, could I implore you to find all the bodies in the Castle and give them a proper burial? It breaks my heart that I cannot do so. I know this is a terrible task, but please—my heart aches for those lost, and there is no one left to do this task.

In the long term, I believe we need to rebuild the Barony, and that starts by finding a new baron. This is the best way for me to gather resources to help you with these *Lost Memories*. Will you help me with this task?

Do you know what happened to Madeline of Wailmoor?

If asked this Christelle pauses for an almost uncomfortable length of time. Finally, she says:

She was proficient with the crossbow. She partook in defense of the courtyard when the demons pressed their final attack. She didn't make it. Her bones are still there. Could you—would you, bury them? Please?

Questions Chrystelle Has for the PCs

- Do you know if the Wailmoor Knight Heleshia is still alive? She is an elf and still has many decades to live, even now (if the PCs informer her of her death, she turns away and takes a moment to compose herself).

- Have you run into any Kandra Witches? If so, what do you know about them?

- The Tower was yanked into the Ethereal before the Castle. Do you know what happened to Silas?

- Do you know what happened to Jackon, too?

- Do you know what Silas and Jackon did to send the Tower and then the Castle to the Ethereal?

- Did you enter the Temple of Dvalin? Was there anyone there?

- How did you undo Silas and Jackon's ritual?

- What has happened in the Wailmoor all these years?

- How did you all meet?

- Can you tell me about all these *Lost Memories* you had? Every single one.

- Is there anyone, anyone at all left alive in Wailmoor?

Running with Harakan

The Dead-Knight Harakan is a right bastard, with the capability to hit above his Challenge Rating if left alone to summon demonic allies to his cause. Alone, at his current rating, CR 8, he can be a deadly encounter depending on how many Level 4 PCs are at the game table. Ultimately, he is behind the Action Economy curve for a well-balanced party with the available magical items, especially a party that can deal radiant damage. When fighting with allies, they take advantage of his hateful auras, and he is a deadly encounter to low-level PCs.

However, his demon summoning has political limits. At a certain point, depending on circumstances, the demons stop considering Harakan as the leader and more as an—annoyance. He's not a demon lord. He can't command respect with his awesome abilities and higher-level Legendary actions, because he doesn't have any.

Harakan hits hard, and with his life-draining lay on hands ability, he can (and will) one-shot low-hit-point PCs. Working with any ally magnifies their abilities with his hateful auras.

But, Harakan has big problems. He's been sold up the river, and to understand how fundamentally shitty his predicament is, it is necessary to examine the properties of the Elven Tower, Olaf's Spell-Engine and Chrystelle.

The Archangel Erebus

The Archangel Erebus, the angel that shepherds the dead, warded the Elven Tower. Specifically, he took the magical wards already in existence, cast by the de Valois elven wizard who lived in the tower so

Intro

Lost at the Beaux Seins

Moortide Rising

The Altar & the Anvil

Castle Wailmoor

Appendix

long ago (he came to study at the Temple of Dvalin) and augmented them with *his own power*. His wards prevent Chrystelle from leaving the tower and what was then her garden, in return for preventing intrusion from outside forces that would take advantage of her immortality. Like demons and undead. And nobody can *teleport, gate, plane shift,* move from the Astral or Ethereal, *dimension door* or use any other types of magical intrusion spells and powers into the Tower.

It is literally impossible for demons and undead to enter the Tower. Orcus himself would be thwarted. There is nothing, nothing at all, that can change this ward except Erebus himself, not even a god or another archangel. Or all the gods and all the archangels. In this, Erebus's power reigns supreme. And he *forgot* about Chrystelle long ago.

Olaf's Spell-Engine

Almost all the information on the dam thus far has been for the DM to provide long-running context for the next module in the series, *Beneath a Dreary Wave*. References for the players should be kept to a minimum, lest they try to continually go there without the engineering blueprints because, without Merisee's books, they'll never be able to get inside.

The dam, however, is a major player in *Curse of the Lost Memories*. The spell-engine inside is what powers the spell effects around the Wailmoor to make them have permeance. Without the dam, Silas and Jackon would never be able to enact their ward stones, and those stones would never have been corrupted.

Olaf V of Wailmoor was Chrystelle's greatest student, and at the time, surpassed her abilities to become an archmage—one of those rare, higher-order casters able to cast the most powerful of spells.

Olaf burned with fury over Chrystelle's predicament. As an archmage, he could literally see Erebus's ward. So, he embarked on a grand scheme and in his studies, became a cleric of Ishtari and thus became a Paragon—a Wizard/Cleric.

He created a great spell-engine within the dam in hopes of powering a ward that could replace the Tower's ward with a different set of limitations. A bit of arcane and divine sleight of hand.

And it didn't work. All it did was make Erebus's ward stronger. It did add a *wall of force*-like effect for the Tower that can be put up and brought down by Chrystelle at will.

Chrystelle

And thus, everything that has transpired has all been for naught. The Witches of Kandra can never get to Chrystelle. Demons can't get to Chrystelle. Orcus can't even get to Chrystelle. *Nobody* can get into the Tower unless Chrystelle lets them in.

That the Wailmoor was effectively destroyed, that all those people died or were driven from their homes, that the Baron was slain, that little Elayne was killed, that the Knights of Wailmoor perished, that Harakan is on her front door—to Chrystelle it was all for *nothing*.

And so, the Dead-Knight Harakan is going to come to a very messy end. Chrystelle is done with the Witches of Kandra. She's going to kill them all from the safety of her Tower. Starting with their minion, Harakan.

CHRYSTELLE'S WANTS AND NEEDS

It is advantageous to Chrystelle that the PCs defeat the Dead-Knight themselves. Not only is she judging them, despite her great power, but she is also limited in the spells she can cast in a pinch because of their short range. If she can't prepare by summoning allies, then she is limited to what she can reach from the top of her Tower. She's always needed allies for this reason. That was primarily the Knights of Wailmoor's function. They were the roaming extension of her will and partners in their shared belief that the Wailmoor and the peoples there deserved their very best.

She desperately wants new allies, and the PCs right now seem to be up to the task—but she is not sure.

3 CONSIDERATIONS FOR THE DM

There are some choices to be made by the DM before proceeding with killing Harakan the Dead-Knight. While the module lists the various options, it's the DM sitting at the table with a thumb on the pulse of the game that is in the best position to present Harakan in a way to bring a rewarding and satisfying conclusion to *Curse of the Lost Memories*.

ARE THE PLAYERS TACTICALLY ADVANCED?

Are the players, by their performance thought the module thus far (and not other modules), advanced enough to handle a deadly encounter? If so, toughen the battle by bringing the CR6 courtyard vrock into the fray with little or no molestation by Chrystelle.

That's a Deadly Encounter for 4th Level PCs. They may need to retreat. If so, that's a good time to get Chrystelle involved.

ARE THE PCS SUPER-BUFFED?

If the PCs had an audience with Chrystelle and gained her trust, and the Dead-Knight is still a contender, it's going to be one hard-hitting, lightning-fast encounter. Add the vrock from the courtyard unmolested by Chrystelle and watch the resultant fireworks.

ARE THE PLAYERS ADVANCED ROLE-PLAYERS?

There are many permutations to dealing with Harakan the Fallen. If the players pulled out the role-playing stops in the campaign thus far, then bringing in Chrystelle should seem like a natural consequence to all their actions. So, if Chrystelle has a chance to blow up Harakan when he is in range of one of her spells, she will.

Meeting her before Harakan is dead is a great role-playing opportunity, but there is a good chance (as not), those good role-players will flail away at him before they meet her.

KILLING HARAKAN

With those three considerations out of the way, it's time for the PCs to assert themselves. This section presents the most common ways PCs can engage Harakan. Adjust according to the overall picture painted by answering the three above questions.

ATTACKING HARAKAN WHEN DISCOVERED IN AREA U5

This is a viable strategy if the PCs burned down the demon pounding on the door in Area U4 and have been avoiding other resource sapping encounters because of their Stealth (for example, the demon dogs could still be roaming the courtyard because they never saw the PCs). It's also viable if the PCs acquired some of the magical loot in Area D12, such as the *frost brand rapier*.

Either way, Harakan's first action is to drop one of his *signal bombs*. This alerts the vrock near the Gatehouse in Area G1 that he previous summoned—if it is still alive. The plan was to have the vrock take off and fly through the cracked window and arrive at the east door at Area U4 in a single round. If the vrock must pause at the window because it was closed and locked, then it takes him 3 move actions instead of 2 to reach Area U4 because it needs to break through the window.

But then Chrystelle casts a *sunburst* at it from the top of her tower from the open window, doing 24d6 radiant damage, with a DC 21 Constitution Save for half. If it saves, this won't kill the vrock, but it's going to arrive at the battle with a lot fewer hit points than it started out with. If it doesn't save (and still alive), the vrock is blinded. And Chrystelle simply does it again, using a 9th Level spell slot.

Consequently, if there are demon hounds still in the courtyard, she simply cuts loose with *chain lightning*, doing it again if necessary.

Either way, the vrock is either completely removed from the battle, and the Dead-Knight is on his own, or

Intro

Lost at the Beaux Seins

Moortide Rising

The Altar & the Anvil

Castle Wailmoor

Appendix

it arrives damaged.

Per the previous section, it's viable to also have the vrock arrive unmolested to pose a challenge to advanced players.

LYING TO HARAKAN

In this instance, the PCs agree to Fake Elayne's or Fake Dragon Knight's story, but Harakan, with his +4 Insight Skill, manages to catch them in a lie.

If that's the case, he follows them to Area U4 (to show them the secret door into the tower) and proceeds with his *signal bomb* plan while attacking, but now he has more space in which to do so.

This is a difficult but not impossible outcome for Harakan. Most likely he will evaluate only one PC (multiple Wisdom (Insight) Checks on his part can play his hand).

If the PCs are successful in leaving Harakan as-is, then proceed with the meeting with Chrystelle and her battle suggestion.

MEETING CHRYSTELLE WHILE HARAKAN IS ALIVE

These conditions can all lead to the same place—a ruse or trick to bring Harakan closer to the tower.

THE PCS FIND CHRYSTELLE BEFORE HARAKAN

Chrystelle will greet them in the most non-threatening manner and ask to talk. She'll propose that the PCs ask a question and she'll ask a question, trying to build trust.

Chrystelle can charm people simply with a look. She tries very hard to preserve the PCs agency, but she doesn't allow them to attack her. She will try to take the measure of the PCs, show them Harakan through her scrying mirror, show them the vrock if it is still alive, and explain that Elayne is not a little girl, but a fell Dead-Knight, etc. Proceed with the meeting with Chrystelle and her battle suggestion.

CHRYSTELLE THE SMOOTH TALKER

Here the PCs are determined to take up the battle with the Evil Witch in the Tower but are talked out of it by Chrystelle. Proceed with the meeting with Chrystelle and her battle suggestion.

TO BATTLE: CHRYSTELLE'S SUGGESTION

Chrystelle tells them everything she knows and explains to the PCs that Harakan came in through a window; he can't traverse the Tower to get to the Upper Floor.

Her plan is simple. You can't *gate* into the Elven Tower, but you can *gate* out. She'll use an *arcane gate* to teleport the PCs from Area T1 to the Hallway in Area U2 just beyond the window. The PCs are to do battle,

but she can be of assistance:

- If the PCs can draw him into the Hallway, she'll snipe at him with *magic missiles* as soon as he shows up in a window. She'll unload with magic missile cast from a 9th Level spell slot. It won't kill him if he is undamaged, but it will do significant damage.

- If the vrock is still alive, she'll unload on that with a *sunburst*, which will do 24d6 damage to it.

- She'll then move to Area U1 at the bottom of the stairs.

- If the PCs can retreat to the stairs in Area U1, she'll kill him outright as soon as he rounds the last corner with a *power word kill* from the bottom of the stairs.

If the players at the table are tactically advanced, have Chrystelle miss the vrock (she's rusty, etc.). With the buffs, expert players should hold their own. PCs will then need to drag both combatants in range of Chrystelle's spells.

THE RUNNING BATTLE

It's possible to get into a running battle with the Dead-Knight and/or the vrock. The PCs could be running with dead companions on the floor, trying to retreat, cutting their losses, making a tactical withdraw, etc. Harakan cannot go into the Tower in Area U1 and is unable to traverse the stairs. He will have to go out the same way he went in, through a window. He'll whistle for his trusty nightmare, Murder Black, who will fly to the window to then run down the PCs. And that will probably be the last thing he ever does. Chrystelle has left a *projected image* on top of the tower and sees his actions, goes back to the tower top, and *sunbursts* them both. Harakan is vulnerable to the radiant damage, and if he fails his Saving Throw it will kill him outright (24d6 of damage, DC 21 Constitution Save at Disadvantage), and significantly damage the nightmare, or kill it too if it doesn't Save.

If by the grace of die rolls Harakan survives, Chrystelle will use herself or her *projected image* to somehow convince the PCs to get into the Tower, so she can buff them and then send them after Harakan (possibly again). He's nearly dead. But the Dead-Knight has his own choice to make:

- If the nightmare didn't make it from the *sunburst*, then Harakan is stuck. The PCs can go in and mop him up. He won't jump out the windows—he'll do his best to take down as many PCs with him as possible. But he's a goner for sure, even with his high armor class, a PC with good damage capabilities can finish

Intro

Lost
at the
Beaux
Seins

Moortide
Rising

The Altar
& the
Anvil

Castle
Wailmoor

Appendix

him off.

- If the nightmare *did* make it, Harakan has Murder Black meet him at the window facing the moor and *not* the Courtyard. He flies around the Castle, looking for the PC who lit him up (not knowing his prize can cast spells from the top of her tower or a doorway)—but it doesn't take long for him to fly within range of Chrystelle. She's out of patience, and simply *sunbursts* him again, expending a 9th Level spell slot, two if necessary, or her spell scroll.

Killing Harakan But Not Finding Chrystelle

Chrystelle can't scry the PCs, but if Harakan is dead, she mops up the vrock and uses a *projected image* to get the PCs into the Tower for a meeting.

The projected image is odd to the PCs: a beautiful half-elf wandering around the Castle going "Hello? Can you come to the Courtyard, so I can see you?" It could take them some time to figure out the image in an illusion, and the scrying attributes of it cannot see the PCs.

The Total Party Kill

The PCs are heroes, and heroes often fail. Otherwise, they would not be heroes.

Events can transpire that Harakan TPKs the group (bad class makeup to fight demons and undead, bad rolls for PCs/good rolls for the DM, PCs expend too many resources to kill the vrock and spike demon, etc.), and it's a bad outcome in many ways, even when the PCs have a death mechanic to resurrect themselves at the Great Tree at the Crossroads Village.

Chrystelle panics, a feeling she hasn't felt in a long time.

She resorts to using her *wish* magic to force the Dead-Knight into range, and simply *power word kills* him. For good measure, she *disintegrates* the body. When the PCs perform their walk-of-shame back to the Castle from the Great Tree where their (now weakened) bodies were revived, they'll find no traces of him—including his incredibly handy gear and magical items.

If the DM is not using the optional *Curse of the Lost Memories* death mechanic, then that's that. Modifying it to a TPK-only recovery mechanism is an option; it is more of a curse, after all.

End Game

At the end of the adventure, PCs, befriend Chrystelle, or at least must *deal* with this very localized power-player. Whatever the new relationship, it's going to take them down many new roads.

The prophecy that leads the old druids to reincarnate over and over to the current year articulates a dramatic course of action—the PCs don't know about this prophecy, but they are coming closer to learning their true nature. At this stage, the prophecy is taking on some semblance of self-fulfillment.

The next module in the *Chronicles of the Celestial Chains* campaign will put PCs at the helm of rebuilding the Barony of Wailmoor or, by choice, keeping it a buffer between them and the civilized lands so they can act without political machination or at the very least prevent what happened in the Wailmoor from happening anywhere else.

Either way, they will face the political dangers—either by bringing the Barony back to life or continuing to let it fallow. How will they handle the Tiamat worshippers of the Duchy of Hardred to the south, who have eyes on the natural resources of the Wailmoor? How will they bring payback to the Witches of Kandra and their leader, the ancient Kavita while not bringing war with the Viscounty? How will they claim the Barony at the court of the King and what will the ruler of Lothmar ask for the exchange of his renewed protection to the Wailmoor Baron? And of course, will the PCs hinder, or help Chrystelle in her desire for vengeance upon the Archangel Narakata?

And, finally, the PCs are not done with the old magic that runs amok in the Wailmoor. Silas's and Jackon's gambit used the ancient dam and its dangerous spell engine. And it sits there, abandoned, looming over the Reservoir, humming with unchecked power seeping into the fabric of reality.

One could say Olaf's Dam, after the Demon War, is the real villain in the Wailmoor. And in *Beneath a Dreary Wave*, the PCs are on their own for fixing it while juggling the political machinations that they set in motion and are fostered unto them by well-meaning, and not-so-well-meaning, neighbors.

Choice: Barony of Wailmoor

The player characters need to make a choice about the Wailmoor. Legally the land is under the purview of the King of Lothmar. It's a feudal protectorate in the Empire.

But the PCs can assert themselves—they are the ones who set out to settle unfinished business in the Wailmoor and finish they did—if they don't realize it, they should—the PCs are power players.

Chrystelle can help them with their new role, she is highly trained and experienced in all manner of diplomacy. Being locked away in the Ethereal Plane has not changed her ability to navigate the complexity of Imperial and Lothmarian factions and politics.

She also explains that she, and they, will need resources. That requires investment. She is running low on paper, ink, spell components, and worse, the tea she is drinking is conjured! She has not had a decent cup of coffee in 150 years. To her, the place is meaningless without people.

Then there is the matter that the Wailmoor magical defenses were overwhelmed because their physical defenses did not match. Castle Wailmoor was breached because it did not have enough towers to defend against an aerial assault, not to mention lacking in professional soldiers. And the Wailmoor, rich in sorcery and magic, had only one Imperial War Wizard, and certainly lacked divine support as most of the Clerics in the Wailmoor were simply priests with political appointments.

She could go on-and-on. Everything that would give the Wailmoor a better chance in war requires a serious commitment to not only go beyond the former Barony's glory but to surpass it in many ways.

This requires infrastructure. A lot of infrastructures.

Take Chrystelle's Advice

Chrystelle makes a plea to have the Wailmoor rebuilt, both from a sense of justice and defiance against the corruptive forces, some still in play, that turned the Wailmoor from a thriving center of education, art, and prosperity and into the abandoned place it is today.

Option: One of the PCs Becomes the Baron

This is the option she suggests and desires greatly. It can be hard, if the PCs have not found the documentation in Mark of Wailmoor's desk, or easy if they have.

Option: The PCs Will Find Another Baron

Chrystelle doesn't recommend this but will support the PCs if they insist. The reason is she believes the PCs need a good deal of freedom to conduct themselves in the future. Beholden to a local Baron is possible. Better if one of the PCs was the Baron or Baroness and appointed a Sheriff or some such and retain the benefits of the feudal position.

Furthermore, it is obvious to her that the fewer people who know about her, the better. Word got out once about her and looked what happened.

If the PCs go down this path, she accepts their decision and implores them to return any items they looted from Castle Wailmoor for the new Baron.

She recommends Sir Carl Walshan. Both he and the Dame have proven themselves. She's been scrying him and is impressed. In fact, she could help the PCs simply reverse the roles—Sir Walshan becomes the Baron, and one of the PCs the Knight of the Crossroads. The Viscount owes them a favor, after all.

OPTION: IMPERIAL SHENANIGANS

Hidden in Mark of Wailmoor's desk is a letter from the Emperor himself, addressed simply to the Baron of Wailmoor. The PCs could decide the best course of action giving them the most independence while maximizing their resources, is to formally join the Empire as an Imperial Realm. They would still have obligations to the King of Lothmar, but his, or his heirs, ability to dictate actions to an Imperial Realm is considerably *less*.

Chrystelle will mention the Imperial Option (and if the PCs have the letter, so much the better), and mention Baron Mark was considering this very course of action before he died. And, she'll point out, that while meeting the standards to join the Empire is both expensive and politically difficult, if the Wailmoor was an Imperial Realm, the Demon War would have proceeded down a much different path.

Chrystelle would love this option—but she will flat out tell the PCs she will need to train them in both advanced diplomacy and advanced rulership—something the previous Barons of the Wailmoor were trained to do since birth.

DON'T TAKE CHRYSTELLE'S ADVICE

Chrystelle will support the decision to not revive the Barony. She's lived long enough to realize the PCs are going to die (and with their curse, probably sooner than later), and she'll just start anew with different folks. Now that the Tower and Castle are back in the Welt, she has the power to impact the world around her. Hopefully learning from the mistakes that lead to the fall of the Wailmoor.

OPTION: SPREAD THE RUMORS

Chrystelle says that she can use magic to obscure the Castle and turn it from a place of abandonment to a place of haunting. She advises that the PCs go back to the Crossroads and report to Sir Walshan (or the Dame, if Walshan died defending the village because the PCs left the Obelisk above it unmolested for too long) and tell him the Wailmoor was a fell, haunted place, that the PCs have dealt with the immediate problems, but for all concerned, it's the best that the place be left alone and given more time to fallow and recover from the terrible Demon War so long ago.

This way, the PCs can use Silas Tower, the Temple of Dvalin, or Castle Wailmoor as their base of operations

without immediate political interference.

But, she'll issue a warning—the Empire is slow but not static. Someday, Imperial pressure will cause eyes to turn to the Wailmoor. All spreading rumors will do is delay the neighbors of the Wailmoor setting their sights on it, not remove it from Empire permanently.

OPTION: TELL THE LICH IN THE TOWER TO GO STUFF IT

The PCs could decide to set up shop away from the Wailmoor. Indeed, they could go off in a random direction based on their character(s) history(s).

Again, Chrystelle will simply bide her time. She'll point out the folly of letting her molder in the Tower, alone, and implore the PCs to help her deal with the Witches of Kandra, their common enemy.

From a campaign perspective, this option is convoluted and illogical, in addition to placing additional burdens of world-building on the DM. It is more suited for a sandbox campaign, rather than the open-world campaign that is the *Chronicles of the Celestial Chains*.

But all roads lead back to the Barony, even if the PCs decide to abandon it. Their previous incarnations' bodies are buried in the Old Graveyard, which is protected by the mighty spell-engine in the dam—which is malfunctioning. Corrupted Obelisks, the Old Elven Tower disappearing, Castle Wailmoor disappearing—those are simply symptoms of a greater problem.

CHOICE: WITCHES OF KANDRA

The PCs killed or defeated a Kandra Witch, a nefarious faction of politically astute warlocks and witches in the wild territories that makes up the Viscounty of Kandra.

While the PCs may not have clued in on the subtle hints, Chrystelle will point out to the PCs that the Dead-Knight flat-out was waiting for them. The first thing he did was enter the Castle and gather intelligence to try to lay a convincing trap by having the PCs unnecessarily fight her.

Chrystelle asks what the PCs are going to do about it. She, personally, is going to war. She states her intentions to kill every Witch in Kandra and if that drives the Viscounty to the brink—so be it.

If the PCs waffle on this, she makes an appeal to authority (her extensive knowledge of warfare)—the PCs need to educate themselves on the matter of war. If they don't think they are at war, then it is only a matter of time before it comes to them.

CHOICE: BASE OF OPERATIONS

With or without embarking on restoring the Barony, the PCs are powerful enough and, probably rich

Intro

Lost at the Beaux Seins

Moortide Rising

The Altar & the Anvil

Castle Wailmoor

Appendix

enough, to have a specific base of operations, and Chrystelle wants that to be in the Barony. While Castle Wailmoor is the obvious choice but given the slaughter that occurred in it 150 years ago, perhaps not. Chrystelle admits her bias, she is lonely and desires the company of real people.

There are other places, she points out, that can serve as a base of operations:

- Silas Tower
- The Temple of Dvalin
- The Waterwheel Forge
- A newly hidden redoubt
- The abandoned copper mine in the Hardred Hills
- A new tower on one of the tors that loom over the Wailmoor

Obviously, the PCs are ultimately safer in Castle Wailmoor. But she says sometimes safe is not better and would like the PCs to seriously consider what matters to them and let her know. She will support them to the best of her considerable ability.

She does admit there are political advantages to occupying Castle Wailmoor.

Insightful PCs will recognize that Chrystelle is conflicted about Castle Wailmoor. Delicate probing will reveal the Castle was built at a time where (non-elven) techniques and architecture were crude and subpar to today's standards. What she really wants is the PCs to rip it down and replace it with a more functional edifice. And put her garden back.

CHOICE: THE RELATIONSHIP

Chrystelle wants to be friends. She is extremely grateful to the PCs for rescuing her. All her power, all her education, all her intellect and wisdom, and she was trapped. For 150-*years*.

Although not as pressing as "hey are we going to kill the Witches or what," PCs need to decide what their relationship with Chrystelle is. She is a very intense person. Her desire to have a decent conversation, to hear about current events, to understand the PCs past, practically floats in the air.

While seemingly a soft frou-frou determination, the PCs relationship with Chrystelle determines her attitude to the PCs—because she is both a high-level Enchanter and a paragon of Skills, PC can't use Diplomacy rolls against her to improve her attitude. Players will need to role-play their desire to become friends or keep her at arm's length. Her disposition towards the PCs, unless they are friendly towards her and do the things that friends do, will fluctuate back and forth from friendly to indifferent in a chaotic manner until the PCs do the right thing and let her

into their circle of friends.

Chrystelle wants all the world to just be a person—this desire drives her interactions inside her inner-sanctum of allies.

Without her, the PCs are beset, without help, by Machiavellian-like neighbors, political pitfalls, dirty secrets and, ultimately, threats to their very existence, sooner rather than later.

But, this isn't Chrystelle's story. *She* wasn't prophesized to storm the Gates of Elysia.

One thing is certain—she needs help, even when all she thinks she wants right now is vengeance. And the PCs are the only people who can help her. How they proceed is a reflection on what kind of heroes the PCs are.

END OF THE ADVENTURE: CHRYSTELLE'S LOST MEMORY REVELATION

Chrystelle said she would get back to the PCs in a few days about their *Lost Memories* and she does.

CHRYSTELLE'S INVESTIGATION ROUTE

Chrystelle is an Enchantress Supreme with considerable Outer Planar contacts, and the entities that owe her favors are many and varied, a spider-web of association that any powerful immortal would build given time, resources, and power—all the things she had aplenty.

And all her agents came up with nothing. One even told her the PCs didn't really exist, that they were just a figment of her imagination. Another told her to kill the PCs immediately.

It didn't take her long to conclude the PCs are cursed in some way. They aren't acting like reincarnates she has knowledge of, and if her contacts, some of them powerful divine servants of the gods, can't divine *anything* about them, then that was some hefty-hinky-bad-juju-right-there.

Then, when she was casting her mind out using *contact other plane*, Chrystelle found herself talking to The Maiden, goddess of War and Battle.

In her bedroom, Chrystelle appears before you with a soft pop of displaced air, appearing apprehensive.

"I have answers," she says simply. "But of course, they all lead to naught but an island made of questions floating in the Sea of Mystery. But first, let me make a point."

The air shimmers and standing before you is something if not dead, then old beyond belief. Thin, almost translucent skin is stretched over a skeleton, her face more a skull than a woman, eyes burning with eldritch fire, a sapphire aura with emerald whips flowing about her body as if the magic is the only thing truly holding her together instead of bone and sinew.

"This is my curse. I would have shown you eventually as we became better friends, but I show you now to make a point." Her voice is hollow, otherworldly.

"In this Tower, I cannot die. Sometimes it drives me to the brink of despair. But all these years, all these centuries, I've kept my memories. They are precious to me, and I would not trade the good nor the bad memories for anything." She pauses, peering at each of you.

"*Your* curse is far worse than mine. You are not simply reincarnated Knights of Wailmoor. You've been reincarnated countless times. Wandering through time, doomed to forget one life and to begin anew, loving, learning, and never reaching a deserved afterlife no matter how pure, how pious your life had been. You have been shut out of Elysia. The gods give you no respite.

You have received no rest from the mortal coil no matter how well deserved."

She pauses again, but this time it's obvious she's trying to regain her composure.

"That you have memories of being Knights of the Wailmoor might be an indication that things may be changing for you. But then again, it is quite possible you've been here before, countless times, trying to break your soul from its cycle of seclusion from the afterlife—and failing each time.

"I thought you my saviors, but it is *you* who need saving. There is much we can learn, but I know one thing—you are destined for war. You were *built* for war. The Goddess of War gazes upon you, and even she despairs."

Here Ends
Curse of the Lost Memories

Appendix 1 - Chronology of The Wailmoor

Dawn of Time: While the everlasting battle between Gods and Demons rages, the Hierophants Druids of the Welt establish a Prophecy about the fall of Elysia to started by a terrible demonic war. They decide to place an all-powerful geas—via nature magic they called The World-Spell—on themselves, causing them to reincarnate, life after life, to be ready to prevent the Prophecy to fulfill itself.

-1000: The Celestial Prince Narakata falls in love with the mortal half-elf Chrystelle de Valois. They promise to cherish each other until the end of time. Narakata blesses his beloved with eternal life: Chrystelle will never age. Both lovers retreat to a small elven tower to host their union on the prime material plane.

-900: The Demon Lord Orcus, Prince of the Undead, takes offense that he was denied dominion over Chrystelle's immortal soul and demands compensation for his loss on the principle that no mortal should be allowed eternal life. Other Celestials, led by the Prince Erebus, agree with the demon prince and ask Narakata to limit Chrystelle's sphere of immortality to her little palace.

-800: After two hundred years, Chrystelle grows frustrated that she could not leave her palace without seeing her great age catch up on her. Narakata spends as much time as he can with her, but his duties lead him outside the tower on multiple occasions. As time passes, frustration turns into resentment, and the two lovers start to grow apart. Narakata visits to the Elven tower on the moor became more infrequent and spaced out.

-600: Chrystelle has not seen Narakata in a hundred years. She curses him. Without being constantly in the presence of the Celestial, her mortal body starts to grow old even if she still cannot die of age. Bored, lonely, and resentful, she starts to use powerful spells to summon creatures to her, looking for company. Guillaume, the shepherd, finds the entrance to her tower as he was leading his herd through the moor.

-590: Chrystelle fully dedicates her time to educate and train the young shepherd that she befriended. He grows into a noble and kind man, trained in the arts of magic and warfare. In a few years, Guillaume becomes a knight and is awarded by the King of Lothmar the lands he used to walk as a shepherd as his own barony.

-580: Castle Wailmoor is built by Guillaume of Wailmoor around the old elven tower. The barony prospers and attracts many commoners under its protection.

-520: Guillaume, Baron of Wailmoor dies of old age. His son Robert becomes the new baron. He is also trained by Chrystelle and continues to grow the influence of the barony. Chrystelle discreetly supports the Wailmoor family from her apartments in the castle. After a few decades of hiding their secret, very few but the Wailmoor Barons are aware of her existence.

-443 to -440 Olaf of Wailmoor the 4th, contracts with the Church of Dvalin to construct a mighty dam for flood control and irrigation. The feat is praised as an engineering marvel and an example of Imperial prosperity. The dedication features the Duke of Hardred and the King of Lothmar, both who praise Olaf for his audacious vision.

-420 The Archmage Olaf of Wailmoor, the 5th places wards and other magical properties on the dam. Olaf's second son, Lenard, creates the Knights of the Wailmoor Order and instills the organization with its shock-and-awe doctrine, magical superiority, and requirements of one or two officers with Imperial War College degrees.

-200: Three hundred years have passed. Generations of barons of Wailmoor succeed each other and with the support of the family's secret, the benevolent immortal lich named Chrystelle, the barony became one of the wealthiest provinces of the Kingdom. Jealous of the Wailmoors, and frightened of their power, various factions within the Kingdom of Lothmar spy upon the Barony, looking for ways to check the Barony's power and influence with the King and the Empire.

-155: The Hierophant Druids continue their cycle of reincarnations. Their mighty World-Spell has done nothing but gathers strength after all this time, and now it is nearing its apex. The reincarnates all become Knights of the Wailmoor, dedicated to protecting the Wailmoor, the Baron, and entrusted with protecting and keeping the secret of Chrystelle

-150: The Witch Kavita, secretly financed by the Viscounty of Kandra and the Duke of Hardred, finally discovers the existence of Chrystelle. She mentions the Wailmoor secret to agents of the demon lord Barbu, a minor ruler in the Abyss. Aware of the story of Chrystelle and Narakata, Barbu thinks he can abduct Chrystelle and bring the lich to Orcus, hoping to gain the Demon Prince favors. With the help of Kavita, Barbu builds a small but terrible army. Baron Mark of Wailmoor calls for help to the blue-robed mage Silas and the Clergy of Dvalin. Neighboring lands contend with much havoc wrought by possessed refugees and are unable to send much assistance. The war in the Barony lasts for two years as the demonic hordes seem to have infinite resources.

-148: Mark, the last Baron of Wailmoor, dies on the battlefield along with more than half of the male population of the barony and almost all his loyal knights.

After the battle, the High Priest Oakheart of Dvalin, The Imperial War Wizard Jackon, the Blue Robed Court Wizard Silas, Knight Heleshia, the Dedicate-Priestess Merisee, and the remaining, hardened soldiers draw out the mighty demon Barbu and slay him with enchanted siege weaponry.

The Wailmoor lands are devastated after being exposed to years of demonic corruption and with the line of Wailmoor extinct, farmers and peasants leave the barony, returning the lands to their primal wilderness or fleeing to the Viscounty to the west. Deep in her tower, Chrystelle is still alive but more alone than she ever was.

-146: Silas the mage, one of the last men to live in the Barony has placed a perimeter of magical stones around its border to contain the demonic taint on the moor and prevent future incursions. Through his studies, he understands the existence of Chrystelle and decides to explore Castle Wailmoor to find her. He triggers the castle's latent magical defenses, trapped when it is pulled into the Ethereal Plane and is killed by demons imprisoned along with him.

Present Days: After they have failed to protect the Barony in their past lives as Knights of Wailmoor, the Hierophants continue to reincarnate, this time as the group of lost, random heroes. Ignorant of their past lives, they keep experiencing strange memories, which draws them to a pub at a crossroads below the abandoned moor plateau.

The Hierophants' Word-Spell taps into the essence of the Welt itself. The spell has kept the Hierophants, even without their memories, intact through countless lives.

It is time.

Intro

Lost at the Beaux Seins

Moortide Rising

The Altar & the Anvil

Castle Wailmoor

Appendix

APPENDIX 2 - COSMOLOGY

"The Emperor not only speaks for us
to the Gods—but stands fast against
the other realms that might interfere
with our right and determination to
live in peace.

"If our civilization rises and then
falls to ashes, at least it will be a fall
of our own doing."

—Jegan Ro, Imperial Scholar
Haswane University
IY 3989

Long has it been said that the gods are protectors of the beautiful world call the Welt from the influences, corruptive or not, of the realms outside. The gods created Mount Elysia, where pious souls go to rest after their arduous, mortal life. They created the celestials to stand firm against all that would interfere with the self-determination of the peoples. They even sent one of their own, The Emperor, to directly shepherd the ranks of mortals to nobler pursuits besides conquest and slaughter.

These things were said so many times, for so long, that it is a Universal Truth.

Even when it might not be.

Appendix Summary

Deities
A 5E summary of the available deities and their spheres of influence.

Ontology
Creation myths and the worlds beyond the Welt (world) and the home of the gods explained, along with what happens to people when they die.

Religion
The organizational aspects of the various religions and in and around the Empire.

Deities

In the pantheon of the Welt, there are the three major deities of law, and then there is everyone else. They are tied loosely in quasi-pantheons and could be considered one unified pantheon because they are either all related, lovers, allies, difficult allies, or any combination thereof.

The deities are unified in opposition to the Lords of the Abyss and the ever-creeping-entropy that threatens to undo the center of creation.

Long have the deities viewed the Welt as a side-show in the grander scheme of things. But it is the Welt where mortal souls are born, prayers made, and prayers answered.

The Three Deities of Law

The Three Deities of Law are represented by the Three Dragons. They are often called *The Saviors of Law* and are worshiped equality throughout the Empire, although some Imperial Realms favor one god over another.

These deities are equal in power and influence over the other gods. Their children view them less as biological parents and more as mentors and tutors (and lovers).

This relationship is frequently strained. None of the three passed on their lawful aspects to their children, and this causes the occasional disappointment amongst the elder dragon gods and even celestials, both of whom view the younger, more chaotic kinship of deities as less than exemplary and never able to obtain the lawful ideal The Three internally chase.

Platine

The Platinum Dragon, or *Father Dragon*, Platine's purview is Law and Good. He is a deity of justice, law, wisdom, and empathy. His symbol is the platinum dragon, and his divine domains are Life, Light, Protection, and Spirit.

Sheresha

Sheresha is often called the *Dragon of Judgement* or the *Dragon of Magic*. His purview is Law and Neutrality. He is a deity of law, magic, protection, loyalty, and honor. His divine domains are Arcana, Life, Knowledge, and Order.

His symbol is a sword with scales as a hilt's cross-guards.

Sheresha appears either as an athletic male or female both to the other gods and worshipers. In dragon form, Sheresha can be male or female.

Tiamat

Tiamat is known as *The Five-Headed Dragon* or, more commonly *The Sea Dragon*. Her purview is Law and Evil. She is a deity of the sea, law, self-reliance, ambition, passion, pride, and power. Her divine domains are Ambition, Strength, and Zeal.

Her symbol is the five-headed dragon.

Dvalin

Sometimes referred to as *Old Dvalin*, the deity is credited with the creation of both dwarves and elves, the two races that do not share the common Welt Creation Myth. Elves no longer worship Dvalin, a bone of contention with their dwarven brethren. Consequently, modern Dvalin's depiction is always dwarf-like.

Dvalin is singled out as his relationship with the other gods is supremely neutral in disposition and seemingly not related, having relations, carnal or otherwise with the other deities. All the females of the pantheon can vouch that they've never slept with him and born his children.

He serves the other deities of law equally but also is the occasional craftsman to other gods. He seems to follow no goals other than his own, and the only thing

he shares with the other deities, besides occasionally making them items of power, is his hatred of demons.

Dvalin's purview is Dwarves and Creation. His divine domains are Forge, Life, Protection, and Strength.

His holy symbol is a hammer and anvil. Dvalin is Neutral Good.

The Kinship

The remaining deities loosely refer to themselves as *The Kinship* and are unified in both their relation to the Deities of Law, each other, and their opposition to the Lords of the Abyss.

Although not biologically accurate and simplistic, The Kinship deities view themselves the adults of the pantheon, with the Three Dragons as the grandparents, and the Celestials as the adolescents and finally the mortal High Priests of the Gods as children.

The Maiden

Often called *The Bitch* both fondly and not-so-fondly, by both mortals and the other gods, The Maiden is the deity of war worshiped by many barbarian tribes, clans, and warriors. Her purviews are War and Battle, and she is the only deity associated with War. Also called the Goddess of War, The Maiden only shares her first name (Anath) with her lovers. She is depicted as a blonde and athletically nubile shield maiden. She is independent and chaotic.

It is said that The Maiden sprang forth from the blood of the Three Deities of Law during a titanic struggle against the Lords of the Abyss.

The Maiden's divine domains are Protection, Strength, and War. Her holy symbol is two battleaxes crisscrossed under a shield, and her alignment is Chaotic Good.

Ishtari

The daughter of Sheresha and Platine, while Sheresha is the God/Goddess of Magic, Ishtari is the goddess of magic *users,* mainly wizards. She is the patron of arcane study and the collection of knowledge, and her purview is Magic and Knowledge.

Ishtari is depicted as a young wizard in revealing robes holding a magical staff. She is sometimes called *The Pantheon's Brat* by the other gods, and while she is easily seduced (by other gods or the occasional mortal archmagi), she soon abandons her current lover for scholarly pursuits.

Her divine domains are Arcana and Knowledge, and her holy symbol is a magic wand over an open floating book. Her alignment is Neutral.

Bastet

Known as *The Mistress,* Bastet is the Feminine Goddess of Sex, Seduction and Pleasure and the daughter of Platine and Tiamat, although she is also the occasional lover of Platine (and many of the other gods, both male and female, when she wants something from them). Her purviews are Lust and Seduction.

Bastet is the only officially protected religion of the Empire, and Bastet acolytes, clerics, and paladins are Imperial Agents, state-sanctioned and protected prostitutes. Her divine domain is Trickery, and she is Chaotic Neutral. Her holy symbol is disembodied cat eyes with long eyelashes.

Bastet appears as an adolescent woman with flowing red hair and enticing green eyes, sometimes appearing as a primal, irresistible nymph and other times a sophisticated, but enticing, noble lady.

Cernunos

Cernunos is the son of Platine and Bastet, and the god most worshiped by elves. His purview is Elves and Nature. He appears as an athletic male elf with stag antlers and outside of the elven lands is a semi-popular deity amongst males. His demeanor is an odd combination from his parents—he has a sense of fairness and empathy from his father, but from his mother, he takes the attributes of care-free, primal living. He is seen both as the elven protector and nature protector amongst elven kind.

Cernunos's divine domains are Life, Nature, and Protection. His holy symbol is the antlers of the stag, and his alignment is Chaotic Good.

Oddly, Cernunos is on better terms with Tiamat than he is with his father and mother, with whom it seems that he is an embarrassment to their not-so-secret incestuous affair. He is formally married to the goddess Rhiannonie.

Rhiannonie

Rhiannonie is the feminine elf deity and is associated with birds and forest animals. She is the devoted wife of Cernunos and sticks by him even when he obviously has another lover. Her purview is Wives and Animals. All the minor primal forest and nature deities are reputed to be the many offspring of Cernunos and Rhiannonie. Otherworldly and spiritual, Rhiannonie sometimes is depicted as naïve and child-like, and other times wiser than the wise. Outside of elven lands, she is a semi-popular deity amongst females.

Her divine domains are Life and Nature. Her holy symbol is a dove of peace. Rhiannonie is Neutral Good. She is friends with Bastet and The Maiden.

Rhiannonie has only born Cernunos one normal child, the god Gwri.

GWRI

Gwri is the god of hunting but appears both as a human or elven male. He is the occasional lover of Ishtari, Bastet, The Maiden, and even Tiamat. His purview is Hunting and Independence. Gwri is depicted as the bad-boy of gods, independent and beholden to no one, sharing only hatred for demons.

Gwri is friendly to his parents and is the only deity that may have a better-than-a-working-relationship with Dvalin. He is also is rumored to walk the Welt disguised as a mortal, having a good time with mortal men, and seducing nubile mortal maidens. His bastard offspring with mortals do not share any divine capabilities or powers, but they are unusually attractive and clever.

Gwri's divine domains are Life and Strength. His holy symbol is the bow and arrow, and he is Chaotic Neutral.

THE LORD OF LIGHT

The god-like entity known only as *The Lord of Light* is the highly magical offspring of Tiamat and Sheresha. Known to mortals as a being that has no resemblance to humans, elves or any other mortal races, his purview is Storms and Light. Seen more of a weapon than an actual person, The Lord of Light does have a small following and the rare church.

His divine domains are Light, Protection, Spirit and Tempest. His followers and clerics are charged with battling undead and demons whenever found. The Lord of Light is no friend of evil and will have no relations, cordial or otherwise, with evil personages, which includes his mother. Out of all the deities, he is the most unpredictable.

The Lord of Light is Chaotic Good. His holy symbol is a sunburst.

MELAINA

Melaina is said to have been born of the gods' collective nightmares after one particularly bad war with the demons, although she does not haunt them *per se* and remains cool towards them all except Tiamat, whom she shares a somewhat sisterly affection. She is reputed to be insane, although she is united with the other gods in opposition to the Lords of the Abyss, for whom she hates with all her being. Melaina's purview is Nightmares and Darkness, and her divine domains are Darkness and Trickery.

While grim and fatalistic, Melaina can appear both extremely attractive and seductive and other times as the stuff of nightmares. A demanding deity, she rewards her devoted and faithful followers with the ability to lucid dream, although often those dreams are dark and disturbing, even if the dreamer is trying to dream of something more pleasant. Passionate and contemptuous of the weak, Melaina is "friends" with Bastet and is reputed to be the occasional lover of The Maiden.

Melaina is Chaotic Evil. Her holy symbol is the medusa's head. Many people who feel trapped and stifled by ever-present lawful aspects of the Empire worship Melaina, along with those that pursue inward mental reflection such as hyper-self-awareness, and self-determination. She has neither bad nor good relations with The Lord of Light.

CASSANDRA

Cassandra is the servant-goddess of The Maiden and daughter of Ishtari. Her father is supposedly Gwri, although Gwri is also reputed to only be able to make mortal women pregnant, a contradiction that leaves Imperial Religious Scholars speculating far into the night, sometimes resulting in fisticuffs.

Sometimes called *the red-headed step-child of the gods*, she is both a warrior and a scholar. Cassandra serves The Maiden as her handmaiden and formal lady-in-waiting. She is friendly towards her mother, not so friendly with Gwri, has googly-eyes for Cernunos, and is secretly friends with Melaina.

Cassandra's purview is Protection and Knowledge and is seen as the patron goddess of women who eschew the traditions of becoming a wife and mother. Her divine domains are Knowledge and Protection, and her holy symbol is a book with a sword as a bookmark.

Cassandra often has insights into the future, although she keeps such to herself, claiming that there is nothing worse than a self-fulfilling prophecy. Cassandra is Chaotic Good.

THE EMPEROR

The man known only as The Emperor and sometimes *The King of Kings* is the son of Platine and Tiamat, sent to the mortal realms to bring law and order to provide a relatively "safe" and "protected" land for mortals to worship the gods. It is through this worship that the gods derive power, which they need to wage war against the Lords of the Abyss.

While of divine origin, the Emperor is not a deity that can grant spells, nor can he listen to or answer prayers. While he retains his immortality, he has no divine power, although is both a 20th Level Wizard and a 20th Level Cleric with the Order domain.

The Emperor's government is efficient and lean. He has few laws, but the ones he does have are absolute, enforced by the Office of Imperial Assassins. His sole

Intro

Lost at the Beaux Seins

Moortide Rising

The Altar & the Anvil

Castle Wailmoor

Appendix

purpose is to bring stability to the continent and thus prevent war between kingdoms (but not necessarily *within* kingdoms). He allows great autonomy to the other kings, opposing them only when one goes against one of the few imperial dictates he has outlined in a document called The Imperial Charter.

The Emperor appears as a forty-year-old human of good health and athletic build, dressed richly but subtly. The Imperial Calendar starts with his reign, and the year is 5011. He is Lawful Neutral and while has the occasional lover, has no wife or children.

Oddly, the gods have no power over the Emperor, probably a condition of living in the mortal realms.

Despite his harsh nature the Emperor is a widely-loved individual and respected greatly even in the chaotic and untamed areas of the Empire.

The *Kingdom of Lothmar Camping Setting* contains more information on the Emperor and the Empire.

THE OLD FAITH

Druids derive their power from nature and the Elemental Planes, not from the gods. Their faith, now called *The Old Faith,* was dominate and supreme before the gods invested the world with the Emperor and the granting of power to the priesthoods.

Such a power-shift was a natural progression and in all but one case, not the result of a war or crusade.

The Old Faith is recognized by the Empire as a valid faith. Druids still hold considerable power in the outer, primal reaches of the Empire, especially in areas that claim to not actually be part of the Empire (but for all intents and purposes to the Emperor, are).

MINOR DEITIES

There are many local deities in the world born out of the constant lovemaking of Cernunos and Rhiannonie.

These deities are nebulous god-like beings of nature that inhabit a mountain, a stretch of river, a large lake, or even a primal forest. They cannot answer divination spells although they can grant cleric power within the divine domain of Nature.

CELESTIALS

It is so difficult moving between Realms that the gods created servants, celestials, to do it for them. Imparted with some of their divine power, celestials cannot derive power from prayers, but they can answer them.

It is against Imperial Edict to worship a celestial, but mortals who die and are dwelling in Purgatory sometimes are recruited as divine agents and granted spells by archangels.

All archangels have a host of lesser celestial servants. Celestials are all Lawful Neutral except for the Archangel of Mount Elysia, who is Lawful Good.

There are seven archangels, but only four are known to mortals.

NARAKATA

Narakata is a warden that helps guard the various realms against demonic intrusion. Powerful and resolute, Narakata has a host of lesser servants who help guard the realms against entropic intrusion.

EREBUS

Erebus is the Shepard of the Dead and protects souls from the desperations of the demons and regulates who goes into and comes out of Purgatory. Erebus helps those who were unable to identify with a deity resolve their inner crisis of faith, purify their intentions, and depart to Mount Elysia. Enigmatic and practical, Erebus is feared on the mortal realms and is sometimes as "The Unbending Darkness."

Deity	Divine Domains	Holy Symbol	Favored Weapon
Platine	Life, Light, Protection, Spirit	The Platinum Dragon	Longsword
Sheresha	Arcana, Life, Knowledge, Order	A sword with scales as cross guards	Any sword
Tiamat	Ambition, Strength, Zeal	The Five-Headed Dragon	Trident
Dvalin	Forge, Life, Protection, Strength	Hammer and Anvil	Warhammer
The Maiden	Protection, Strength, War	Two battleaxes crisscrossed under a shield	Any martial melee weapon
Ishtari	Arcana, Knowledge	Magic wand over a floating spell book	Quarterstaff
Bastet	Trickery	Disembodied cat-like eyes with long eyelashes	Stiletto
Cernunos	Life, Nature, Protection	Stag antlers	Greataxe
Rhiannonie	Life, Nature	Dove of peace	Quarterstaff
Gwri	Life, Strength	The Bow and Arrow	Longbow
The Lord of Light	Light, Protection, Spirit, Tempest	Sunburst	Warhammer
Melaina	Darkness, Trickery	Medusa's Head	Glaive
Cassandra	Knowledge, Protection	Book with a sword as a bookmark	Longsword

Michael

The Archangel Michael is the Warrior Angel, able to traverse the realms to righteously smite agents of Entropy and Demons. He is the General of the Gods and is feared by Demon Lords, the other angels, and even the more Chaotic of the Three Dragon's offspring, except the Goddess of War, who, out of all the other gods, understands Michael's resolute and unbending nature. The Maiden and Michael are reputed to sometimes be lovers, a scandal that pleases no one except Bastet.

"You know what I fear? I fear the War Bitch and Michael get it on one time too many, and she pops out some war machine from her Nethers that destroys both Law and Chaos alike. We're talking the End Beyond the End. Can some other slutty goddess attend to his needs? Seriously."—The Demon Lord Orcus.

Arealial

Arealial is the Archangel of Mount Elysia. She guards its gates (both into it and leaving it for the Next Realm) and ministers to those who suffered greatly in life (but are not impure), easing their mortal burdens until only the desire to live with the gods remain. Many mortals refer to her as the "Eternal Virgin of Purity," but there has been more than one Imperial Scholar over the years that have looked at the family tree of the gods and wonders how anyone could think that was possible.

Ontology

There are various Realms within the grand cosmology that surrounds the Welt, viewed through the mortal lens of persistent myth. In the Empire, most people view their nature of being as highly spiritual.

The Realms

The Reams are loosely connected via the Astral Sea. There is no alignment wheel of god lands off the Astral, only individual realms. Only the four elemental realms are in proximity to each other and are accessible from any of the other Realms.

The Realms are contested between the gods in the Next Realm and the Lords of the Abyss in their twisted, infinitely corrupted Realm of Chaos and Evil. The gods, specifically the Three Deities of Law, view all the Realms as under their protection and responsibility.

The Welt

The World, or sometimes referred to The Mortal Realm.

Mount Elysia

Where pious and deserving souls go when they die to rest and come to grips with the end of their mortal life, rewarded by entry to the Eternal Paradise. There, they are then sent on to their final journey to be with their chosen deity in The Next Realm. Pure souls that do not identify with a deity are provided gentle guidance until they are ready to embark on their final journey.

Souls not pure enough for Mount Elysia goes to Purgatory first.

The Next Realm

The realms of the gods. Each god has their own "sub-realm" within the Next Realm, both infinite (stretching on in possibility forever) and finite (appearing as a super earth-like planetoid) depending on a celestial and religious point of view.

Most mortals have a difficult time understanding the non-linear nature of the Next Realm, and therefore Mount Elysia is a more understandable, and desirable aspiration.

Purgatory

The realm where souls that are not pure enough for Mount Elysia go to be cleansed. Souls endure educational trials in which they must admit their shortcomings and learn from their mistakes. Purgatory is not seen as a pleasant place and winding up there is taught to be a failure of sorts. It is a place of trials, designed to strip away all the hindrances a mortal has imposed between themselves and the gods' purviews.

Purgatory is never punishment. It's simply a place where worshipers go who did not meet their gods' standards of Mount Elysia's reward.

The Four Elemental Realms

The four elemental realms float in the astral sea in the proximity of each other with The Welt squarely in the middle, separated between themselves and The Welt by the Aether (Ethereal) Barrier.

Within are elementals both great and small, some of which have power supreme. Those elemental lords cannot grant divine spells but are the primary mechanism in which druids obtain allies. When a druid summons an elemental, the various lords of the elemental planes are ready to do their part in protecting The Welt from dangers within and without.

- **Vzduchu**, the Realm of Air.
- **Terra**, the Realm of Earth.
- **Oceanna**, the Realm of Water.
- **Feu**, the Realm of Fire.

Intro

Lost at the Beaux Seins

Moortide Rising

The Altar & the Anvil

Castle Wailmoor

Appendix

LIMBO

The Realm of Chaos, and the "closest" Realm to the Abyss. It is reputed that not even celestials navigate Limbo, but rather recruit their own agents to do so.

NIAIS

The Realm of the Fey Courts, an infinitely wild and primal realm, where the capricious Fey Lords mainly keep to themselves.

It is theorized it was the Fey Court that turned the elves away from Dvalin.

CYSGODOL

The Realm of Shadow, mysterious and misunderstood. Sometimes called the Realm of Apathy, Cysgodol is ruled by no entity and populated by enigmatic creatures that desire to be left alone.

Melaina is said to be able to enter Cysgodol unmolested, able to traverse "the space between dark and shadow."

THE ABYSS

The realm of demons. Souls of demon worshipers go directly to the Abyss when they die. Demons consume souls, although it was never a part of their purpose or mission. Entropy and the opposition to Law is always the goal of the Demon Lords. Evil is simply their means to this end.

Although Chaotic, the Demon Lords follow certain rules of warfare with the gods. Partly because it allows them more flexibility than it does the gods and celestials, partly because the last thing any of them want is Michael waging a holy vendetta in their personal realm—and partly because the demon lords feel the gods too, try to avoid Michael's wrath.

OTHER REALMS

A seemingly endless series of worlds accessible only from the Astral Sea through great and dangerous confabulations called Astral Tunnels.

Imperial Scholars know of these other planets, and some of them have been to one or two, but mortal travel between realms often runs afoul of Narakata and his agents.

COSMOLOGY NON-CONCEPTS

There is no "hell" or place of torment for souls. Souls deemed unworthy of the gods, heretics and apostate were sent to Purgatory where they were gently shown what was real and what was simply a fantasy of their own making, needing to pass a series of test before ascending to Mount Elysia.

There are several evil deities more than happy to be the home of souls of the mortals in life that pursed evil ends. It is a great honor for many men and women of diabolical morals and ethics to be with Tiamat in the afterlife, for example, and murders and thieves are happy under the "care" of Melaina.

Lost souls are preyed upon by demons, who corrupt and twist them into horrifying parodies of life.

CREATION MYTH

There are two primary creations myths: one for the dwarves and the elves, and the other for everyone else. Both share the common theme of how the world was created, however.

HOW THE WELT WAS MADE

The world, as the myth goes, was "pulled from the sun and the two moons" in half biological, half fantastical description that sounds a lot like sex.

This creation myth of the Welt is consistent amongst many people, leading Imperial Religious Scholars to believe that is what was taught by the druids of the Old Faith in the time before the Empire.

LIFE MYTH

Life, the creation myth further explains, begotten from the constant love from the sun and moons, products of their devotion to the Welt. Between the three they would capture great balls of ice in the void of space and fling them on the world, and thus the world was given water. Out of water came plants and insects and then animals, and finally, people.

Humans, gnomes and halflings share this world-view creation myth. For a very religious, god-centric world, the myth of creation as handed down by the druids has oddly never left the various races civilizational memory and is incorporated into the various religions today. People view the gods (except for Dvalin) as powerful beings that found the people of The Welt and, through commandments of the Three Deities of Law, protected their lives and souls from the forces of Entropy that would consume all.

OLD DVALIN

The exceptions to the Life Myth are dwarves and elves. For them, it is said that Dvalin came upon the Welt and decided it needed *more* life. He created the dwarves and elves to live upon the world, hardy and graceful people to share in the wonderment that was The Welt.

Dvalin does not seem to care a bit that the elves no longer worship him and instead have turned to other deities, although racially the two people are at odds, with the dwarves viewing the elves as ungrateful little snots rejecting the wise tutelage of their father, and the elves feeling Dvalin was a parent letting their children make their own choices and that the dwarves need to grow up and "leave the nest."

Some Imperial Religious Scholars believe that both races come from one, and it was only through a dramatically different world-view that they diverged into the dwarf and elf today. This belief is not shared by dwarves and elves and is seen as insulting and patronizing.

Religion

Viscounty of Kandra

In the Viscounty, formal churches are not allowed as a circumstance (and Imperial Treaty) of when the Kingdom of Lothmar went to war with the (then) non-Imperial Land of Kandra, a druidic nation. The druids won, and the Emperor himself brokered a peace deal in which the lands would become a quasi-independent Viscounty under the Kingdom of Lothmar's domain—the druids, while victorious, decided they would do better under the Empire's protection than they would if they retained their full independence. In return, there would be no formal churches of the gods in the Viscounty.

Over time, the people of the Viscounty became highly religious anyway (as the Emperor knew they would) by establishing a distributed method of worship. Each Godsday, services are held in a house or business that rotates to a different place each week until the pattern starts over again, the sermon usually given by an acolyte, a village elder, or the occasionally wandering priest. Priests of the gods live in simple houses or monasteries that never serve as a place of worship amongst the common folk.

It is this reason why the rite of passage for an adult in the Viscounty includes obtaining or earning a silver holy symbol.

There are many druids in the Viscounty, still, which is by design (also by the Emperor). These druids are responsible for the export of Pride of Viscounty Horses, the best warhorses in the Empire. They are also the primary healers of each village, although in large cities and towns priests of the gods usually provide healing services to the masses.

Duchy of Hardred

The Duchy of Hardred worships Tiamat more so than any other gods. Her temples are grand and extensive, and her priests carry profound influence throughout the Duchy. The Duke himself is a die-hard Tiamat worshiper, an ambitious, cunning, and passionate man of martial and diplomatic talent.

Duchy of Lothmar

The King's own Duchy primarily worships Platine, although there are many other churches to the gods, especially in larger towns and cities.

Intro

Lost at the Beaux Seins

Moortide Rising

The Altar & the Anvil

Castle Wailmoor

Appendix

Appendix 3 - Chrystelle de Valois

I was once the most beautiful woman in the whole Welt. It only brought trouble and despair. I wish I had lived the life of a normal woman... But I will do the best with what was given to me, paying the price for my vanity.

And vanity is the cruelest of sins. The price of vanity is loneliness, the most terrible of afflictions.

— Chrystelle de Valois

The Early Years

The 16-years old half-elf Chrystelle de Valois was already one of the most beautiful women of the Welt—taking most attractive features of both races and distilling it down to one impossibly gorgeous Lady. She was often called Chrystelle the Enchantress and at the court of the Emperor, bards and storytellers composed songs about her elegance, grace and how wise men became foolish and enthralled when her blue-eyed gaze landed on them.

While suitors lined up to meet her and provide the most amazing gifts to her family, the fame of her beauty reached as far as Mount Elysia, and the angels themselves came down to admire her in secret. Even the powerful Celestial Prince, Narakata, descended to the Welt on his immaculate Pegasus to see with his own eyes the wonder everyone in Celestia was talking about.

And he fell in love.

It is always complex to describe the emotions of a celestial, and one as such powerful as Narakata even more. Men do not really know what celestial love is, or whether it compares to the feelings most mortal express. But Narakata was obsessed by Chrystelle. He wanted to be with her, always and was growing jealous of other men who continued to court the young woman.

One day he decided he would make Chrystelle his own, and that he will be the only one to have her. Her family had an old tower, even for elves, and he would take Chrystelle and make the tower her domain, so no other men will ever lay their filthy and concupiscent eyes on her.

Chrystelle fell in love with Narakata, of course. No mortal can resist a Celestial Prince. She followed her lover to the elven tower on the moor and then he made her immortal. Not that she asked for it, but Narakata, in his obsession, feared for Chrystelle to grow old and suffer the consequence of her mortal state: death.

For hundreds of years, the two lovers lived on the moor, in the Elven tower, in peace and harmony.

The Price of Undeath

While the gods and the demons fought a constant cold-war over the souls of the inhabitants of the Welt, they all knew that the universe is built around laws that cannot be challenged—the nature of death and its consequences is one of them. When Orcus, the demon prince of the undead, became aware that a celestial granted a mortal eternal life, he got offended and asked Erebus, another Celestial Prince, for compensation. Even though demons and gods were at constant conflict, there was certain respect amongst immortals.

Erebus agreed with the demon on the principles of the law and ordered Narakata to return Chrystelle to her mortal state—angry both for having to agree with his nemesis, Orcus and Narakata for his secretive pride. Narakata entered a great fury, threatening Mount Elysia and the Abyss alike. Erebus could not calm him and thus proposed a compromise: Chrystelle would remain immortal, but her immortality would be restricted to the elven tower on the moor.

Orcus agreed on the compromise, for he was afraid of Narakata and did not want to risk further escalation for the fate of one mere soul. But he was still offended and swore he would act behind the scenes to take back that undeserved gift from Chrystelle should Narakata turn his eyes away from her.

The Benevolent Lich

Hundreds of years after Narakata lost interest in her, Chrystelle became a powerful immortal, kept alive by the power of the tower—but it was terrible immortality. Outside of the presence of Narakata, her body withered with time until only the magic of the tower could keep her alive. While she was now isolated from Narakata, she was also isolated from the corruptive forces that usually prey upon mortals that try to live forever. Even after all these years of abandonment and the frustration of being imprisoned in her own tower, she still has the kind heart and passion for her mortal kin that she had when she was 16-years at the court of the Emperor.

Chrystelle is not suicidal. She never tried to run out of the tower and let all these years catch up on her. She never grew bitter and angry at the world for her condition but does succumb to a few dark nights where she wished she would cut Narakata's throat or strangle his pompous and condescending neck, or various other physical maladies women dream of when spurned.

Roleplaying Chrystelle

Chrystelle is a recurring character in the campaign and has centuries of practice in arcane arts. The Demon War tore at her very heart and being trapped in her Tower, and the Ethereal Plane has her, for the first time in all her existence, questioning her sanity.

At first, she is suspicious of the PCs and does not know of their reincarnating identities or whether they might be demons in disguise trying to trick her.

Once she understands the PCs to be her strongest allies, she should grow into behaving like a powerful source of support and lore for the players.

Intro

Lost at the Beaux Seins

Moortide Rising

The Altar & the Anvil

Castle Wailmoor

Appendix

At the beginning of the Campaign, Chrystelle has not seen a living soul in 150-years since the Tower and trapped her in the Ethereal Plane. She is very lonely and frustrated with her prisoner condition. As the PCs step inside Castle Wailmoor, she does not know why the castle has been freed from the Ethereal Plane and suspects PCs to be demons—that is until the PCs start doing battle with the demon's agent sent to enter the Tower now that it is back from its Ethereal banishment.

Currently, Chrystelle is deeply saddened by the Demon War. Everything she had carefully built came crashing down, from her point of view, in an instant. She burns with the dual desire for vengeance and desire to rebuild, both without the mistakes she made in the past.

CHRYSTELLE'S POWER

Chrystelle has never stopped learning. She has a keen understanding of people and their motivations and is an expert in many useful subjects such as engineering, geology, medicine, and even warfare. She is a patient teacher and a wise counsel.

Chrystelle's true power is her passive ability, through her philosophy, benevolent nature, and limitations to her movement, to impact the world around her.

Ironically, Chrystelle is the Enchantress Supreme. She reached the limits of arcane power long ago. Like herself when she was but a young lady, Chrystelle can charm and beguile with merely a glance. But now it has nothing to do with beauty, but a vast and all-powerful connection to the arcana allowed by her immortality.

CHRYSTELLE'S STAT BLOCK

Take a magically gifted woman, lock her in her tower for centuries with nothing but arcane studies, and the result is someone who's reached the height of her chosen magical field: enchantment. Her mere presence is literally beguiling. She is extraordinarily clever and has spent a long time gaining wisdom.

Inside her tower, Chrystelle reigns supreme. However, her real threat to anybody attempting to defile her sanctum is her vast expertise in battle. She has gone so far as contracted with the various elemental lord to have their minions assault her home. She has put out multiple contracts on her life and done battle with high-level assassins and hit squads. She has done favors for multitudes of personages beyond the Welt in return for battle practice.

In all her existence, only one person was able to penetrate the Castle (not even her Tower) and pose a real threat: the demon-possessed Aether Witch. And even then, Chrystelle ripped the demon on of her

body, sent it screaming back to the Abyss, yanked the woman into her tower, and blew the witch into the Deep Ethereal.

Chrystelle is so good at self-defense that it bores her. And thus, her abilities are now static—they are the limits of her power. Even her access to *wish* magic cannot move her abilities upwards.

Her powerful abilities are specific to her lair. Outside of her lair, she must resort to more subtle means to impact the world that she can see but now can never touch.

Chrystelle de Valois

Female Half-Elf Wizard 20 — Medium humanoid, chaotic good
Armor Class 16 (robe of the white archmagi) — **Hit Points** 152
Speed 30 ft.

Statistics

STR	DEX	CON	INT	WIS	CHA
10 (+0)	12 (+1)	14 (+2)	20 (+5)	18 (+4)	13 (+1)

Feats Elemental Adept, Observant, Ritual Caster
Saving Throws Int +11, Wis +10, Advantage on Saving Throws for spells *(scarab of protection)*
Skills Acrobatics +7, Animal Handling +10, Arcana +11, Athletics +6, Deception +7, History +11, Insight +10, Intimidation +7, Investigation +11, Medicine +10, Nature +11, Perception +10, Performance +7, Persuasion +7, Religion +11, Sleight of Hand +7, Stealth +17 (Advantage on checks to move silently), Survival +10
Damage Resistances bludgeoning, piercing, and slashing from nonmagical weapons
Senses darkvision 60 ft., truesight 60 ft., passive Perception 20
Languages Abyssal, Auran, Celestial, Common, Draconic, Dwarvish, Elvish, Gnomish, Halfling
Challenge 23 (50,000 XP)

Spells

Signature Spells. Cast spell without preparation or spell slot usage: *vampiric touch* (1/day), *lightning bolt* (1/day)

Spell Mastery: Cast spell without preparation or spell slot usage at will: *protection from evil, misty step*

9th— (2 slots) *time stop, power word kill, imprisonment*
8th— (1 slot) *telepathy, sunburst, power word stun*
7th— (2 slots) *symbol, project image, mage's sword*
6th— (2 slots) *true seeing, globe of invulnerability, disintegrate, chain lightning, arcane gate*
5th— (3 slots) *scrying*
4th— (3 slots) *stone skin, greater invisibility*
3rd— (3slots) *lightning bolt, haste, dispel magic, counterspell*
2nd— (3slots) *suggestion, hold person*
1st— (4 slots) *sleep, mage armor*
Cantrips— *fire bolt, mage hand, message, prestidigitation, shocking grasp*

Abilities

Ring of Three Wishes (3 charges). While wearing this ring, Chrystelle can use an action to expend 1 of its 3 charges to cast the *wish* spell from it. The ring becomes nonmagical when she uses the last charge.

Hypnotic Gaze (DC 21 Wis). As an action, Chrystelle can choose one creature that she can see within 5. If the target can see or hear her, it must succeed on a Wisdom Saving Throw or be charmed by

Chrystelle until the end of her next turn. The charmed creature's speed drops to 0, and the creature is incapacitated and visibly dazed.

On subsequent turns, she can use her action to maintain this effect.

Instinctive Charm (DC 21 Wis). When a creature Chrystelle can see within 30 feet of her makes an attack roll against her, she can use her reaction to divert the attack, provided that another creature is within the attack's range. The attacker must make a Wisdom Saving Throw against her wizard spell save DC. On a failed save, the attacker must target the creature that is closest to it, not including Chrystelle or itself. If multiple creatures are closest, the attacker chooses which one to target. On a successful save, Chrystelle can't use this feature on the attacker again until a long rest.

Creatures that can't be charmed are immune to this effect.

+3 Staff of Absorption. This quarter staff acts as a magnet, drawing spells or spell-like abilities into itself. The magic absorbed must be a single-target spell or a ray directed at either the character possessing the staff or her gear. The staff then nullifies the spell's effect and stores its potential until the wielder releases this energy in the form of spells of her own. She can instantly detect a spell's level as the staff absorbs that spell's energy. Absorption requires no action on the part of the user if the staff is in hand at the time.

This staff operates as a rod of absorption when held, and absorbed spells can be used to cast spells. Its absorption ability is thus far unused.

Elemental Adept (Lightning). Spells Chrystelle casts ignore resistance to damage of the lightning elemental type. All 1 on a damage die is as a 2.

Alter Memories (DC 21 Int). Chrystelle can make a creature unaware of her magical influence on it. When she casts an enchantment spell to charm one or more creatures, she can alter one creature's understanding so that it remains unaware of being charmed.

Iron Flask. This iron bottle has a brass stopper. Chrystelle can use an action to speak the flask's command word, targeting a creature that she can see within 60 feet of her. If the target is native to a plane of existence other than the one she on, the target must succeed on a DC 21 Wisdom Saving Throw or be trapped in the flask. If the target has been trapped by the flask before, it has Advantage on the Saving Throw. Once trapped, a creature remains in the flask until released. The flask can hold only one creature at a time. A creature trapped in the flask doesn't need to breathe, eat, or drink and doesn't age.

Scarab of Protection (12 charges). If Chrystelle fails a Saving Throw against a necromancy spell or a harmful effect originating from an undead creature, she can use her reaction to expend 1 charge and turn the failed save into a successful one.

Boots of Elvenkind. Chrystelle's high-heeled boots make her sneaky. Her steps make no sound, and she has Advantage on Dexterity (Stealth) checks that rely on moving silently.

Fey Ancestry. Chrystelle has Advantage on Saving Throws against being charmed, and magic can't put her to sleep.

Observant (Wisdom). If Chrystelle can see a creature's mouth while it is speaking a language she understands, she can interpret what it's saying by reading its lips.

Ritual Caster (Wizard). Chrystelle is a ritual caster of many spells.

Arcane Recovery (10 levels, 1/day). Chrystelle has learned to regain some of her daily magical energy by studying her spellbook. Once per day when she finishes a short rest, she can choose expended spell slots to recover.

Boon of High Magic. One extra 9th-level spell slot.

Boon of Immortality. In her tower, Chrystelle cannot die from old age.

Boon of Skill Proficiency. Chrystelle has proficiency with all skills.

Boon of Truesight. Chrystelle has truesight with a range of 60 feet.

Boon of Undetectability. Chrystelle gains a +10 bonus to Dexterity (Stealth) checks, and can't be detected or targeted by divination magic, including scrying sensors.

Legendary Actions

Chrystelle can take 3 legendary actions, choosing from the options below. Only one legendary action option can be used at a time and only at the end of another creature's turn. Chrystelle regains spent legendary actions at the start of her turn.

Archmage Supreme (0 Actions). Chrystelle casts a cantrip.

Ethereal Dance (1 Action). Chrystelle *Misty Steps* anywhere within range of the spell if the destination is in her tower.

Enthralling Presence (2 Actions). Two subjects are the target of the *suggestion* spell (DC 21 Wisdom Save)

Lair Actions

On initiative count 20 (losing ties), Chrystelle can take a lair action to cause one of the following effects; she can't use the same effect two rounds in a row:

Olaf's Gambit. A *wall of force* covers the entire outside of the Old Elven Tower for any length of time. This effect can be dispelled at will.

Ethereal Ejection. DC 21 Intelligence Save or target in her line-of-sight is ejected from the Old Elven Tower into the Deep Ethereal.

The Dark Heart of Erebus. Any creature that Chrystelle is aware of in her lair is subject to a *power word kill*, no range limitation.

Scion of Wailmoor. Any good creature in Chrystelle's lair (including Chrystelle) is healed up to 100 HP. Creatures less than 100 HP are healed their maximum.

Actions

+3 Staff of Absorption. Melee Weapon Attack: +9 to hit, reach 5 ft., one target.
Hit: 6 (1d6+3) bludgeoning damage or 7 (1d8+3) bludgeoning damage if used with two hands to make a melee attack.

Unarmed Strike. *Melee Weapon Attack:* +6 to hit, reach 5 ft., one creature.
Hit: 1 bludgeoning damage.

Spell Book

Chrystelle's spell books contain every wizard spell. If the spell can be cast as a ritual, she has a corresponding ritual book.

Intro

Lost at the Beaux Seins

Moortide Rising

The Altar & the Anvil

Castle Wailmoor

Appendix

APPENDIX 4 - SEALING THE CRYPT OBELISK LOST MEMORY

Heleshia observes as Jackon and Silas complete the ceremony, and the warding Obelisk fades until it is mostly transparent.

"This is so fascinating! Don't see magic like this every day," Merisee the Priestess quips, writing in her ever-present book. She has followed Jackon and Silas around like a puppy, an immature trait from the vastly out-of-place priestess of Dvalin. Merisee is an elf and a young one at that.

Silas and Jackon turn to her, both appearing worn and frazzled from the powerful magic of the ritual.

"I would like to protest again that it is unwise to write the secrets of the Obelisk down in a book," says Silas.

The young elf maiden simply raises an eyebrow. "My lord, I can assure you this book cannot fall into the wrong hands. First, we'll lock it away behind a portcullis that can only be unlocked via two special keys forged from wolfram, a metal known only to a few esoteric smith-priests of Dvalin. To do so requires special tools, the special mold, and a magical crucible. The metal, tools and the crucible are locked away and guarded separately from all the other temple reliquaries. Then, after unlocking the portcullis, only a cleric, paladin or Dedicate to Dvalin can traverse the warding glyph. And *then*, this book is written in Old Dvalin, which is a language only Dvalin scholars know. But there's more!" She pauses.

"Go on," Jackon says, annoyed.

"I've written it in Dedicate Code. You have to know the cipher to decode it."

"Is there a way to get the code other than from someone like yourself?" Silas asks.

"Ha! No—wait, yes. Theoretically, any worshiper of Dvalin with a proper holy symbol can start putting together the key to the cipher—the key is in the Radiant Chapel, after all, and all they need to do is match the bottom symbol on the columns to the symbol key on a silver holy symbol—but they'll have to traverse the Realm of Dreams to see the correct symbol correlation on the columns!" Merisee says the last with a gleam in her eye.

Both Silas and Jackon exchange glances, and both sigh at the same time.

Appendix 5 – Pride of Viscounty Warhorses

All the warhorses gifted by the Viscount come with barding. Each is trained for battle, but the training assumes the rider is a competent lancer. Untrained PCs could be in for a difficult time if they engage in mounted combat. PCs familiar with mounted combat will instantly recognize these warhorses are of the caliber normally reserved for Viscounty Officers and nobles.

The Viscount brought six warhorses. If there are over six PCs, some will be left out. Merris will go out of his way to recommend which horse should go with which PC.

If there are less than six PCs, the party doesn't get the extra warhorses. They only receive one each.

PCs that are small in stature could be in for a long acclimation process. There is no *Pride of the Viscounty War Ponies*.

About Viscounty Horse Culture

The political power structure in the Viscounty of Kandra is a confederation of horse-lords ruled by a viscount, appointed by the King of Lothmar. Druids and Witches are also power players, with the druids playing a larger role as the group directly responsible for raising and training the horses.

Amongst Viscounty humans, horse ownership is a symbol of masculinity. Neither women nor men will not look favorably at a man who does not own at least a riding horse. Men with warhorses are classified as warriors and thus receive added respect (and attention from the ladies). At the top of the horse-status pyramid are those with special, noble steeds bred for Viscounty Officers and the horse-lords and their respective families. These warhorses are called *Pride of the Viscounty*.

One shortcut to horse ownership is becoming a Lancer. Lancers receive a warhorse if they don't already have one. It is theirs to keep for their term of service. If maimed or killed in battle, the horse is replaced.

The Viscounty is composed of 30% halflings. Halflings do not share this view of horse-ownership status and take umbrage if such a "weird-human-thing" is attributed to their status. "We live under the tyranny of horses," is a Viscounty halfling saying. While many halfling males have ponies, most will admit they have one to simply keep up with their human friends.

Intro

Lost at the Beaux Seins

Moortide Rising

The Altar & the Anvil

Castle Wailmoor

Appendix

Brute the Warhorse

Male Warhorse Fighter 1 Large beast, unaligned
Armor Class 14 (studded leather) — **Hit Points** 30 — **Speed** 65 ft.

Statistics

STR	DEX	CON	INT	WIS	CHA
20 (+5)	12 (+1)	13 (+1	4 (-3)	12 (+1)	(-2)

Saving Throws Str +7, Con +3
Skills Acrobatics +3, Athletics +7, Perception +3
Senses passive Perception 13
Languages Can understand some Common but can't speak
Challenge 1 (200 XP)

Abilities

Trampling Charge. If the horse moves at least 20 feet straight toward a creature and then hits it with a hoof attack on the same turn, that target must succeed on a DC 14 Strength saving throw or be knocked prone. If the target is prone, the horse can make another attack with its hooves against it as a bonus action.

Second Wind (1/short rest). On his turn, can use a bonus action to regain hit points equal to 1d10 + 1.

Actions

Hooves. *Melee Weapon Attack:* +7 to hit, reach 5 ft., one target. *Hit:* 12 (2d6+5) bludgeoning damage.

Description

Brute is a good, loyal warhorse. He takes umbrage of smaller people and animals (which is most people and animals) not getting out of his way if he wants to walk somewhere. He will casually "bump" them out of the way. His name comes from his strength and size.

Dancer the Warhorse

Male Warhorse Fighter 1 — Large beast, unaligned
Armor Class 15 (studded leather) — **Hit Points** 30 — **Speed** 65 ft.

Statistics

STR	DEX	CON	INT	WIS	CHA
18 (+4)	14 (+2)	13 (+1)	4 (-3)	12 (+1)	7 (-2)

Saving Throws Str +6, Con +3
Skills Acrobatics +4, Athletics +6, Perception +3
Senses passive Perception 13
Languages Can understand some Common but can't speak
Challenge 1 (200 XP)

Abilities

Trampling Charge. If the horse moves at least 20 feet straight toward a creature and then hits it with a hoof attack on the same turn, that target must succeed on a DC 14 Strength saving throw or be knocked prone. If the target is prone, the horse can make another attack with its hooves against it as a bonus action.

Second Wind (1/short rest). On her turn, can use a bonus action to regain hit points equal to 1d10 + 1.

Actions

Hooves. *Melee Weapon Attack:* +6 to hit, reach 5 ft., one target. *Hit:* 11 (2d6+4) bludgeoning damage.

Description

Dancer is highly nimble for a bloodthirsty warhorse. He can make jumps and turns most other horses, including trained ones, would avoid.

Slaughter the Warhorse

Male Warhorse Fighter 2 — Large beast — Neutral Good
Armor Class 16 (scale mail) — **Hit Points** 41 — **Speed** 65 ft.

Statistics

STR	DEX	CON	INT	WIS	CHA
18 (+4)	12 (+1)	14 (+2)	4 (-3)	12 (+1)	7 (-2)

Saving Throws Str +6, Con +3
Skills Acrobatics +3, Athletics +6, Perception +3
Senses passive Perception 13
Languages Can understand some Common but can't speak
Challenge 2 (450 XP)

Abilities

Trampling Charge. If the horse moves at least 20 feet straight toward a creature and then hits it with a hoof attack on the same turn, that target must succeed on a DC 14 Strength saving throw or be knocked prone. If the target is prone, the horse can make another attack with its hooves against it as a bonus action.

Action Surge (1/short rest). Can attack twice, instead of once, whenever he takes the Attack action on his turn.

Second Wind (1/short rest). On his turn, can use a bonus action to regain hit points equal to 1d10 + 2.

Actions

Multiattack. Slaughter makes two melee attacks.

Hooves. *Melee Weapon Attack:* +6 to hit, reach 5 ft., one target. *Hit:* 11 (2d6+4) bludgeoning damage.

Description

Slaughter is the best warhorse out of the six the Viscount brought with him. Whereas many warhorses can function in battle, Slaughter seems to like it. A lot.

Slaughter is intelligent enough to be picky on his riders. If the PC doesn't look and act like a knight (paladin or fighter armored like a knight), he'll toss the rider off at first opportunity. Assuming the un-cavalier-like PC can get close to him. He will bite or kick anybody he deems unworthy of his devotion.

Slaughter also has a rudimentary understanding of morality. If he witnesses an evil act, he'll disapprove or take other actions to the best of his ability to do so.

Sneaky Wind the Warhorse

Male Warhorse Rogue 1 — Large beast, unaligned
Armor Class 12 — **Hit Points** 28 — **Speed** 65 ft.

Statistics

STR	DEX	CON	INT	WIS	CHA
18 (+4)	14 (+2)	13 (+1)	4 (-3)	12 (+1)	7 (-2)

Saving Throws Dex +4, Int -1
Skills Acrobatics +4, Athletics +6, Insight +5, Perception +3, Sleight of Hand +4, Stealth +8
Senses passive Perception 13
Languages Can understand rudimentary Thieves' Cant but can't speak.
Challenge 1 (200 XP)

Abilities

Trampling Charge. If the horse moves at least 20 feet straight toward a creature and then hits it with a hoof attack on the same turn, that target must succeed on a DC 14 Strength saving throw or be knocked prone. If the target is prone, the horse can make another attack with its hooves against it as a bonus action.

Sneak Attack. Sneaky Wind adds 1d6 additional damage when landing a successful sneak attack.

Actions

Hooves. *Melee Weapon Attack:* +6 to hit, reach 5 ft., one target. *Hit:* 11 (2d6+4) bludgeoning damage. 1d6 added damage for a sneak attack

Description

Sneaky Wind will absolutely steal anything valuable left alone and then hide it. He will even go so far as to put things in his saddlebags if given a chance. Even amongst the druids, his ability to move silently for such a large animal is a marvel.

He's a warhorse, though. He is trained for battle. Sneaky doesn't neigh or nicker, and constant noise bothers him.

Swifttail the Warhorse

Male Warhorse Fighter 1 — Large beast, unaligned
Armor Class 14 (studded leather) — **Hit Points** 30 — **Speed** 70 ft.

Statistics

STR	DEX	CON	INT	WIS	CHA
18 (+4)	12 (+1)	13 (+1)	4 (-3)	12 (+1)	7 (-2)

Saving Throws Str +6, Con +3
Skills Acrobatics +3, Athletics +6, Perception +3
Senses passive Perception 13
Languages Can understand some Common but can't speak
Challenge 1 (200 XP)

Abilities

Trampling Charge. If the horse moves at least 20 feet straight toward a creature and then hits it with a hoof attack on the same turn, that target must succeed on a DC 14 Strength saving throw or be knocked prone. If the target is prone, the horse can make another attack with its hooves against it as a bonus action.

Second Wind (1/short rest). On his turn, can use a bonus action to regain hit points equal to 1d10 + 1.

Actions

Hooves. *Melee Weapon Attack:* +6 to hit, reach 5 ft., one target. *Hit:* 11 (2d6+4) bludgeoning damage.

Description

Swifttail is stupid fast. He would be a racehorse, but in the Viscounty, only mares and geldings can be racehorses.

Warhorse Raven the Sure

Male Warhorse Fighter 1 — Large beast, unaligned
Armor Class 14 (studded leather) — **Hit Points** 30 — **Speed** 65 ft.

Statistics

STR	DEX	CON	INT	WIS	CHA
18 (+4),	12 (+1)	13 (+1)	4 (-3)	12 (+1)	7 (-2)

Saving Throws Str +8, Dex +5, Con +5
Skills Acrobatics +3, Athletics +6, Perception +3
Senses passive Perception 13
Languages Can understand some Common but can't speak
Challenge 1 (200 XP)

Abilities

Trampling Charge. If the horse moves at least 20 feet straight toward a creature and then hits it with a hoof attack on the same turn, that target must succeed on a DC 14 Strength saving throw or be knocked prone. If the target is prone, the horse can make another attack with its hooves against it as a bonus action.

Second Wind (1/short rest). On his turn, can use a bonus action to regain hit points equal to 1d10 + 1.

Actions

Hooves. *Melee Weapon Attack:* +6 to hit, reach 5 ft., one target. *Hit:* 11 (2d6+4) bludgeoning damage.

Description

Raven is sure on his hooves and has a balance many other horses lack.

Intro

Lost at the Beaux Seins

Moortide Rising

The Altar & the Anvil

Castle Wailmoor

Appendix

Next from Griffon Lore Games

Beneath a Dreary Wave

Watch for the sequel to *Curse of the Lost Memories* and the second module of the Campaign! In **Beneath a Dreary Wave** (CC2), players must decide how to support the rebirth of the barony of Wailmoor. Either they have a seat of power with one player choosing to be the new Baron and work with the rest of the PCs to face the dangers and the political intrigue coming at them or support whomever Chrystelle de Valois will name as the new heir to the Wailmoor dynasty.

Threats will come from all over the Kingdom of Lothmar, with viscounts and dukes eyeing the once rich and powerful barony. How will the PCs handle the Covens of Kandra and the evil witch Kavita? Will they entreat and find a political compromise with the Tiamat-worshipping Duke of Hardred? Should the Barony stand on its own and seek support in swearing fealty to a bigger, more powerful estate?

And just when they are knee deep in political shenanigans, they must penetrate the secluded dungeon inside the old dam by the reservoir before its run-away magical spell-engine destroys everything they've just gained. They'll have to seek out the Dvalin Dedicate-Priestess Merisee and convince her to give up her secrets, but her price will rock the PCs to their very core.

One way or the other, the PCs will need to stop reacting and start becoming masters of their own fate—or their *Lost Memory* curse will consume them for all eternity.

The Kingdom of Lothmar

Discover the Kingdom of Lothmar is this upcoming new campaign setting guide from Griffon Lore Games! The **Kingdom of Lothmar Campaign Guide** (KoL) covers everything you need to know to run the *Chronicles of the Celestial Chains* campaign with even more depth, or simply run your own adventures in the Welt!

The Viscounty of Kandra to the west of the Wailmoor is a wild place lead by a mischievous, ambitious couple that contends with aggressive horse lords, witches, and druids. In Lothmar, the Viscounty yields considerable economic weight from its immense expertise from raising and selling warhorses throughout the Empire.

The Duchy of Hardred, the wealthiest province of the Kingdom and arguably the Empire, is run by the tight fist of the Duke Holdar and the High Priest Salazar of the Church of Tiamat, but all their power sometimes seems for naught—the Duke's eldest daughter went missing on her wedding day, and no amount of divination will reveal her fate. And the ever-present merchant guilds seem unstoppable with their constant power growth and tangle everyone in their web of political intrigue.

The guide covers these provinces and more, twelve in all, with descriptions of the Elven Protectorate of Shaeniss, the King Lands, the Sun Counties of Ghon and others—including a description of the Empire. Included is a guide to the Gods of the Welt, their faiths, and clergy, as well as an in-depth review of the merchant guilds and other factions in Lothmar.

Redman, Sean K reynolds, F. Wesley Schneider, Amber Scorr, Doug Seacat, Mike Selinker, Lisa Stevens, James L. Sutter, Russ Taylor, Penny Williams, Skip Williams, Teeuwynn Woodruff.

Pathfinder Roleplaying Game Advanced Class Guide © 2014, Paizo Inc.; Authors: Dennis Baker, Ross Byers, Jesse Benner, Savannah Broadway, Jason Bulmahn, Jim Groves, Tim Hitchcock, Tracy Hurley, Jonathan H. Keith, Will McCardell, Dale C. McCoy, Jr., Tom Phillips, Stephen Radney-MacFarland, Thomas M. Reid, Sean K Reynolds, Tork Shaw, Owen K.C. Stephens, and Russ Taylor.

Pathfinder Roleplaying Game Advanced Player's Guide. © 2010, Paizo Publishing, LLC; Author: Jason Bulmahn

Pathfinder Roleplaying Game Advanced Race Guide. © 2012, Paizo Publishing, LLC; Authors: Dennis Baker, Jesse Benner, Benjamin Bruck, Jason Bulmahn, Adam Daigle, Jim Groves, Tim Hitchcock, Hal MacLean, Jason Nelson, Stephen Radney-MacFarland, Owen K.C. Stephens, Todd Stewart, and Russ Taylor.

Pathfinder Roleplaying Game Monster Codex. © 2014, Paizo Inc.; Authors: Dennis Baker, Jesse Benner, Logan Bonner, Jason Bulmahn, Ross Byers, John Compton, Robert N. Emerson, Jonathan H. Keith, Dale C. McCoy, Jr., Mark Moreland, Tom Phillips, Stephen Radney-MacFarland, Sean K Reynolds, Thomas M. Reid, Patrick Renie, Mark Seifter, Tork Shaw, Neil Spicer, Owen K.C. Stephens, and Russ Taylor.

Pathfinder Roleplaying Game Villain Codex © 2016, Paizo Inc.; Authors: Alexander Augunas, Logan Bonner, Paris Crenshaw, Dan Dillon, Crystal Frasier, Amanda Hamon Kunz, Eric Hindley, Mikko Kallio, Dale C. McCoy, Jr., Stephen Radney-MacFarland, Thomas M. Reid, Alistair Rigg, Alex Riggs, Mark Seifter, and Linda Zayas-Palmer.

Pathfinder Roleplaying Game: Ultimate Equipment (OGL) © 2012, Paizo Publishing, LLC; Authors: Dennis Baker, Jesse Benner, Benjamin Bruck, Ross Byers, Brian J. Cortijo, Ryan Costello, Mike Ferguson, Matt Goetz, Jim Groves, Tracy Hurley, Matt James, Jonathan H. Keith, Michael Kenway, Hal MacLean, Jason Nelson, Tork Shaw, Owen KC Stephens, Russ Taylor, and numerous RPG Superstar contributors.

CPSIA information can be obtained
at www.ICGtesting.com
Printed in the USA
BVHW022203210619
550898BV00004B/3/P